MW01711400

VENTURA

DESKTOP PUBLISHING, STYLE SHEETS, FONTS, LAYOUT, MULTIPLE-FRAME DOCUMENTS, AND GRAPHIC DESIGN

Rob Krumm

MIS: PRESS

MANAGEMENT INFORMATION SOURCE, INC.

COPYRIGHT

1107 N.W. 14th Avenue
Portland, Oregon 97209
(503) 222-2399

First Printing

ISBN 0-943518-37-7

Library of Congress Catalog Card Number: 87-12388

DEDICATION

To Chris,

The best days are ahead.

TABLE OF CONTENTS

INTRODUCTION

By reading and working through this book, you will learn how to use, control, and create documents with Ventura Desktop Publisher. Like all powerful computer applications, Ventura Desktop Publisher has a long list of commands, features, and special effects that can appear overwhelming to even an experienced user. This book organizes the features and abilities of Ventura into a series of examples that build from the most basic operations to the most complex. Some experience with a word processing program (e.g., Word, WordPerfect, WordStar, Multimate) is helpful since you will need to create some of the example documents in a word processor before loading them into Ventura.

This book is intended to offer you a practical yet educational experience. Because of its tutorial structure, this book provides more than a list of commands with hints and tips. Each chapter consists of step-by-step instructions that tell you how to create a specific type of document. During the process of creating these example documents, you will encounter various tasks and problems you are likely to encounter in any future documents on which you will work. Included are details covering both the operations needed to solve these problems as well as the thinking behind those operations.

The book begins with simple documents and operations and builds, step by step, to advanced document operations and structures.

You will encounter four types of information in this book:

1. **Informational Text**. The text of the book supplies the background information on how Ventura works and how you can learn to control the look of your documents.

2. **Keyboard Instructions**. Keyboard instructions are commands or text you will need to enter while you are working through the chapters. The keyboard commands are separated from the text and appear in **bold** print. Specific keystroke commands are enclosed in square brackets. For example, the notation

   [return]

indicates that you should press the Return key. You also will use a variety of special keystroke combinations. For example, you can save a chapter by pressing and holding down the **Ctrl** key while simultaneously pressing the letter **s**. In this book, such key combinations will appear as follows:

[Ctrl/s]

Any information in parentheses to the right of keystroke instructions indicates an explanation to the reader and should *not* to be entered.

3. **Mouse point and click instructions.** The majority of operations in Ventura require you to use the mouse to point at and select various items. In this book, a picture of a mouse will appear in the margin next to each paragraph that contains mouse instructions.

4. **Screen Images.** To make the procedures in this book as clear as possible, many full-screen images are included to show you how your screen will look during various operations.

By working through this book, you will receive a full course in Ventura Desktop Publisher. The commands and procedures appear within the context of specific examples, which enables you to see how all of the small operations tie together to form the printing effects you want to produce.

This book will not teach you the *right* way to perform your desktop publishing assignments; rather, it will help use the power of Ventura to express your own ideas and creativity.

CHAPTER 1

BASIC CONCEPTS

The goal of this book is to teach you to create documents using Ventura desktop publishing software. After you learn to use Ventura, the ideas expressed in your documents will be more organized and have greater clarity and impact than if they had been created by ordinary word processing programs. After all, it's not just *what* you say that's important, but *how* you say it.

You must understand, however, that features of a program like Ventura are a means to an end – better communication with your audience. Whether your audience is a company's board of directors, the local Rotary club, or the readership of a magazine, Ventura provides the tools to present ideas in ways not previously possible. This book will teach you to control Ventura so you can produce the product you want for the people in your market. The book is not intended as a course in graphic design or typesetting, and references to technical aspects of publishing have been kept to a minimum. The book emphasizes the creative potential of Ventura.

THE SCREEN DISPLAY

After you have installed Ventura, you are ready to begin.

Ventura displays a screen that may seem unusual if you are accustomed to the standard text displays of word processing and spreadsheet programs. Ventura uses high-resolution graphics to create a screen display combining text and graphics.

The display contains several different areas with special meanings and uses.

The center of the screen – the **page window** – is a blank area or window through which a Ventura document is viewed. Surrounding the window are the following special areas:

Menu Bar The **menu bar** lists the major commands used in Ventura. When you point the mouse at any of the words on the Menu bar, Ventura displays a list of commands related to that menu choice.

Document Window The center of the screen display consists of a blank square named the **document window**. The text of a document appears in this window. This part of the screen display will change as you enter and format text.

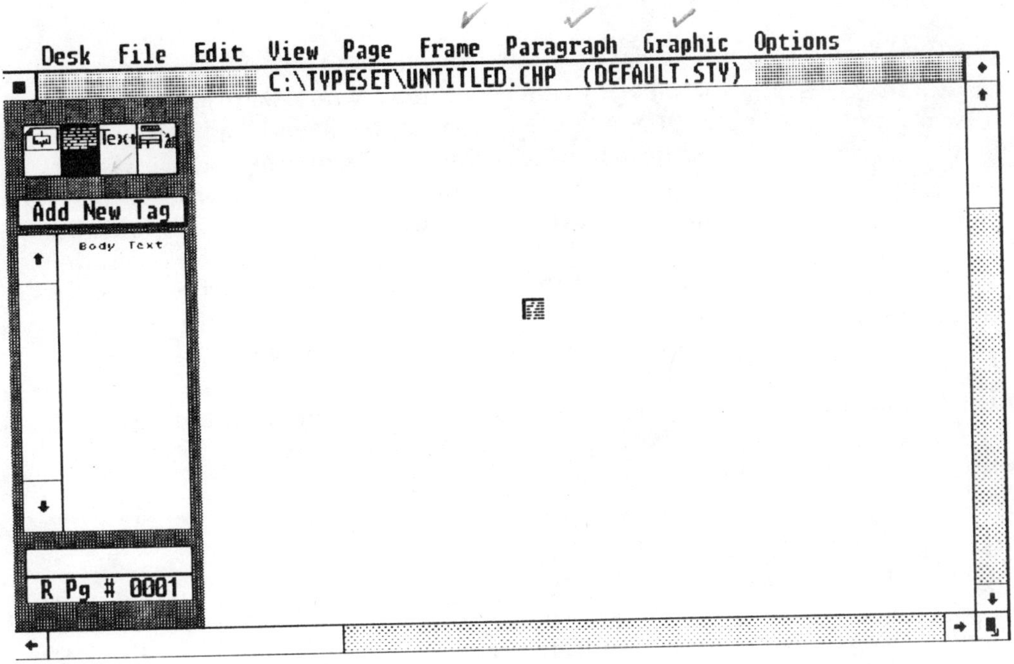

Figure 1.1

Mode Indicator

The **mode indicator** consists of four boxes – one for each of the operational modes available in Ventura. The four modes are the **Frame** mode, the **Paragarph** mode, the **Text** mode, and the **Graphics** mode.

Side Bar

The **side bar** presents a list of options that can be selected in the mode currently activated. Each of Ventura's modes displays a unique side bar.

Page Counter

The **page counter** displays the number of the page currently displayed on the screen. If the document contains right and left pages, Ventura indicates the page type with an R or an L.

Document Name

This bar shows the name of the current document and style sheet file. Ventura displays the name UNTITLED.CHP when you do not have a document loaded.

Vertical Bar

The **vertical bar** indicates the relative position on the page of the document window. The entire bar represents the length of the page. The solid or white part of the bar represents the section visible through the document window. The gray part indicates the portion of the page not visible in the window. As you move up and down the page, the position of the solid part of the bar will change to indicate how far the text displayed in the window is from the top or bottom of the page.

Horizontal Bar

The **horizontal bar** indicates the horizontal position of the display window on the page.

COLUMN GUIDES

The blank window may seem misleading when you begin to enter text. Ventura automatically maintains margins on the page. When you enter text, it is forced to fit inside the margins.

Ventura can display an on-screen guide of the page's top, bottom, left, and right margins. To display the column guide, use one of Ventura's options located on the **Options** menu.

Point the mouse at the Options menu heading, and the Options menu appears:

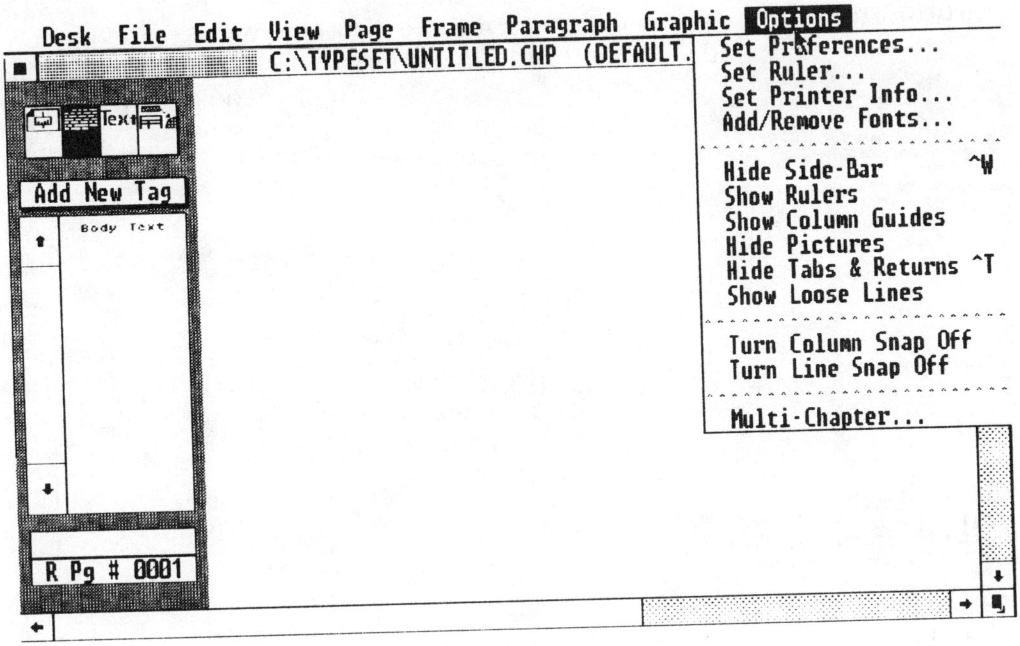

Figure 1.2

In the center of the list, you will find the **Show Column Guides** selection. Point the mouse at this selection.

When you point at a selection, Ventura reverses its color. When the Show Column Guides selection is reversed, click the mouse button. Two dotted lines appear on the screen (see Figure 1.3).

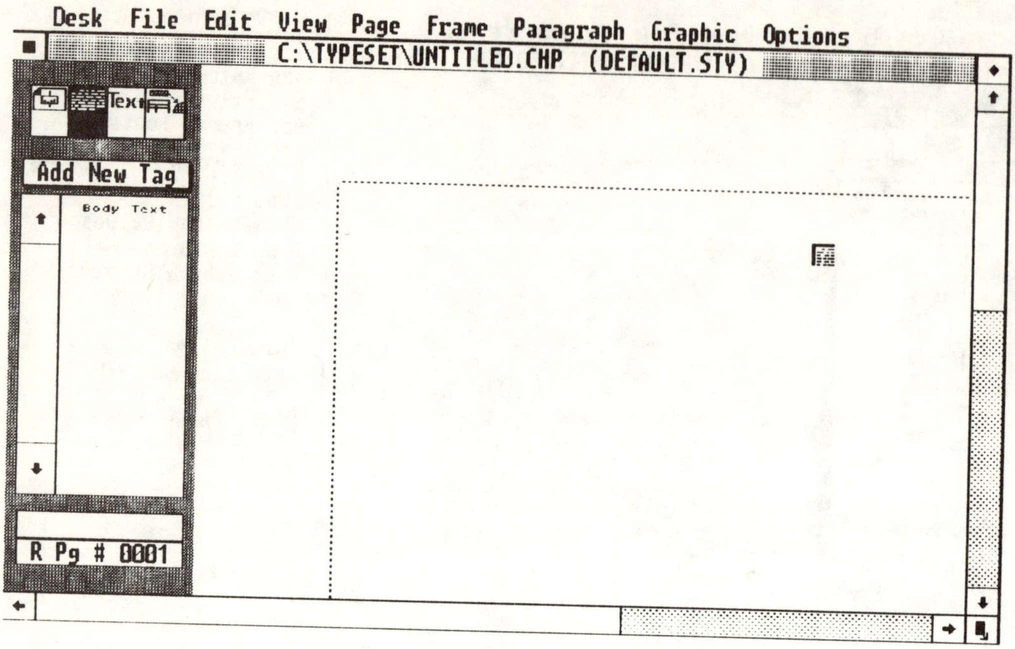

Figure 1.3

The lines indicate the page's margins. At this point, the lines form a right angle indicating the upper left-hand corner. Keep in mind that you will not see the column guides in the document window if your document window is positioned in the center of your document (too far from a margin for the column guides to be displayed).

The lines are referred to as **column guides** because Ventura allows text displays containing more than one column on each page. In such cases, you will see several sets of column guides indicating margins for the separate columns. For now, all text will be entered into a single column.

VIEWS

The document window area can display a document in four different ways or **views**. Views specify the amount of a document that fits into the window. The four views are as follows:

Enlarged This view displays text at maximum enlargement and is used to display and work with small details in the text.

Normal This view displays text at about half the size of the enlarged view. Because the text is smaller, you can see twice as much of the page as you can in the enlarged view. This view is the most commonly used view and can be used for making format changes to text when in the Paragraph mode.

Reduced This view reduces the text so that an entire page can be displayed at one time. This view can be used to examine a full-page layout, including headers and footers.

Facing Pages This view reduces text even more so that two pages – a left and a right – can be seen at one time. This view is used to compare formatting differences between left- and right-side pages.

The first three views – enlarged, normal, and reduced – can be controlled from the **View** menu or by using Ctrl/key combinations, which means you press and hold the Ctrl key while simultaneously pressing another key. For example, to place Ventura into the Normal view, press

[Ctrl/n]

The document area displays a larger area. Press

[Ctrl/r]

The document area displays the outline of an entire page.

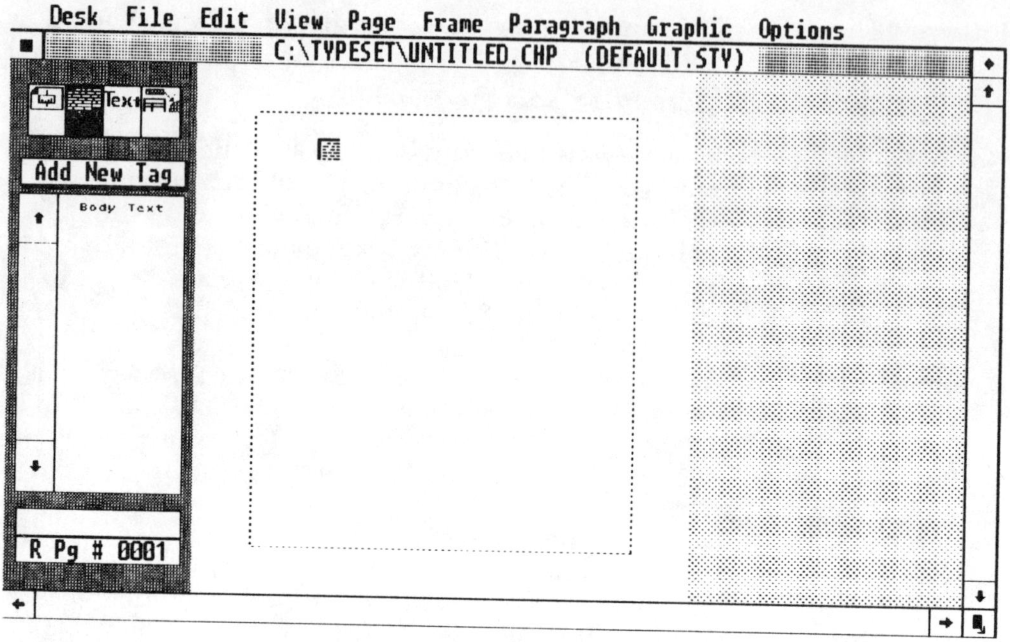

Figure 1.4

Instead of using Ctrl/key combinations, you can also change the view by using the menu; point the mouse at the View menu title. The menu will appear as in Figure 1.5.

Note that a check mark appears next to the Reduced View selection to indicate that this view is active. The Facing Pages view is assigned no Ctrl/key combination and can only be entered by using the menu (see Figure 1.6).

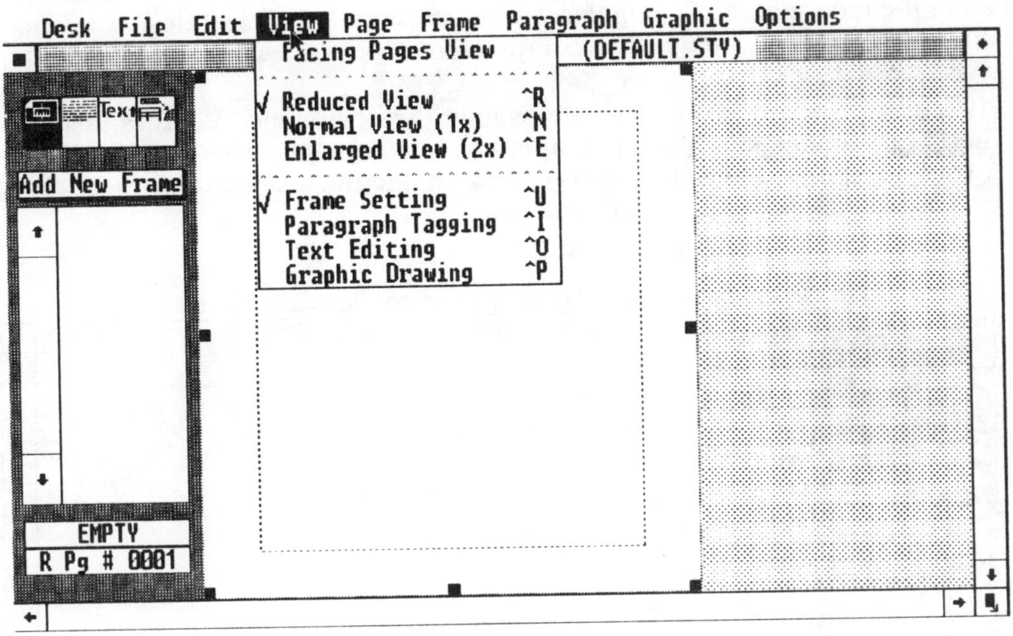

Figure 1.5

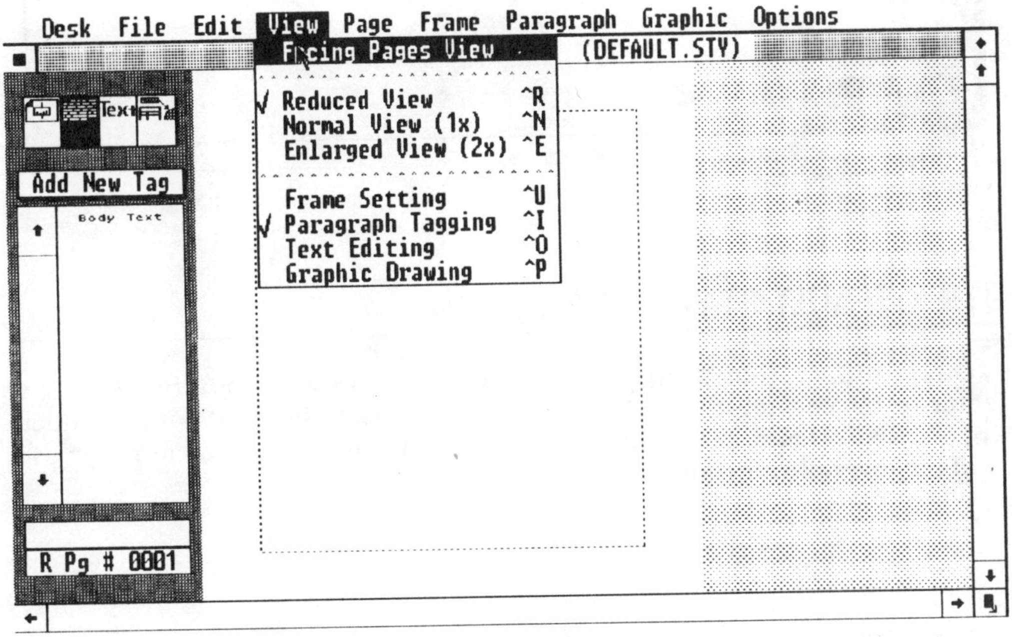

Figure 1.6

Point the mouse at the Facing Pages View selection. To select that view, click the mouse button. The view is compressed to display two pages.

At this point, there is only a single page in the document. Ventura assumes that the first page in any document is a right-side page. The space in which the left page would be displayed is blank. In documents including more than one page, both pages are displayed.

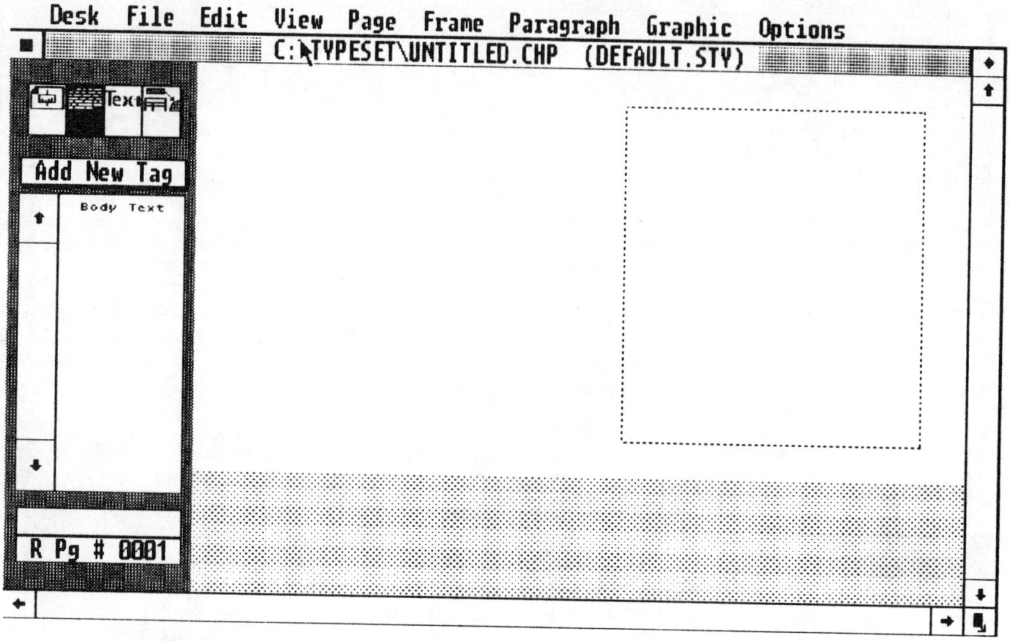

Figure 1.7

THE DEFAULT STYLE

Ventura differs from word processing programs in which the first step is to enter text. You must first decide the **style sheet** to be used with the document. Style sheets determine a document's formatting characteristics; they will be covered in detail later in this book.

Begin by loading the DEFAULT style sheet. When you first load Ventura, the program automatically assumes you want to use the style sheet last used; thus, the active style sheet depends on who used the computer last and what that user was working on. It may be that the DEFAULT style is already active. To load the DEFAULT sheet, first display the **File** menu. Point the mouse at the File menu title. The File menu appears as follows:

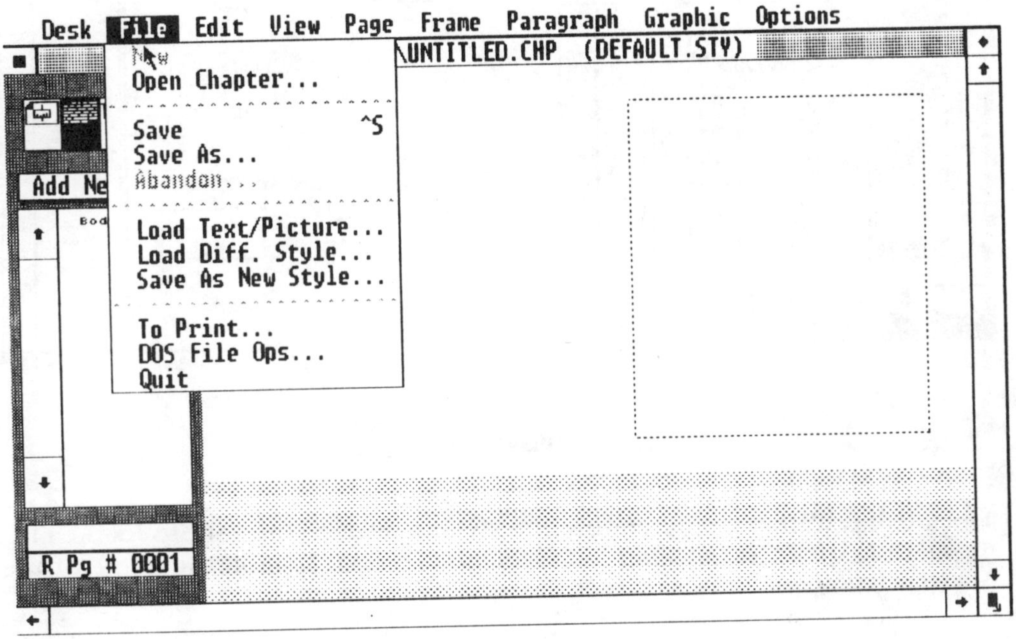

Figure 1.8

The File menu is divided into four sections separated by dotted lines. The first two sections are used to load and save Ventura chapters. The third section is used to load files that support chapters (such as text, picture, and style files). The last section contains the Print, DOS File Options, and Quit commands.

At this point, however, you want to load a specific style sheet.

Point the mouse at the Load Diff. Style selection and click the button. The ITEM SELECTOR box appears as follows:

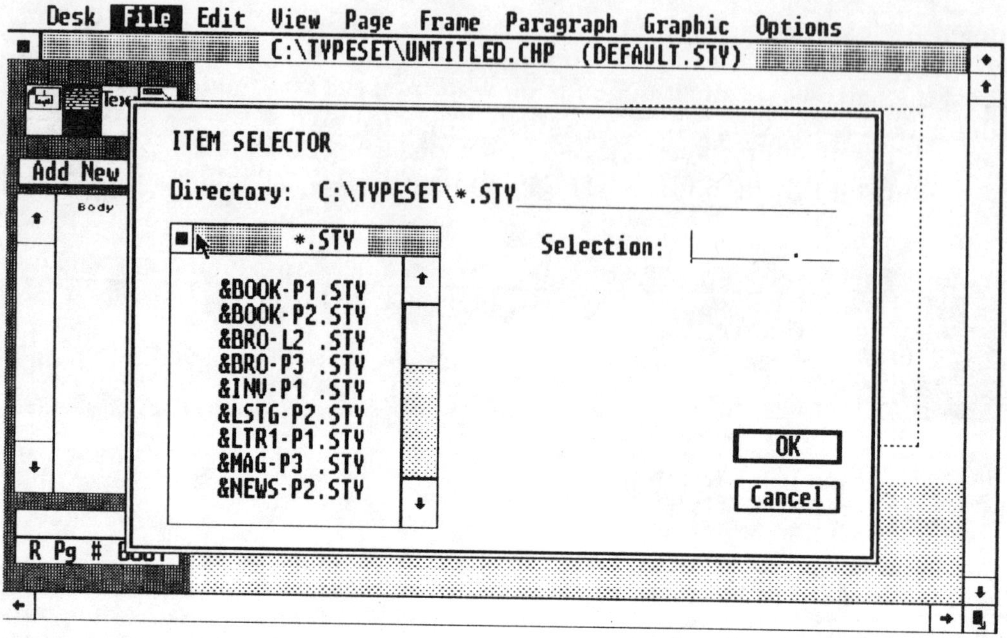

Figure 1.9

This display allows you to choose the style sheet file you want to load. This display is explained in detail later; for now, simply type in the name of the file that you want. Type

default

and press the Return key (noted throughout this book as [return]). The style sheet is loaded. At the top of the screen, the name of the style sheet file—DEFAULT.STY—appears to confirm the change.

You are now ready to begin creating a document.

VENTURA DOCUMENTS

Before beginning to enter text into a Ventura document, you must understand some important concepts fundamental to all Ventura operations.

How Ventura Differs from Word Processing

Many people using Ventura have previous experience with microcomputer software. Most commonly, this experience is with word processing programs such as WordStar, Multimate, WordPerfect, PFS Write, and Microsoft Word. These programs allow you to create, revise, and check the spelling of documents. Ventura is *not* intended as a replacement for word processing programs. Word processors allow you to check spelling and edit, revise, move, and copy text more efficiently than does Ventura.

ENTERING TEXT

When using Ventura, you will almost always prepare the text of the document with your favorite word processing program. It is possible, however, to directly create a document in Ventura's master frame.

When you execute a document in this way, Ventura creates a separate file for your text. This step is helpful because text entered into a master frame is saved in a file that can be easily accessed by a word processor, even though it was created in Ventura. Later, you can use your word processor to edit or spell-check a Ventura document.

To enter text, you must first place Ventura into the Text mode. As mentioned previously, Ventura contains four basic operational modes:

Frame mode	In this mode, operations involving the creation, editing, and positioning of frames can be executed.
Paragraph mode	Operations involving paragraph styles (for example, indenting, character size, font style, and line spacing operations) are executed in this mode.
Text mode	In this mode, Ventura allows you to enter and delete text. You can also underline, boldface, and change the capitalization of text. The Text mode operates in a manner similar to most word processing programs.
Graphics mode	This mode is used to add graphics such as boxes, circles, and lines to your document.

You can determine the active mode by examining the **mode indicator** box near the top left corner of the screen. Currently, the Paragraph mode is active. Because modes are so important, there are three methods for switching between them:

Mode indicator	You can change modes by pointing at the mode indicator you want to activate and clicking the mouse button.
View menu	The View menu lists the four modes. You can select a mode by pointing to the View menu heading, highlighting the name of the mode to be activated, and clicking the mouse button.
Control keys	Ventura also allows you to select operational modes by using the following Ctrl/key combinations:

[Ctrl/u]	selects the Frame mode.
[Ctrl/i]	selects the Paragraph mode.
[Ctrl/o]	selects the Text mode.
[Ctrl/p]	selects the Graphics mode.

To change to the Text mode, enter

[Ctrl/o]

The mode indicator changes; the text symbol is highlighted. Note that the cursor has changed to a new shape. The mouse cursor changes shape depending on the current mode. Regardless of the current mode, the mouse cursor changes to an arrow when you point at any of the menu headings or side bar displays. The mode controls the shape of the mouse cursor only when the cursor is located in the document area.

ZOOMING ONTO A PAGE

In the Reduced View, you can change to more detailed display modes by using the cursor and control keys. If you position the mouse cursor on the part of the page you want to enlarge, Ventura will enlarge that area when you change display modes.

Point the cursor in the upper left corner of the page.

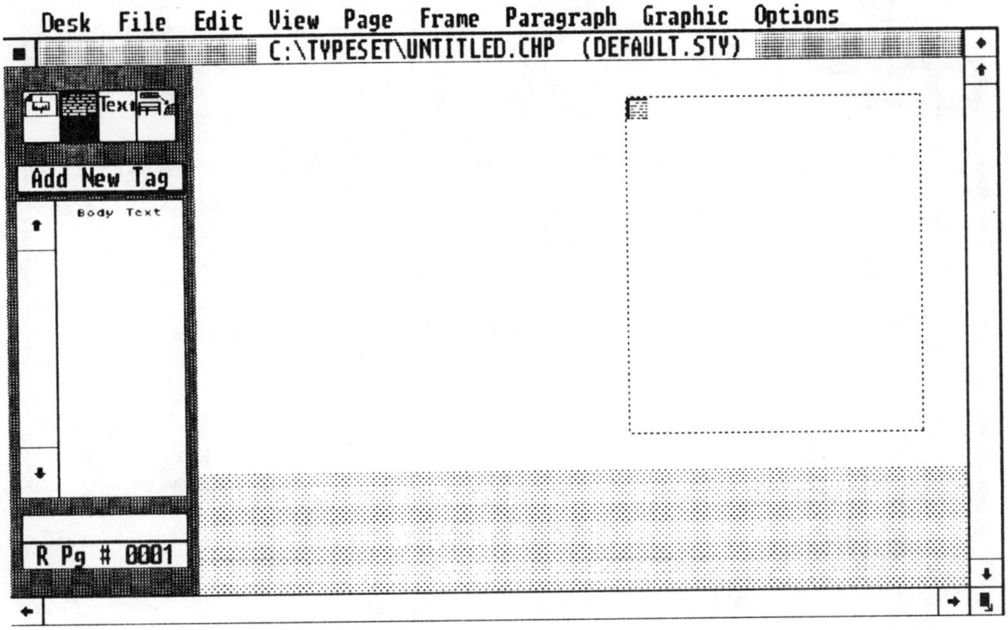

Figure 1.10

To change the display to Enlarged View, enter

[Ctrl/e]

Ventura enlarges the upper left corner of the screen.

Now that the screen display has zoomed in on the beginning of the page, position the mouse cursor once again as close as possible to the upper left-hand corner of the page. To instruct Ventura that you want to enter text at that position in the frame, click the mouse button.

The program displays a message box in the center of the screen:

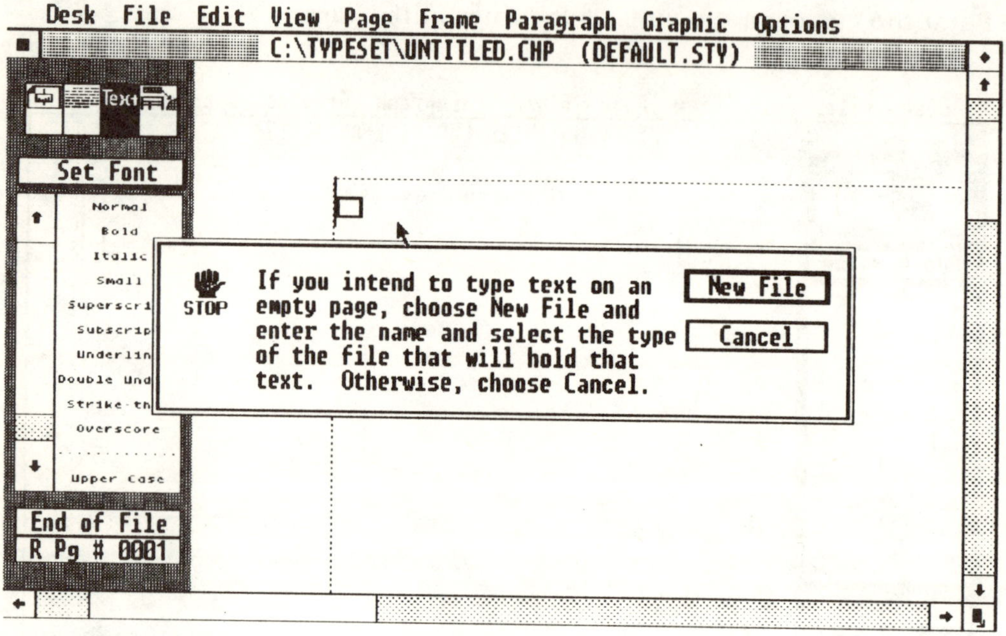

Figure 1.11

The box indicates that you are attempting to enter text into a frame without first creating a text file with a word processor. Ventura allows you to create a text file directly.

Point the mouse at the New File option and click the button.

The next box to appear is used to select the file's name and format type. Ventura does not have a special dialogue box for creating a new text file; instead, the **File Type/Rename** selection in the **Edit** menu is used. This option is most commonly used to change a file name or format, but, in this case, it serves as a file creation menu.

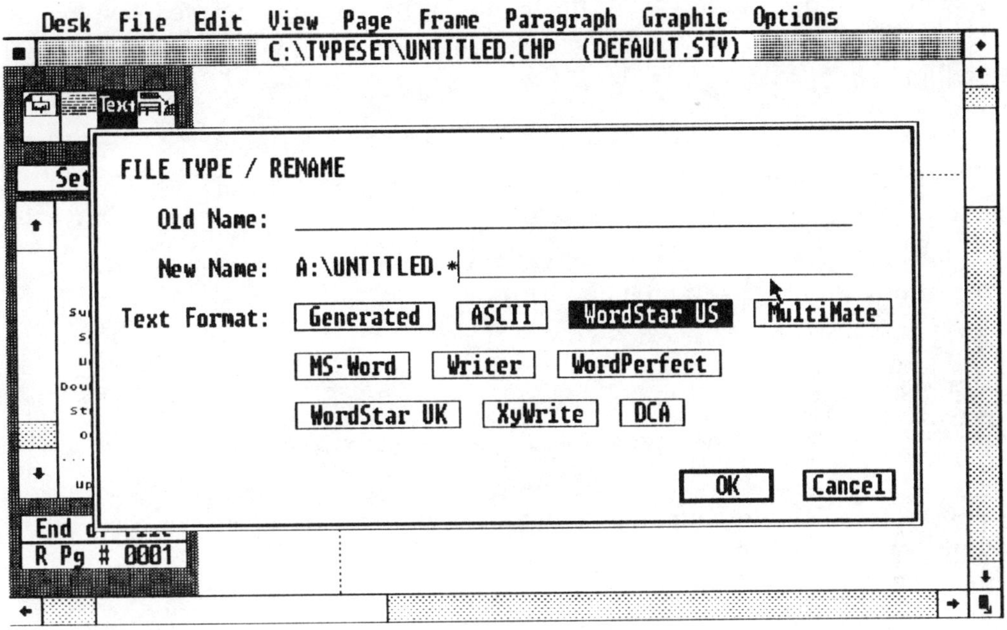

Figure 1.12

Ventura displays the 10 different file formats it recognizes, including eight of the most popular word processing programs used on the IBM PC and compatible computers.

In addition, Ventura recognizes a standard ASCII text file format, such as those produced by most spreadsheet and data base programs. For more information about Ventura and other applications such as Lotus 1-2-3 and dBASE III PLUS, see Chapter 8.

The **Generated** format is used for files produced by Ventura. These are usually text files for tables of contents or indices.

When Ventura creates an index or table of contents, it creates an ASCII text file that can be used with most word processing programs, which allows you to later edit and spell-check the document with a word processing program.

Choose a format that matches your word processing program, or choose ASCII if you don't have a preference. For this example, point the mouse cursor at WordPerfect and click the button.

The next step is to enter the file name. The name is entered on the line labeled **New name:**. The line currently contains the name UNTITLED.*. To clear the line for a new entry, press

[Esc]

Enter the name of the text file. Since this is the first document you are creating, name the file FIRST.DOC. Enter

first.doc
[return]

The normal Ventura display returns, including a small square box in the upper left corner of the page.

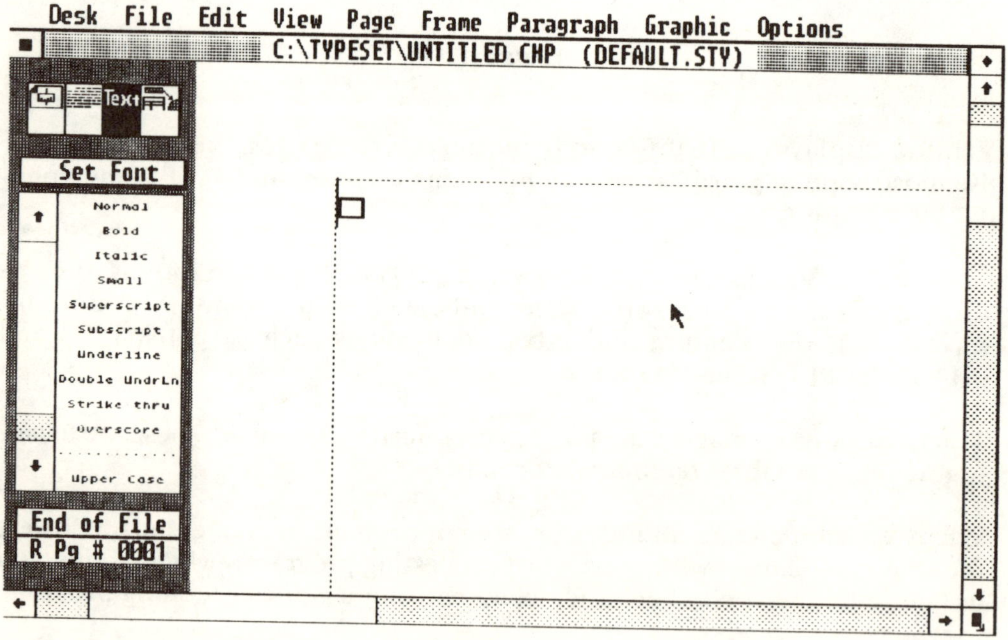

Figure 1.13

Next to the box is a blinking straight line referred to as the **text cursor**. There are now two cursors on the screen—the text cursor and the **mouse cursor.** The text cursor appears only in the Text mode and functions much like a cursor controlled by arrow keys in a word processing program. The mouse cursor remains where it was last positioned. Remember, you last used the mouse cursor to select a file format from the Edit menu. Ventura leaves the mouse cursor at that position even after the dialogue box has disappeared.

Next, enter the following text:

Microcomputer Software
[return]

The text appears on the screen as it is entered.

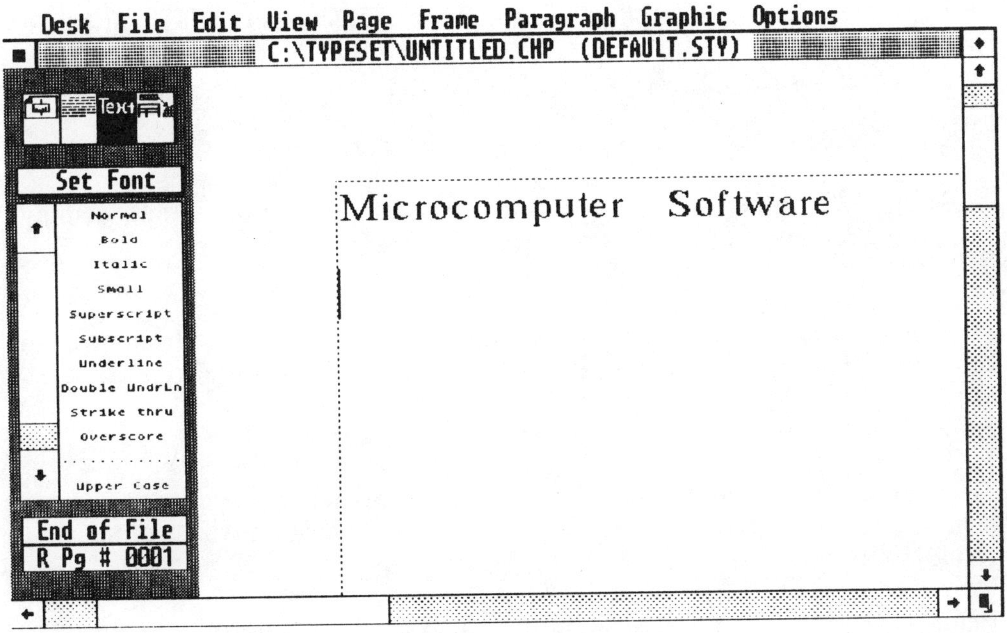

Figure 1.14

The text cursor moves along with the text much like a word processor cursor; the mouse cursor's position is unaffected. Continue by entering the following text:

Since 1981 when the IBM PC was introduced

Note that the word "introduced" doesn't appear on the screen. Because you are currently working in the Enlarged View, Ventura displays only a small section of the screen. Ventura does not automatically scroll the screen display to the right as you type; instead, you must manually change the position of the work window.

The current text is wider than the present screen can display. In effect, you typed off the right edge of the screen. The text *is* entered, but it is not currently visible on the screen.

To see the "invisible" text, you must change the screen display. There are two ways to display the text:

- Change the display mode to reveal more of the page.
- Stay in the same display mode and use the scrolling bars to display a different section of the page.

To illustrate the difference, try both methods. The bar at the bottom of the screen controls the horizontal position of the page display and represents the entire width of the page (including margins). The solid part of the bar represents the currently displayed portion of the page.

To display the right side of the page, point the mouse cursor at the solid portion of the bottom bar. When you do this, the mouse cursor symbol changes to an arrow.

Press and hold down the mouse button. The solid bar's border changes from a solid line to a dotted line.

With the button held down, move the cursor to the right approximately one inch. As you move, the solid portion of the bar is dragged to the right.

Release the mouse button. The screen display adjusts to the right, showing you the right portion of the line.

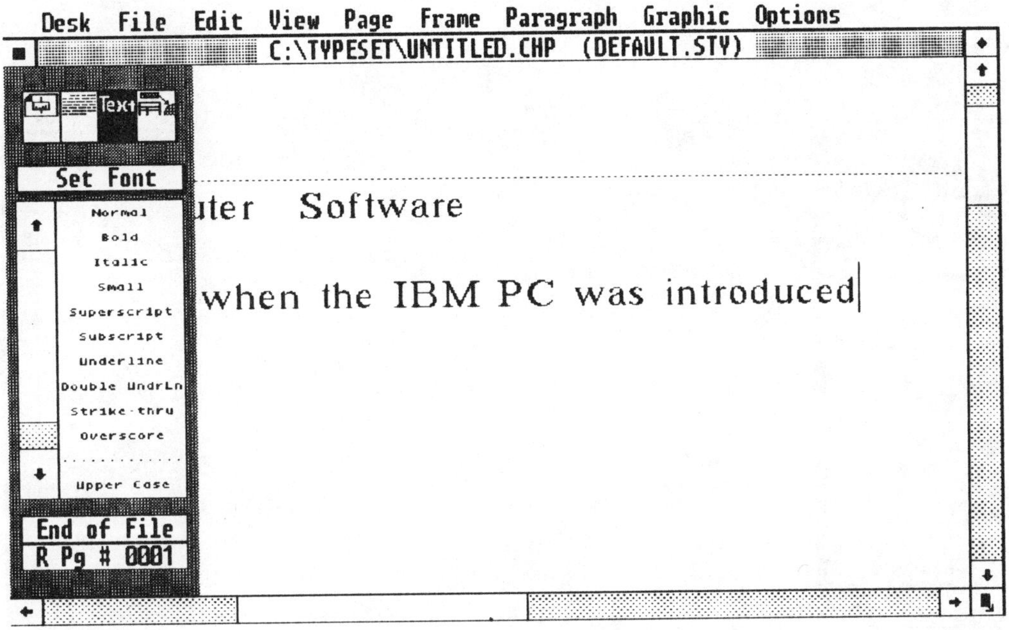

Figure 1.15

The text cursor remains in the same place. You can now continue the entry. Remember to put a space after the word "introduced." Enter

the quality and

Again, it seems that you are typing beyond the edge of the page. This time, change the display mode to reveal more of the page.

First, place the mouse cursor on the name "IBM." This cursor position provides Ventura with a point of reference so that when you zoom out, you will still see this part of the page. Next, enter the command to change the display to the Normal View mode by entering

[Ctrl/n]

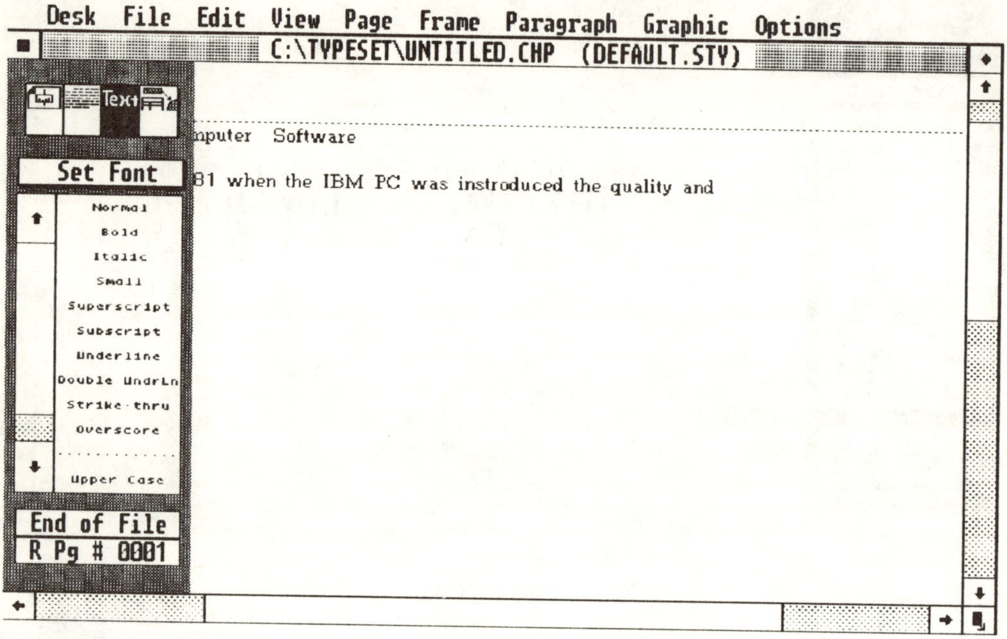

Figure 1.16

You can now see twice as much of the screen display. Enter

quantity of software programs

You may appear to be running out of room again. One way to move the display to the right is to use the bar to slide the display; however, this method can become tedious. You can combine both ways into a shortcut using the following method.

Point the mouse cursor at the word "software."

Enter

[Ctrl/n]

The screen display scrolls to the right. The position of the mouse cursor is used by Ventura as a guide to determine what part of the screen will be displayed. By placing the mouse cursor on the word "software," you can adjust the display based on that position by entering a [Ctrl/n] command.

[Ctrl/n] is the command for the normal display mode, which is already active. When you enter the [Ctrl/n], Ventura evaluates the screen display and adjusts the position based on the location of the mouse cursor. Continue the entry. Type

has

This time, you have typed to the right margin. Much like a word processor, Ventura automatically creates a new line when you reach the end of the current line. As a result, you should shift the display view to the left side of the page, which provides you with an opportunity to learn yet another way to change the display position.

Examine the bar at the bottom of the display. On the ends of the bar are arrows pointing left and right.

Point the mouse at the left arrow and click the button. The screen display moves to the left about .5". Click the mouse button again. The screen display again shifts left .5". Continue to click the mouse button until the solid bar shifts entirely to the left.

Pointing and clicking the mouse button at the arrows on the ends of the bars—both horizontal and vertical—moves the display one step toward the direction in which the arrows point. If you point at an arrow and hold the mouse button down, the click will automatically repeat until you release the button.

Continue entering text, pressing the Return key at the end of each line:

increased dramatically. Examples are:
Lotus 1-2-3 Release 2
WordPerfect 4.2
dBASE III Plus Version 1.1

Your screen should resemble the following:

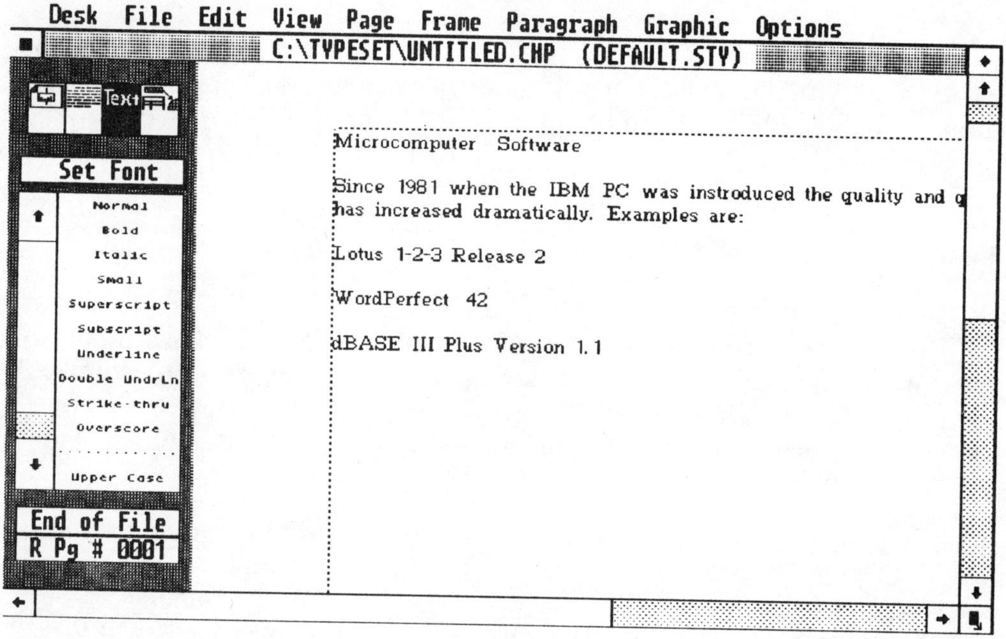

Figure 1.17

SAVING A FILE

You have now created a simple Ventura **chapter**. Ventura documents are referred to as chapters to distinguish them from documents produced with word processing programs. The main difference between a word processing document and a Ventura chapter file is that a chapter file ties together data stored in several types of files; a word processing document is a single computer file.

Ventura chapters consist of at least four files with different extensions:

.CHP This file—the main chapter file—contains a record of all other files used to create the finished document.

.CIF The Chapter Information File is designed to help other programs work with Ventura chapters.

.STY This file contains the style sheet. All chapters must have an associated style sheet file.

.DOC This is the document file that contains the text of the document. This file is a word processor file in a format compatible with Ventura. The DOC extension is optional. Some programs like Multimate and Microsoft Word expect document files to have DOC extensions. Others, like WordStar and WordPerfect, can accept any extension or none at all.

To save the text as part of a chapter file, enter

[Ctrl/s]

or select **Save** from the File menu. Ventura displays the ITEM SELECTOR dialogue box.

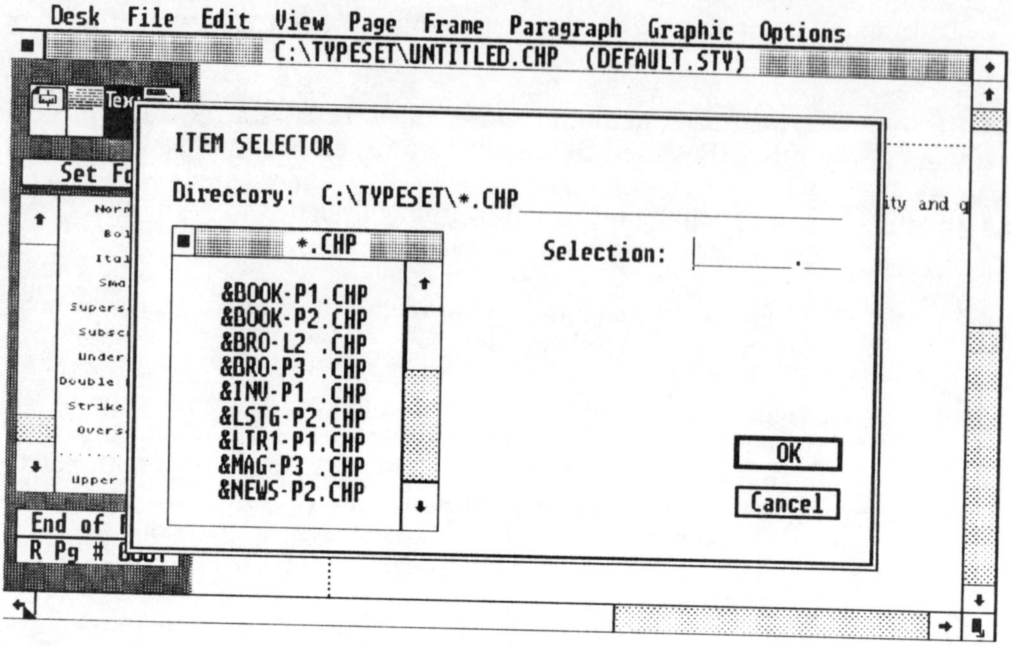

Figure 1.18

You will learn more later about the dialogue box. For now, simply enter the name of the chapter:

software
[return]

The chapter file is saved, and Ventura returns to the screen display exactly as you left it. The only change is the name of the chapter, SOFTWARE.CHP, which appears at the top of the display. The full name that appears at the top of the display is C:\TYPESET\SOFTWARE.CHP. C:\TYPESET\ refers to the current DOS volume and directory settings. For a full discussion of related DOS concepts, refer to Appendix A.

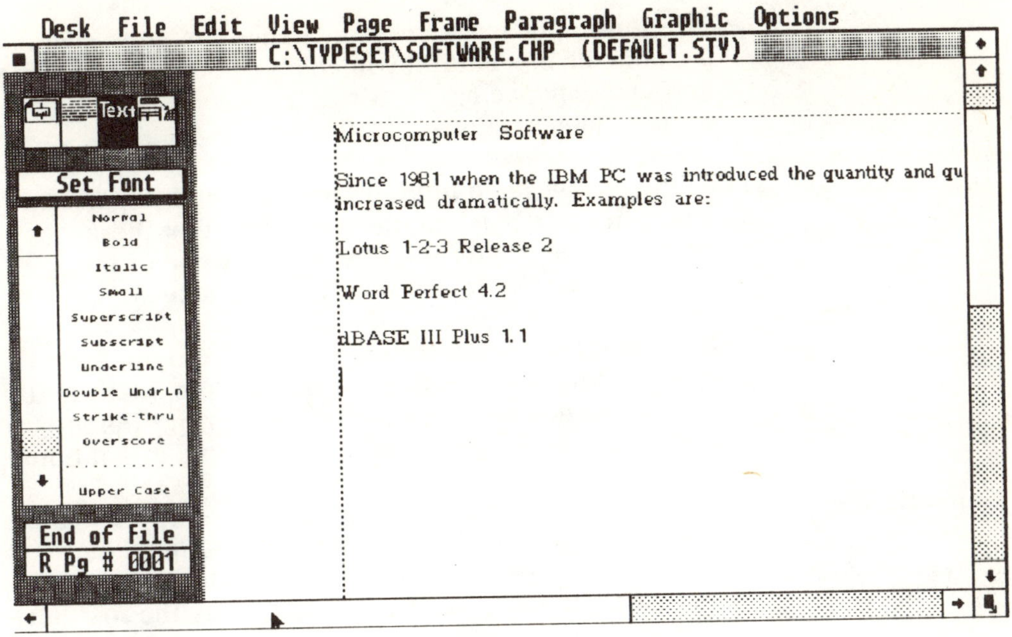

Figure 1.19

TEXT ENHANCEMENTS

So far, you have created a document consisting of a single type of text. In Text mode, Ventura allows you to add a number of character enhancements. The side bar located on the left side of the screen lists the enhancements Ventura can perform. They fall into three groups:

Set Font — This option changes the print character font and point size. The term **font** refers to the shape and style of characters. Some print styles, such as Dutch (Times-Roman), use various line thicknesses to form characters. Other fonts, such as Swiss (Helvetica), use a consistent line thickness throughout characters. **Point size** refers to the size of characters; the larger the point size, the larger the character.

Keep in mind that when you change the point size of a character in Ventura, you change both the horizontal and vertical spacing. You will learn more about fonts in later sections.

Text Modifications

These changes add bold, underline, italic, superscript, and other attributes to the text. Note that these changes do not alter the font or point size of the text; they modify fonts already on the screen.

Italic and bold print are implemented only in fonts that support those features. For example, small fonts usually do not support bold or italic print. Large fonts used for headlines may be available in bold only.

Capitalization

This feature is used to change the case—upper and lower—of text. You can change to all uppercase or all lowercase text. Ventura also provides an option named **Capitalize**, which capitalizes only the first letter of each word.

Highlighting Text

Ventura is an **object-oriented** program, which means that you must first select the part of the text to be changed. The selected area is the object. Then, you must choose an enhancement from the side bar to be carried out on the selected text.

Suppose you want to indicate bold type for the letters "IBM PC." The first step is to highlight the letters you want to change.

Position the mouse cursor on the "I." Hold down the mouse button and move the mouse to the right.

As you move the mouse, the color of the selected text reverses. Move the mouse until "IBM PC" is highlighted. Release the mouse button.

The text should resemble the following:

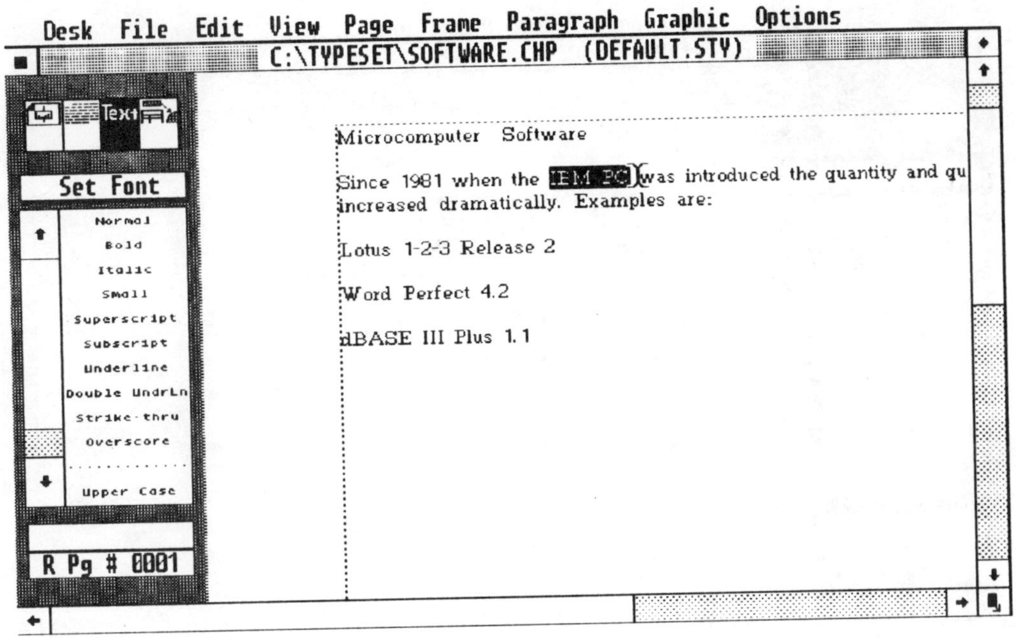

Figure 1.20

Moving the mouse too far – or in the wrong direction – won't cause a problem. As long as you hold the button down, you can expand or contract the amount of highlighted text.

If you highlight the wrong part of the text, you can remove the highlight by placing the mouse cursor anywhere in the document window and clicking the button.

Now that the text is highlighted, you can select text enhancements from the side bar.

To change the highlighted text to bold, point the mouse at the word "Bold" on the side bar and click the button.

Because the text is still highlighted, the bold effect may be difficult to see. You can remove the highlight by pointing the mouse anywhere in the document window and clicking the mouse button. The text should resemble Figure 1.21.

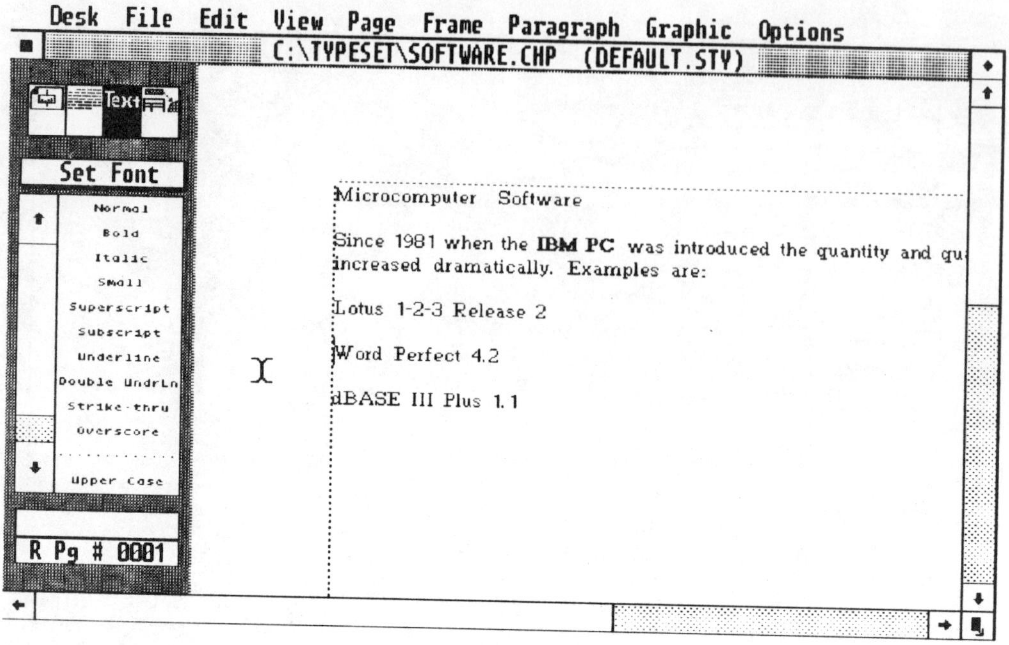

Figure 1.21

The next step is to change the names of software programs to italic text.

Use the mouse to highlight all text beginning with the word "Lotus." You needn't be very precise when pointing at a block of text. For example, you can begin highlighting by positioning the mouse cursor to the left of the word "Lotus" in the margin area on the left side of the screen. Next, hold down the mouse button and move in a diagonal direction toward the lower right corner of the text block – the phrase "Plus 1.1."

As you move the mouse, you will see that the highlight covers all text between the two points. When the entire block is highlighted, click the mouse button, and the screen will return to normal.

To change the text to italic, point the mouse at the Italic option and click the button. The text is italicized.

Another option is to change the capitalization of the text. You might want the title "Microcomputer Software" to appear in uppercase.

Highlight the two words. The next step is to choose the capitalization enhancement you want to use. At this point, only one option – **Upper Case** – is visible on the side bar display. Notice, however, that the side bar display contains its own positioning bar with arrows at both ends.

This bar works in much the same way as the horizontal and vertical window position bars; its purpose is to reveal additional options in the side bar display.

Note that a small portion of the bar just above the down arrow is shown in gray, which indicates that the displayed list is only a partial list of possible options. Some options – those below Upper Case – are not visible at this time.

To display the additional options, point the mouse cursor at the down arrow and click the button. The display shifts down one line, revealing a new option – **Capitalize**.

Click the mouse button. Another option – **Lower Case** – appears. Also note that the solid portion of the bar has now reached the bottom of the bar, indicating that you have reached the end of the option list. The gray portion of the bar is now at the top, indicating that there are options at the top of the list that are not currently visible.

This type of bar system enables Ventura to display options in windows of a fixed size. By examining the gray portions of the bar, you can determine if parts of the list are currently hidden from view. If the bar is completely solid, the displayed list is a complete list of all available options.

In this case, you want to change the entire text to uppercase. Point the mouse at Upper Case and click the button. The text is changed to all uppercase (see Figure 1.22).

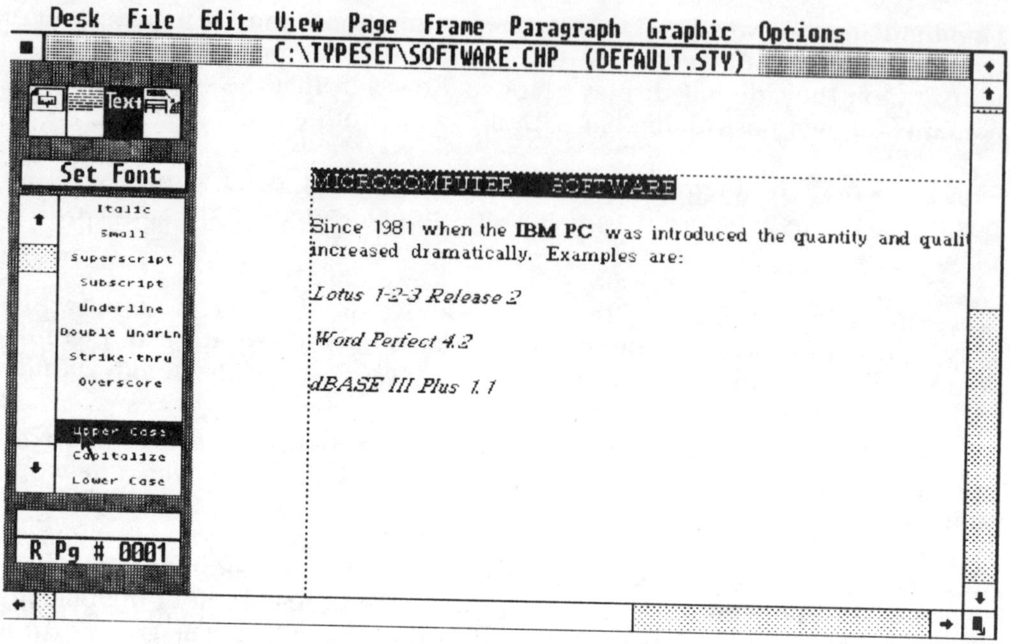

Figure 1.22

Ventura does not automatically remove a highlight from text after you select a text enhancement. Rather, the highlight remains on that portion of text until you select another area by clicking the mouse button, which is useful because you can easily change a text enhancement by selecting a different option.

Suppose you are not sure which way you like the title. To examine the title with only the first letter of each word in uppercase, select the Capitalize option. Point the mouse at Capitalize and click the button.

The text is altered according to your selection. You can switch back and forth as many times as you like. Change the text back to all uppercase. Point the mouse at Upper Case and click the button.

You might also want the text underlined. Point the mouse at **Underline** and click the button.

The text is underlined. Suppose you want to remove a text modification. The first option, which is not currently visible, is **Normal**. To display the top of the option list, point the mouse at the text enhancement box arrow (pointing up) and click the button twice.

To remove the underline, point the mouse at the Normal option and click the button.

Changing text to Normal removes *all* print modifications previously assigned to a section of the text. For example, suppose you selected Underline and Italic, but you want only Italic. When you change the text to Normal, both the underline and italic attributes are removed. You must then select the Italic option again to display the text as you want.

Choosing Normal has no effect on the capitalization type you have selected. The text is still highlighted, which means that it is still selected for further modification.

Changing Fonts

So far, you have used two of the three text enhancement options available in the text mode—text modifications and capitalization. The third function is controlled through the **Set Font** box that appears just above the side bar display.

Font changes alter the size and shape of the characters entered into the document.

To change the font of the highlighted text, point the mouse at Set Font and click the button. You can also activate the Set Font option by pressing [Ctrl/2].

Ventura displays the FONT SETTING FOR SELECTED TEXT dialogue box (see Figure 1.23).

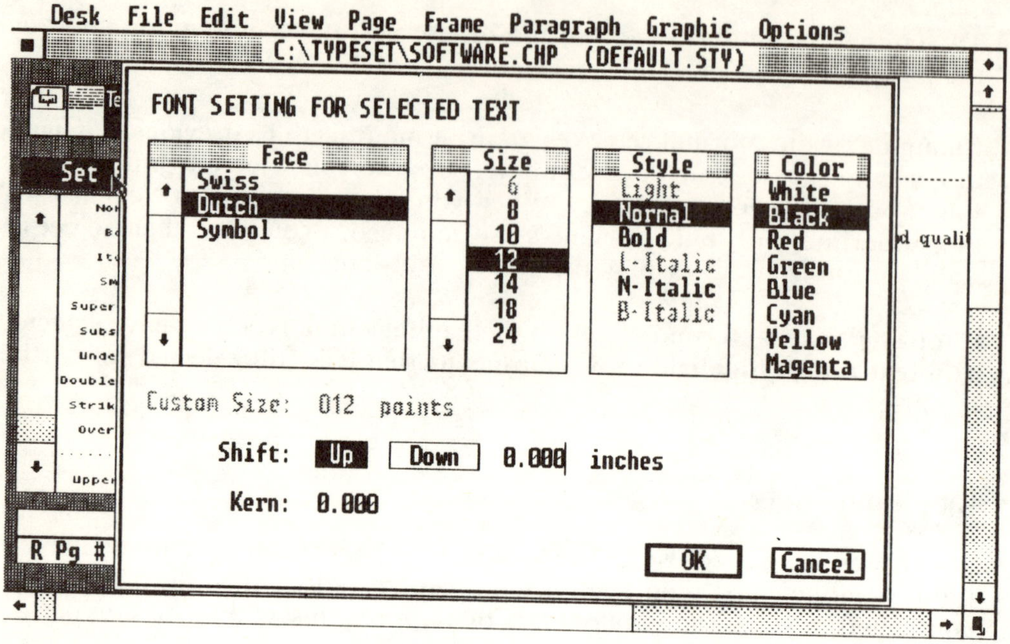

Figure 1.23

The following specifications can be selected for the highlighted text:

Face This selection refers to the style and shape of the characters. The **Face** box lists the names of the fonts available. The list will vary depending on the printer in use. In this example, three fonts – Swiss, Dutch, and Symbol – are listed. Your printer may have a different list of fonts. When fonts selected in this book are not available on your printer, choose the closest font as a substitute. To simplify selection, only two fonts types are used in this book: Dutch (also referred to as Times-Roman) and Swiss (also referred to as Helvetica). Most laser printers support at least these two fonts.

Size

The size of the letters in the fonts is measured in **points.** Points is a term used in printing and typesetting and is not familiar to most people. Points are measured as follows:

Printers divide an inch into 6 parts or **picas.** A pica is divided into 12 parts or points. In summary,

one inch = 6 picas
one pica = 12 points
one inch = 72 picas

While these measurements may seem strange if you are not acquainted with printing terminology, many computer users know that most computer printers print six lines of text in each inch of vertical space. In other words, each line is 1/6" in height. Printers and typesetters refer to each line as one pica, or 12 points, in height.

Suppose you want the title to stand out from the rest of the text. Swiss (Helvetica) fonts are usually good for headings and titles because their lines are of uniform thickness. To select the Swiss font, point the mouse at Swiss and click the button.

The highlight moves from Dutch to Swiss. Next, change the point size to 18. Point the mouse at 18 and click the button.

Note that the Style box changes to display fewer style options. Large fonts are usually limited to one or two style options. In this case, the Swiss 18-point font is supplied only in bold, so it is not necessary to select bold. The screen reflects the selections you have made (see Figure 1.24).

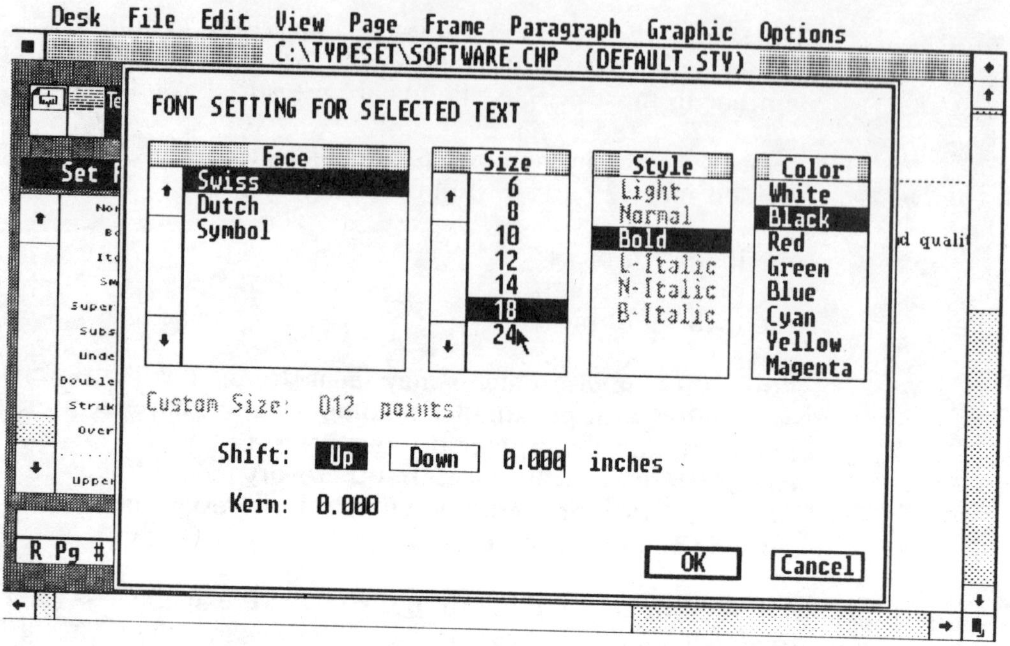

Figure 1.24

Now that you have selected the font you want to use, you can complete the entry in one of two ways:

OK box Point the mouse at the **OK** box and click the button.

[return] Press the Return key.

In this case, press

[return]

The document is displayed with the text in its new font:

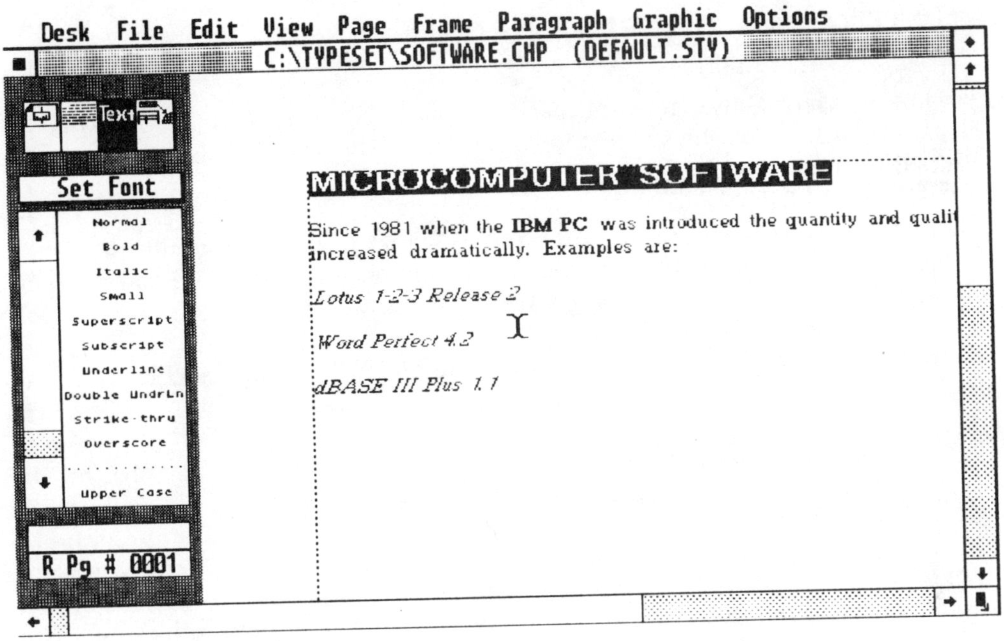

Figure 1.25

Ventura displays the text as closely as possible to the final printed product. Text set for large fonts appears in proportion to the small text, just as it will when printed. This ability is often referred to by the acronym **WYSIWYG**, which stands for "what you see is what you get." Keep in mind that the correspondence between the screen display and the final product is only approximate. The screen display of most computers does not contain enough pixels to emulate the resolution of a laser printer; however, the text does appear in the approximate proportions it will appear in the final printed product.

Note that increasing the point size of the title increases both its height and width.

Ventura is an intelligent program when it comes to changes in fonts because it adjusts the layout of each page to accommodate changes in the size and shape of any text element. As you learn to create more complex formats, you will appreciate this ability more and more.

THE TEXT AND MOUSE CURSORS

Normally, when Ventura is in the Text mode, two cursors appear on the text display. The mouse cursor is controlled by the mouse and the text cursor is controlled by arrow keys.

The text cursor allows you to enter and edit text just as you would in a word processing program in which the left and right arrow keys move character by character, and the up and down arrow keys move line by line.

The mouse cursor is independent of text lines and columns and responds to any movement you make with the mouse.

There may, however, be times when you want to achieve with the mouse cursor the character-by-character control of the text cursor. For example, in the name "dBASE III PLUS," the characters "BASE III PLUS" are usually printed in a larger font than the other characters. In other words, you must highlight those seven characters to change their font. You can use the mouse cursor, but it might be easier to use the arrow keys to control selection. This is especially true when the existing font is of a small point size.

To control the mouse cursor with the arrow keys, enter

[Ctrl/right shift]

You must use the Shift key on the right side of the keyboard; the left Shift key will not work properly.

Ventura issues a beep. The mouse cursor is now controlled by both the mouse and the arrow keys. Press

[down arrow]

This time, the mouse cursor moves down a line. Use the arrow keys to position the mouse cursor on the letter "B" in the word "dBASE."

To select this letter as the beginning of the highlight, click the mouse button.

Next, use the Right Arrow key to move the mouse cursor to the space following "III."

To select the intervening text, hold down the Shift key and click the mouse button. The text is highlighted. The font can be changed from the font selection box, which can be accessed from the keyboard or by pointing the mouse at the Set Font box and clicking the button. Access the FONT SETTING box from the keyboard by pressing

[Ctrl/2]

The FONT SETTING menus appear. To change the font size, point the mouse at 14 and click the button. Then, press

[return]

The highlighted text is enlarged to 14-point type.

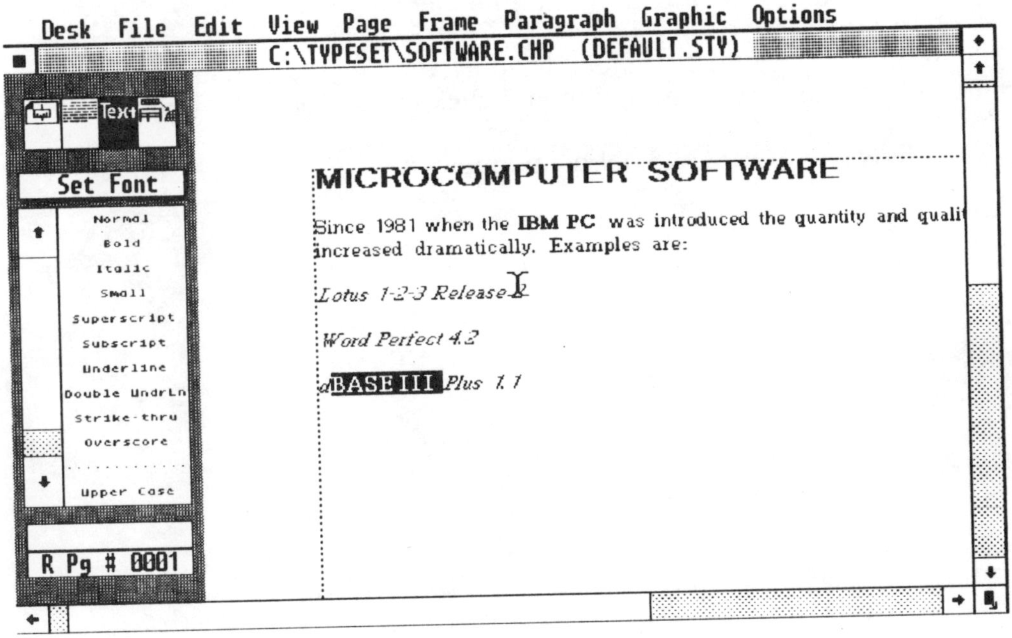

Figure 1.26

To release the mouse cursor from the control of the arrow keys, enter

[Ctrl/right shift]

Once again, Ventura issues a beep. The arrow keys – not the mouse cursor – now control the text cursor.

PRINTING A DOCUMENT

You have now explored the basic editing and text enhancement functions of Ventura, which only scratches the surface of this program's power. You have, however, established a good understanding of basic Ventura techniques.

The next step is to print the created document and see the final results of your work.

The **Print** command is found on the File menu, which is used for all commands involving the input or output of information. Since printing is an output operation, it is included on the File menu.

Point the mouse at the File menu heading; the File menu is displayed. Point the mouse at the To Print option and click the button.

The PRINT INFORMATION menu appears:

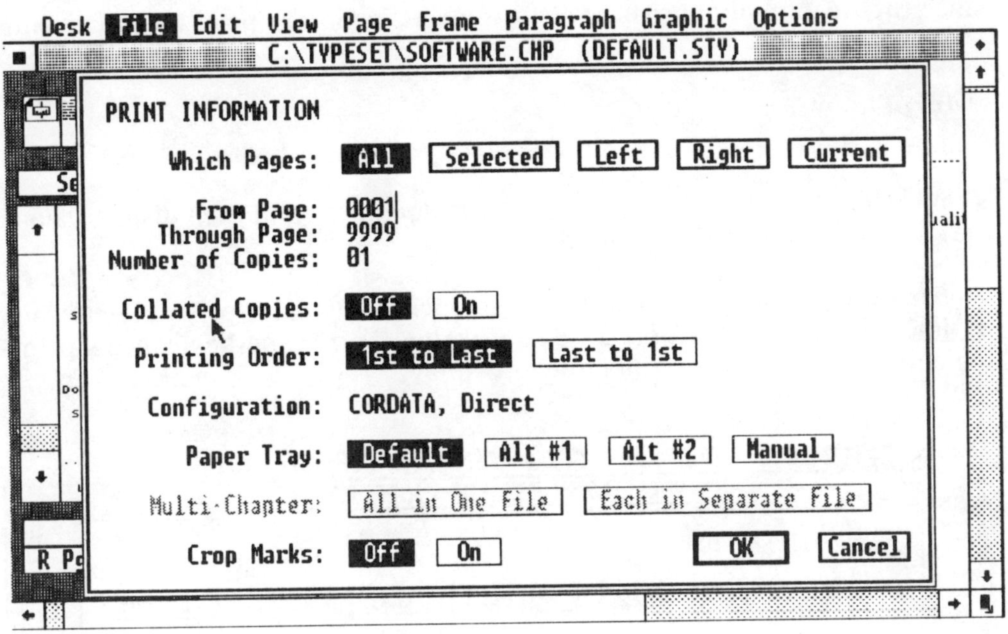

Figure 1.27

Ventura allows you to select the pages to be printed; you have five choices:

All Prints all pages in a chapter.

Selected Prints a selected range of pages. The beginning and ending page numbers must be manually entered.

Left Prints only left pages. In Ventura, all left pages are even-numbered. This option is useful when you want to print on both sides of the paper. With laser printers, you can first print all left pages on one side of the paper and then use the same paper again to print the right pages on the other side.

Right Prints only right pages, which are odd-numbered pages.

Current Prints only the page currently displayed on the screen.

Since the document consists of a single page, begin the printing by pressing

[return]

Ventura loads the files needed to print the document and then displays a box indicating the page being printed.

This feature is handy for printing large documents; it helps you keep track of how far printing has progressed. Pressing the Escape key cancels printing and returns you to the document display.

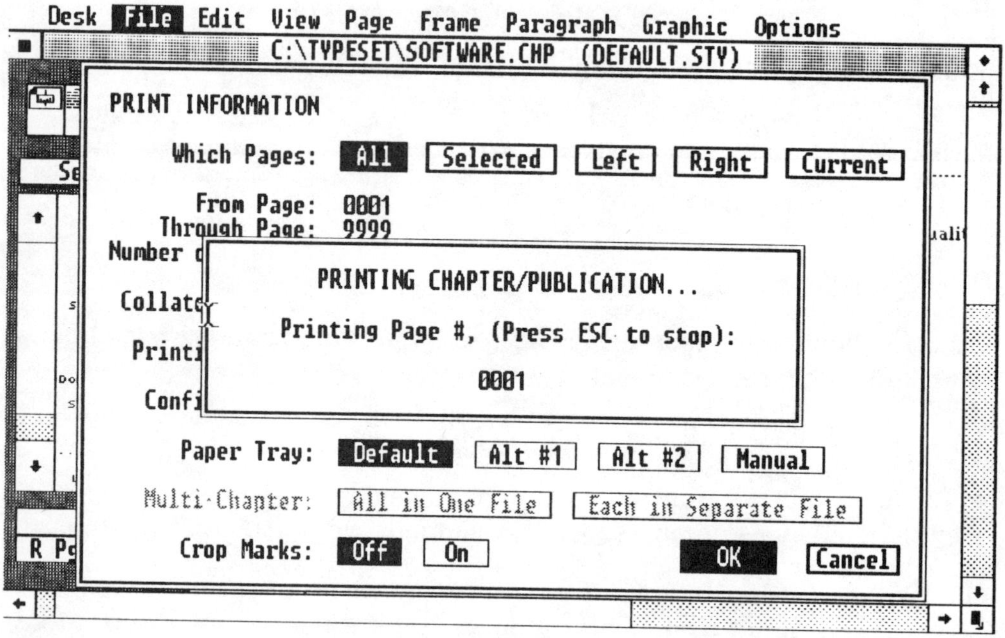

Figure 1.28

When the printing is complete, the normal display reappears. To complete this first chapter, exit the Ventura program by pointing the mouse at the File menu heading; then, point the mouse at Quit, and click the button.

Ventura keeps track of whether or not your chapter has been saved. In this case, Ventura reacts to text enhancements added to the text since you last saved the chapter by displaying the following dialogue box:

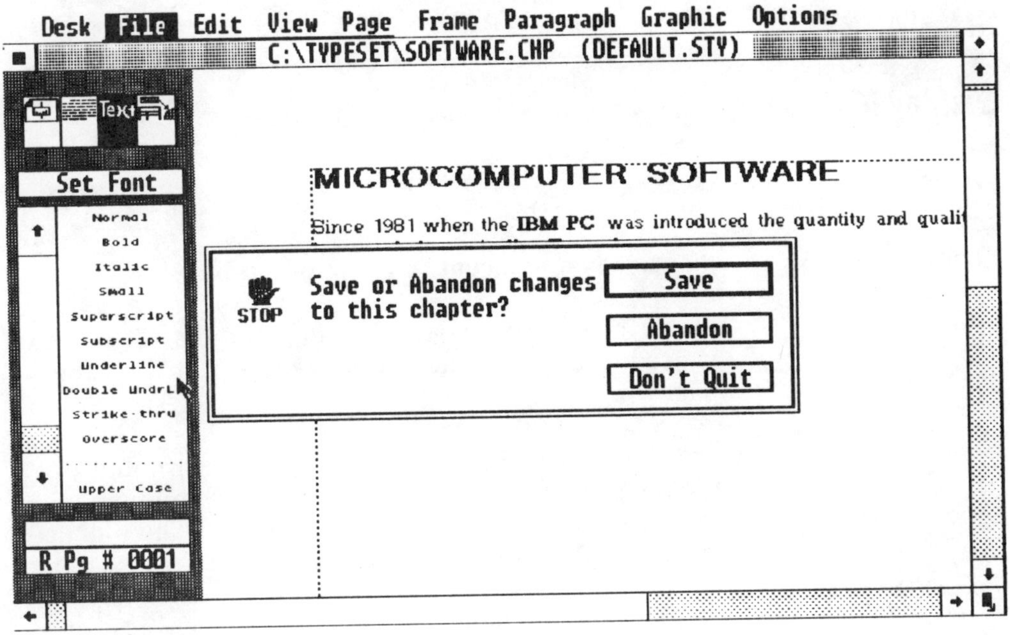

Figure 1.29

You are presented with three options: save the changes, abandon the changes, or cancel the Quit option and return to Ventura. In this case, you want to save the changes.

Point the mouse at Save and click the button.

The chapter is saved, and the program returns you to the operating system level. You have now completed your first Ventura document.

SUMMARY

Display Modes

Ventura's screen display uses the following four modes:

Facing Pages	displays two adjacent pages at one time.
Reduced	displays an entire page including margins. This view is used to evaluate the overall layout of text on the page.
Normal	used for text entry and formatting. The amount of text displayed in this mode depends on the type of screen display used with the computer. The higher the resolution, the more text can be viewed.
Enlarged	displays the document at double the magnification of Normal mode. This mode is used to examine a document's details.

The modes can be changed by using the View menu or—with the exception of the Facing Pages mode—by entering a Ctrl/key combination from the keyboard as follows:

[Ctrl/r]	Reduced
[Ctrl/n]	Normal
[Ctrl/e]	Enlarged

Operational Modes

Ventura contains four basic operational modes. You can activate a mode by using the mouse to click on the mode's symbol on the side bar or by using Ctrl/key combinations.

Frame

Ventura automatically establishes a master frame for each chapter you create. You can use the master frame alone or add more frames to the chapter. Pressing [Ctrl/u] places Ventura in the Frame mode.

Paragraph

Paragraph mode is used to create and modify paragraph style tags, which are discussed in more detail in Chapter 2. Pressing [Ctrl/i] activates the Paragraph mode.

Text

Text mode allows you to add, edit, and revise text. This mode operates much like a typical word processor. You can add text enhancements such as bold, italic, and underlining in this mode. Pressing [Ctrl/o] activates the Text mode.

Graphics

Graphics mode allows you to add nontext items such as lines and boxes to your chapter. Pressing [Ctrl/p] activates the Graphics mode.

Highlighting

In the Text mode, Ventura selects text for modification by highlight. Once text is highlighted, you can choose enhancements from the side bar display. Text mode modifications include font changes, print modifications, and capitalization options.

CHAPTER 2

TEXT FORMATTING

In Chapter 1, you learned the basic text editing and text enhancement functions of Ventura. This chapter goes beyond those basic concepts and teaches you the fundamental aspects of Ventura's ability to control the format of your text. **Format** refers to the way the text is actually placed on the page and includes indents, line spacing, tab alignments, page breaks, and ruling lines. Ruling lines are straight lines that are added to the text display to visually mark text. In addition, you can associate text enhancements, such as those used in Chapter 1, with a specific type of paragraph formatting called **styling.**

It is in the concept of styling where Ventura dramatically departs from the standard word processing concepts found in programs like WordStar, Multimate, and WordPerfect. Microsoft Word, however, contains a styling feature that operates similarly to Ventura. If you understand Word style sheets, you will find that Ventura operates in an almost identical fashion. Most word processing programs allow for formatting of paragraphs, tabs, indents, and, to some degree, changes in font and point size. But all of these features are implemented *manually.* You must manually enter the commands to change each paragraph format or group of paragraph formats each time you want to vary from the default margins and tabs. If you want to replicate identical formats in two different places in one document, you must remember the exact settings and enter them manually each time you want that format.

This system has a number of drawbacks. Since it is *your* memory, not the computer's, that keeps track of the settings, it is hard to consistently format a document, let alone a series of related documents such as chapters in a book. Even worse, if you decide to change a format, you must manually search for each location in the document where that formatting occurs. Once you find it, you must change the setting each time to match the new setting.

Ventura takes a different approach. With styling, it separates from any specific area of the text the settings used to create a specific format. Ventura stores the settings in a **stylesheet** file that is separate from the text file. A Ventura chapter is essentially the combination of two files: one that holds the text and another that holds the style specifications.

This chapter will show you how styles are created, used, and stored and what advantages they provide over the manual formatting concept found in most word processing programs.

THE TEXT FILE

In the last chapter, you created a document by entering text directly into the master frame. While it is possible create documents directly in Ventura, it is generally recommended that text be prepared with the aid of a word processing program, preferably one that is directly compatible with Ventura. Such word processing programs include WordStar, WordPerfect, Microsoft Word, Multimate, Displaywrite III or IV, XYWRITE, or Xerox Writer. If you use a different word processing program, you can still import text into Ventura by converting your text files into ASCII format. For example, PFS Write allows you to store text in ASCII format. Another method is to convert your word processing files to a format Ventura recognizes. For example, WordStar 2000 users can convert their files to WordStar, which can then be used by Ventura.

There are many advantages to creating text with a word processor as opposed to the direct entry method discussed in Chapter 1. Word processing programs have greater facilities for making entries and corrections, such as search and replace functions, spell checking, and block move and copy operations. Word processing programs can handle files faster than Ventura because they use the built-in characer set of the computer. Ventura uses its own typographical fonts, which operate more slowly. Word processing programs also can generally handle larger files than can Ventura. Some advanced programs such as Microsoft Word and WordPerfect allow you to work on more than one document at a time.

With that explanation in mind, as the next step you need to use a word processing program to create the text of your document. For example, the document you will create here is a balance sheet showing the assets and liabilities of a business. This type of document normally requires figures aligned into columns; however, with the word processor, you need only enter the bare text without being concerned with text alignment. The alignment of the column can be left for Ventura and will be accomplished after the column has been loaded into that program from the word processor.

Figure 2.1 contains the text of the document you will prepare. The arrows show the places in the document where [return]s should be entered.

```
A PERSONAL INVITATION←
ULTRAMATH 4-D←
We would like to introduce you to what we believe is the new look
and feel for Spreadsheet software for the year 2000.←
Your hosts are←
Walter La Fish and Carl Lafong of Independent Computer Support
Associates.←
This is a personal invitation to a Private Preview for very
important computer uses at the ICSA hospitality suite 8657.← ←
The Regal Regency Marquis Hotel, 1770 Main Street, Fort Wayne,
IN.←
Buffet and Bar from 12:00 noon to 12:00 midnight Tuesday,
Wednesday and Thursday, September 1st, 2nd, and 3rd.←
Come and enjoy our hospitality and our ongoing product
demonstration.←
```

Figure 2.1

Note that you should not leave blank lines between paragraphs. In Ventura, spacing between paragraphs is handled as part of the paragraph formatting options you will learn about as this chapter, as well as the book, progresses.

The example document in Figure 2.1 uses the WordPerfect text processor; however, you can still prepare the same text in Word, WordStar, or Multimate. The default margins may be different from those in WordPerfect, but that difference is irrelevant as long as the [return]s are entered at the correct positions. Ventura will reformat the lines to match its own margins.

Save the file as **INVIT.WP**. Remember that WordPerfect does not automatically add the WP extension; you must enter it manually. While it is not necessary to add this extension to a document prepared with WordPerfect, it is a good habit to get into so you can identify WordPerfect document files when they appear later in a directory display.

Once you have completed and saved the document, return to the root directory by entering

cd
[return]

Start Ventura by entering

vp
[return]

LOADING A TEXT FILE

The benefit of using your favorite word processor to create a document is that you can take advantage of its text editing, thesaurus, and spelling features, and reserve Ventura for the formatting tasks.

Most word processors use the text mode of the IBM PC and compatibles to display text because that display is usually easier to read. The computer can display large amounts of text at a much higher rate of speed in the IBM PC mode than it can in Ventura, which must calculate the exact visual proportions of all the characters it displays.

Now that you have the text file prepared, you can load it into a Ventura page.

Point the mouse at the File menu title. Then point the mouse at the Load Text/Picture selection and click the mouse button.

Ventura displays the Load Text/Picture menu box (see Figure 2.2).

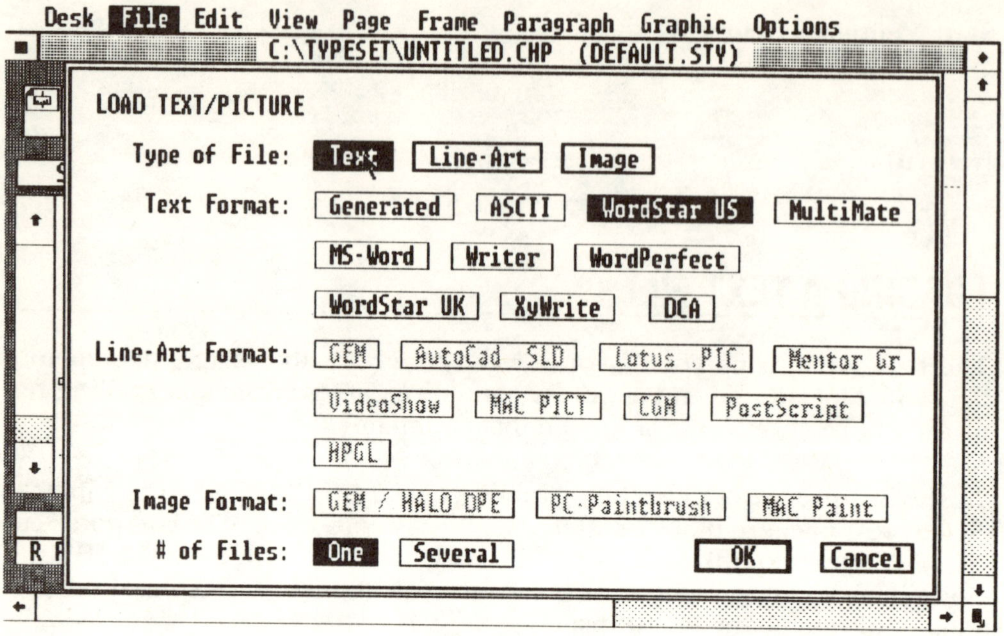

Figure 2.2

This display is important; you will see it quite often when working with Ventura. This menu allows you to load three types of files:

- **Text**. Text files are created with a word processor, a text editor, or applications that convert data to standard ASCII text files. The ASCII setting on the Load menu refers to files that end paragraphs with two carriage returns. These files should be loaded using the WordStar format. Many popular programs can create ASCII text files that contain at least part of the information they usually store in their own file format. For example, Lotus 1-2-3 can copy spreadsheet values and labels (not formulas) to a print file with a PRN extension. These files can be loaded as WordStar files. The procedure used to format Lotus 1-2-3 print files is covered in detail later in this book.

- **Line-Art.** Line-art refers to a special type of graphic structure used to create picture files. Line-art comes from programs such as Lotus 1-2-3, AutoCad, MacPaint, and Gem Draw and consists of vector instructions that can be calculated in order to create an image. Line-art images can be scaled up or down with little loss of resolution.

- **Image.** Image files are bit-mapped images that consist of a pixel-by-pixel description of the image.

To load a text file, highlight the Text box by pointing the mouse at Text and clicking the button.

Note that when you select Text, all the options for the other two file types, line-art and image, appear in gray to indicate that those options cannot be used at this time.

The next step is to select the Text format. In this book, WordPerfect is the text format used. If you use a different word processor, select the one you used to create the text file.

Point the mouse at WordPerfect and click the button.

With the setting correctly selected, press

[return]

Ventura displays the Item Selector menu.

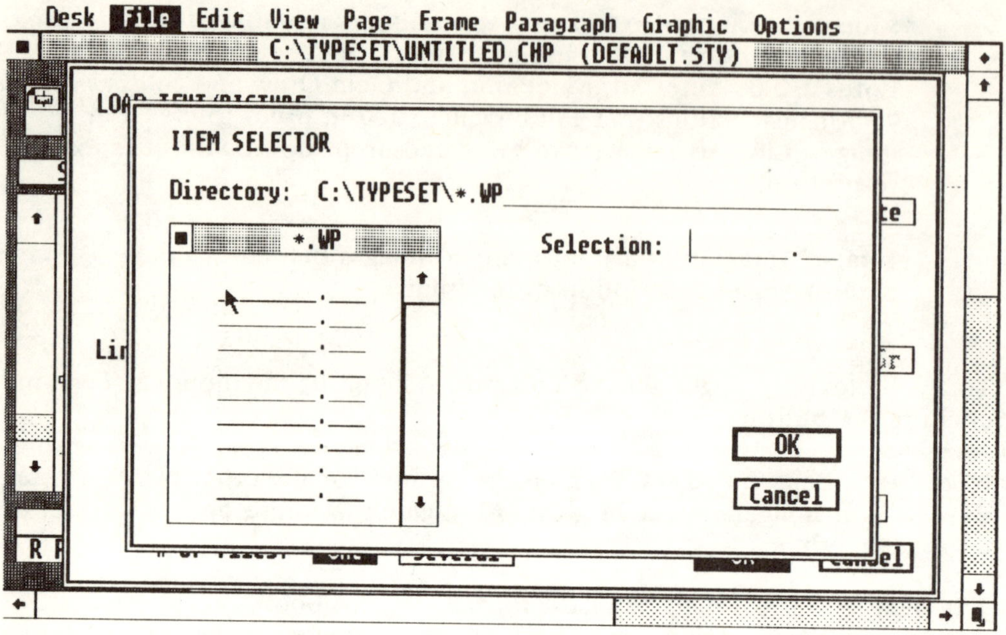

Figure 2.3

The ITEM SELECTOR menu is also an important one to understand since Ventura uses it to represent the DOS concepts of drives, directories, and files. (If you are not familiar with DOS drives, directories, and files, a discussion of these items can be found in Appendix A.) The display is divided into three parts, with the top line displaying the name of the active directory. In this example, the active directory is C:\TYPESET.

Ventura also includes a DOS wild card specification, ***.WP**, which selects only files with the WP extension. Note that since Ventura assumes WordPerfect documents have a WP extension, you must manually add WP extensions to your WordPerfect file names.

The selection line is where you enter the name of the file to be loaded.

The next part of the display, the selector box window, is more visual. The upper left corner of the box contains the **up level button**, which is used to move back one DOS directory level. The center includes a listing of files that qualify under the current file specification. On the right side is a bar that indicates if the list is longer than the nine files that can appear in the window at any one time.

In most cases, your word processing program is stored in its own directory on the hard disk. For example, WordPerfect is usually stored in a directory called \WP, Microsoft Word in a directory called \WORD, and WordStar in a directory called \WS. You may install these programs into any directory you like; the ones suggested are only those typically used.

Ventura currently displays the contents of the TYPESET directory, which was created automatically when you installed Ventura. Ventura always defaults to the last directory used during the previous session. If your directory display does not show TYPESET, the last person using the program accessed some other directory.

Because you saved your text document, INVIT.WP, in the directory \WP, not \TYPESET, change the directory display by using the up level button. Point the mouse at the up level button, and then click the mouse button.

The display in the selector box changes to reveal the contents of the root directory of your hard disk. Note that your directory's contents will differ from the one displayed here (see Figure 2.4).

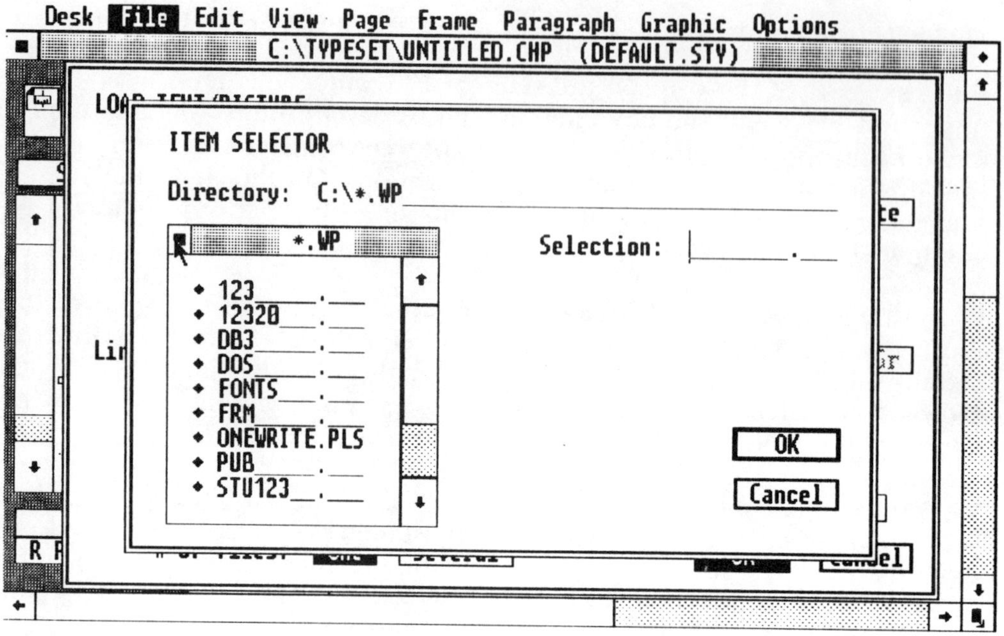

Figure 2.4

The diamond that appears in front of the items indicates that these items are directories, not individual files. The file you require is located in the WP directory. If the WP directory is not visible, scroll the display in the selector box by pointing the mouse at the down arrow and then clicking the mouse button.

Continue clicking until the WP directory is visible (see Figure 2.5).

When you have displayed the directory, you can display its contents in the selector box by pointing the mouse at WP, and then clicking the mouse button. The selector displays those files in the WP directory with the WP extension, one of which should be INVITE.WP. If your file doesn't appear on the screen, scroll the display by clicking the down arrow at the bottom of the selector window bar (see Figure 2.6).

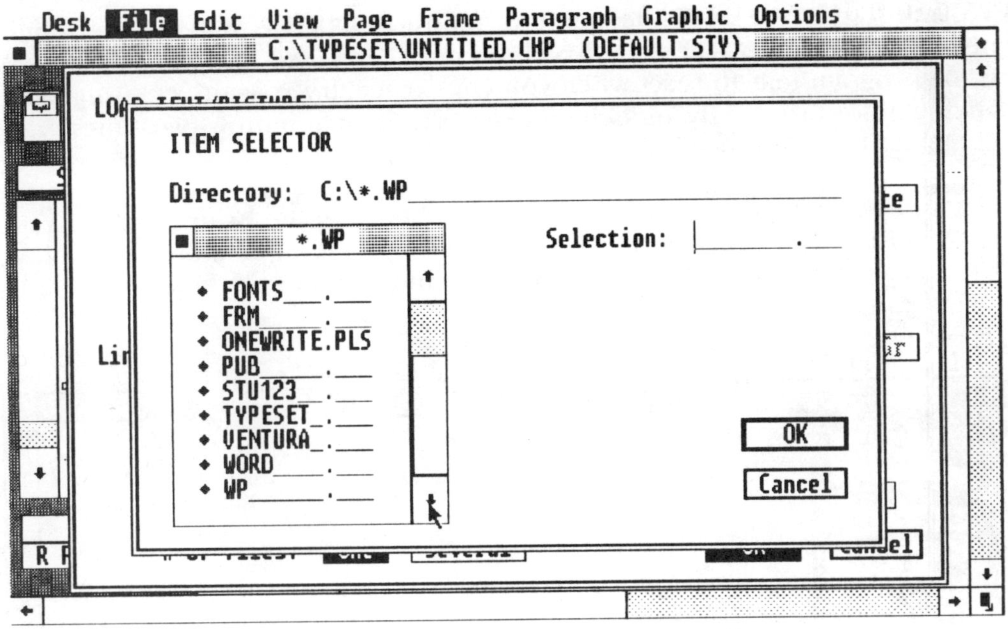

Figure 2.5

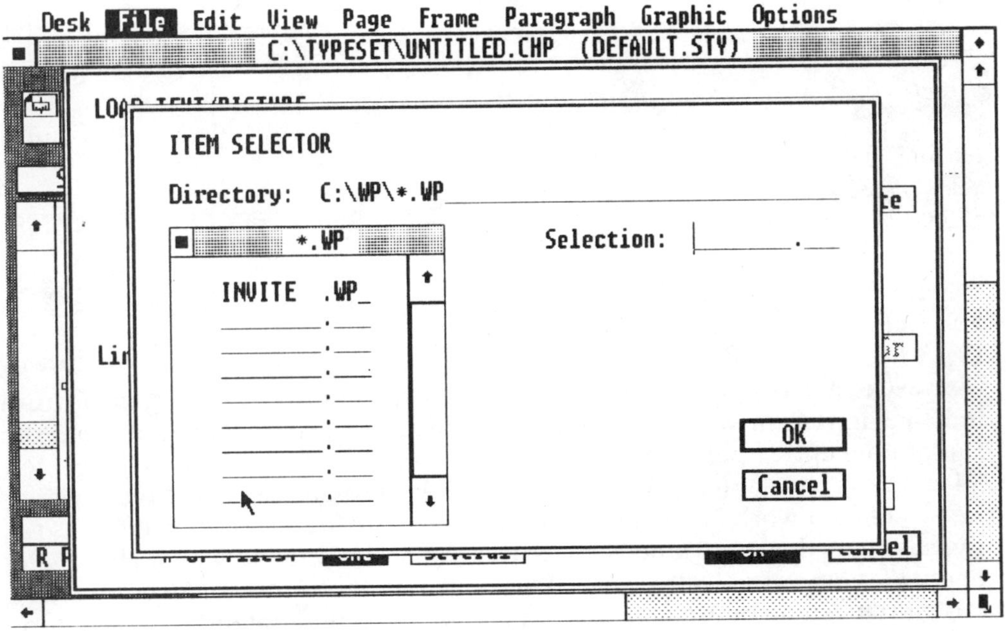

Figure 2.6

To select the INVITE.WP file, point the mouse at INVITE.WP, and then click the mouse button twice. The two clicks must be issued in rapid succession. If the program fails to react when you click twice, try it again, entering each click a little faster. By quickly clicking the mouse button two times, you eliminate the need to select OK or press the Return key.

Ventura has loaded your text file, and switched into the **Frame** mode. You can confirm that your file has been loaded by looking at side bar display, where you should see the name of the text file listed in the box.

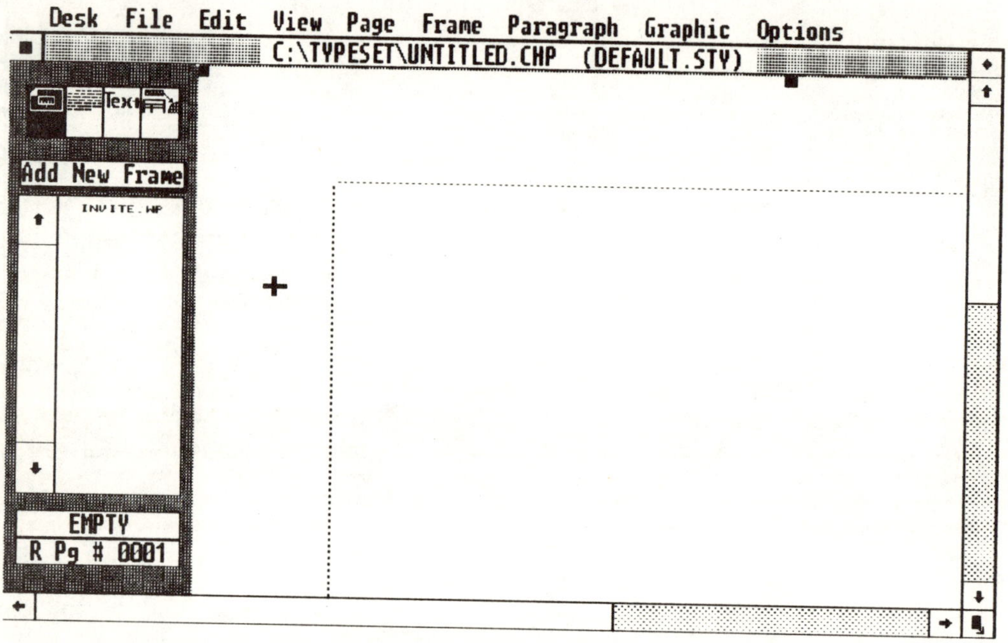

Figure 2.7

The text is not displayed on the page; rather, Ventura waits for an instruction that tells it in which frame it should insert the text. Ventura uses the frames concept to place text and pictures at specific locations in a chapter. All chapters have at least one frame, which is automatically generated whenever you begin work on a chapter document. This frame is referred to as the **underlying** or **master** frame because it is the basic frame to which all the elements of Ventura are attached. This text uses the terms **underlying frame** and **master frame** interchangeably. (The Ventura manual only uses the term **underlying frame.**)

In a simple document, all the text can be placed directly into the master frame by selecting the name of the text file from the side bar display. First, make sure the frame is active (border buttons are displayed). If the frame is not active, point the mouse anywhere in the frame and click the button. Then point the mouse at INVITE.WP, and then click the mouse button twice.

The text is displayed in the page frame exactly as if you had typed it there.

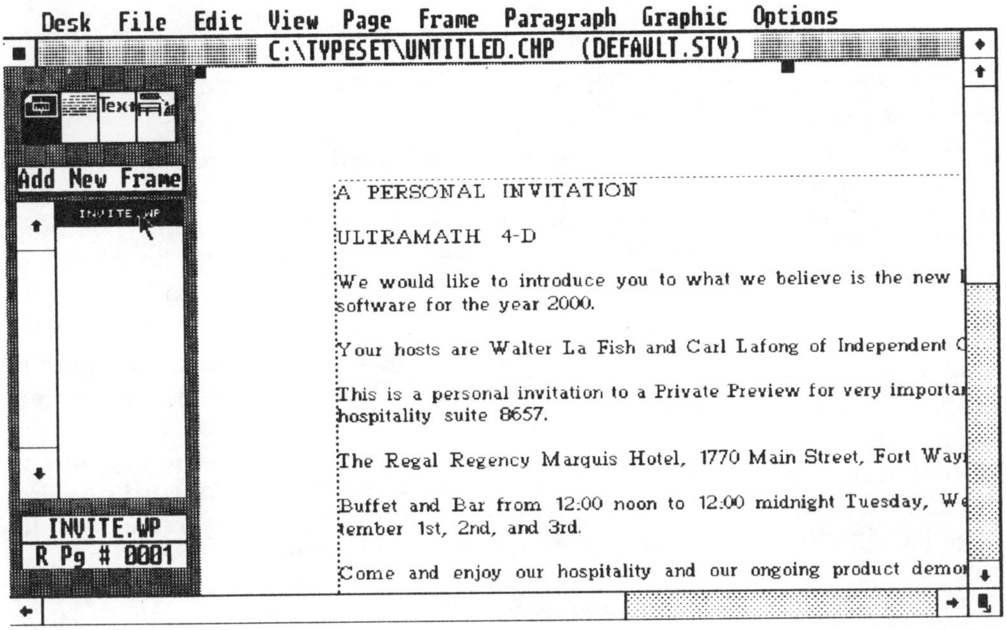

Figure 2.8

The text then can be edited by placing Ventura into the **Text** mode, [Ctrl/o], and using the methods discussed in Chapter 1.

CREATING A STYLE TAG

Since you have correctly entered the text, the objective now is to change the text from a plain expression into a more dramatic presentation, which requires that you change the format of some of the paragraphs.

For example, the first two lines of text should be more vivid than the rest. There are a number of ways to enhance this text: change fonts, center the text, increase the amount of space between lines, or add ruling lines. All of these options require that you create a **style tag**. A style tag is a specification that communicates to Ventura how you want the text to appear.

Style tags are created and altered in the Paragraph mode. Currently you are in the Frame mode. Change modes by entering

[Ctrl/i]

The mode indicator highlights the Paragraph symbol. In addition, the side bar displays another style tag, **Body Text**. As with frames, Ventura creates a master style tag that is automatically assigned to every paragraph. You must always have a Body Text style tag; however, you can change the format of that tag any way that you like.

For the moment, leave the Body Text style tag as it is. Your objective is to create some new styles for the parts of the text that need to stand out. Select the first line of text for formatting. Since formatting affects an entire paragraph, you can point the mouse at any part of the paragraph to select it. Note that the term "paragraph" is used in the same sense as in word processing, that is, to indicate all the text from one [return] to the next [return]. The term paragraph has no grammatical significance in computer technology. A short line, such as the first line in the example, is considered a paragraph because it ends with a [return] character.

To select the paragraph, point the mouse at "A" in the first line of text, and then click the mouse button. The entire paragraph is highlighted.

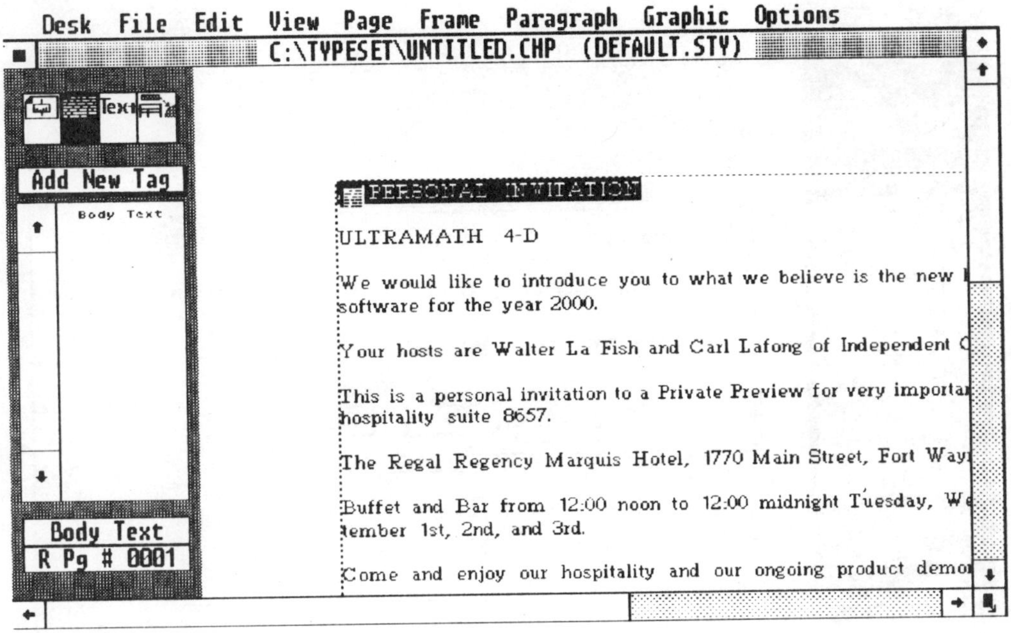

Figure 2.9

Now, instruct Ventura that you want to establish a new style tag by using the **Add New Tag** box that appears just above the side bar display. Point the mouse at Add New Tag and click the mouse button. Ventura displays the ADD NEW TAG dialogue box (see Figure 2.10).

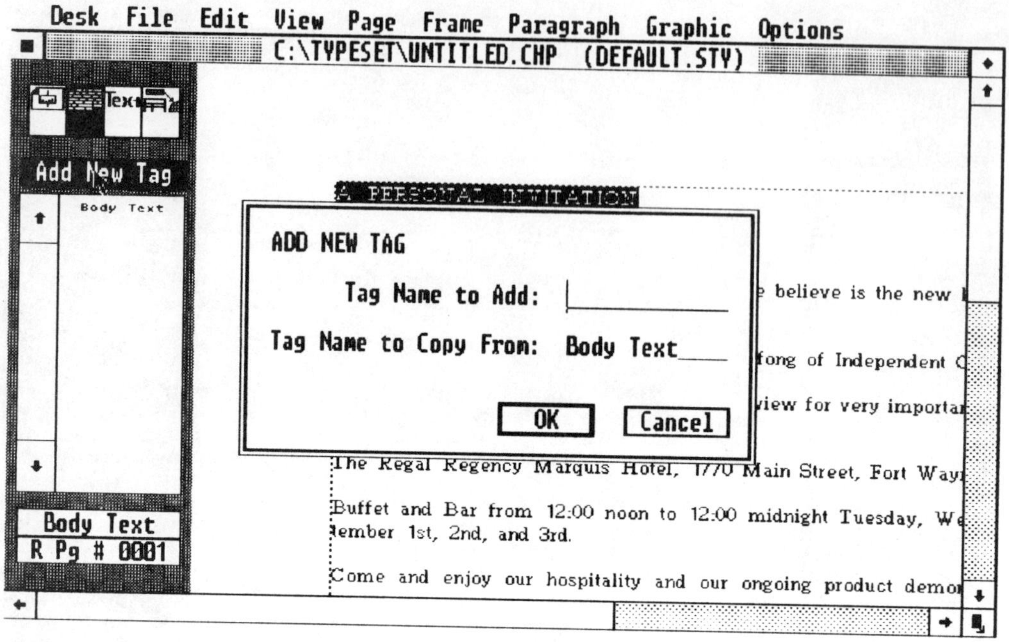

Figure 2.10

You can now type in the name of the new style tag. The names of tags can be up to 13 characters long and can contain spaces. Don't confuse tag names with file names, however. Tag names can contain spaces because they are used only by Ventura. File names are used by Ventura and DOS, and must therefore conform to DOS file name conventions, which forbid the use of spaces in file names. The names should reflect, as much as possible, the purpose or appearance of the style, which is not always easy to accomplish in 13 characters. But don't be too concerned. Ventura allows you to rename tags at a later time should you think of a better name. In this case, enter

greeting
[return]

If you look only at the text, you won't see that much has been accomplished. But there are some other important changes. The side bar now contains two names, Body Text and Greeting, indicating that a new style tag has been added to the chapter. Also, the box above the page number displays "Greeting," indicating that the paragraph currently highlighted is formatted using the Greeting style.

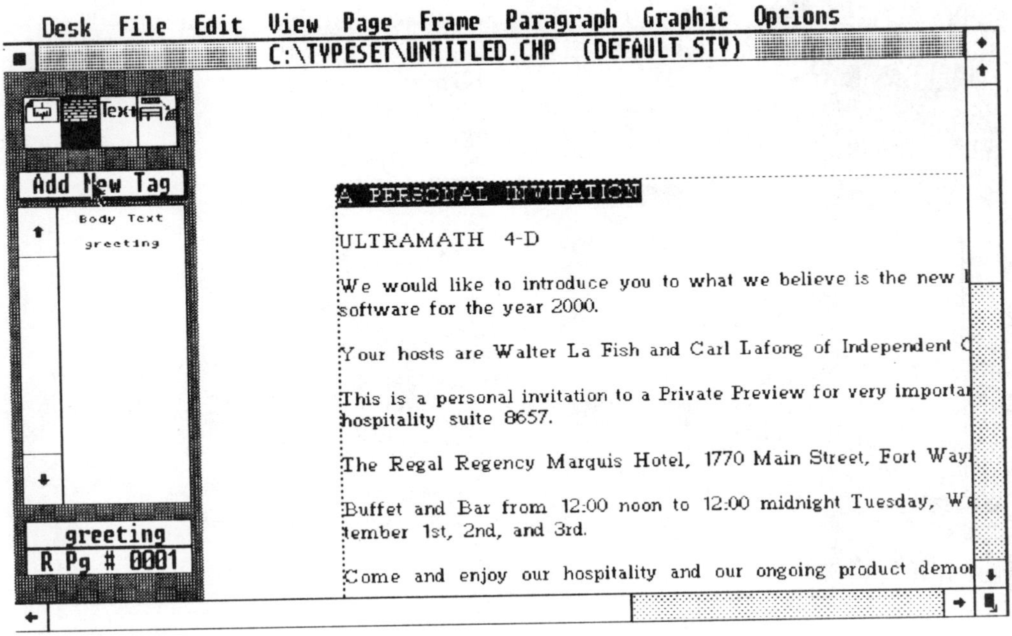

Figure 2.11

But the highlighted paragraph doesn't seem to differ from the other text because when the Greeting tag was created, that tag copied all its format settings from the only other tag that existed, Body Text. At this point, both tags consist of the same settings; however, now that you have tagged the first paragraph, you can change the setting and, consequently, the look of the text. Tag settings are controlled from the Paragraph menu. So point the mouse at the Paragraph menu heading and click the mouse button. The Paragaph menu appears as in Figure 2.12.

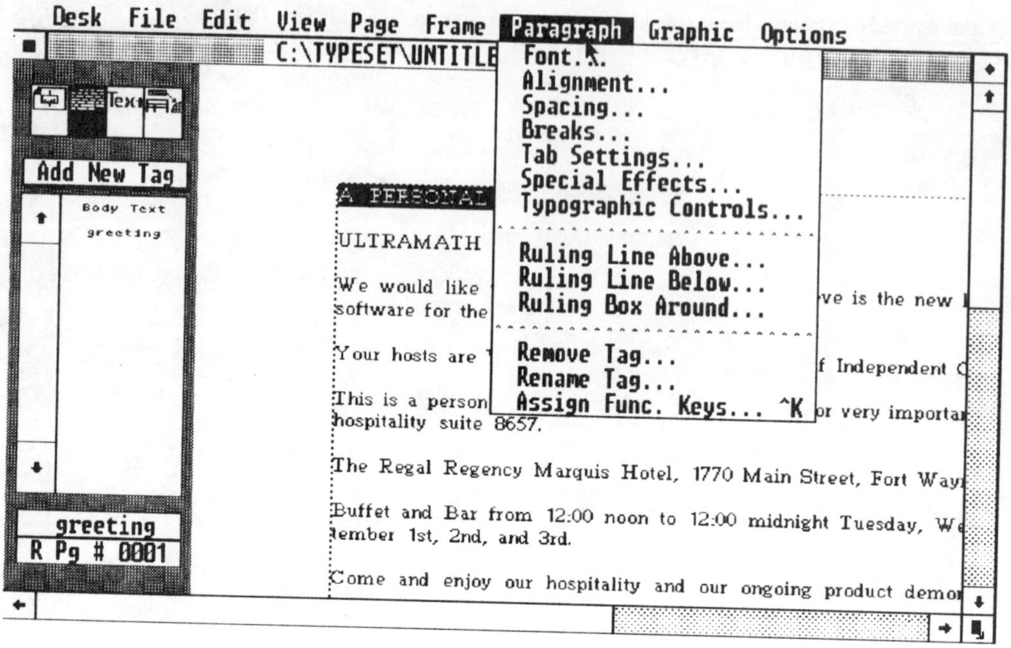

Figure 2.12

Ventura's Paragraph menu consists of three parts:

- **Paragraph Format**. These operations stress paragraph items such as margins, tabs, line spacing, text alignment, and some special paragraph formats available in Ventura.
- **Ruling Lines**. Ventura can add ruling lines to your text. These lines can be placed above, below, and around text. If the text is divided into multiple columns, vertical lines can be added between the columns.
- **Tag Operations**. These functions allow you to remove or rename a style tag. You can also assign a specific style tag to a function key so you can more quickly enter a commonly used tag.

Begin by changing the font of the text. Point the mouse at the Font selection and click the button. Ventura displays the "Greeting" Font menu, exactly the same menu that appeared when you chose the Set Font option in Chapter 1. The only difference is that this time, the font you select will affect all of the text in any paragraph with the selected style tag, in this case, Greeting.

For example, to select Swiss 14-point font, point the mouse at the Swiss option and click the button. Then point the mouse at 14 and click the button.

To complete the selection, press

[return]

The paragraph now appears as Swiss 14-point text.

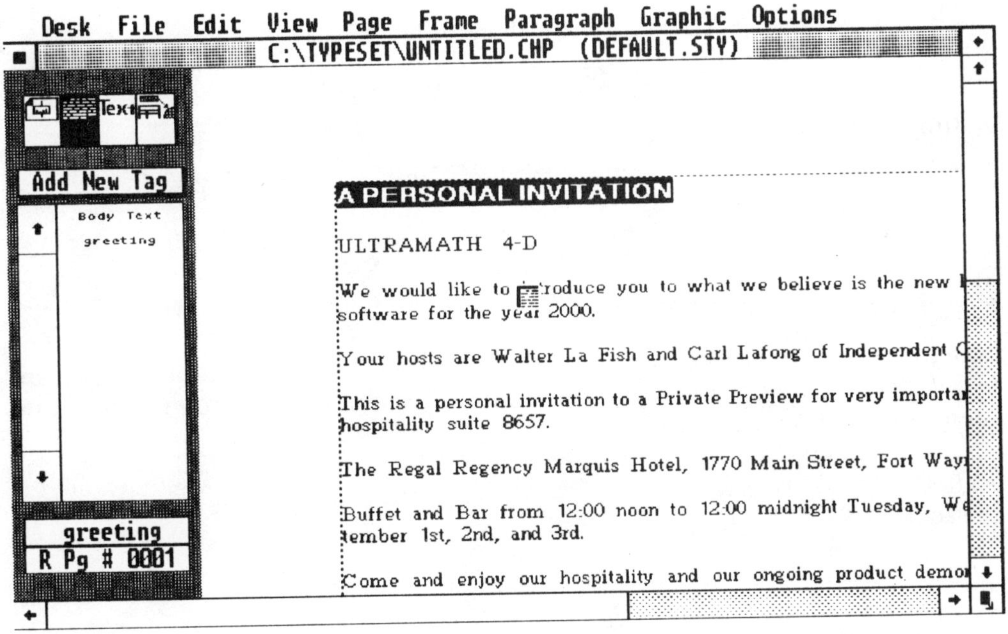

Figure 2.13

For a more dramatic effect, the greeting should be centered. Centering is a characteristic that Ventura groups with the Alignment function. To center the text, point the mouse at the Paragraph menu title. Then, point the mouse at the Alignment selection and click the button. Ventura will display the ALIGNMENT menu.

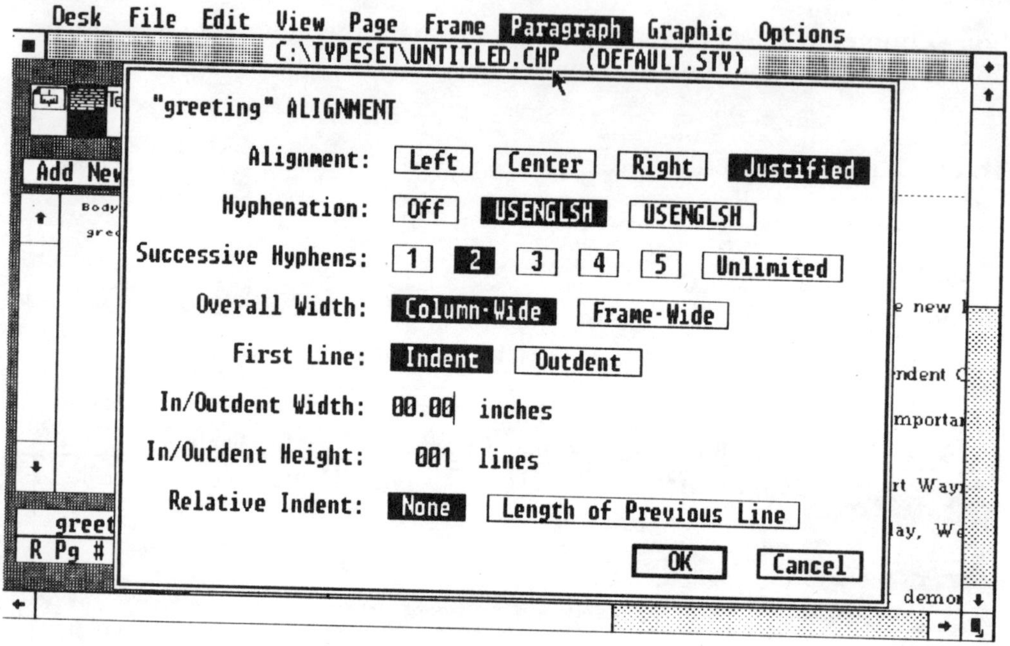

Figure 2.14

The first series of options on the menu controls the text alignment. To center the text, point the mouse at the Center option and click the button. Complete the entry by pressing

[return]

The paragraph is now centered.

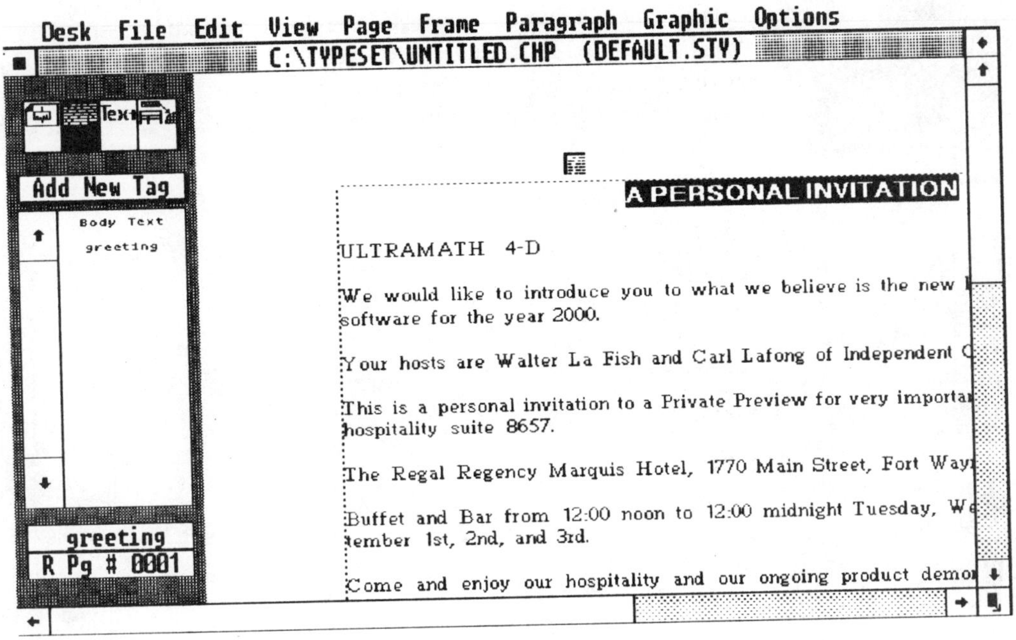

Figure 2.15

APPLYING A STYLE TAG

You have now prepared a style tag that carries with it the specifications you have selected from the Paragraph menu. The advantage of creating a style tag, as opposed to formatting just the highlighted paragraph, is that you can apply that tag to other paragraphs.

Suppose you want the next line of text to have the same formatting. You can simply apply the Greeting style tag just created.

First, highlight the paragraph you want to tag. Point the mouse at "ULTRAMATH" and click the button.

Ventura removes the highlight from the first paragraph and places it in the second. To apply a style tag, you will use the mouse to select one of the names displayed on the style bar. Point the mouse at the Greeting tag and click the button.

Now the second paragraph has the same font and alignment as the first paragraph.

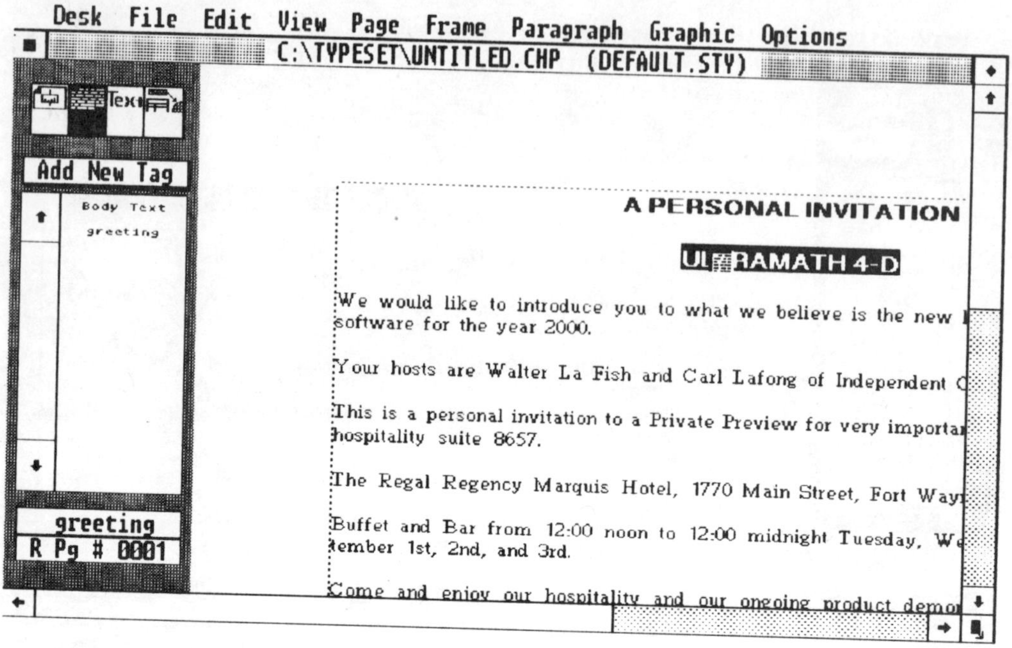

Figure 2.16

Now tag the next paragraph. Point the mouse at "introduce" and click the button. Then point the mouse at the Greeting tag and click the button.

The text should be formatted exactly like the two preceding paragraphs; however, this look probably isn't what you intended. This paragraph was probably better off as body text. Fortunately, Ventura makes it simple to correct blunders. Point the mouse at Body Text and click the button. The text reverts to its previous format.

SAVING A NEW STYLE

Since you have created a special style tag to format this document, you can save it as part of a style file for later use.

Ventura can store as many style files as you want to create. The current style file, called DEFAULT, was created by the manufacturer. While it is possible to change this style file, it is better to leave it as it is. The DEFAULT should be used to start new styles from scratch. You are better off creating a new file with a new name to store the formats that you will use with this invitation.

You could wait until you complete the document before you save the style, but there is a compelling reason to save the style file now. When you reach the end of your work, it is easy to forget that Ventura saves the style under DEFAULT. To avoid misnaming your style file, you should create a new style file as soon as you begin to alter an existing style sheet.

First, point the mouse at the File menu heading. To save the style sheet, point the mouse at the Save as New Style selection and click the button.

The ITEM SELECTOR menu appears.

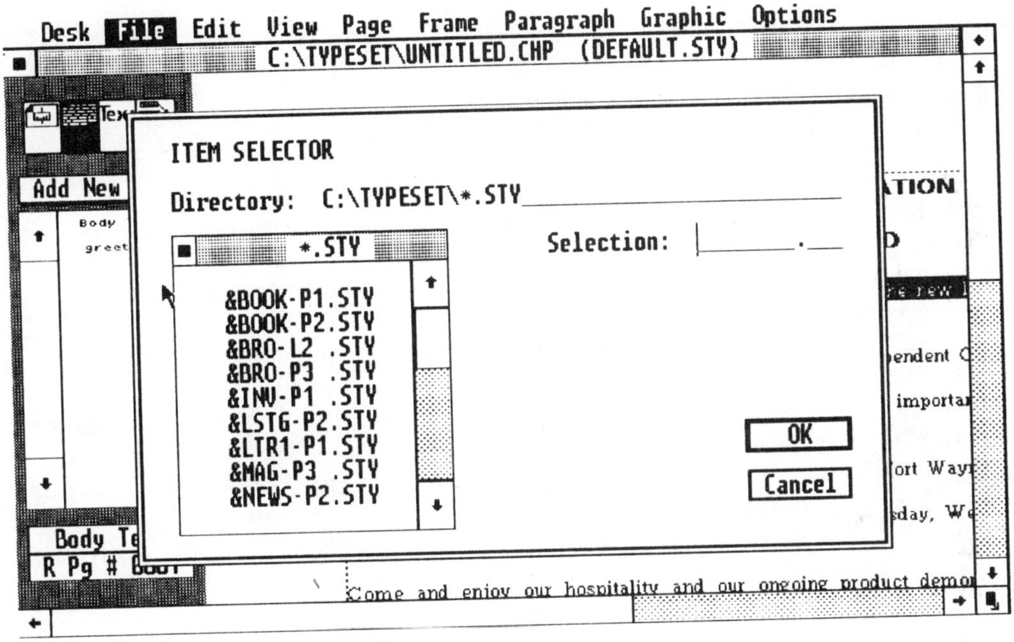

Figure 2.17

Enter

invite
[return]

The new style sheet is created. Note that the top of the screen shows the name of the style sheet as INVITE.STY.

At this time, save the chapter you are working on so you won't lose what you've accomplished so far. Enter

[Ctrl/s]
invite
[return]

The top of the screen shows the name of the file, INVITE.CHP, and the style sheet, INVITE.STY.

CHANGING THE BODY TEXT STYLE

Since this example document you are formatting is an invitation, you may want to create a standard body text that is different from normal body text.

For example, you may decide to center all the lines and print them in a font that is different from the one in which they are now displayed. Since all the paragraphs in the text, with the exception of the first two, are formatted as body text, you can change the format of all of these paragraphs by changing the Body Text style. Keep in mind that you should alter the Body Text style only when you are certain that you want the standard paragraph formatted in a special way. Ventura automatically formats a paragraph as body text unless you specifically request a different tag. In this example, the change is justified because printing on invitations is often centered for the entire text.

Point the mouse at "We would" and click the button.

The first paragraph is highlighted. To check for the style that is currently in effect for this paragraph, look at the box directly above the page number box. You can see the tag's name, Body Text; therefore, to determine what style was used for a paragraph, highlight the paragraph and check the name that shows in this box.

To change the text to centered, point the mouse at the Paragraph menu heading. Then point the mouse at the Alignment selection and click the button.

To select centered text from the Alignment menu, point the mouse at the Center option and click the button.

Complete the entry by pressing

[return]

The entire document should now be centered.

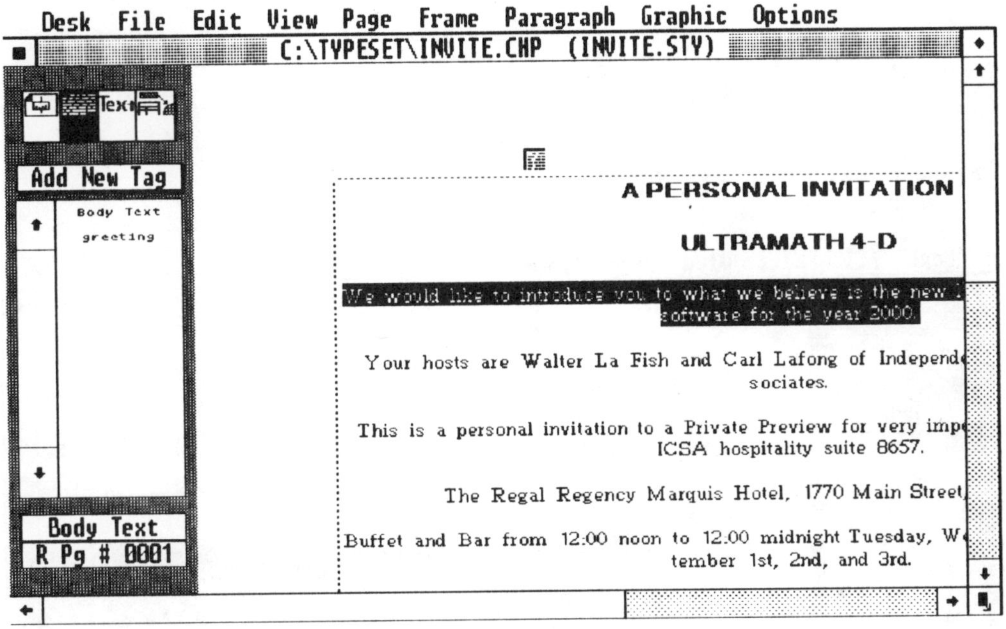

Figure 2.18

Note that when the format of the highlighted paragraph changed, the format of all the paragraphs that had the same style tag also changed. Any changes made to a single paragraph with the Body Text style, in turn, affect all of the paragraphs in the document with that same style tag. Keep in mind that any other documents that use the same style sheet will also be affected the next time they are loaded. It is important to remember which styles are used in what documents so that you do not accidentally change the format of a document. You can see how powerful changes in style tags can be when a tag is applied to a large portion of the text.

Next, change the font of the Body Text tag. Point the mouse at the Paragraph menu; then point the mouse at the Font selection and click the button.

To change all the text to italic, point the mouse at N-Italic (the N stands for Normal Italic; some printers offer Light-Italic and Bold-Italic print as well) and click the button.

To complete the change, press

[return]

Now the text appears centered and italicized.

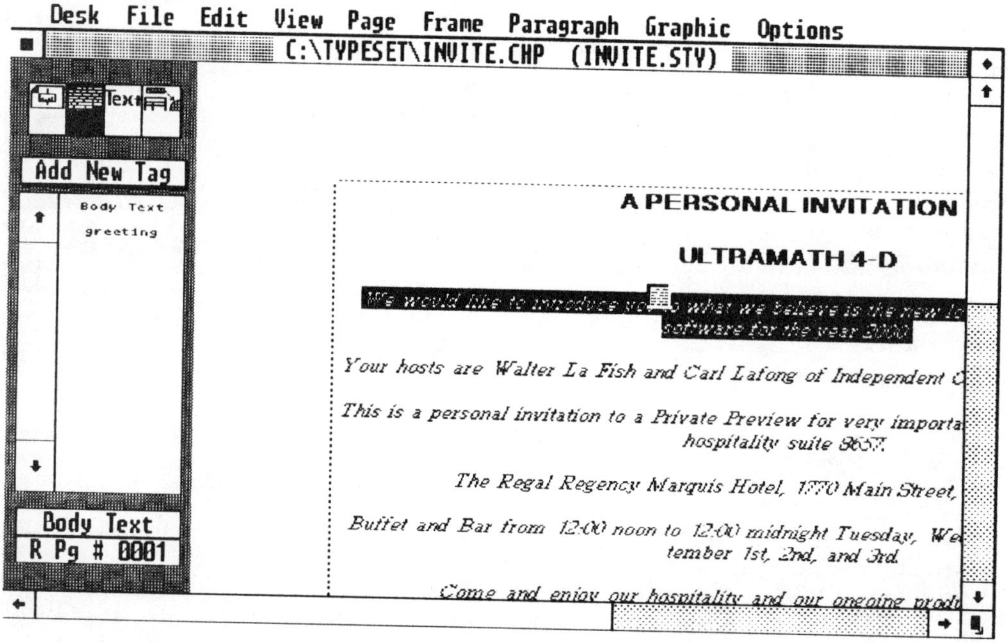

Figure 2.19

SPACING AND RULING LINES

By employing the Font and Alignment options, you have used styles to layout the basic look of your document. Ventura offers a number of other options that can change a document's appearance. Two very important ways to enhance the look of a document are to add spacing and ruling lines to vary the texture.

As an example, look at the second paragraph in the example invitation, the one that begins "Your hosts are. . . ."

To emphasize the names of the hosts, you could split the text into two parts following the word "are." Doing so allows the names of the hosts to be more noticeable because they begin a new line of text. To make this change, place Ventura into the Text mode by entering

[Ctrl/o]

Point the mouse cursor at the space between the words "are" and "Walter" and click the mouse button.

Create a new line by entering

[return]

Spacing

The next goal is to use spacing to make this line stand out. Because you want to vary the spacing of this line only, and not all paragraphs with the Body Text style, you will have to create a new tag for this line. Enter the Paragraph mode by pressing

[Ctrl/i]

Point the mouse at "Walter..." and click the button.

To create the tag name, point the mouse at Add New Tag and click the button.

Enter the name of the new tag:

hosts
[return]

Because "hosts" was copied from Body Text, the format of the new tag is identical to the way it was when it was tagged Body Text. You are now ready to change that format by altering the line spacing.

Point the mouse at the Paragraph menu heading. Then point the mouse at the Spacing selection and click the button. The SPACING menu appears.

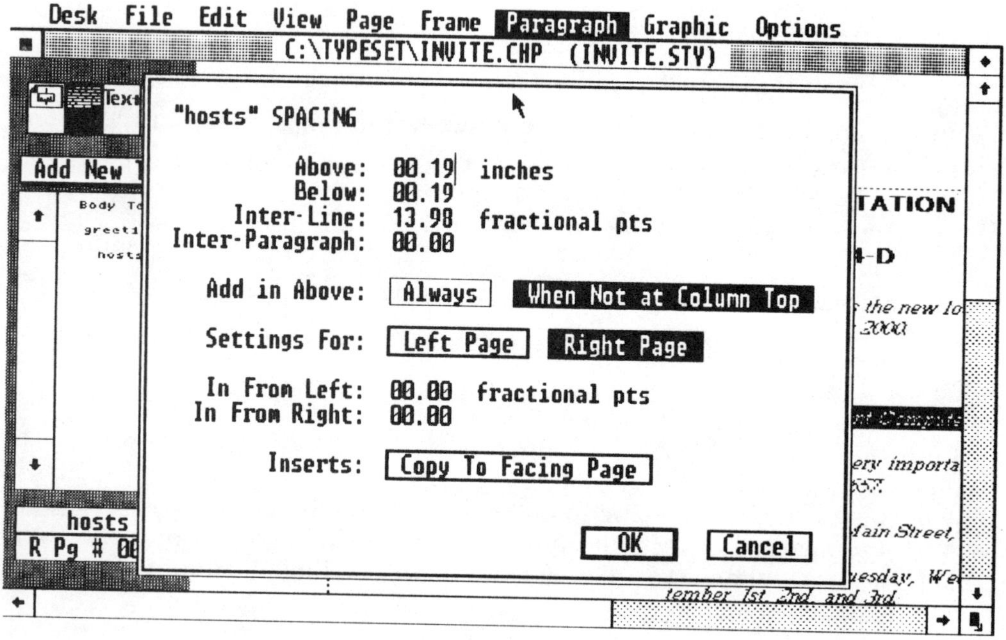

Figure 2.20

Ventura specifies four types of spacing between lines:

- **Above**. This option controls the amount of space left above a tag. The above spacing is used only when the previous paragraph has a different style tag. When paragraphs have the same style tag, inter-paragraph spacing controls the spacing.

- **Below**. This option sets the amount of space that follows a paragraph. Like the above spacing, below comes into effect only when the following paragraph has a different style tag than the current paragraph.

- **Inter-paragraph**. This spacing appears between paragraphs of the same style tag.

- **Intra-line**. This spacing is used to separate lines of text within the same paragraph and is similar to the line spacing specifications used by word processing programs.

In the Spacing menu, you also can see the ways Ventura measures spacing. Instead of using one method of measurement, Ventura allows you to choose one of four types of measurement:

- **Inches**. Space is measured in inches with two-decimal-place precision.

- **Centimeters**. Space is measured in centimeters with two-decimal-place precision.

- **Picas** and **Points.** Space is measured in terms used by printers: points and picas. In the printing business, a different form of measurement is used than in other areas of society. Usually inches are divided into parts by dividing by 2, i.e., halfs, quarters, eighths, sixteenths, etc. Printers divide an inch into six parts. Each 1/6th of an inch is called a **pica**. The pica is in turn divided into 12 smaller parts called **points,** which means that an inch consists of 72 points or 6 picas. The use of picas and points is consistent with the basic idea that a typical line height is 1/6" rather than 1/4" or 1/2". Printers have evolved a measuring system consistent with their needs to measure lines of text.

- **Fractional Points.** Because computers can provide great numeric accuracy, Ventura can convert traditional point measurement, 72 points per inch, into more precise decimal values that measure values as small as 1/100th of a point, or .0001388 of an inch. Of course, today's screen displays and laser printers are not capable of reproducing this fine a measurement; however, fractional points are the most accurate of Ventura's measuring system.

Spacing in Ventura is a complicated subject. You will encounter more information about spacing as you proceed through the chapters. For now, the task at hand is to increase the amount of space surrounding a particular line in the text.

To increase space, you will increase the value for the Above and Below spacing fields. Enter

[backspace]
[backspace]
5
[down arrow]
[backspace]
[backspace]
5
[return]

The new spacing widens the gap before and after the line to 1/2".

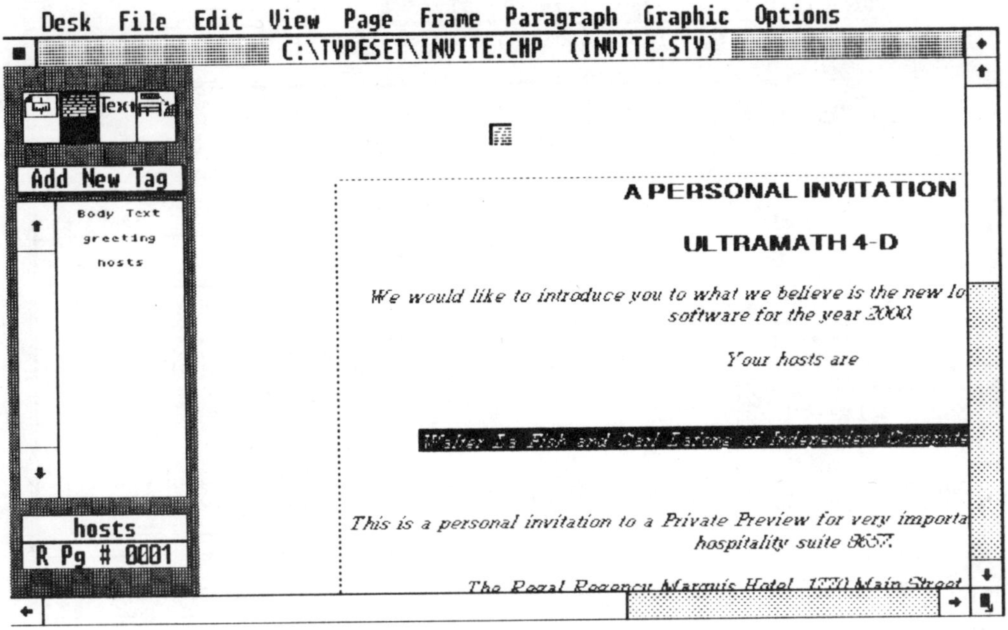

Figure 2.21

Ruling Lines

Another way of attracting attention to an area of a document is to divide the space using ruling lines. A ruling line is simply a straight line that is drawn in the text area. Ventura allows you to create horizontal and vertical ruling lines, which you can specify to be drawn above and/or below a paragraph. Vertical ruling lines are used with text that is formatted in several columns. To create a horizontal ruling line, point the mouse at the Paragraph menu heading. Then, point the mouse at the Ruling Line Above selection and click the button. The RULING LINES ABOVE menu should appear as in Figure 2.22.

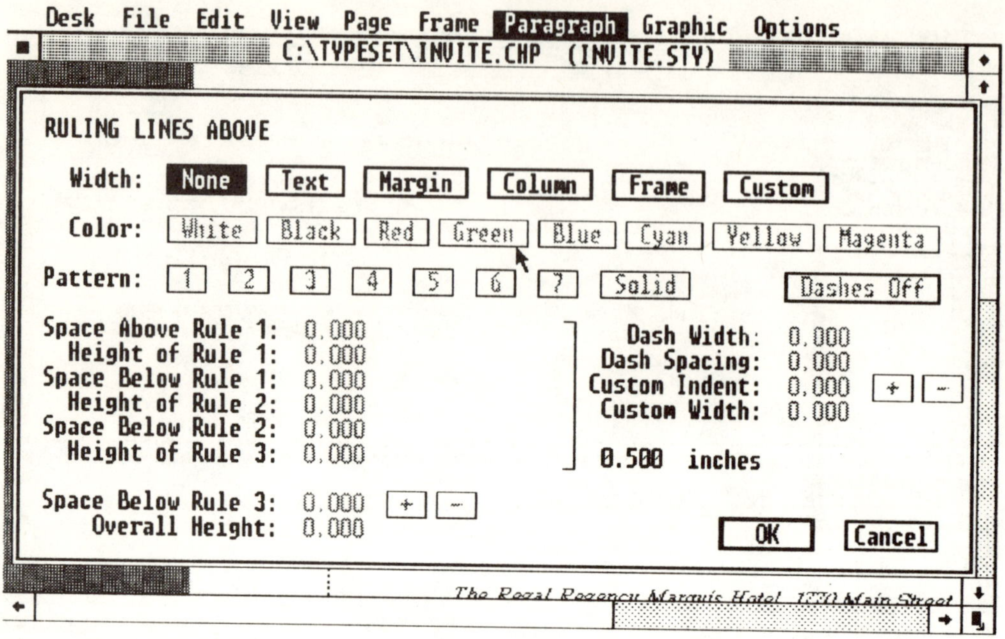

Figure 2.22

In this example, draw the line to match the length of the text. Point the mouse at the Text option and click the button.

The next section of the menu controls the thickness of the line. The ruling line can consist of up to three individual lines that vary in their individual thickness and the amount of space between each line. In this first attempt, you will draw a simple, single line.

The Pattern option is automatically set to solid, meaning that the line will be a solid black line.

The bottom portion of the display reflects the exact measurements used to calculate the thickness and spacing of the lines. The text cursor is positioned on the first line of the display, which controls the space above the first rule line.

To start, draw a simple line. Move the cursor to the Height of Rule 1 line by pressing

[down arrow]

Set the line thickness at 5/100" by entering

[backspace]
[backspace]
5

Ventura immediately displays a line to help you visualize what the line will look like in the text, which is helpful when you create a ruler that consists of more than one line.

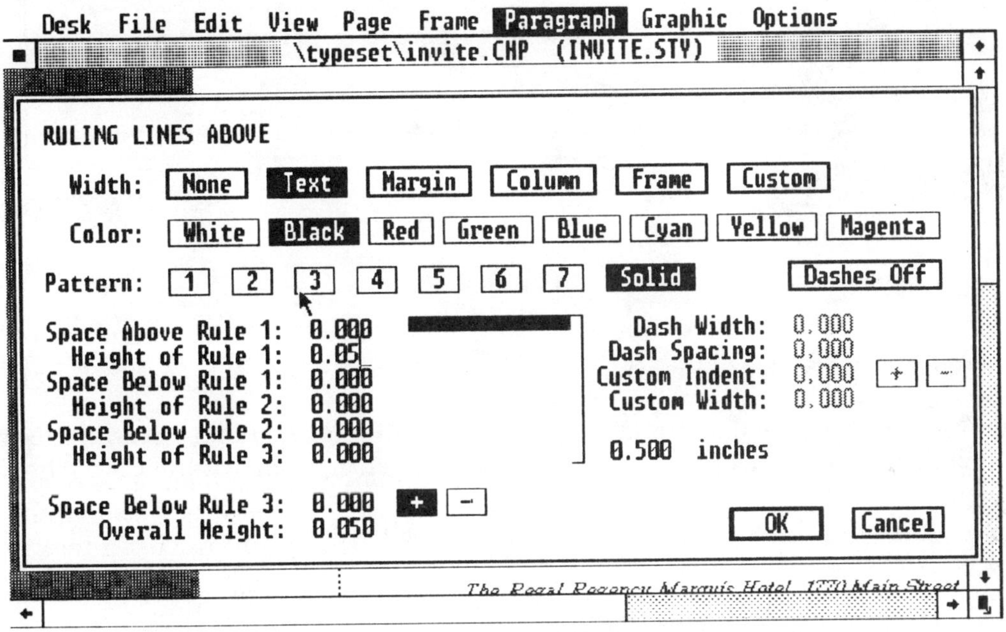

Figure 2.23

To see what the text looks like with this ruling line, press

[return]

Because you selected Text as the line width specification, the line is drawn immediately over the text and extends only as far as the text extends.

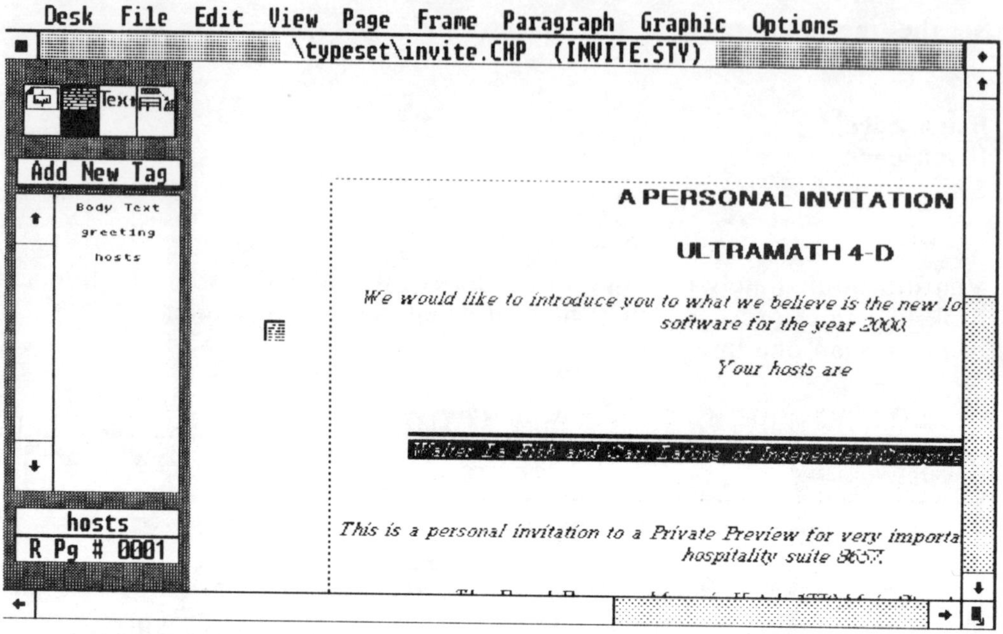

Figure 2.24

Space Below Ruling Lines

The line just added to the text appears too close to the text and would look better if there were more space in between. Return to the Ruling Line Above menu by pointing the mouse at the Paragraph menu. Then, point the mouse at the Ruling Line Above selection and click the button.

Note that when you go back into a menu, the previous settings are displayed. This display can help you ascertain how a paragraph or style tag was created. By displaying the options on the Paragraph menu, you can see the settings used for that style tag.

Because the ruling line is drawn above the text, the setting you want to work with is the one at the bottom of the display, Space Below Rule 3, which controls the amount of space that appears following the ruling line or lines. By increasing this value, you can place more space between the text and the ruling line. In this example, you will add 1/4" more space between the ruling line and the text.

Use the Down Arrow key to place the text cursor on the Space Below Rule 3 line. Enter

[backspace] (3 times)
25
[return]

The text and the ruling line are separated by 1/4" of space.

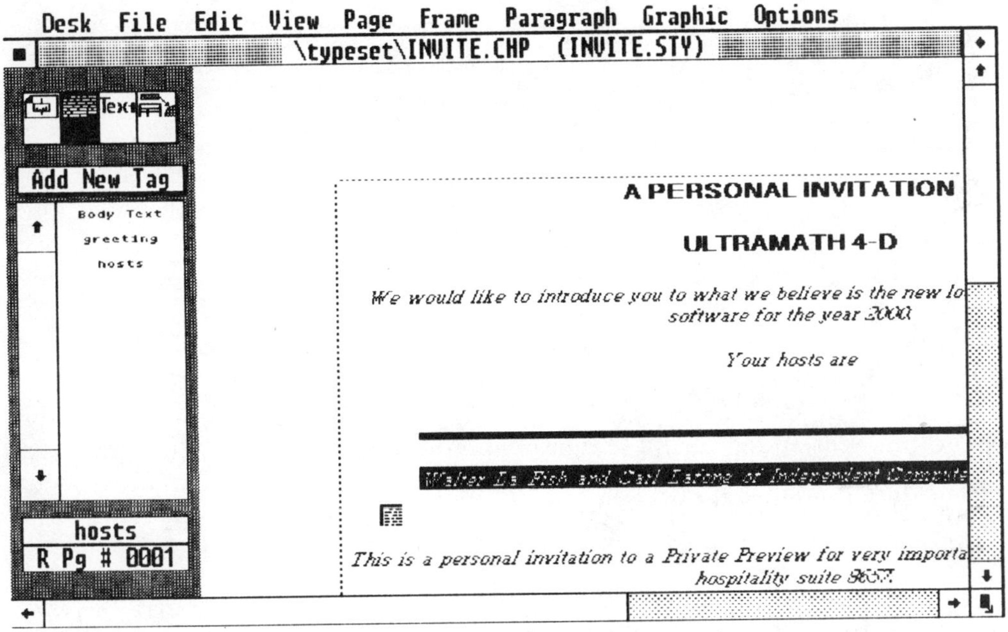

Figure 2.25

Next, add a similar line below the text. Point the mouse at the Paragraph menu heading. Then point the mouse at the Ruling Line Below selection and click the button.

Note that this menu is exactly the same as the Ruling Line Above menu. Once again, select Text as the width by pointing the mouse at the Text option and clicking the button.

Your goal is to place a 5/100" ruling line 1/4" below the text. Since Ventura measures distance as above or below the ruling line, enter a space of .25" in the Space Above Rule 1 line. Keep in mind that the Space Above Rule 1 refers to the space below the text and before the ruling line. Enter

[backspace] (3 times)
25
[down arrow]

Next, enter the height of the ruling line:

[backspace]
[backspace]
5

Complete the entry by pressing

[return]

The text now shows the ruling line above and below the text.

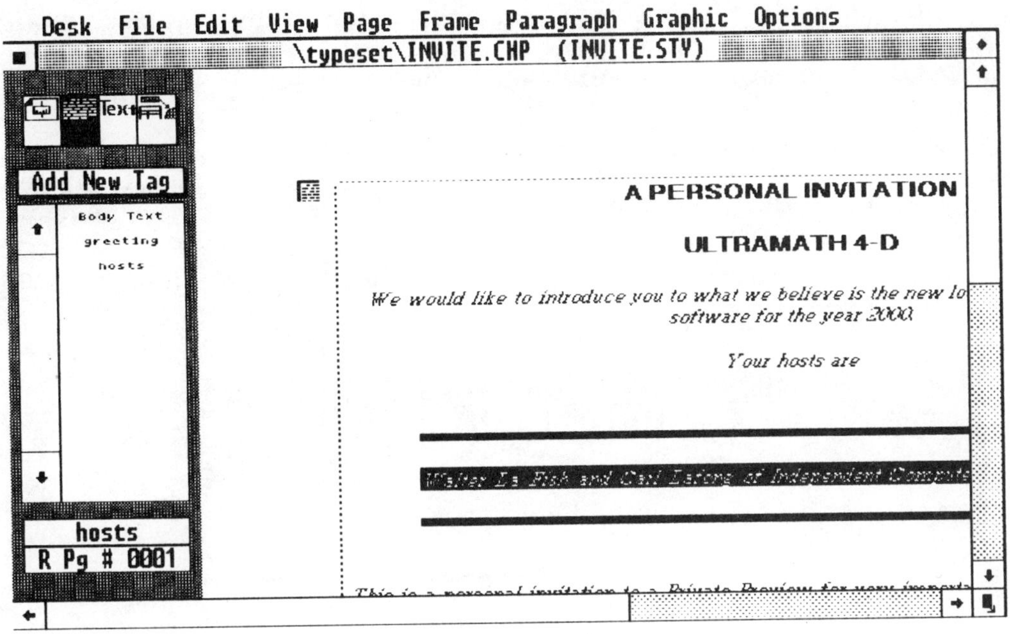

Figure 2.26

Thus far, you have added the following formatting modifications to the Hosts style tag:

- **Spacing:** 1/2" above and below the paragraph.
- **Ruling Lines:** a ruling line 5/100" thick, 1/4" above and below the text.

Now that you have created this tag, you can apply it to any line in the text. To find another place in the document to try this tag, move the display window down to reveal more of the text. Use the vertical bar on the right edge of the display. The bottom of the bar contains a down arrow.

Point the mouse at the down arrow and click the button. The screen display moves down a small amount. Click the button again and continue clicking until you see the line that begins "The Regal Regency." Point the mouse at "Regal" and click the button.

You can format the highlighted paragraph with any of the tags listed on the side bar display by pointing the mouse at one and clicking. For this example, select the Hosts style tag by pointing the mouse at Hosts and clicking the button.

The paragraph is formatted with the same spacing and ruling lines that were used with the other paragraphs tagged as Hosts. Because you have increased the amount of spacing, you may need to click the down arrow on the vertical bar a few times. When you have the paragraph in view, it should resemble the following:

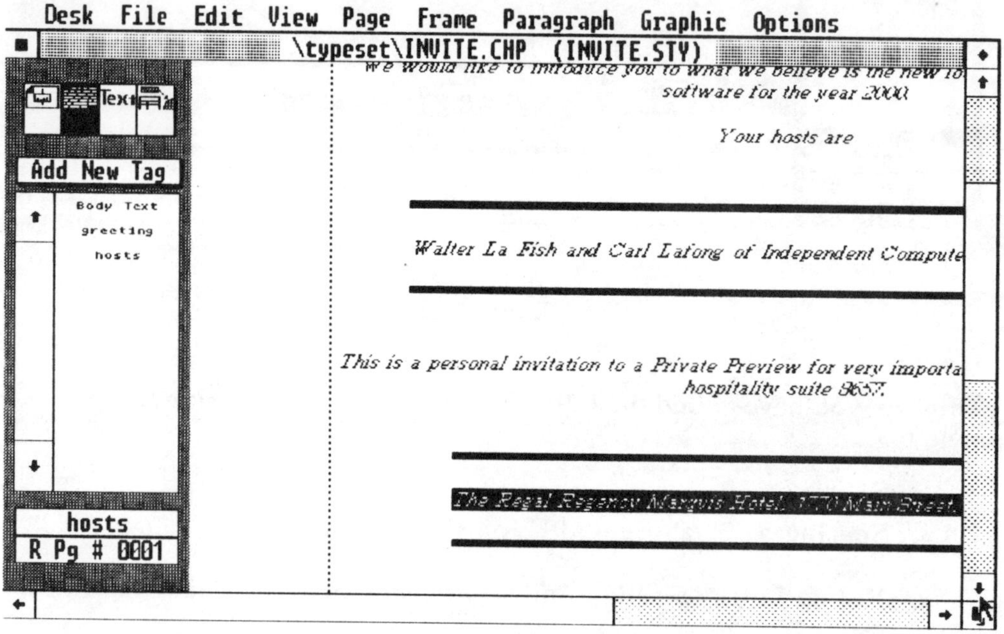

Figure 2.27

FRAME OPERATIONS

Up to this point, all changes have been made on the paragraph level. The final step in formatting this document is to consider the frame of reference in which the document will print. The frame of reference is the *master* frame into which the text of the document was loaded.

To get a better idea of how the text with its new formatting fits into that frame, place Ventura into the Reduced View mode. Enter

[Ctrl/r]

You can now see the way the text fits into the master frame. In this view, the text is probably too small to read; however, this reduced size shouldn't create a problem because your purpose is to examine the overall layout of the page, not the individual text items. Note that special monitors, such as the Wyse 700, have sufficient resolution to make text readable even in the reduced mode. Most CGA, Hercules, and EGA monitors will display something similar to Figure 2.28.

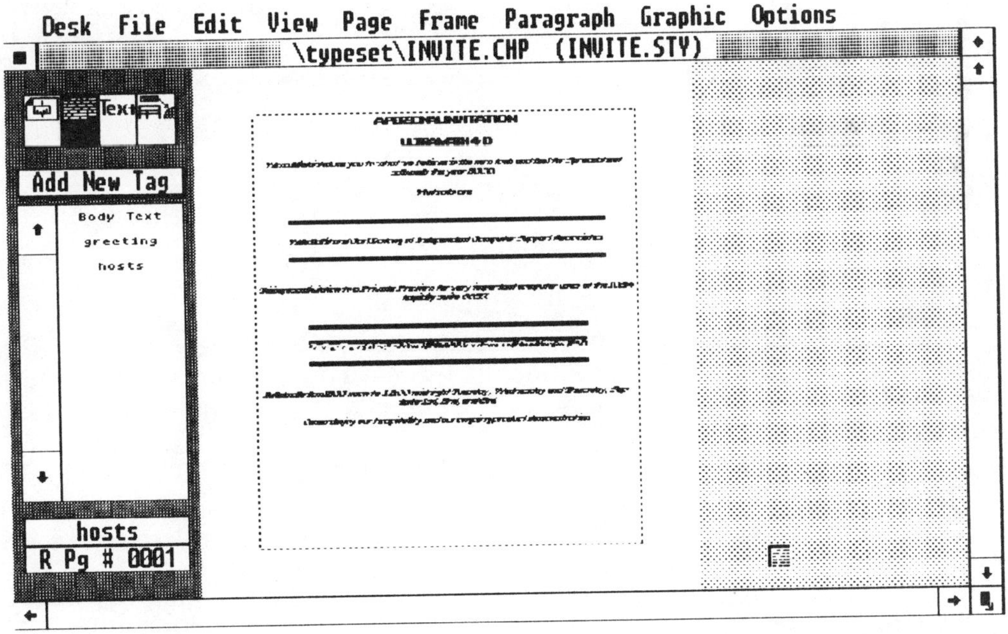

Figure 2.28

Now place Ventura into the Frame mode by entering

[Ctrl/u]

In the Frame mode, the selected frame is indicated not by a highlight, but by the presence of buttons located around the perimeter of the frame.

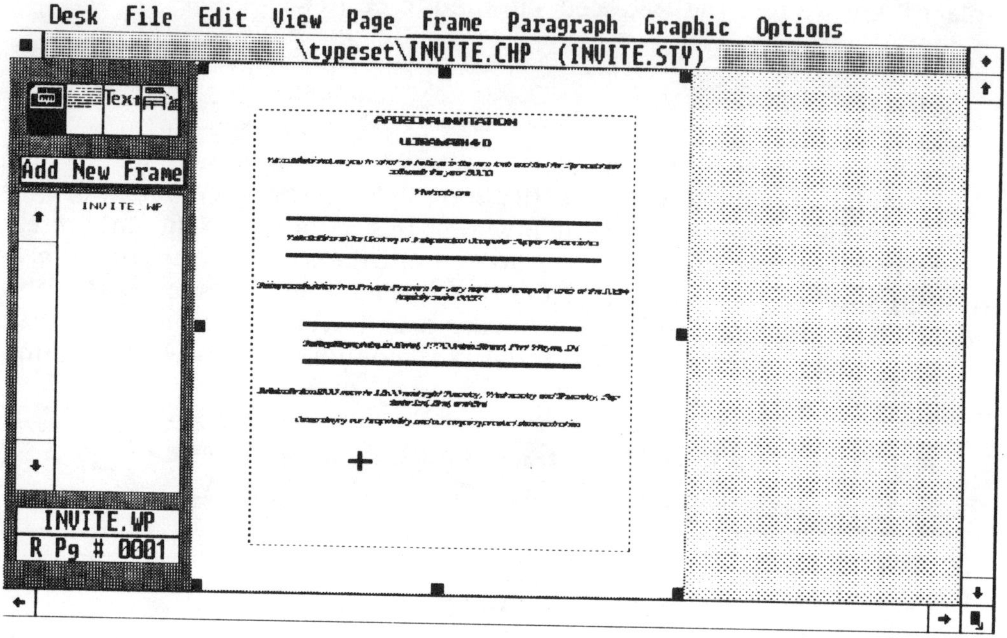

Figure 2.29

The dotted line that forms a box inside the frame is called the **column guide**, which shows you the text area inside the frame. The area outside the column guide is the margin area that appears as white space on the final printed document.

The column guide does not appear when the page prints, but is only displayed on the screen as a point of reference. If you would like to see how the screen will look when it is printed, you can turn off the column guide display by pointing the mouse at the Options menu heading. The menu resembles Figure 2.30.

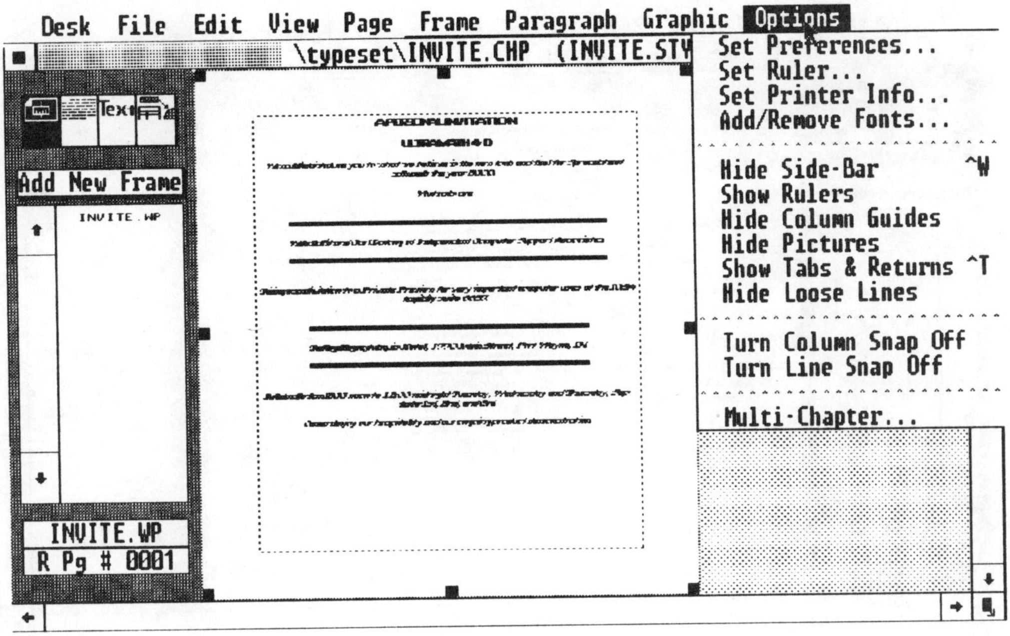

Figure 2.30

To turn off the column guide, point the mouse at the Hide Column Guides selection and click the button.

The document appears just as it will look when printed (see Figure 2.31).

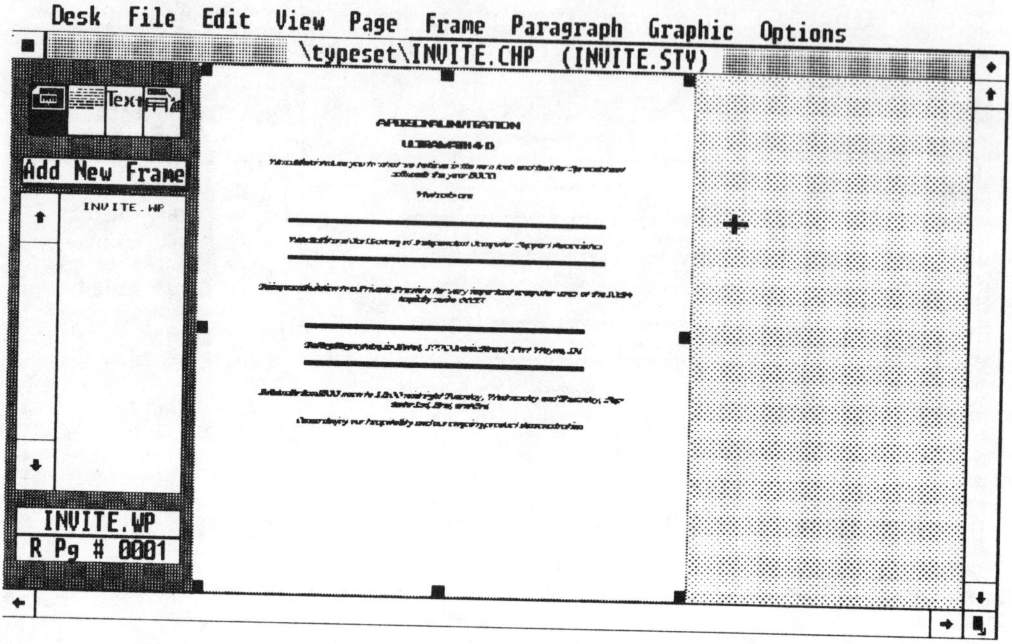

Figure 2.31

Margin Changes

Since the current document is too small to fill up the entire page, you may want to alter the margin so that the text appears more centrally placed on the page. Margin operations are handled under the Frame menu, not the Page menu because, unlike word processing programs, Ventura allows you to have more than one frame of reference on each page. In this simple example, there is only one frame, the master frame used on this page.

To change margins, point the mouse at the Frame menu, which will resemble Figure 2.32.

To change the margin settings, point the mouse at the Margins & Columns selection and click the button.

The MARGINS & COLUMNS menu will resemble Figure 2.33.

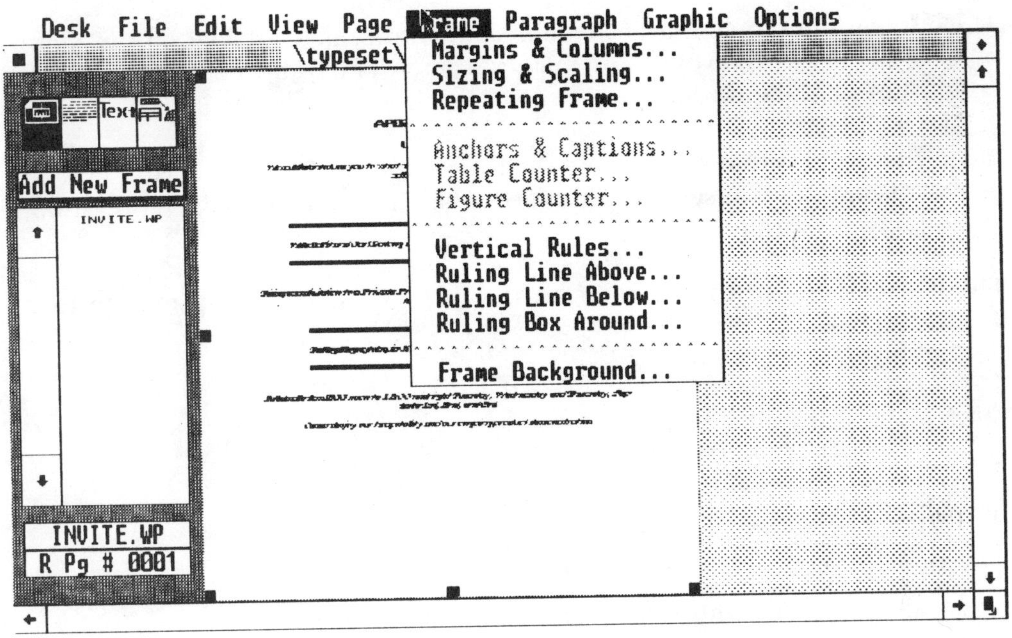

Figure 2.32

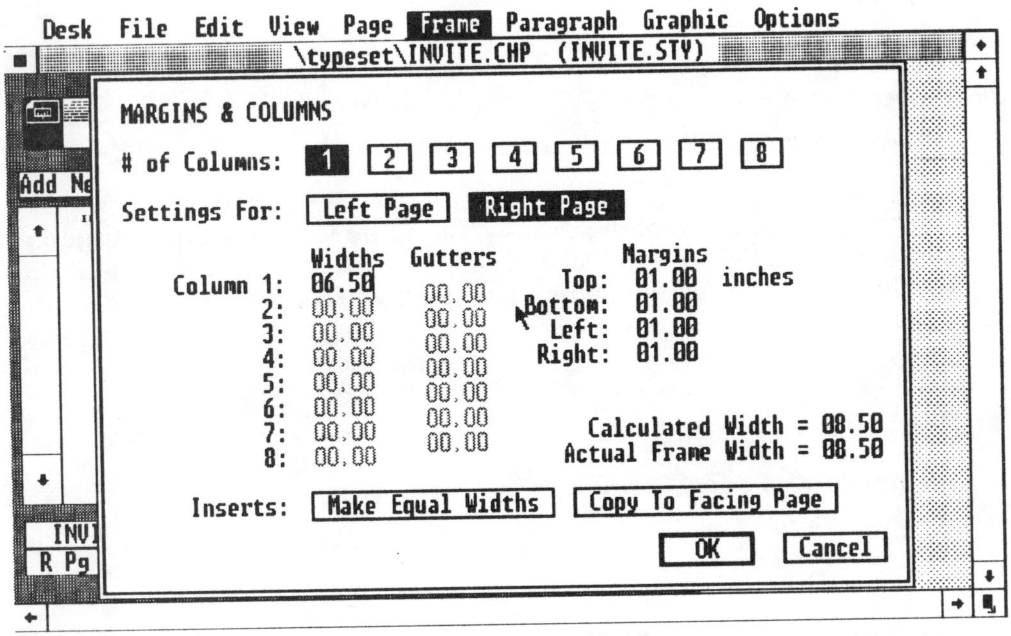

Figure 2.33

The current margin settings for the master frame, as displayed on the menu, place a 1" margin all around the master frame. The frame consists of a single column of text 6.5" wide.

Begin the process that will change the top margin to 2" and the side margins to 1.5". Point the mouse at the last zero in the line, which reads "Top: 01.00," and click the button.

The text cursor will then appear on the line. Change the top margin to 2" by entering

[backspace] (3 times)
2
[down arrow]
[down arrow]

Now change the left and right margins to 1.5" by entering

[backspace]
[backspace]
5
[down arrow]
[backspace]
5

If you look at the left side of the display, the value for the width of Column # 1 has automatically been reduced to 5.5" because you have increased the margins by 1". Conclude the margin changes by pressing

[return]

The document now appears with the increased margins.

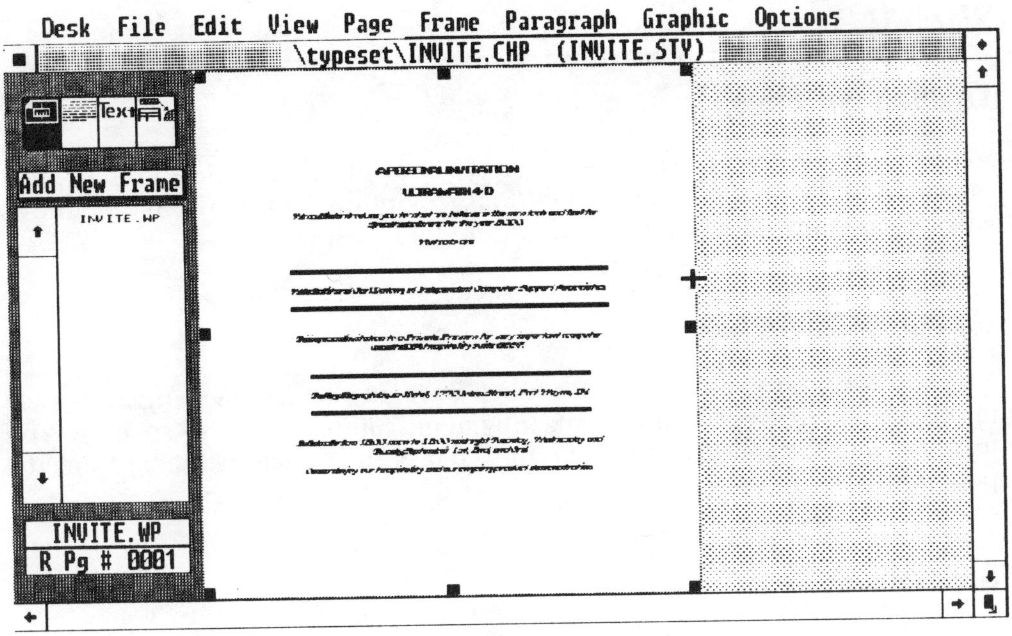

Figure 2.34

Save the document by entering

[Ctrl/s]

Finally, print the chapter by pointing the mouse at the File menu. Then point the mouse at the To Print selection and click the button. Next point the mouse at OK and click the button. Ventura prints the document, and you can quit the program by pointing the mouse at the File menu heading, pointing the mouse at the Quit selection, and clicking the button.

SUMMARY

Loading Text Files

Ventura allows you to combine three types of files: text files, line art, and bit-mapped images. The **Load Text/Picture** option on the File menu allows you to select the files you want to add to your chapter.

Paragraph Style Tags

You can format text in Ventura through **paragraph tags**. A paragraph style tag contains settings for tabs, fonts, aligment, ruling lines, and spacing. You format documents by creating the required tags and attaching them to specific paragraphs.

Style Sheets

All of the tags you create for a given document can be saved for use with other documents. Ventura saves **style sheets**, which are separate and distinct from the chapter file. Each document may have a unique style sheet of its own or use a style originally created for another document.

Body Text

Ventura automatically creates a style called **Body Text**. All paragraphs loaded from a word processor text file are automatically assigned the Body Text style. You can use the Paragraph mode to change the style of paragraphs.

Spacing

Ventura controls the spacing of text by the spacing definitions specified as part of a style tag. You can specify values for above, below, and between paragraphs.

Measurement

Ventura can display measurements as inches, centimeters, points, and picas, or fractional points.

Ruling Lines

In creating a style tag definition, you can add **ruling lines** to be drawn above, below, or around paragraphs.

Margins

Margins are a characteristic not of individual paragraphs, as is the case in word processing programs, but of frames. Margins are changed from the Frame menu.

CHAPTER 3

TABS AND INDENTS

Chapters 1 and 2 outline general but fundamental concepts of Ventura document creation. This chapter concentrates on a specific type of formatting problem and then goes into greater detail about several of Ventura's paragraph formatting abilities.

In particular, this chapter focuses on how text is aligned into columns and how tabs are controlled in Ventura. As an example, a financial balance sheet document will be created.

This type of document raises an important point about the relationship between work performed with a word processing program and the methods Ventura uses to format documents. Because of Ventura's advanced formatting abilities, you may discover that many of your word processor's features are not necessary for documents intended as text files for Ventura chapters.

Load your word processing program and prepare to create a document, which you will name BALANCE.WP if you are using WordPerfect. If you are using another word processor, adjust the name of the file accordingly. Microsoft Word users should name the document BALANCE.DOC; WordStar users should name it BALANCE.WS.

The document to be prepared – a financial balance sheet – contains indented headings as well as text aligned in three different columns. Financial statements typically consist of three columns of numbers: the first column shows subtractions such as depreciation values; the second contains account totals; and the third lists totals and subtotals.

Do not be concerned with the physical location of text entered into this document. For example, to place a value into the second column, typical word processing programs require that you create three tabs stops. In this case, the tabs would be decimal-aligned tabs so the amounts would be right-justified. Most word processing programs allow you to distinguish between normal (left-aligned) and decimal (right-aligned) tab stops. If you are using WordPerfect, note that WordPerfect 4.2 and WordPerfect 4.1 use slightly different methods to establish decimal tabs, but the differences are not important for this example.

When you enter text, pressing the Tab key positions the cursor at the appropriate tab stop. With most word processing programs, pressing the Tab key inserts a character into the text that instructs the word processor to align text on the next tab stop. WordPerfect and Microsoft Word insert tab characters that Ventura recognizes. WordStar, on the other hand, does not insert tab characters when the Tab key is used; the program inserts a series of spaces to fill the spaces between tab stops. Ventura interprets these spaces as space characters instead of tab instructions. If you are using WordStar, text documents do not format correctly when loaded into Ventura. To correct this, edit the spaces out of the text after it has been loaded into Ventura and replace the spaces with tab characters. For more information about the differences between Ventura and word processing programs, see appendix A.

In the following document, it is not the position of the text, but the fact that a tab character is inserted between the heading and the value that is important. Ventura determines actual physical locations of the heading and the value when you create style tags for those particular lines. When using the word processor, you need only be concerned that the proper characters—text *and* tabs—are inserted in the proper order.

Following is the text of the document you must create. The text is shown as a series of keystrokes to be entered. The **[Tab]** symbol designates positions in which tab commands must be entered. Remember, the text will not line up correctly in columns when you enter it in a word processing program, but this does not present a problem. You will control the alignment from within Ventura.

It is important that tab characters be inserted between the text items. The tab character is entered by pressing the Tab key. You need make no special effort to distinguish decimal- or left-aligned tabs. If you use WordStar—even version 4.0—this technique will not work, because WordStar inserts spaces instead of a tab character when the Tab key is pressed. Remember to press the Return key at the end of each line.

Central Hardware
Balance Sheet
December 31, 1986
Assets
Currect Assets
Cash [Tab] 1,000
Accounts Receivable [Tab] 3,000
Notes Receivable [Tab] 1,500
Inventory [Tab] 40,000
Supplies [Tab] 1,000
Total Current Assets [Tab] 46,500
Plant Assets
Land [Tab] 5,000
Buildings [Tab] 76,000
Less Accumulated Depreciation [Tab] 3,000 [Tab] 73,000
Store Equipment [Tab] 20,000
Less Accumulated Depreciation [Tab] 6,000 [Tab] 14,000
Total Plant Assets [Tab] 92,000
Investments [Tab] 50,000
Patents [Tab] 10,000
Good Will [Tab] 5,000
Total Assets [Tab] 203,000
Liabilities
Current Liabilities
Accounts Payable [Tab] 15,000
Notes Payable [Tab] 5,000
Accrued Taxes [Tab] 3,000
Total Current Liabilities [Tab] 23,000
Long-term Liabilities
Mortgages Payable [Tab] 50,000
Notes Payable [Tab] 20,000
Total Long-term Liabilities [Tab] 70,000
Total Liabilities [Tab] 93,000
Capital
Walter La Fish, Capital [Tab] 110,500
Total Liabilities and Capital [Tab] 203,500

When you finish entering the document, save it as BALANCE.WP (for WordPerfect users) or BALANCE.DOC (for Word or Multimate users). After the text has been created, you can exit the word processing program. You are then ready to format the document in Ventura.

LOADING THE TEXT

After the document has been created and saved, load Ventura in the usual manner. Although the chapter is assigned (by default) the name UNTITLED.CHP, the current style sheet file is INVITE.STY. Remember, Ventura retains the last style file worked with and automatically loads that style file the next time the program is loaded.

To load the text from the BALANCE.WP file into the master frame, point the mouse at the File menu title. Then, point the mouse at the Load Text/Picture option and click the button.

The setting on the LOAD TEXT/PICTURE box retains the set of options last entered (in this case, Text as the file type and WordPerfect as the text format). If you are using a different word processor, the selections should reflect that program. If the current options displayed on your screen are different, use the mouse to select the correct ones for this example.

To continue, press

[return]

The ITEM SELECTOR display indicates the last directory used to load a text file. This should be the same directory – C:\WP – you used to load the INVITE.WP file in the previous chapter.

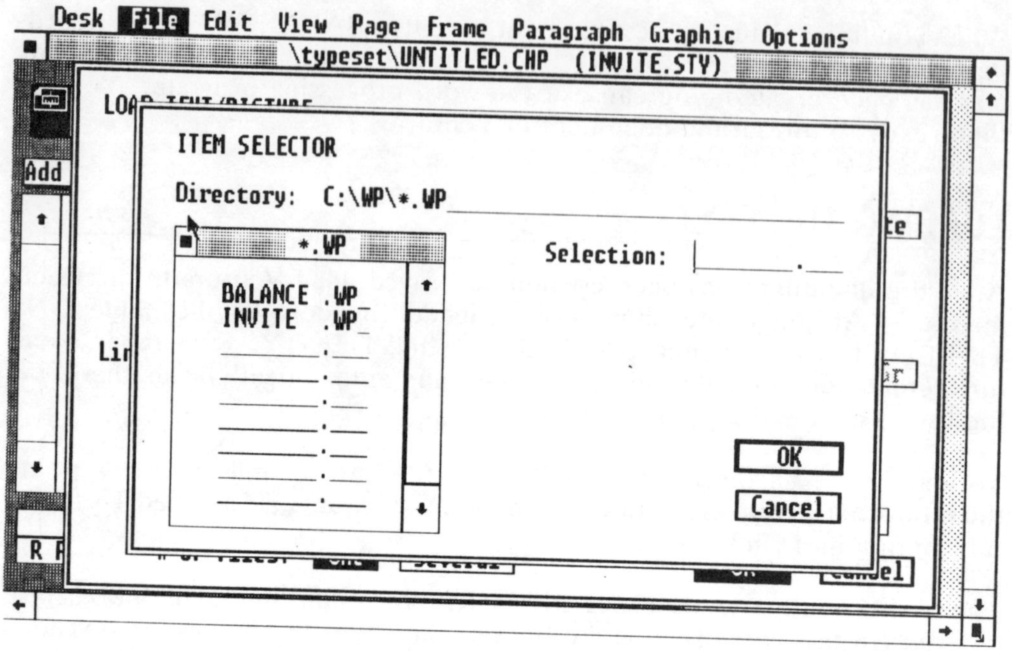

Figure 3.1

Point the mouse at the BALANCE.WP entry and click the button. If necessary, click the mouse button inside the text area to highlight the frame, point at the BALANCE.WP file listing in the side bar, and click the mouse button twice in rapid succession. The file name will appear in the side bar. Make sure the master frame is active (the frame buttons appear). Then, point the mouse at BALANCE.WP in the side bar and click the button. The text will appear in the master frame.

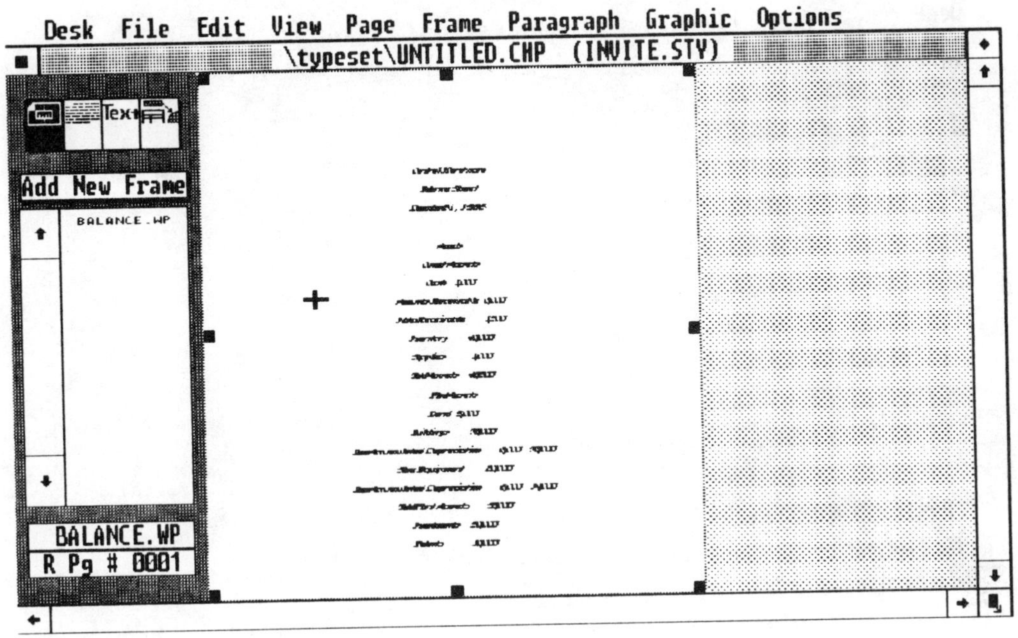

Figure 3.2

The current style sheet file (INVITE.STY) uses center-aligned, italic text as the Body Text style tag; the text is formatted according to those specifications. Any text loaded into the master frame will be automatically formatted in this way.

Since the financial document differs in purpose from the invitation created in Chapter 2, create a new style sheet for it. Begin by loading the DEFAULT style sheet to create the new tags for the financial document.

Point the mouse at the File menu title. Then, point the mouse at the Load Diff. Style option and click the button.

Enter the name of the style file:

default
[return]

The DEFAULT.STY style sheet file loads.

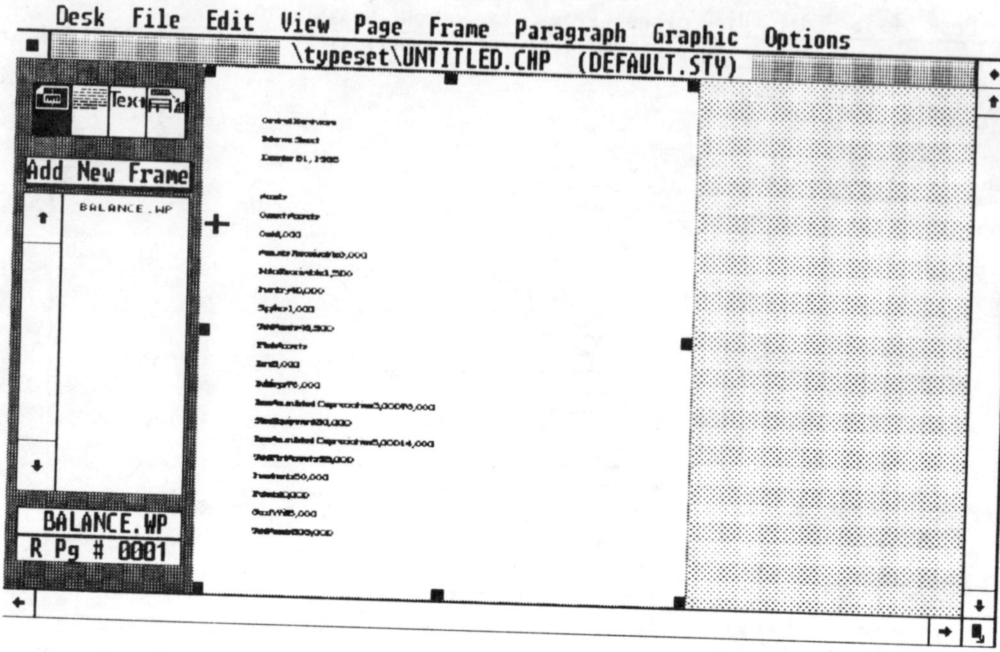

Figure 3.3

The text is now formatted in a manner similar to that of a word processing program – with left-aligned text in the normal font.

Because you are creating new tags, assign this style sheet a new file name. Point the mouse at the File menu title. Then, point the mouse at the Save As New Style option and click the button. Enter the name of the new style sheet file:

finance
[return]

The resulting tags will be stored in the FINANCE.STY file.

Activating the column guide display helps you become oriented while formatting the text. At the end of the last chapter, this display was turned off so you could view the document as it would appear on the printed page; Ventura retains that setting from the last session.

Point the mouse at the Options menu title. Then, point the mouse at the Show Column Guides selection and click the button. You are now ready to begin formatting the text.

CHANGING VIEWS

To view text more clearly for formatting purposes, place Ventura into the Normal View mode. You can use the mouse cursor as a guide when changing modes.

Point the mouse at the upper left corner of the text area. Change modes by pressing

[Ctrl/n]

MULTIPLE TAGGING

The first three lines of text consist of headings for the balance sheet. Ventura allows you to highlight more than one paragraph at a time, which is handy because in this case, you want to format all three paragraphs with the same style tag.

Place Ventura in the Paragraph mode by entering

[Ctrl/i]

Highlight the first line of the text. Point the mouse at "Center," and click the button. (When pointing in the Paragraph mode, the mouse cursor is a square. Place the top of the square in the middle of the word at which you are pointing.)

To include another paragraph in the highlighted text, you must hold down one of the Shift keys while you click the mouse button. Point the mouse at "Balance," hold down a Shift key, and click the button.

Both paragraphs are highlighted. Now, add the third paragraph. Point the mouse at "December," hold down a Shift key, and click the button.

All three paragraphs are highlighted.

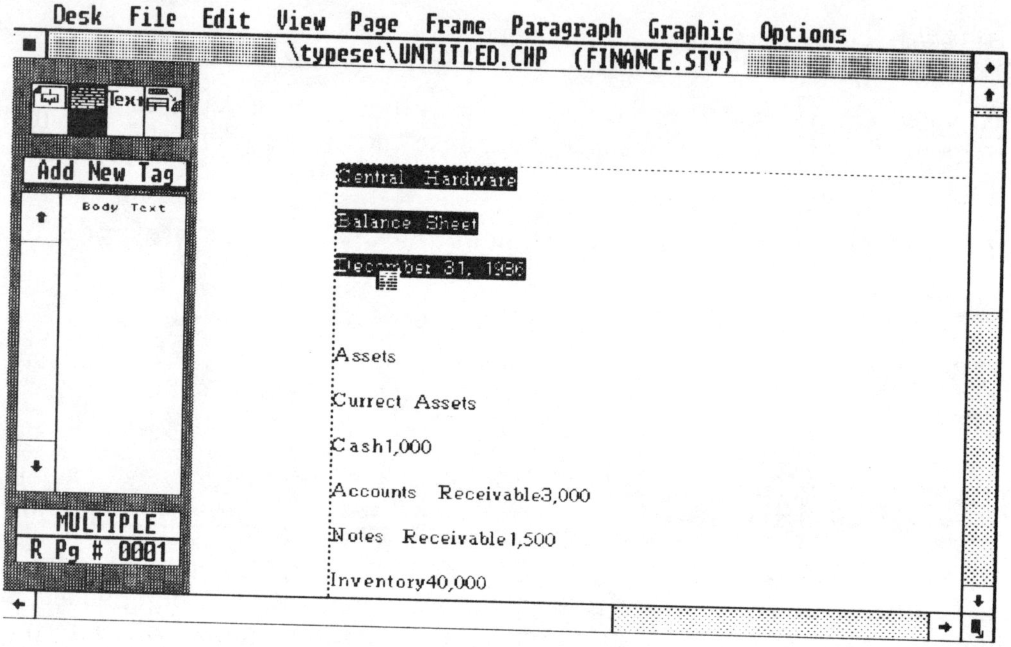

Figure 3.4

You can include in the highlight any paragraph on the page. Take, for example, the line that reads "Current Assets." Point the mouse at "Current," hold down a Shift key, and click the button.

To remove the highlight from one of the paragraphs, all you must do is select it again. This time, the highlight will be removed. Point the mouse at "Current," hold down a Shift key, and click the button.

The highlight is removed from the paragraph, but the other three paragraphs remain highlighted. If you click the mouse button without holding down a Shift key, Ventura removes the highlight from all paragraphs, and you must reselect the paragraphs to be highlighted.

ADDING A NEW TAG

The next step is to create a new tag for the title lines. Point the mouse at the Add New Tag box, and click the button.

Enter the name of the new style tag:

Title
[return]

In this example, make the title's style italic and center-aligned. Point the mouse at the Paragraph menu title. Then, point the mouse at the Font selection and click the button.

To select italic text, point the mouse at the N-Italic selection, and click the button. Then, press

[return]

To center the paragraphs, point the mouse at the Paragraph menu title. Then, point the mouse at the Alignment option and click the button. Next, point the mouse at the Center selection, and click the button.

Note that only the first paragraph has actually been affected by the style changes; however, since all three paragraphs are highlighted, you can apply the changes made to the Title tag to all paragraphs by selecting the tag from the side bar display.

Point the mouse at the Title tag and click the button. The three lines are now centered and italicized.

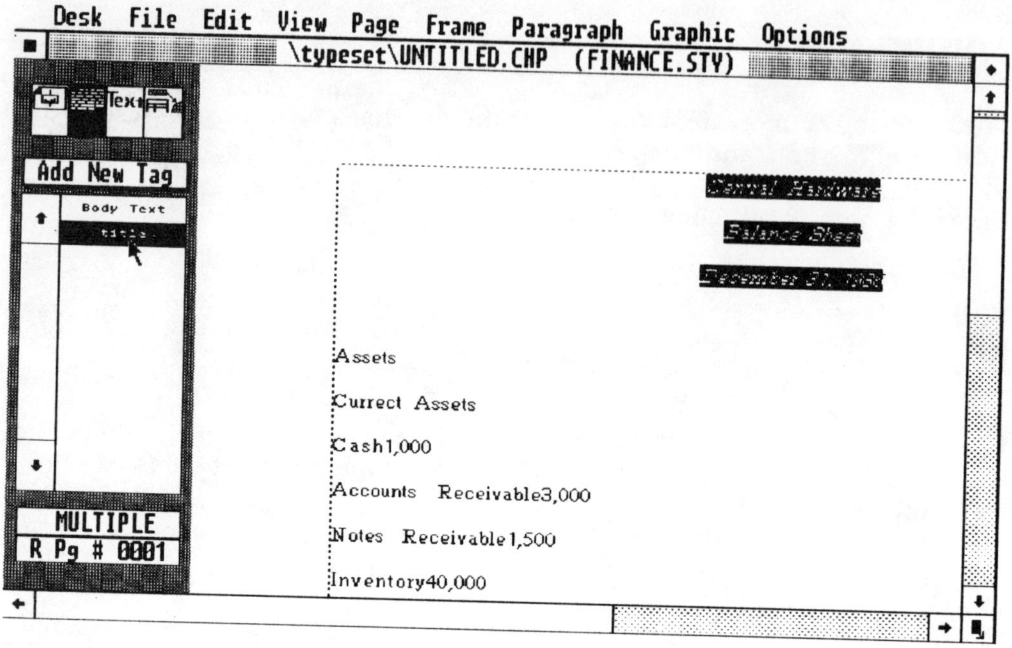

Figure 3.5

CREATING TAGS FROM OTHER TAGS

The next step is to create a tag for the major headings that occur in financial statements, such as Assets, Liabilities, and Capital. In this example, use the same format applied to the Title tag, but make the text bold instead of italic. Thus, you can create a new tag starting with attributes already added to the Title tag.

Point the mouse at "Assets," and click the button.

To create a new tag, point the mouse at the Add New Tag box, and click the button. Enter the name of the new tag:

Major Heading

Note that Ventura automatically indicates Body Text as the style tag from which to copy. In this instance, the name should be changed to Title. Enter

[down arrow]

Clear the name Body Text from the line by pressing

[Esc]

Next, enter the tag from which the new tag is to be copied:

Title
[return]

At this point, the two tags—Title and Major Head—are identical. You can change the font characteristic of the new tag to differentiate major headings from titles.

Point the mouse at the Paragraph menu title. Then, point the mouse at the Font option and click the button.

Change the font to 14-point bold. Point the mouse at 14, and click the button. Note that 14-point text is automatically assigned as bold. Complete the selection by pressing

[return]

The heading is now formatted as 14-point bold text.

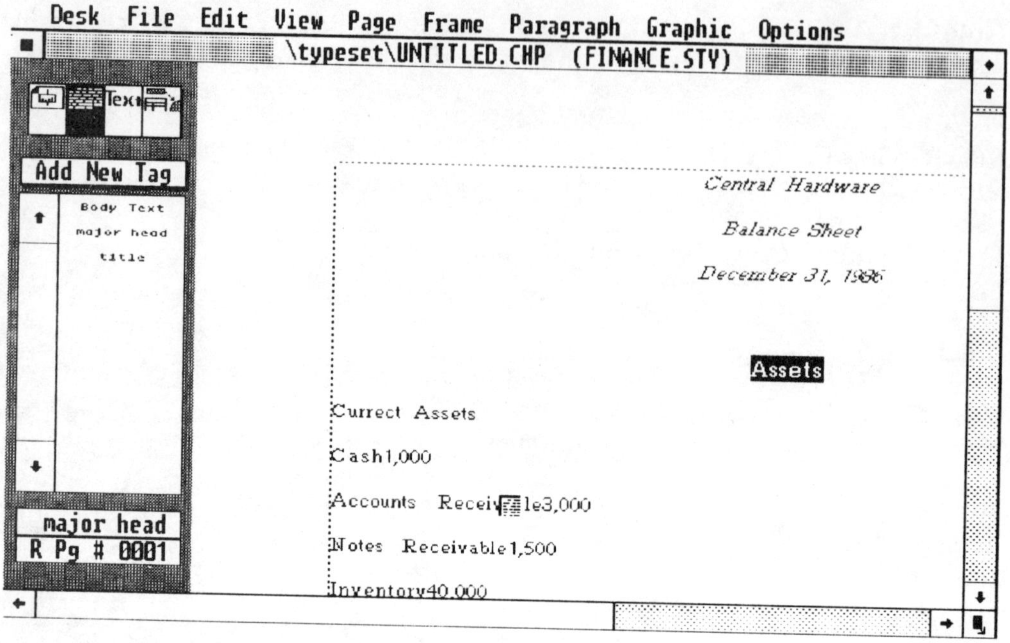

Figure 3.6

FORMATTING TAB STOPS

The next line in the text reads "Current Assets." In this occurrence, it is formatted as Body Text, which is adequate for this line.

The next component—the lines comprising the body of the financial statement—contains a heading and one or more values. The lines should be formatted so the heading is indented and the value is aligned at the proper tab location.

In a financial statement, there are three types of value lines: one for category values, one for depreciation figures, and one for totals and subtotals.

Highlight the first line of this type. Point the mouse at "Cash," and click the button.

The line that reads "Cash1,000" is misleading. In the document prepared in WordPerfect, a tab character was inserted between the word "Cash" and the number "1,000." That character remains, but Ventura does not normally display characters that are not part of the alphanumeric character set. You can change Ventura's display mode to reveal formatting characters such as tabs and carriage returns. Press

[Ctrl/t]

Ventura changes the display to show symbols representing return and tab characters. Arrow symbols indicate tabs.

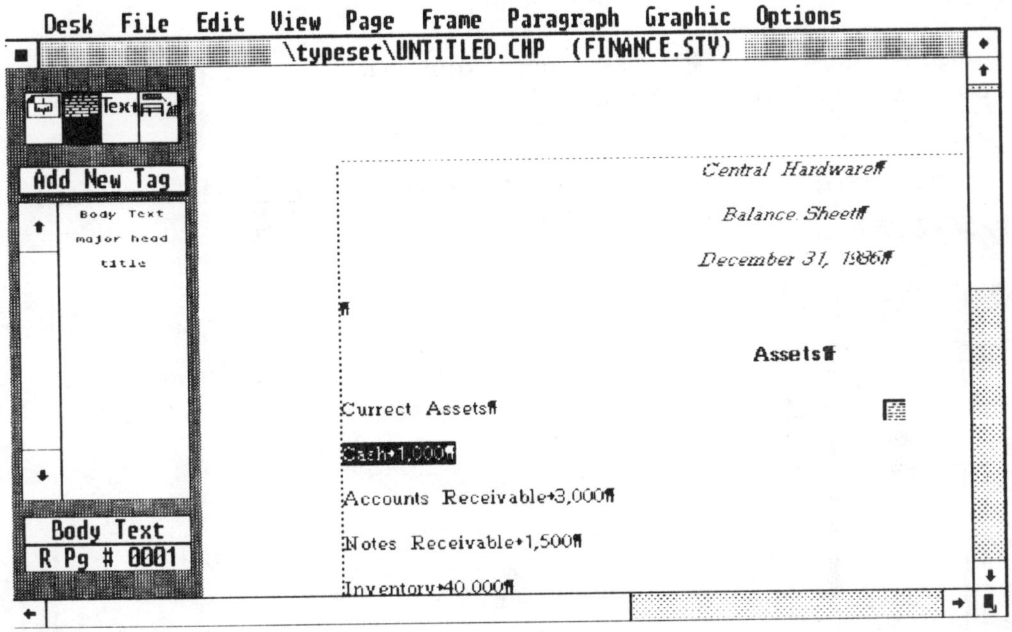

Figure 3.7

The tab commands are in the text, but they do not separate the headings from the values because tabs will not take effect until you define tab stops on which they are to align. Create a new tag for this paragraph, and name it "Values."

Point the mouse at the Add New Tag box, and click the button. Enter the name of the tag:

Values
[return]

The Values tag should include some special characteristics: text should be indented and the corresponding number aligned at a tab stop.

Ventura allows you to display ruler markings on the sides of the text window. These rulers display actual measurements (in inches) and allow you to translate screen displays into actual locations on the printed page. The ruler can be activated from the Options menu.

Point the mouse at the Paragraph menu title. Then, point the mouse at the Font option and click the button. The screen should resemble Figure 3.8.

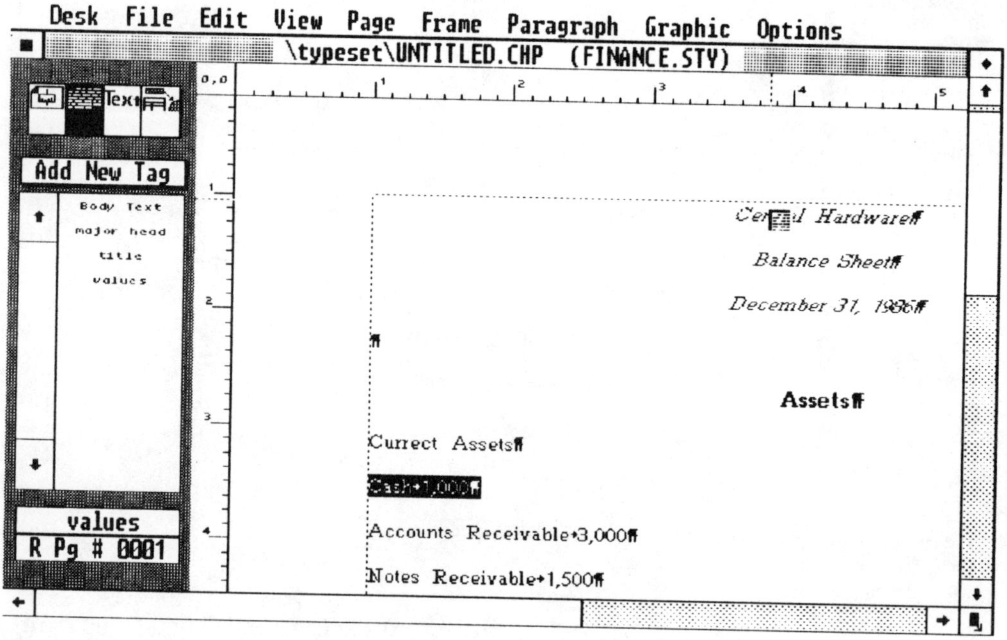

Figure 3.8

The rulers appear on the top and left sides of the document window. If you look carefully, you will see a dotted line in each ruler, indicating the current location of the mouse cursor. The lines move as you move the mouse.

Point the mouse at "Cash." The dotted line in the vertical ruler moves to about 3.5"; the horizontal line moves close to 1". This suggests that if you were to print the text, the word "Cash" would appear 3.5" from the top of the page and 1" in from the left of the page. Ruler lines help compensate for differences in screen displays because they translate screen location into concrete measurements.

First, select an indent for the paragraph. Point the mouse at the Paragraph menu title. Then, point the mouse at the Alignment option and click the button.

The ALIGNMENT menu appears. The first step is to select left-alignment. Point the mouse at the Left selection, and click the button. Note that Ventura *will not* align text at tab stops if the paragraph is set for justified alignment.

The text cursor is positioned at the line that reads "In/Outdent Width." Enter the size of the indent on this line. Just above the line are two boxes – Indent and Outdent – that determine whether the width entered on the width line indents or outdents the paragraph's first line of text. **Outdent** is the opposite of **indent**. In an indent, the text of the first line is pushed a specified distance to the right of the existing margin. An outdent allows the first line to extend a specified distance to the left of the existing margin. The default selection is Indent. Specify an indent of 1/4". Enter

[Esc]
.25
[return]

The text is indented 1/4" from the margin.

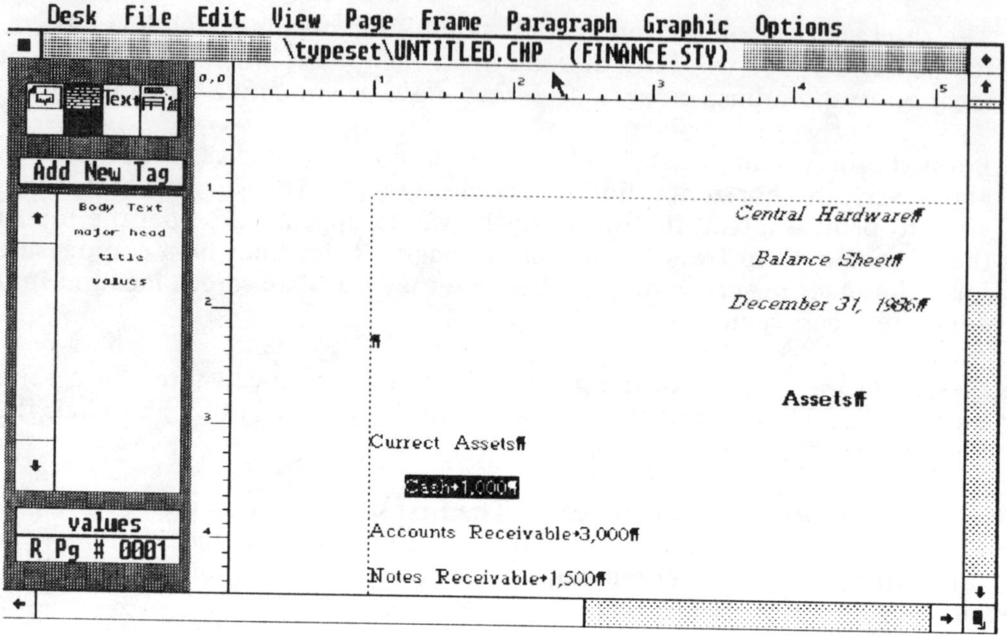

Figure 3.9

The tab can also be handled from the paragraph menu. Point the mouse at the Paragraph menu title. Then, point the mouse at the Tab Settings option and click the button.

The TAB SETTINGS menu appears:

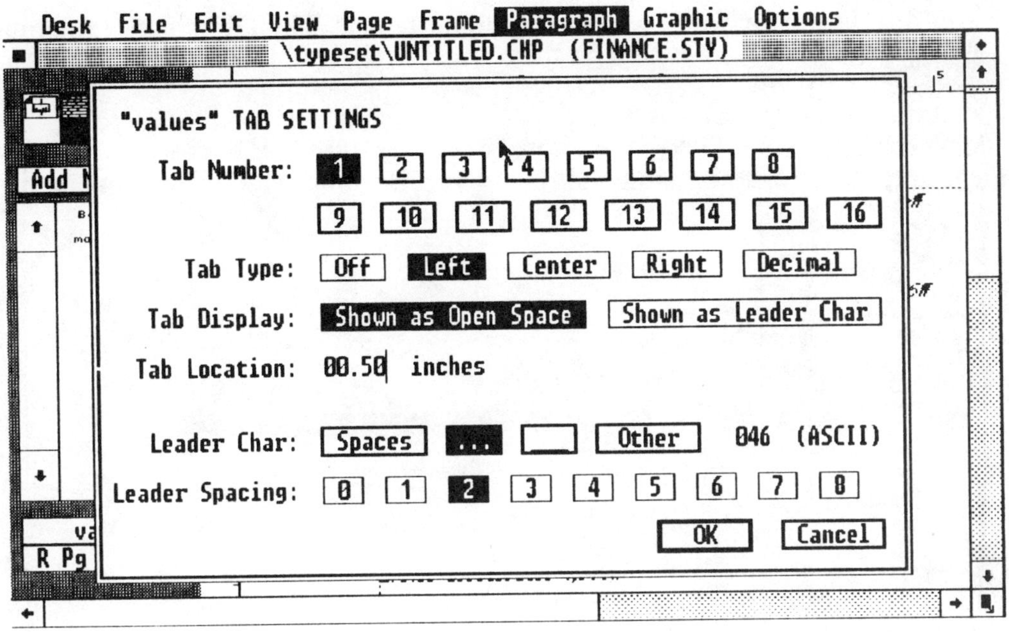

Figure 3.10

Ventura allows you to set up to 16 tab locations for each paragraph. The tabs can be set for left-, center-, right-, or decimal-alignment. You can also elect to display blank spaces or other characters – such as dots – before tabs.

In this case, you will want to set a right-aligned tab 3.5" from the margin. Remember, tab locations are measured from the left margin – *not* the edge of the frame. For example, to create a column 4.5" from the edge of the paper, you must consider the current left margin setting. Currently, the left margin is 1", which means the tab setting should be 4.5" - 1", or 3.5".

Select the tab as right-aligned. Point the mouse at the Right selection, and click the button.

The current location for the first tab setting is .5". Change it by entering

035
[return]

Ventura automatically inserts the decimal point. The tab is now expanded so that the value is aligned 3.5" from the margin.

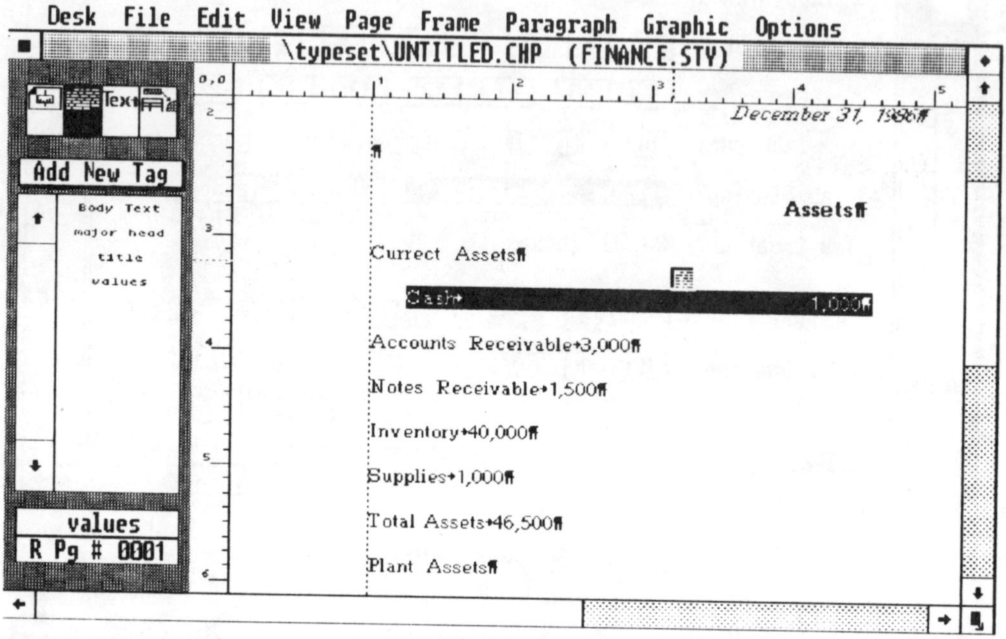

Figure 3.11

After you have established the style tag for the values, extend the highlight to include the next five lines. Remember to hold down a Shift key before you click the mouse button while the cursor is on the paragraph. If your screen display does not show the entire line, scroll the display down one line at a time by clicking the mouse button while the cursor is on the down arrow symbol at the bottom of the vertical display bar.

When all six paragraphs are highlighted, select the Values paragraph tag. Point the mouse at the Values tag, and click the button. All paragraphs align in the same way (see Figure 3.12).

To set this section off from the heading, you can reduce the amount of space between each paragraph. Point the mouse at the Paragraph menu title. Then, point the mouse at the Spacing option and click the button. The SPACING menu appears (see Figure 3.13).

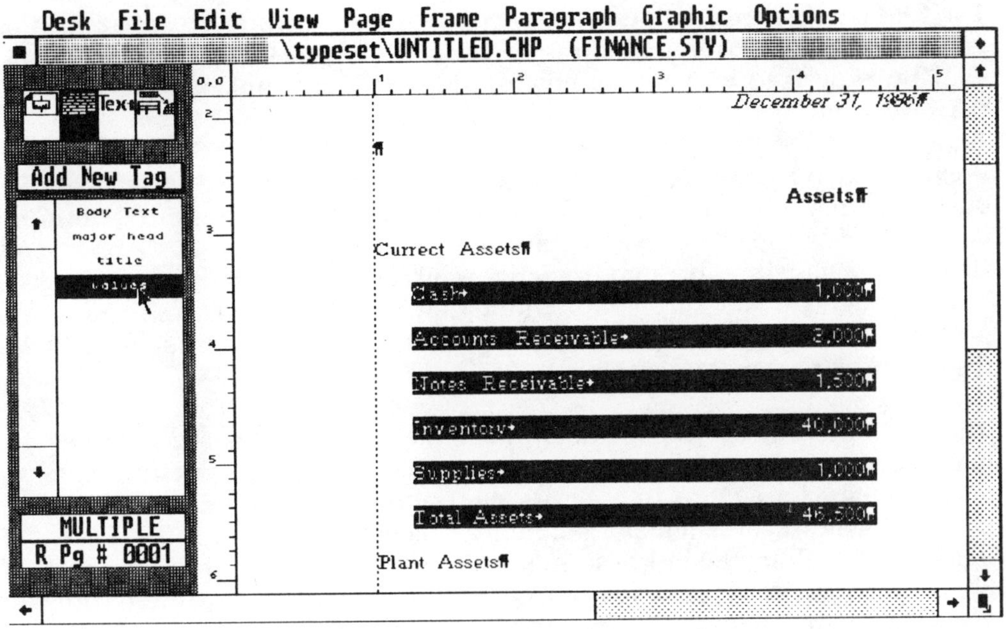

Figure 3.12

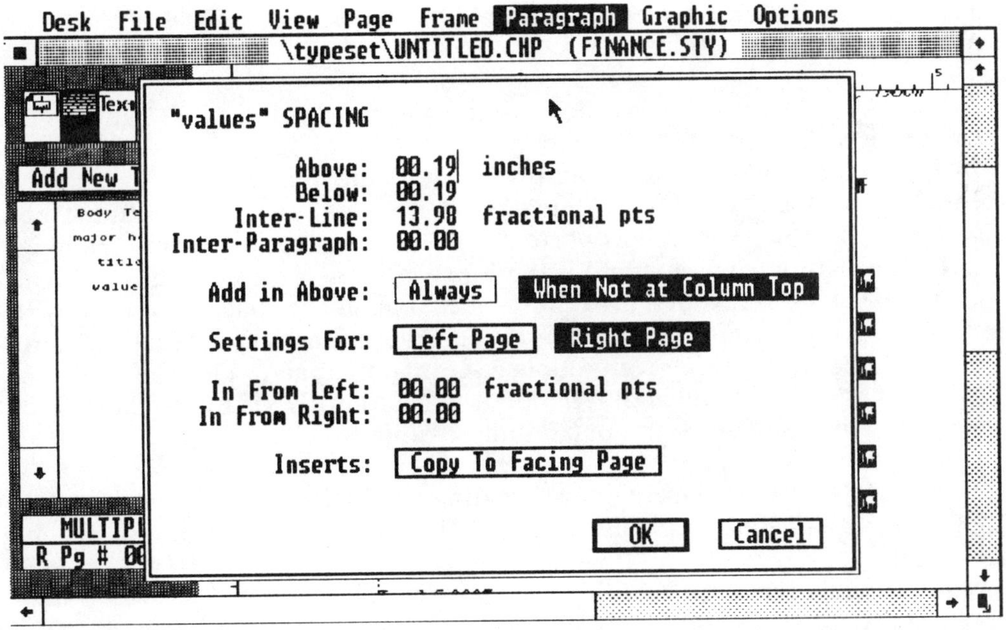

Figure 3.13

The SPACING menu expresses some of the most complicated relationships in Ventura and is covered later in great detail (also see Chapter 2). For now, your purpose is to understand how to reduce the amount of space between the value lines.

Previously, you learned that the SPACING menu controls the vertical distance between lines of text. Each paragraph uses four settings to determine the amount of space between lines. The first two settings – Above and Below – are usually expressed in inches. Currently, the values are set at .19". The second two measurements – Inter-Line and Inter-Paragraph – are expressed as **fractional points.** The current value for Inter-Line spacing is 13.98; the setting for Inter-Paragraph is 0.

The Inter-Line measurement determines the amount of space between the baseline of one line of text and the baseline of the next. **Baseline** refers to an imaginary horizontal line across the bottom of most characters. Some characters, however, such as "g" and "y," have tails, or **descenders**, that fall below the baseline; the tail descends below the baseline established for most characters. (A few years ago, most dot matrix computer printers did not allow descenders below the baseline, which made text look awkward. Today, all printers except very inexpensive ones are capable of printing text with decenders.) The Inter-Line spacing value should be large enough to allow characters to print without overlapping each other. Printers generally follow a rule that the space between lines should be approximately 20% of the height of the characters.

As stated previously, printers measure text height in points (1/72" units). The current font is set at 12-point. If you add 20% to 12 points, you arrive at 14.4 points as the suggested value for Inter-Line spacing, but Ventura has entered 13.98 as the value. Remember, Ventura allows you to choose bold and italic printing – as well as normal text – in the same point size. Bold text is thicker than normal text and is therefore taller as well as wider. Italic text is printed at a slant, which also causes a change in the space taken up by the character. To allow for these technical considerations, Ventura sets the inter-line spacing to a smaller value than you might expect. The difference between 14.4 and 13.98 is about 1/100", which is hardly visible to the eye, but Ventura tries to achieve the maximum possible precison.

Thus, the Inter-Line spacing is approximately 20% more than the height of the characters. Next, consider the .19" values for Above and Below spacing.

The values appear to vary widely because they are expressed in two different systems of measurement. Ventura can display spacing measurements in any of the measuring systems you prefer. To change a measurement system, click on the name of the measurement. For example, to determine the value in inches of 13.98 fractional points, point the mouse at "fractional," and click the button.

The measurement system changes from fractional points to inches, revealing that 13.98 fractional points is equal to approximately .19". The conversion makes clearer the relationship between Inter-Line and Above and Below spacing. Ventura automatically assigns approximately the same spacing value to Above and Below as it assigns to Inter-Line spacing.

Change the measurement system once again. Point the mouse at "inches," and click the button. This time, the measurement appears in centimeters; .19" is approximately .49 centimeters.

Point the mouse at "centimeters," and click the button. The value is now expressed in picas and points. Point the mouse at "picas & points," and click the button. The fractional points value appears once again. Ventura allows you to switch between measurement systems as often as you like.

Fractional points is the default measurement system because it is the most accurate. If you select inches, centimeters, or picas and points, Ventura rounds the actual values. To show exact values for Inter-Line spacing, Ventura uses fractional points. Displaying Above and Below values in inches implies that these measurements are not as crucial (in terms of accuracy) as the Inter-line spacing value.

Manipulating the amount of space between two paragraphs is one of the most complex aspects of Ventura, and the procedure requires that you follow a special set of rules.

Ventura determines the amount of space by comparing values of pairs of paragraphs. For example, suppose Ventura was trying to determine the space between two paragraphs named A and B. Assume that paragraph A is entered just above paragraph B.

To determine the space between A and B, Ventura compares the Below value in A to the Above value in B. If the Below value in A is greater than the Above value in B, Ventura will then use the Below value in A as the space between paragraphs. In this case, the Above value in B will be ignored.

Suppose there is a paragraph C. If the Above value of C is larger than the Below value of B, the Above value of C will be used.

It is important to understand that you cannot change spacing unless you consider the relationship between both paragraphs involved. For example, suppose you think B and C are too far apart. You might think that reducing the Below value of B will correct this problem, but reducing B's value won't have any effect. Since the Below value of B is already smaller than the Above value of C, Ventura ignores the Below value of B. Because of the relationship between paragraphs, you can reduce the space by changing the Above value of C. Note, however, that if you change the Above value of C so much that it becomes smaller than the Below value of B, Ventura switches priorities and begins to control spacing based on the Below value of B, which has become the larger of the two values.

This concept of spacing is quite complicated, but, in the long run, the system makes sense and creates documents with more consistent spacing. Remember that spacing requires thought and planning. Each spacing operation described in this book will cover a different aspect of this complex subject.

In this case, you want to reduce the amount of space between all Values tags by changing both the Above and Below values to a smaller number. For example, changing the values from .19" to .10" reduces the amount of space between the paragraphs.

Create the new values by entering

[Esc]
.1
[down arrow]
[backspace]
[return]

All of the lines tagged as Values now have less space between them:

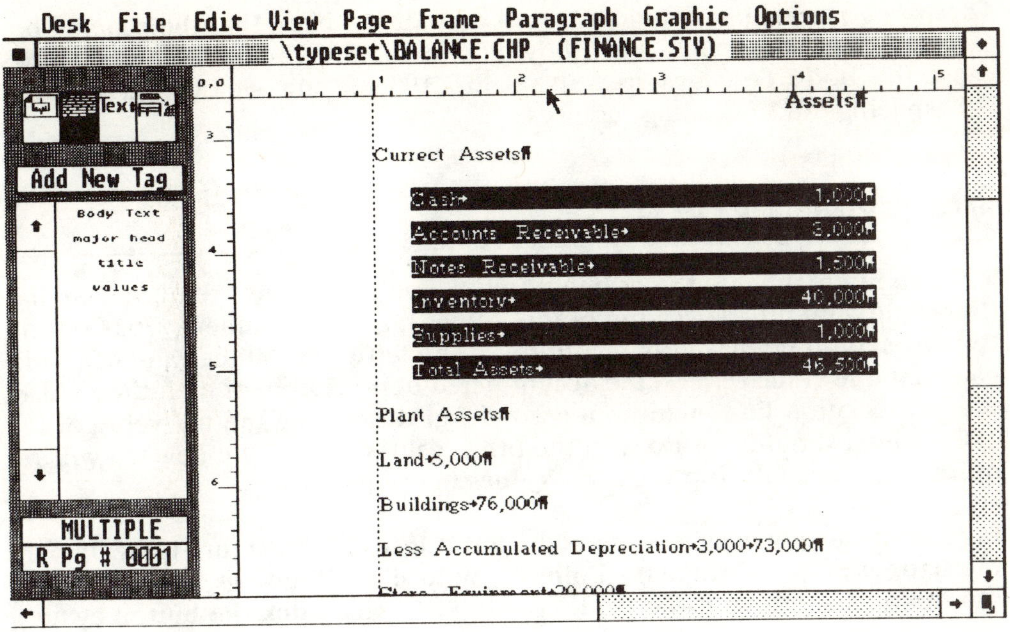

Figure 3.14

Now that the Values tag has been established, you can apply it to other lines that require the same style. To scroll the display down the page, use the cursor position in combination with a view command.

Point the mouse at the word "Plant." Enter

[Ctrl/n]

Two lines in this display also require the Values tag. Point the mouse at "Land," and click the button. Next, add the following line to the highlight. Point the mouse at "Store Equipment," hold down the Shift key, and click the button.

Select the Values tag for these paragraphs. Point the mouse at Values and click the button.

These two paragraphs are now tagged as Values. Note that the spacing between Values paragraphs and Body Text paragraphs remains the same because the Body Text tags are still set for .19" spacing, which overrules the .10" spacing the Values tag requires.

MODIFYING A STYLE

The two nonhighlighted lines between the highlighted ones require a similar (but slightly modified) version of the Values tag. The numbers "76,000" and "3,000" should be placed in a column to the left of the other values to indicate that one value reflects the accumulated depreciation of the other. Also, the depreciation line includes a second figure showing the net value of the asset, which should line up with the other values. Thus, the new tag will require one more tab stop than the Values tag requires.

Instead of starting over from scratch, you can instruct Ventura to begin with the settings of an existing tag. Point the mouse at "Buildings," click the button, point the mouse at the Add New Tag box, and click the button again.

Enter the name for the tab, but do not press Return. Name the tag "Deprc" (for depreciation entries). Type

Deprc

Ventura assumes that you want to begin with the attributes of the Body Text tag. Change the name of the tag from which to copy by entering

[Down arrow]
[Esc]
Values
[return]

The paragraph is formatted with the Values tag setting; however, your task is to change the tab settings for this tag.

Point the mouse at the Paragraph menu title. Then, point the mouse at the Tab Settings option and click the button.

The first tab stop in this style tag should appear to the left of the current setting of 3.5". Change the setting by reducing the measurement by .75". Enter

[Esc]
02.75

To set another tab, you must select the number of the tab. Point the mouse at "2," and click the button.

You can see by reading the settings in the box that tab 2 is currently a left-aligned tab positioned 1" from the left margin. Change the tab to a right-aligned tab. Point the mouse at Right, and click the button.

This tab should be in the same location as the tab in the Values tag—the second number in the Deprc column and the first number in the Values column should line up in the same column. Enter

[Esc]
03.5
[return]

Tag the next line with the new style tag. Point the mouse at "Depreciation," and click the button. Then, point the mouse at the Deprc tag listing, and click the button again. The text lines up correctly (see Figure 3.15).

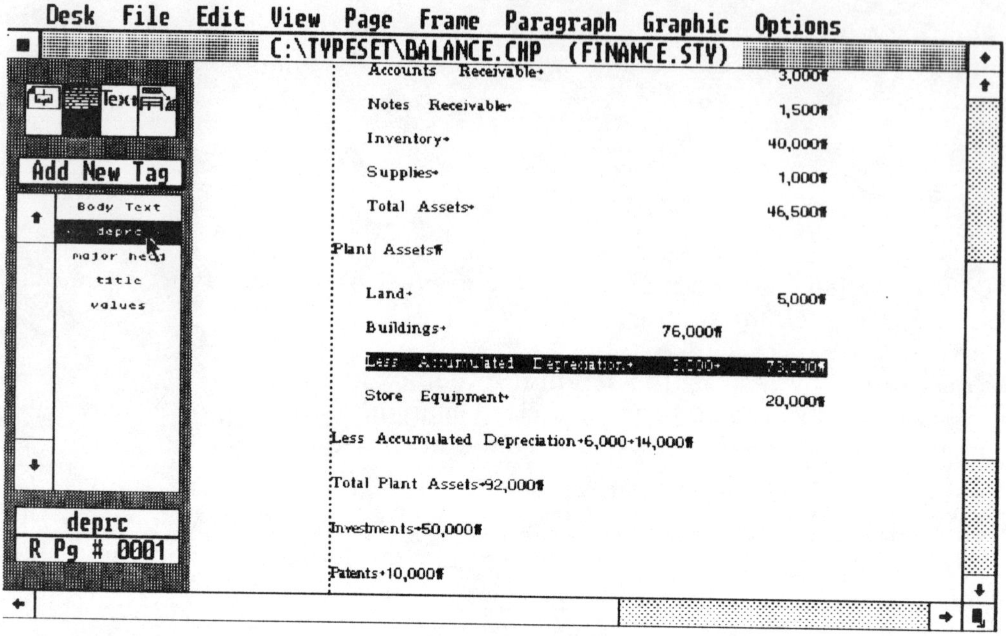

Figure 3.15

Tag the next two lines, "Store Equipment" and "Less Accumulated Depreciation," with the Deprc style tag.

TOTAL LINES

The next line in the balance sheet reads "Total Plant Assets." This line represents a total of all values under the heading "Plant Assets." Since totals on a financial statement are usually placed in a column to the right of the values, you should create a tag for the lines including totals. First, select the line that requires the new tag.

Point the mouse at "Total Plant," and click the button.

To create a new tag, point the mouse at the Add New Tag box, and click the button. In this instance, name the new tag "Total" and copy the style settings from the Values tag. Enter

Total
[down arrow]
[Esc]
Values
[return]

The tag requires two changes: the text should be indented farther to the right, and the tab stop should be moved to a column position farther to the right. The first change can be accomplished through the Alignment option in the Paragraph menu.

Point the mouse at the Paragraph menu title. Then, point the mouse at the Alignment option, and click the button. The current indent setting is .25". Increase this setting to .5" by entering

[Esc]
.5
[return]

The line you are working on is indented .5" from the left margin. The next step is to change the location of the tab stop so "92,000" is moved to a new column position.

Point the mouse at the Paragraph menu title. Then, point the mouse at the Tab Setting option, and click the button.

Change the tab stop from 3.5" to 4.5" in from the left margin. Enter

[Esc]
04.5
[return]

The Total line now stands out from the other numbers in the financial statement.

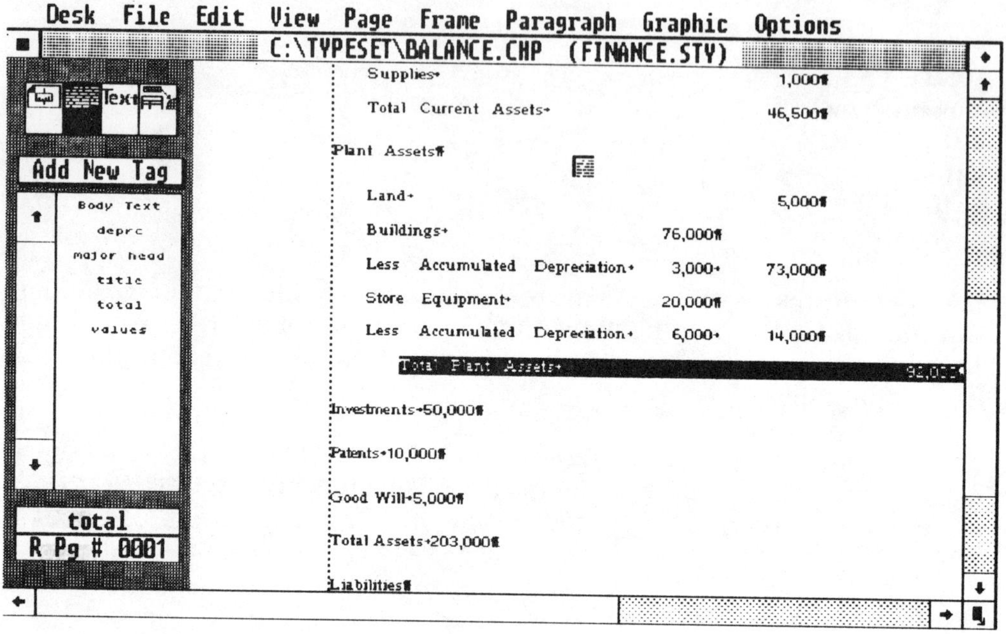

Figure 3.16

Careful inspection of the document reveals that a Total line – "Total Current Assets" – is tagged with the Values tag and not the Total tag. Correcting such mistakes is easy in Ventura because of how style tags work. If a tag exists, it is simple to assign it to a paragraph or change your mind and assign the same paragraph a different tag. While it may take time to determine the correct settings for a tag, once the tag is established, it is easy to apply that tag to one or more paragraphs.

To correct this oversight, point the mouse at "Total Current," and click the button. Point the mouse at the Total tag, and click the button again.

The total for current assets aligns with the total for plant assets. Style tagging is much more accurate than setting individual margins and tab stops for each paragraph, since you need only remember the name of the tag – not the exact settings contained in the tag description.

Now that you have created the Total tag, you can tag the next three items on the financial statement—"Investments," "Patents," and "Good Will." When you have finished, the document should resemble the following:

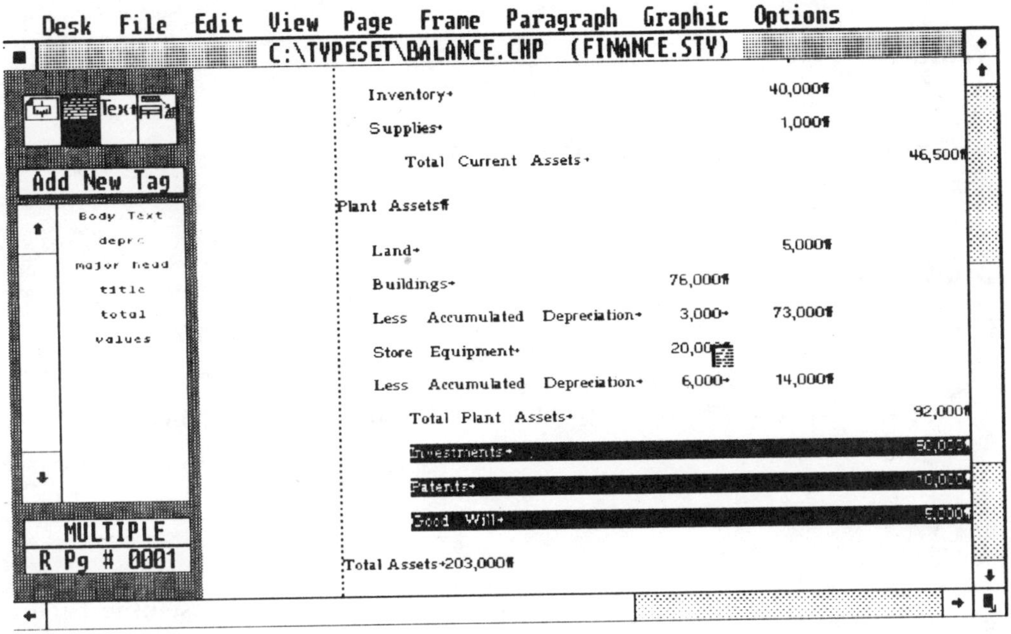

Figure 3.17

Although you have accomplished a great deal in formatting this document, there are still some additional changes you should make. The three lines currently highlighted are tagged with the Total tag just as the "Total Plant Assets" values are. These lines are slightly different because they are not totals of summarized figures on the statement; they are totals of individual balance sheet items. The names should not be indented but should align on the left margin as the "Plant Assets" values do.

To accomplish this format, you must create a new tag with the same settings as the Total tag but with the line indent removed. Name this new tag "Values 2." Point the mouse at the Add New Tag box and click the button. The ADD NEW TAG menu appears. Enter the name of the tag to be added:

Values 2

Make sure that the Tag Name to Copy From reads "Total." If it does not, clear the line for a new entry by pressing

[down arrow]
[Esc]

and enter the name of the tag from which the new tag is to be copied:

Total

When you have completed the task, the document should resemble Figure 3.18.

You have now created all the tags necessary to format the balance sheet. The rest of the work consists of applying the tags to the remainder of the document. You can see that style tagging requires that you spend time creating tags at the beginning of a job. After you decide on style tags, formatting documents can be done very quickly. You can also see that copying and modifying existing style tags is much faster than always beginning a style tag from scratch. When you create a new tag, examine the list of existing tags to see if you have created one similar in style to the one you want to create.

The last line of the assets section of the balance sheet is a Total line. Point the mouse at "Total Assets" and click the button. Then, point the mouse at the Total tag and click the button again.

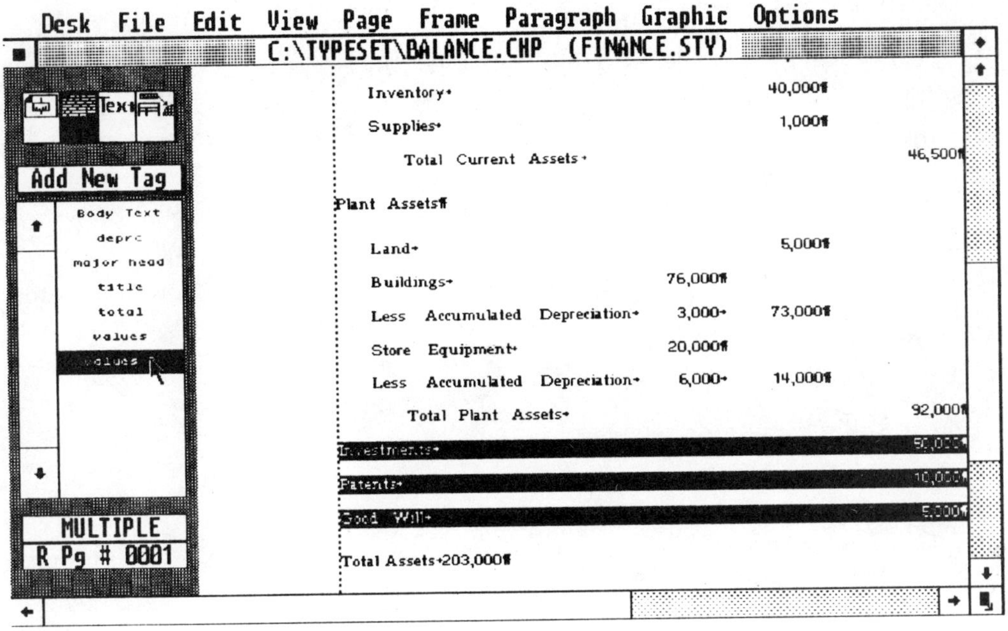

Figure 3.18

You can make one last addition to this part of the document. The figure "203,000" is the bottom line value for the assets. Traditionally, this value is double-underlined.

To add this enhancement to the document, you must change from the Paragraph mode to the Text mode. Press

[Ctrl/o]

You can add the double underline by highlighting the text you want to enhance and choosing **Double UndrLn** from the side bar display. Remember that in Text mode, highlighting is accomplished by pointing the mouse just to the left of the first character, holding the mouse button down, and moving the highlight to just beyond the last character. When your highlight includes the correct text, release the mouse button.

Highlight "203,000," point the mouse at Double UndrLn, and click the button. Return to the Paragraph mode by entering

[Ctrl/i]

Due to the resolution of some screen displays, the double underline may appear as a solid line. For a closer look at the double underline, you can change to the Enlarged View mode. Remember that before changing to Enlarged View mode, it is important to place the mouse cursor on the part of the text you want to appear in the upper left corner of the window.

Point the mouse at "203,000." Enter

[Ctrl/e]

You can see that Ventura has correctly placed the double underline below the text.

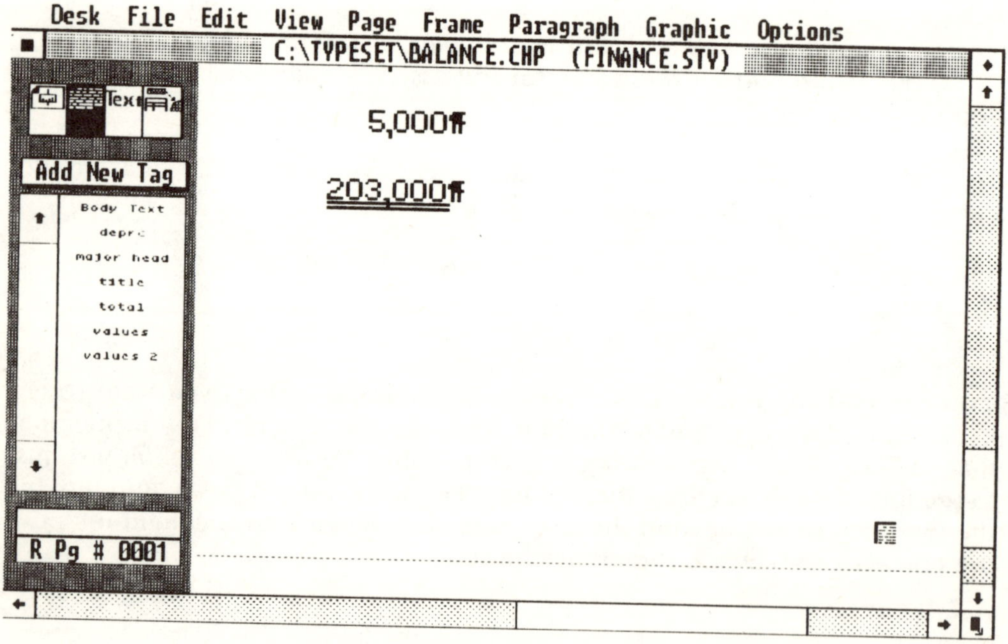

Figure 3.19

To see the current layout of the document, change to Reduced View mode. Enter

[Ctrl/r]

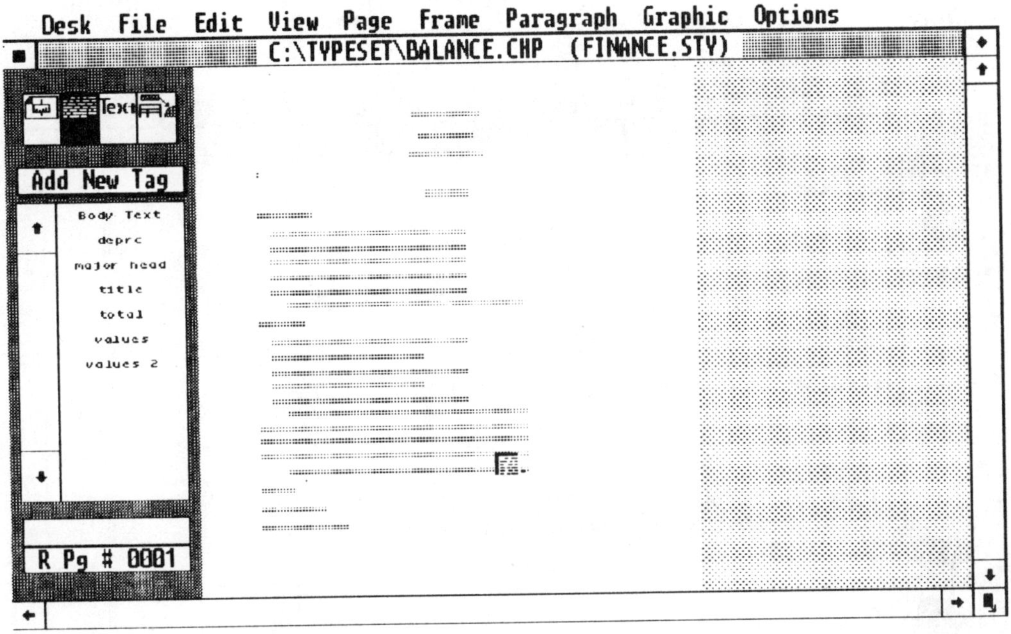

Figure 3.20

The document is displayed, but the text appears **greeked** – displayed as gray lines instead of individual characters. There are two advantages to this type of display. First, pages can be displayed faster because the computer does not need to paint each individual character. Also, a greeked display emphasizes basic formatting structure by showing the outline of the text instead of the text itself.

There are, however, times when you want to see the actual characters, even in the reduced display. In this example, the alignment of the numbers in columns cannot be seen when the text is greeked because the gray area includes the spacing between tab stops. To see the actual text, you must display the Options menu.

Point the mouse at the Options menu title. The first option on the menu is Set Preferences, which contains the setting for greeked text. Point the mouse at the Set Preferences selection and click the button.

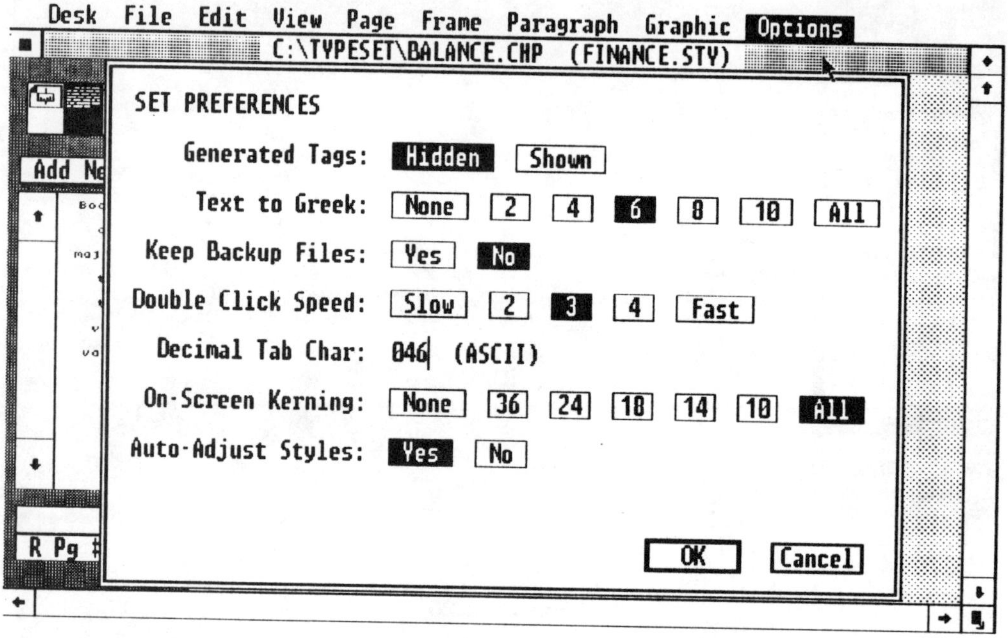

Figure 3.21

The setting for greeked text contains two words – None and All – separated by the numbers 2, 4, 6, 8, and 10.

Ventura allows you to select the amount of text to be greeked when you select the Reduced View mode. Greeked text affects only the Reduced and Facing Pages View modes. Text is always displayed normally in Normal and Enlarged View modes. Selecting "All" indicates greeking for all text, while selecting "None" instructs Ventura to display all text in actual characters. The number values between "All" and "None" are used to combine greeked text with normal character display. For example, choosing "10" instructs Ventura to greek all text in a 10-point or smaller typeface but to display all text with a point size larger than 10. Ventura's ability to mix text and greeked characters varies depending on the screen display in use. Some screens display all greeked text even when a combination is specified.

In this case, select None. Point the mouse at None, and click the button. Complete the entry by pressing

[return]

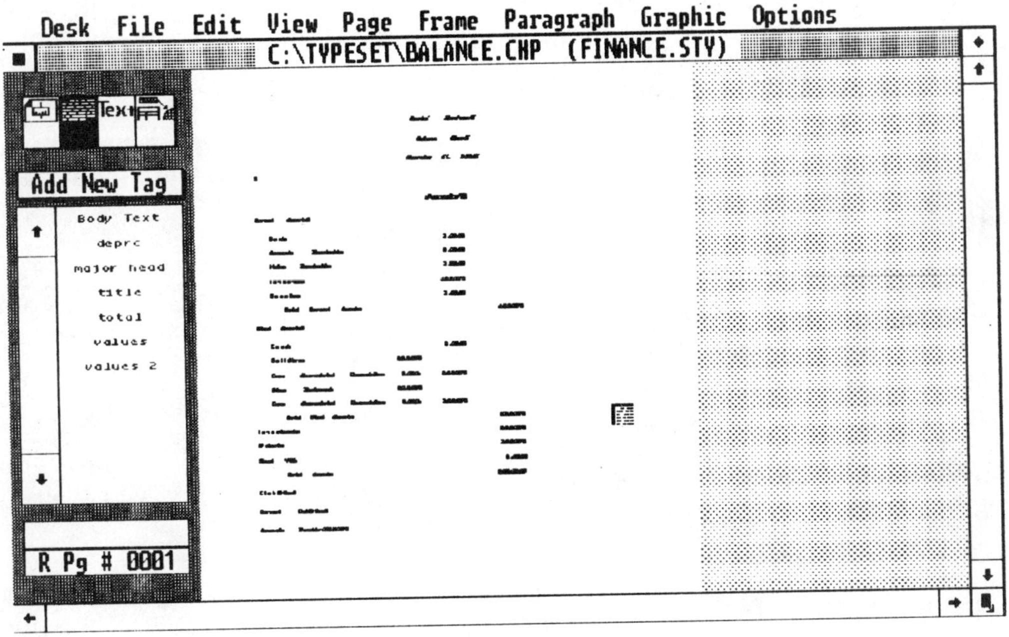

Figure 3.22

Ventura now paints the characters in their actual positions on the page. The characters are usually too small to read; however, the alignment of text in tab columns is revealed because you can now see the difference between the text and the blank space on each line.

Return to the Normal View mode. Point the mouse at the lower left corner of the text. Enter

[Ctrl/n]

FORCING A NEW PAGE

You have arrived at the bottom line of the assets section of the balance sheet. The Reduced View mode shows that you have almost filled the first page with the asset section of the document. It seems logical to begin the liability section of the document on the next page, but, since Ventura has not been instructed to do this, it places the next three lines at the bottom of page 1.

To change this page break, you must indicate that a new page should begin following the "Total Assets" line. Most word processing programs allow you to insert a page break command in the text at the point at which you want to force a new page (in WordStar, a .PA command; in WordPerfect, a [Ctrl/return]; and in Word, a [Ctrl/Shift/return]).

Ventura, however, approaches page breaks in a different way. Ventura considers a page break command to be part of the characteristics of a given tag, which means that you do not insert page breaks directly into the text but instead assign page breaks to specific style tags.

At first, this may seem confusing and inconvenient, but Ventura allows you to perform a number of sophisticated operations in which you can control line and page breaks rather easily.

Because page breaks are assocated with tags, you need to create a new tag instructing Ventura when to start a new page. Page break tags are the same as any text tag, but they contain an additional setting that forces Ventura to start a new page. In this instance, you can modify the total tag and name it Bottom Line.

First, highlight the paragraph that is to be assigned the page break. Point the mouse at "Total Assets," and click the button.

Create a new tag. Point the mouse at the Add New Tag box, and click the button.

Enter the name of the new tag. Note that Ventura assumes you want to copy the settings from the tag already specified for this paragraph. Enter

Bottom Line
[return]

The next step is to display the page-breaking options found on the Paragraph menu. Point the mouse at the Paragraph menu title. Then, point the mouse at the Breaks option and click the button.

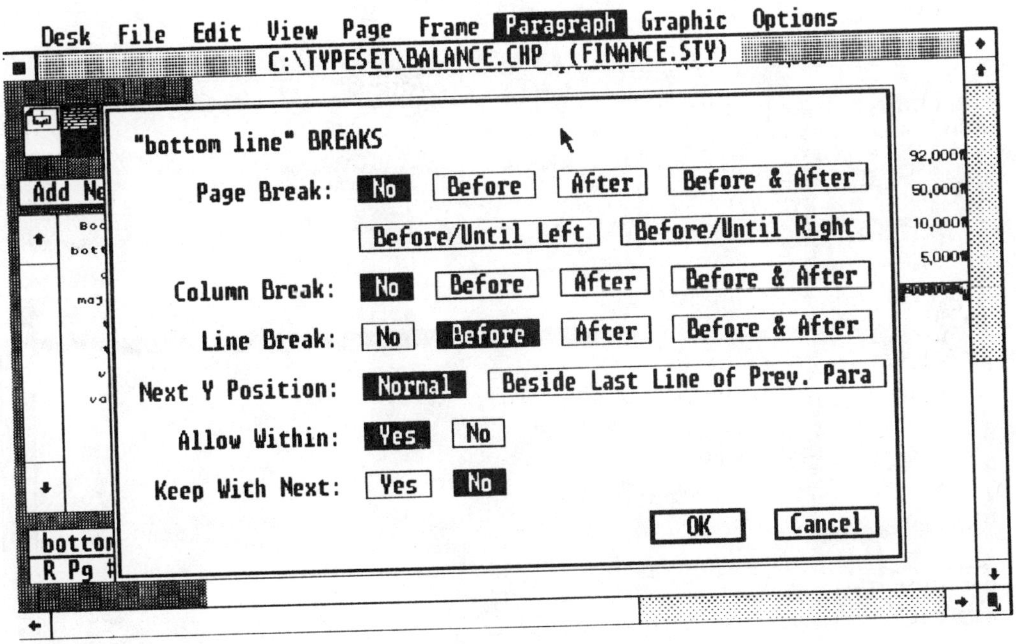

Figure 3.23

The BREAKS menu appears. Ventura allows you to control both page and line breaks. **Line breaks** refer to the way Ventura reacts to carriage return characters in the text. Normally, Ventura starts a new line before each new paragraph; however, you can create paragraph tags that suppress the start of a new line even when you enter a [return] in the text, which allows you to create special effects. Normally, line breaks correspond directly to returns entered in the text. In this case, you want Ventura to create a page break after the current paragraph.

Point the mouse at "After," and click the button. Complete the selection by pressing

[return]

Ventura clears the bottom of the page by placing the next line at the top of page 2.

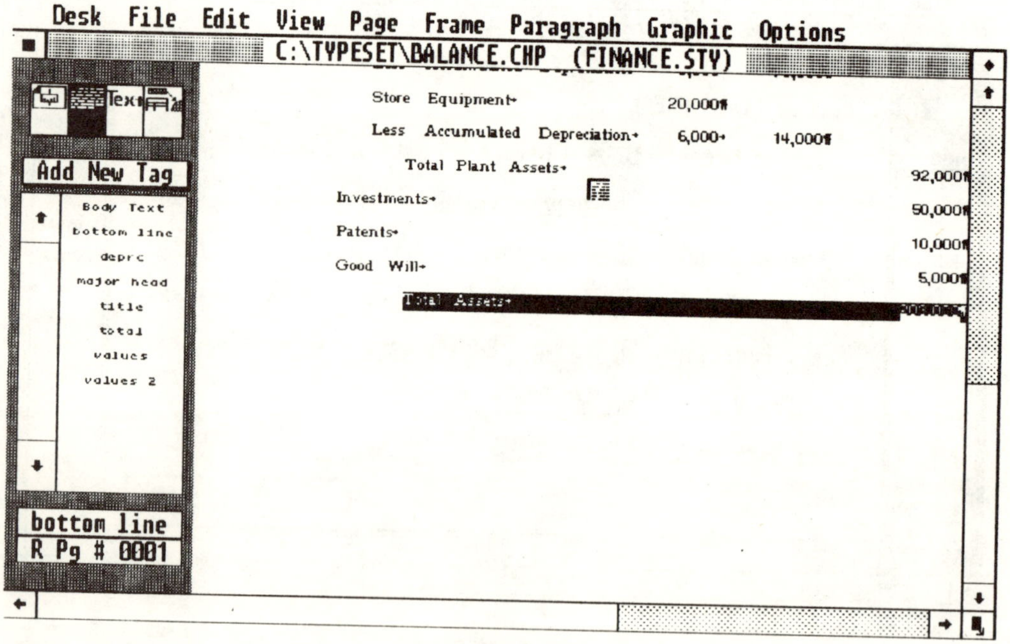

Figure 3.24

View the entire page by activating the Reduced View mode. Press

[Ctrl/r]

The PgDn (page down) key will move the cursor to the next page. Press

[PgDn]

You can now see the remainder of the text. Note that you can determine the current page by examining the page number indicator.

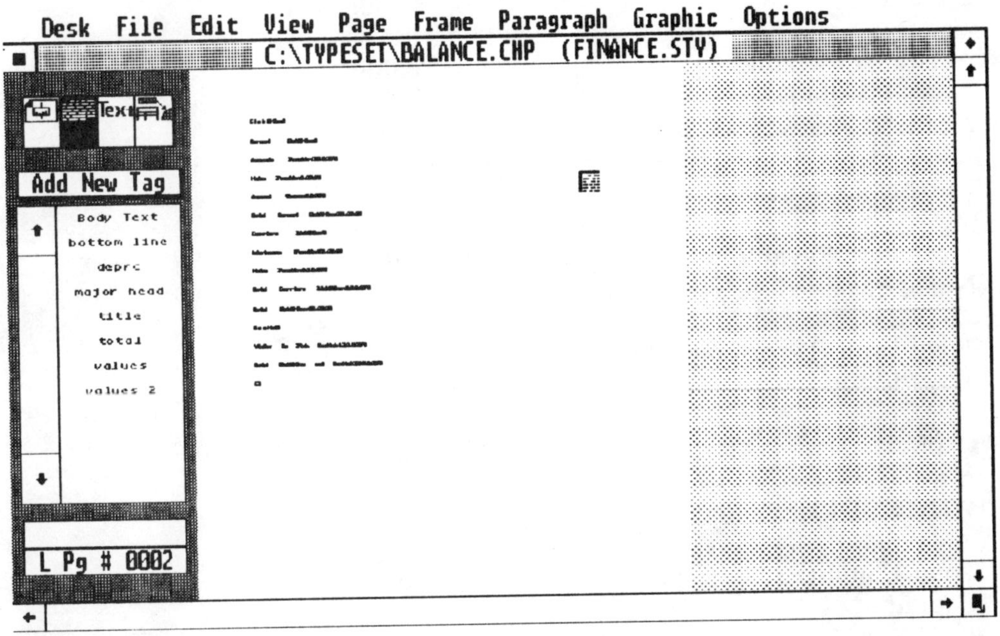

Figure 3.25

The second page can be formatted quickly because you have already defined all the necessary tags. First, place Ventura in the Normal View mode. Point the mouse at the upper left-hand corner of the text. Press

[Ctrl/n]

Now that you know how to tag paragraphs and have defined a set of tags, assign the following tags to the following text items. Remember to scroll the screen down to see more text when necessary:

Text	Tag
"Liabilities"	Major Head
"Accounts Payable" "Notes Payable" "Accrued Taxes"	Values
"Current Liabilities"	Total
"Mortgages Payable" "Notes Payable"	Values
"Total Long-Term Liabilities" "Total Liabilities"	Total
"Capital"	Major Head
"Walter La Fish"	Total
"Total Liabilities" "Capital"	Bottom Line

To place the double underline under the Bottom Line figure, you must change from the Paragraph mode to the Text mode. Press

[Ctrl/o]

Highlight the value "203,000," point the mouse at Double UndrLn, and click the button.

The document is now complete. To see the overall layout of the second page, place Ventura into the Reduced View mode by entering

[Ctrl/r]

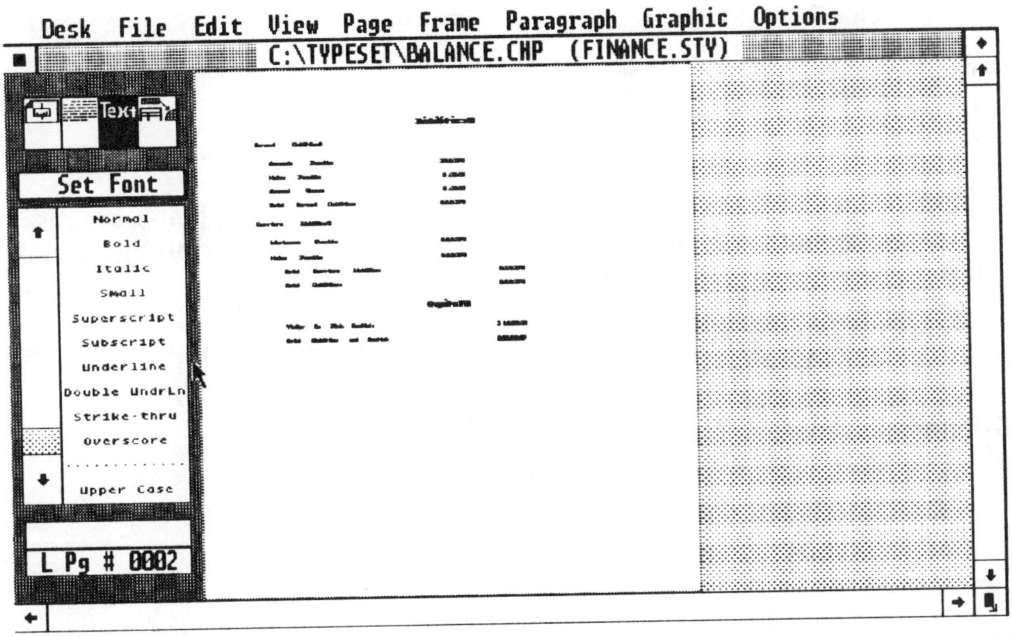

Figure 3.26

This exercise demonstrates how quickly you can format a document once you have established the necessary tags. Just as significantly, the style sheet you have created can be used with any number of text files that contain similar information. By attaching this style sheet, you save the time required to create new tags. Of course, you can change or add to the tags if the situation requires different formats.

As you create more style sheets, you will accrue a library of formats based on your experience in creating various documents.

Save the document as a new chapter named BALANCE. Enter

[Ctrl/s]
balance
[return]

Print the document by pointing the mouse at the File menu title, then pointing the mouse at the To Print selection, and clicking the button.

To print both pages, press

[return]

Your printer probably prints three pages; the third page is blank because of the way the bottom line tag is defined and the fact that you probably ended the last line of your text with a return.

To better understand the problem, focus on the last item in the document, the value "203,500."

Point the mouse at "203,500" and press

[Ctrl/e]

The line ends with the paragraph end symbol (see Figure 3.27). Point the mouse at the paragraph symbol, and click the button.

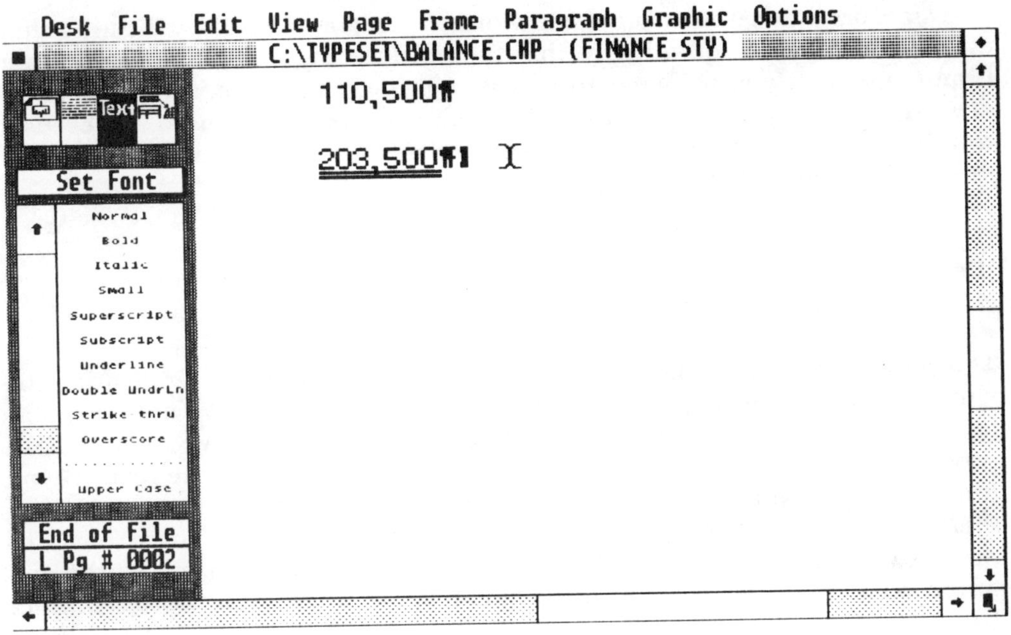

Figure 3.27

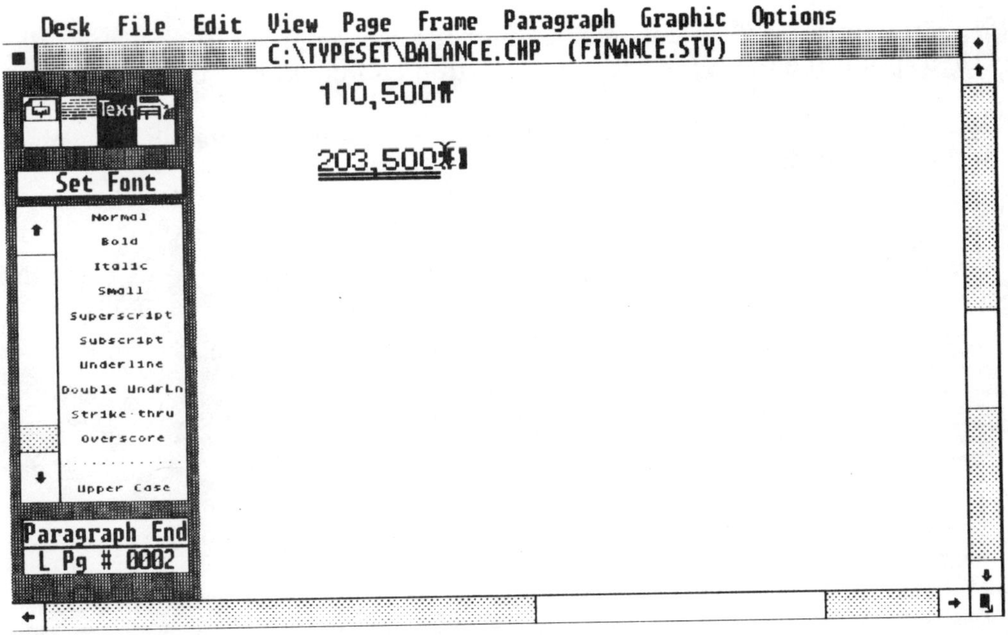

Figure 3.28

The side bar indicator displays the words "Paragraph End," indicating that the mouse cursor is pointing at that symbol (see Figure 3.28). The Bottom Line tag, which you assigned to this paragraph, causes Ventura to begin a new page following that line; as a result, an extra page is printed. There is a solution; you must delete the paragraph end and allow the end-of-file marker to end this line. Press

[Del]

The paragraph end marker is removed and the square block, indicating the end of the file takes its place. Ventura assumes that you have not accidentally entered additional blank lines into your text file, which is a common word processing mistake and will cause your results to vary from the text. If you find that when you delete the paragraph end, another one takes its place, there are extra return characters at the end of your text. To correct this problem, simply continue to delete until the end-of-file marker is at the end of the final line. The box below the side bar will display the words "End of File."

With the end-of-file marker on page 2, Ventura will not print the extra page.

To prepare for a new document, point the mouse at the File menu title. Then, point the mouse at the New selection and click the button.

Ventura monitors changes and displays a box warning you that changes made to the chapter have not been saved.

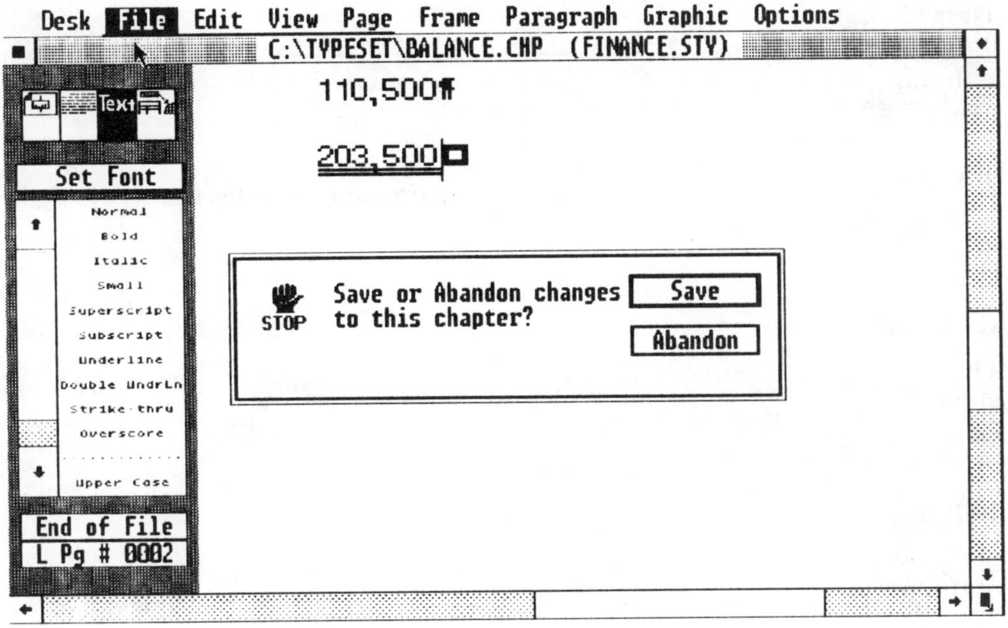

Figure 3.29

Point the mouse at the Save option, and click the button.

The screen is now clear; you can begin a new document. Note that the new style sheet, FINANCE, is still active. Ventura automatically retains the style sheet last used and loads that style sheet for any new documents. Remember to load a different, pertinent style sheet if necessary.

SUMMARY

New Tags

When you create a new tag, you can copy the settings from any existing tag in the style sheet, which makes it simpler to create new styles that vary slightly from existing tags.

Ruler Lines

Ventura allows you to display special ruler lines that show in inches the location of text on the page.

Indents

Paragraphs can be assigned specific indent values as part of a paragraph style tag. Indents are found on the Alignment option of the Paragraph menu.

Tabs

Ventura allows you to define tab stops as part of a paragraph style tag. Tabs are set in inches and are measured from the left margin of the frame. You can select left-, center-, right-, or decimal-aligned tabs.

Spacing Rules

Ventura follows a complicated set of rules to determine line spacing between paragraphs. Ventura compares the space below the top paragraph and the space above the bottom paragraph to determine which setting is larger. The larger of the two settings is used for the spacing. Remember, spacing is not determined by any one paragraph setting but by the relationship between the settings of any given pair of paragraphs.

Page Breaks

Page breaks in Ventura are assigned as part of a paragraph's style tag, which means that to insert a page break, you must define a special tag containing the page break setting. Page breaks are selected from the Breaks option of the Paragraph menu.

CHAPTER 4

GRAPHICS—CREATING FORMS

Even with the dominance of computers, businesses still use a wide variety of paper forms. With Ventura, you can create all types of forms, such as invoices, order forms, and letterheads. Your only limitation is your imagination.

In this chapter, you will learn some of the basic techniques available in Ventura for creating standard forms. The example presented in this chapter will be an invoice form; however, the principle used to create it can be applied to almost any type of form you might want to produce.

In this example, you will begin entering text directly into Ventura. Since the amount of text that appears on a form is minimal, you will find it fairly simple to enter the text directly into a Ventura document rather than using a word processor first.

The first step is to load the DEFAULT style sheet. If you have been working though this book, the last style sheet you used was FINANCE.STY. To change to the DEFAULT style sheet, point the mouse at the File menu heading. Then, point the mouse at the Load Diff. Style selection and click the mouse button.

Note: since it is simpler to give an instruction in the form of a keyboard entry, this book will use commands entered from the keyboard whenever possible. Keep in mind that you can also use point-and-click mouse operations to accomplish the same task most of the time. If you prefer to use mouse operations, feel free to substitute those actions for keyboard entries when appropriate.

From the Load Diff. Style menu, you can now select the DEFAULT.STY style sheet from the selector window or simply type in the name. Enter

default
[return]

Place the program in Normal View mode by entering

[Ctrl/n]

You are now ready to start creating the form.

USING RULER MEASUREMENTS

Because Ventura is so visually oriented, the tendency is to rely on your eye for making placement decisions. The accuracy of this type of placement will vary from individual to individual, depending on that person's acuity and artistic sense.

Ventura allows you to use rulers to help you more accurately judge alignment characteristics. In Chapter 3, you learned how to use the Options menu to turn on the ruler display. If your ruler lines do *not* appear at the top and left edge of the document window, turn the rulers on. If your rulers are visible, skip the next step.

Point the mouse at the Options menu heading. Then point the mouse at the Show Rulers selection and click the button.

The rulers measure the page, beginning in the upper left-hand corner of the paper. The ruler is divided into eighths of an inch.

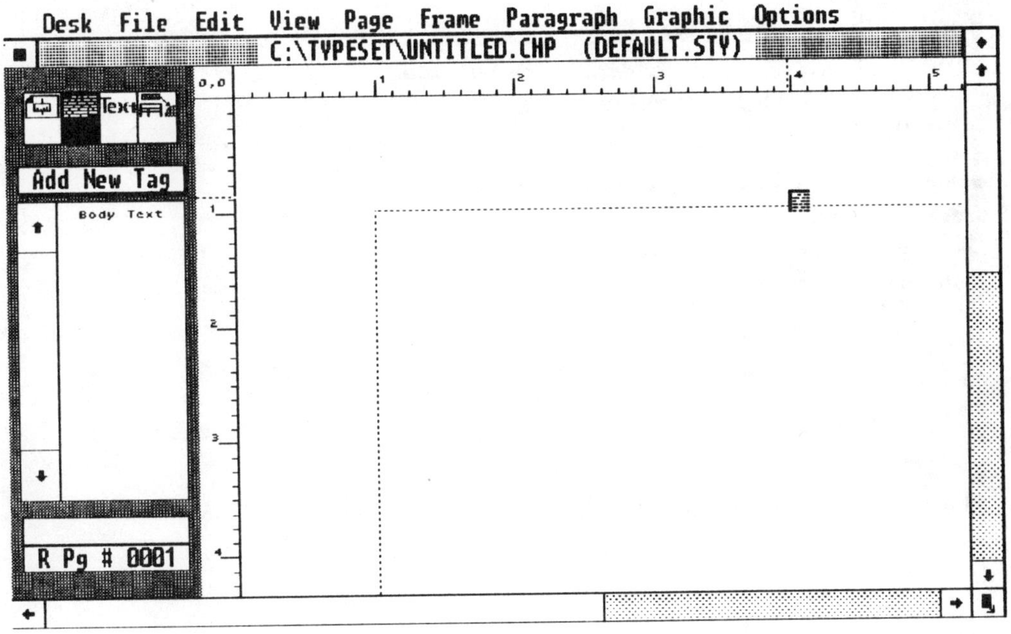

Figure 4.1

The ruler line is currently set to measure the page beginning at the page's edge; however, since there is a 1" margin around the entire page, you may find it more useful to begin the measurements at the margin location rather than at the edge of the page. You can adjust the ruler lines to fit the margins.

First, point the mouse at the Options menu heading. Then, point the mouse at the Set Ruler selection and click the button.

Ventura displays the SET RULER menu.

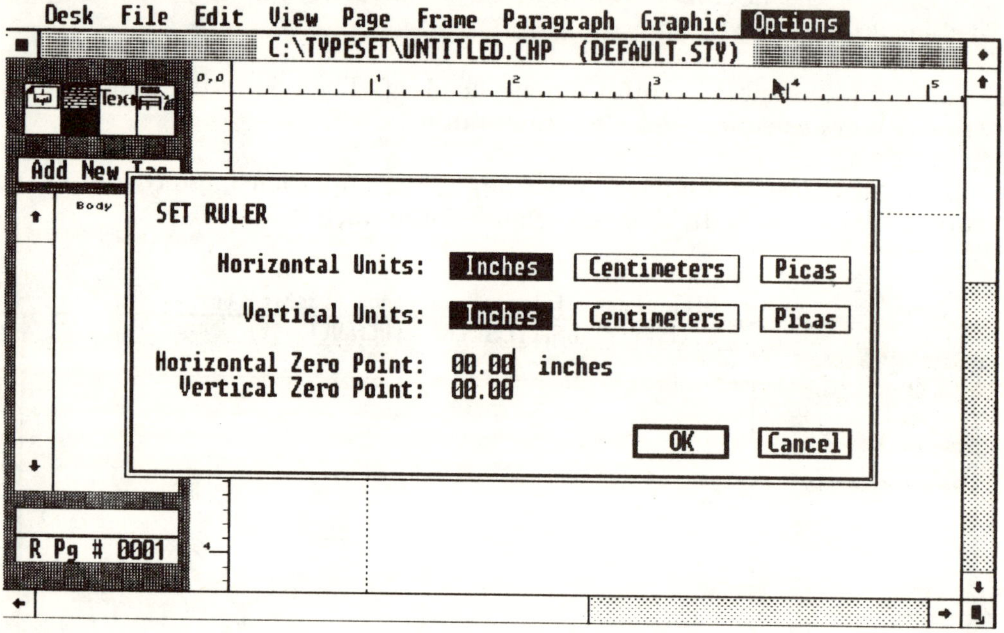

Figure 4.2

The menu consists of two options. The first choice is the unit of measurement (inches, centimeters, or picas), and the other choice sets the beginning ruler location. In this case, you can leave the unit of measurement at inches; however, you do want to change the location at which the rulers begin. Since the top and left margins are set at 1", enter

[Esc]
01
[down arrow]
[Esc]
01
[return]

Ventura has shifted the ruler line measurements so that zero is at the edge of the left margin rather than at the edge of the page. By changing the rulers, you eliminate the need to mentally add an inch each time you try to calculate a location.

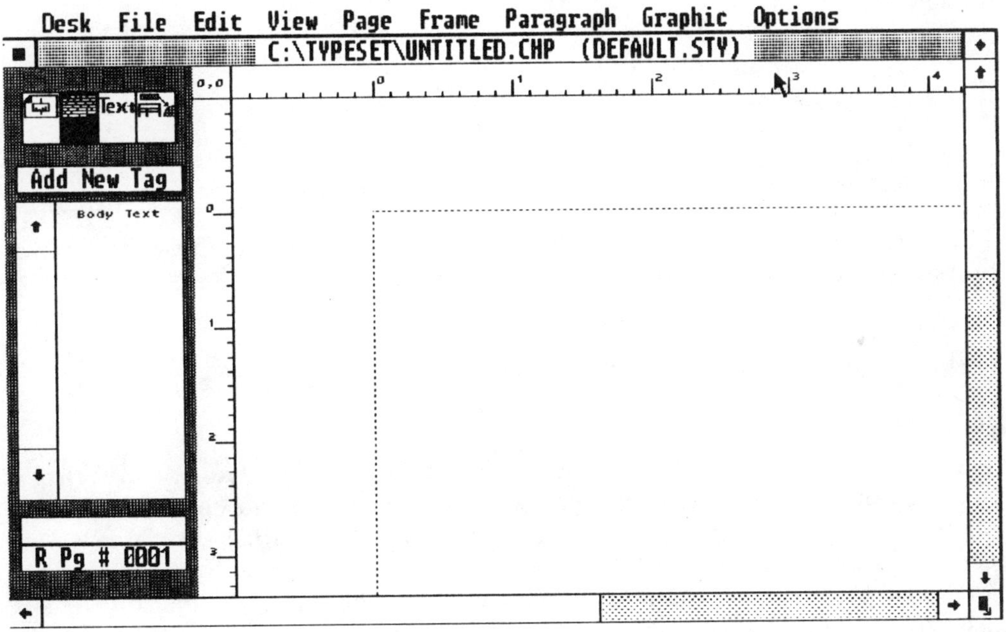

Figure 4.3

The first step in developing your invoice document is to place the company name and address at the top of the form. This action requires that you switch to the Text mode. Enter

[Ctrl/o]

Because you have not previously created a text file to load, you must create one through Ventura.

Point the mouse at the upper left corner of the column guides. Then, click the mouse button. Ventura warns you that you are about to create a new file.

Point the mouse at the New File option and click the button. Then, enter the name of the new file:

[Esc]
ltrhead
[return]

LINE ENDINGS

You can now enter the name and address of the company; however, do *not* press a [return] at the end of the line. Enter

La Fish Enterprises

The end of this line will be treated in a new way. Instead of entering a [return], or end-of-paragraph command, you will enter an end-of-line command. In most word processing programs, short lines are treated as paragraphs and end with a [return]. But more sophisticated programs, such as Ventura and Microsoft Word, allow a subtle but useful distinction. If you are typing several short lines that belong together as a unit, such as an address block, you can terminate the lines with **line end** commands instead of **paragraph end** commands.

Line ends occur between short lines that belong to the same style tag. The purpose of a line ending command is to treat a group of short lines as if they were full lines of text in a paragraph, which means that all the lines will use the same style tag. More significantly, Ventura will space the lines more closely together than it would if they had paragraph endings at the close of each line. To create a new line, enter

[Ctrl/return]

Ventura displays a character that looks like an arrow pointing down and left to indicate that a line end command has been entered.

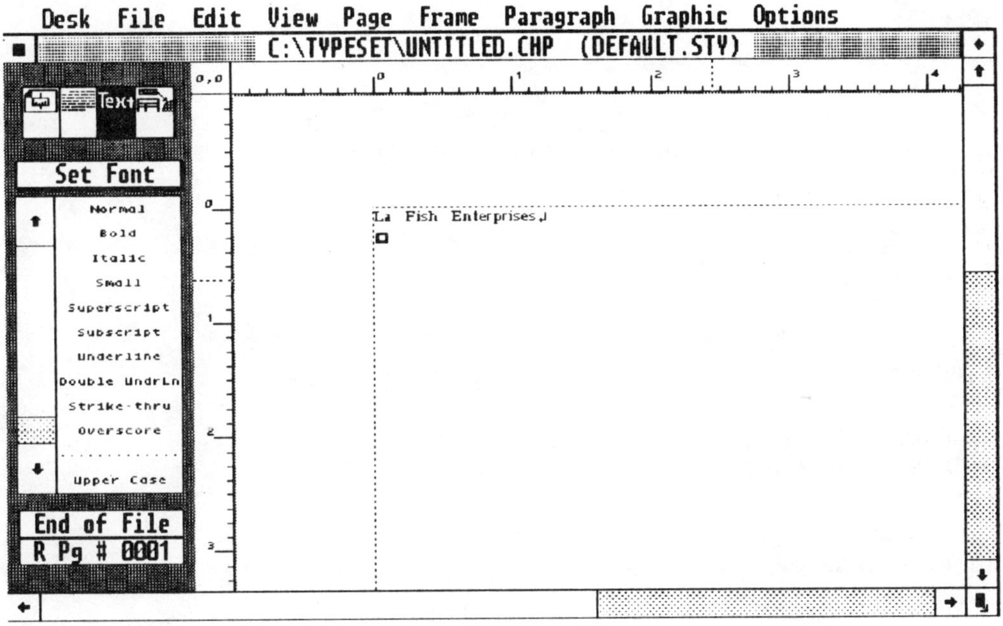

Figure 4.4

Note that the spacing between the lines is small, the same spacing that would be used when full lines are entered. To see the contrast between paragraph and line spacing, remove the line end and replace it with a paragraph end. Press

[backspace]
[return]

Depending on your screen display, this type of editing may cause some lines or dots to remain on the screen in the wrong place. You can tell Ventura to repaint the screen. Press

[Esc]

You can now see that a paragraph end creates a much larger vertical space than does a line end. Put the line end back by entering

[backspace]
[Ctrl/return]

Complete the address block by entering the following:

1250 Walnut Blvd.
[Ctrl/return]
Suite 1000
[Ctrl/return]
Pine Creek, CA 94596

TAGGING A BLOCK

With the address entered, you are ready to format the text. Place Ventura in the Paragraph mode by entering

[Ctrl/i]

Point the mouse at "La Fish" and click the button.

Ventura highlights all the lines that end with line end characters. The line ends make it easy to format a series of related short lines. You will want to change the font and alignment of this group of lines, which means you should create a new tag.

Point the mouse at Add New Tag and click the button. Enter

logo
[return]

Next, change the font by pointing the mouse at the Paragraph menu heading. Then, point the mouse at the Font selection and click the button.

From the Font menu, select Swiss 14-Point Bold by pointing the mouse at Swiss and clicking the button. Then, point the mouse at 14 and click the button.

Complete the entry by pressing

[return]

Next, center the text by pointing the mouse at the Paragraph menu heading. Then, point the mouse at the Alignment selection and click the button. Finally, from the Alignment subment, point the mouse at the Center option and click the button.

Complete the entry by pressing

[return]

The text should resemble the following:

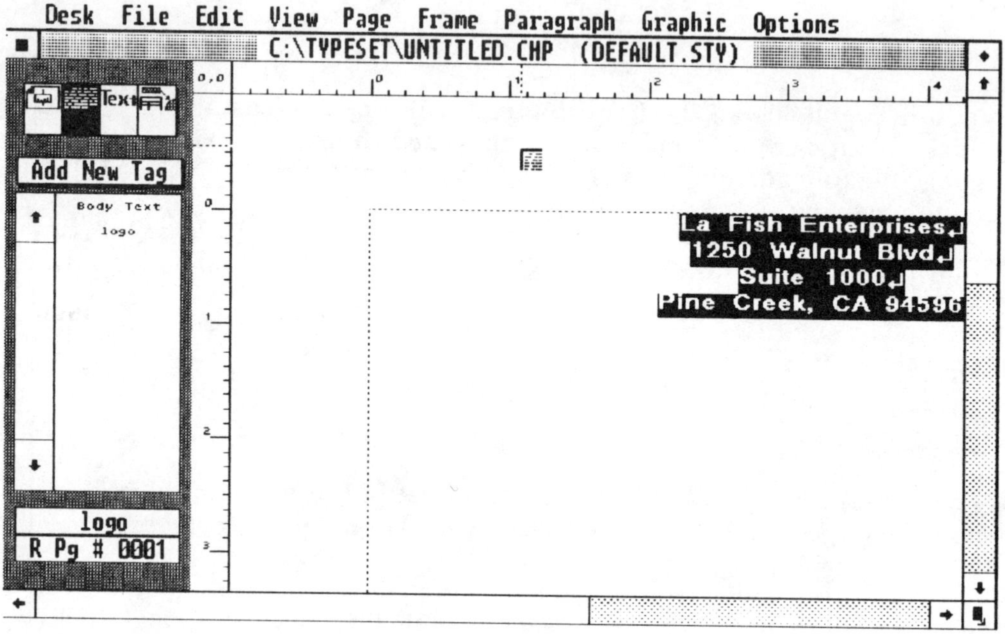

Figure 4.5

USING BOXED TEXT

Up to this point, all the text formatted with Ventura has been paragraph-oriented text that was formatted in lines between margins, which is similar to the way word processing programs work with text. But Ventura has the ability to place text at any location on the page. One method for placing text at specific locations is called **boxed text.** Boxed text is text that is typed into a small box, or mini-frame, that can be moved to any location on the screen. Ventura can also create documents that have multiple frames. Frames are different from boxed text, however. In Chapter 5 you will learn about multiple-frame documents.

Boxed text is implemented through Ventura's Graphics mode. To place Ventura in the Graphics mode, enter

[Ctrl/p]

The Graphics mode changes the display in the side bar.

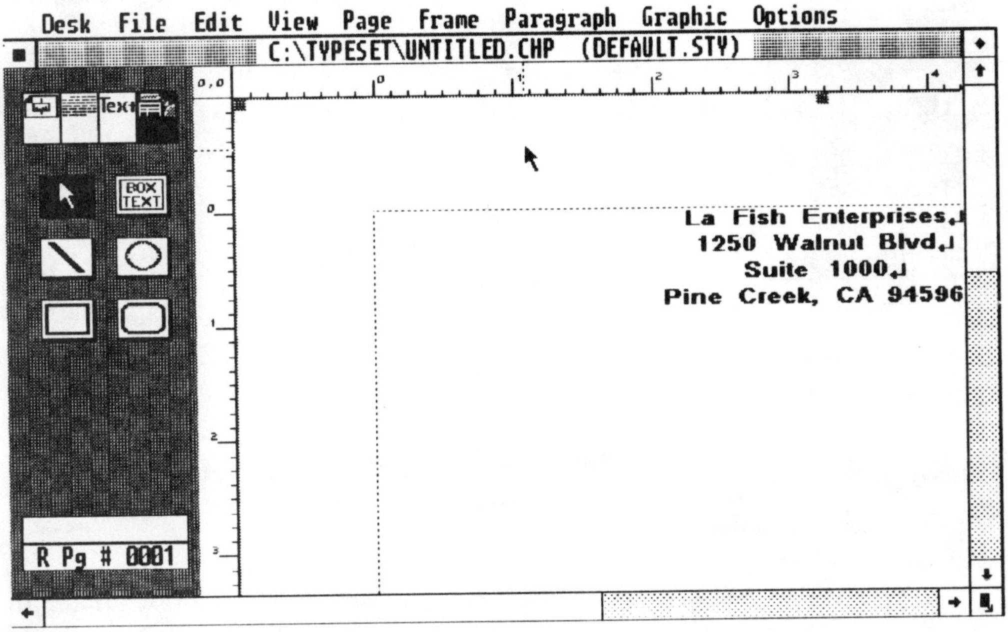

Figure 4.6

The side bar shows six figures that represent the graphics options. Point the mouse at the Box Text option and click the button.

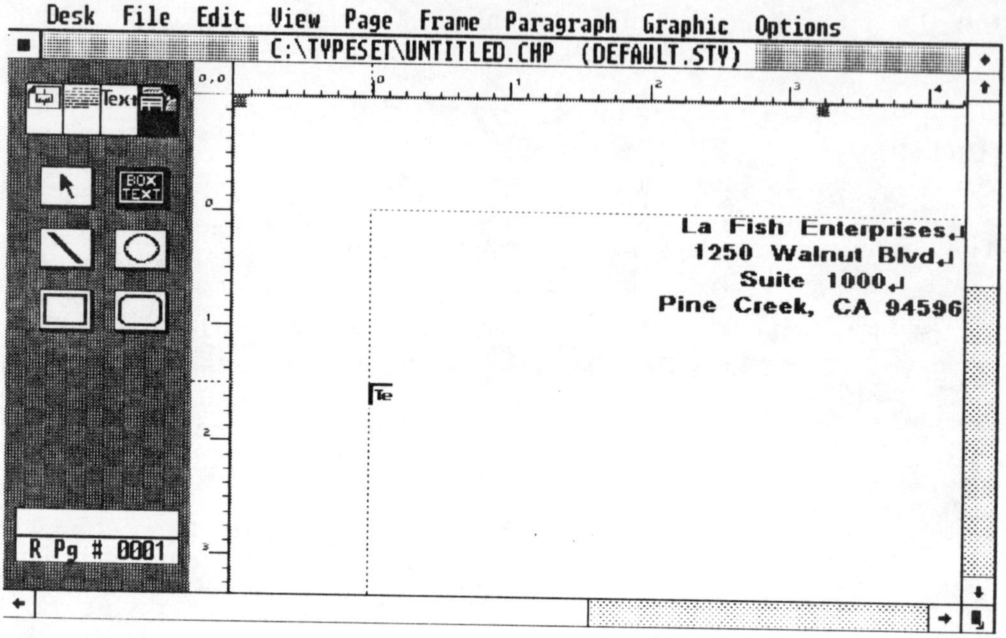

Figure 4.7

Point the mouse at "La Fish" but *do not* click the mouse button. Note that the mouse cursor now takes a new shape, which indicates that the boxed-text drawing mode is active.

The invoice form you are about to create will consist of a number of small text boxes. Each box will contain the name of some data item that you want to fill in. For example, one box should be designed for the date, another for the PO number, another for the company name, and so on.

To begin, create a box for the date. The date box should begin at the left column guide, about 1.5" from the top. The ruler lines can come in handy here. As you move the mouse, the line in the ruler will keep track of your location.

Point the mouse 1.5" down on the column guide, but, again, *do not* click the mouse button yet. The edge of the cursor should fall in the column guide line.

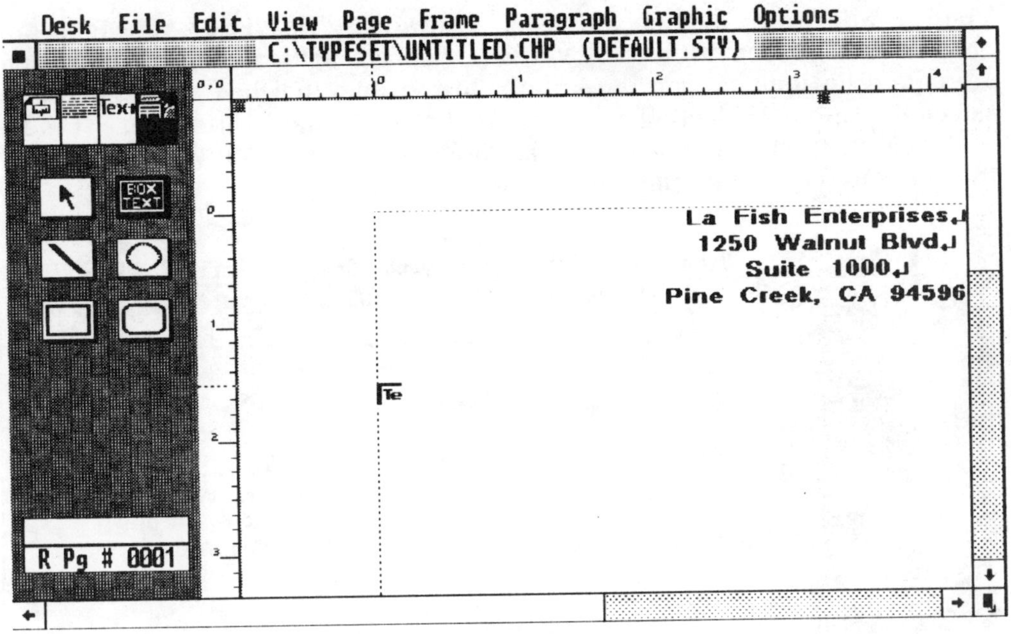

Figure 4.8

To create a box, press and hold the mouse button and drag the mouse down or to the right. As you move the mouse, Ventura draws the box. As long as you hold down the button, you can change the size and shape of the box by moving the mouse. When you design the correct box, let go of the button, and the box is complete.

In this example, draw the box from the current cursor location to 2" down on the column guide. Then, drag across 2" to the right, which will create a box 2" wide and .5" high.

Ventura will draw a box on the page. The words "Box Text" appear in the box. On the border of the box, Ventura displays eight smaller boxes, which are called **buttons.** When the buttons are visible, that box is the currently selected graphic. Selecting a graphic is similar to highlighting text. It indicates that the commands you issue will affect that box, not any other box that may be entered in the same document.

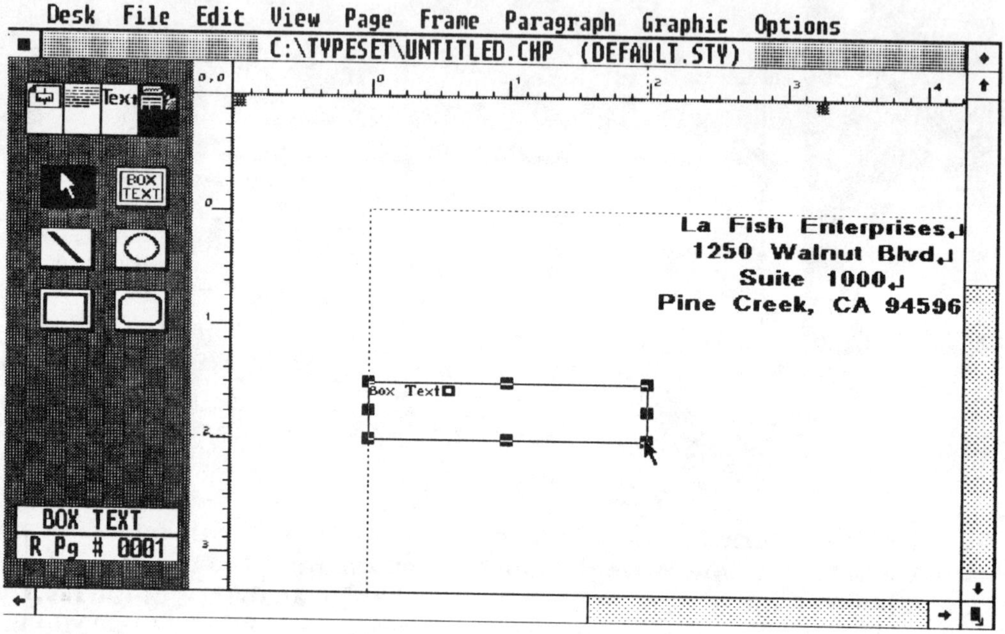

Figure 4.9

Editing Boxed Text

Ventura automatically enters the words "Box Text" into each box you create. This label helps you gauge the location and size of the text relative to the size of the box. The text will be erased and replaced with the actual text you want to place into the box.

Box text is edited from the Text mode just like paragraph text. Change to the Text mode by entering

[Ctrl/o]

Note that when Ventura is in the Text mode, the box buttons disappear. Graphics commands cannot be used in the Text mode, so the buttons have no function and are removed from the screen display.

The first step is to delete the words "Box Text." Point the mouse at end of the word "Text" and click the mouse button.

The cursor should be positioned at the end of the phrase. If you look at the box above the page number, it should read "End of File." Ventura treats each boxed text as if it were an individual text file.

Use the Backspace key to delete the words "Box Text." Now enter

DATE:

The screen should resemble the following:

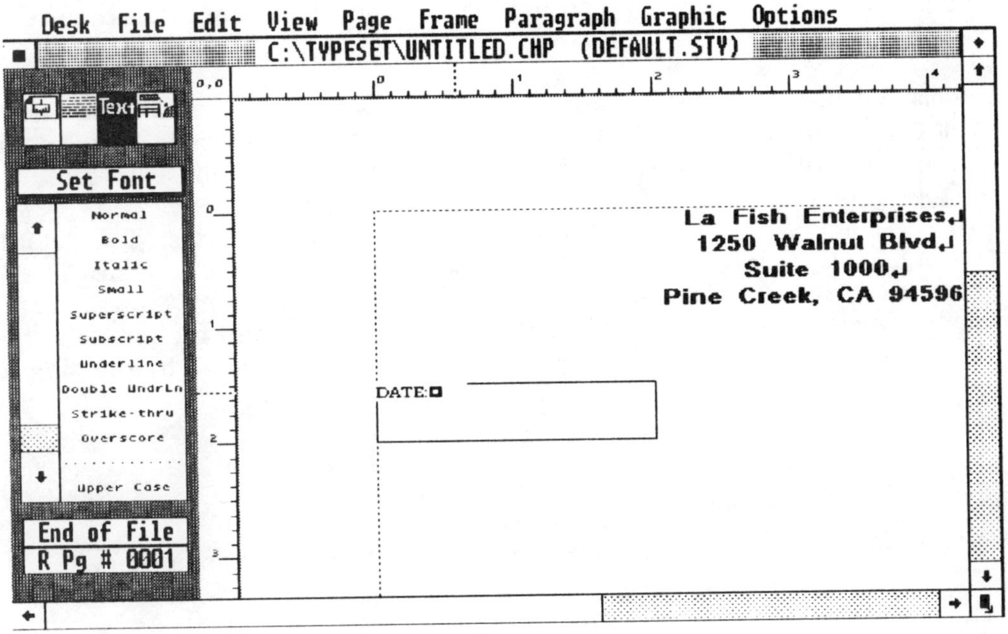

Figure 4.10

Formatting Boxed Text

Now that you have entered text into the box, you will want to select format options—font, spacing, etc. Change Ventura to the Paragaph mode by entering

[Ctrl/i]

Point the mouse at "DATE:" and click the mouse button.

Look at the box above the page number. It shows "Z__BOXTEXT." Ventura automatically tags all boxed text as Z__BOXTEXT. You might wonder where this tag came from since your style sheet shows only Body Text and Logo as tags. Ventura keeps a set of special tags reserved for special features, such as boxed text, page headers, and footnotes. These tags are automatically included in every style sheet, but they are not normally displayed in the style sheet list. Ventura calls these tags **generated tags** because they are automatically created when you implement a special feature that requires a tag.

Ventura will display the generated tags along with your user-defined tags if you request it. Point the mouse at the Options menu heading. Then, point the mouse at the Set Preferences selection and click the mouse button.

The first item on the Set Preferences menu is Generated Tags. The default setting for Generated Tags is Hidden, which means that the names of the generated tags will not appear on the side bar display along with the user-defined tags. Instead of accepting the default setting, point the mouse at the Shown option and click the button. Complete the command by pressing

[return]

The name Z__BOXTEXT now appears in the side bar listing of tags.

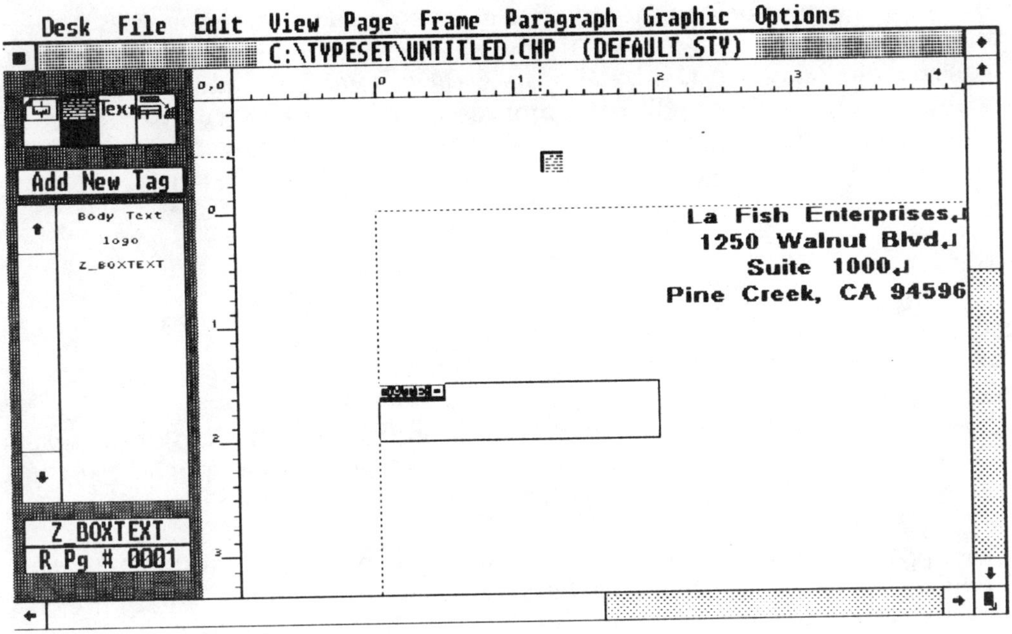

Figure 4.11

The next step is to select the font you want to use in the boxed text. Point the mouse at the Paragraph menu heading. Then point the mouse at the Font selection and click the button. Select Swiss 14-Point Bold by pointing the mouse at Swiss and clicking the button.

Finally, point the mouse at the number 14 and click the button. Complete the entry by pressing

[return]

The text should be formatted for that font. Changing the Z__BOXTEXT tag will affect all the text entered in text boxes, which means that when you create the next box, the text will automatically be formatted as Swiss 14-Point. If you had wanted to change only this one box and leave the rest as regular body text, you would need to create a new tag instead of modifying Z__BOX-TEXT.

Before you continue, you should once again stop and save this new style sheet that you are developing under a new name. Remember that at this point, you are changing the DEFAULT style sheet. Point the mouse at the File menu heading. Then, point the mouse at the Save As New Style selection and click the button. Enter

invoice
[return]

Now all the settings will be stored as INVOICE.STY.

One problem remains. You have probably noticed that the top of the text is aligned with the top line of the box. The text would look much better if it were more centered between the top and the bottom of the box.

This problem can be solved by using the Spacing option on the Paragraph menu. Point the mouse at the Paragraph menu heading. Then, point the mouse at the Spacing selection and click the button. The SPACING menu will appear as follows.

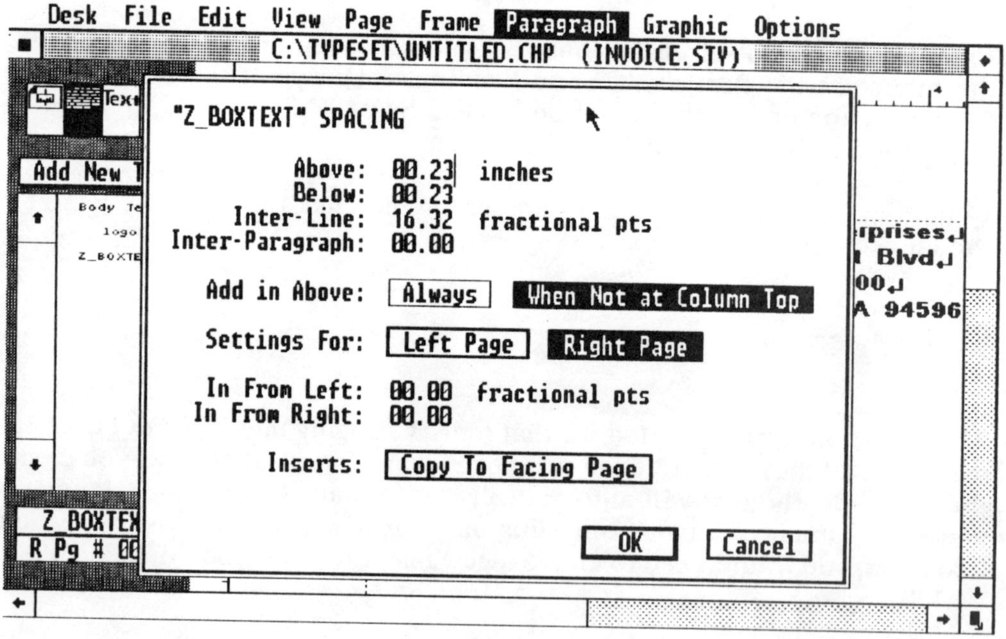

Figure 4.12

In the center of the box, you will see the Add in Above setting, which has two options: Always and When Not at Column Top. The currently selected setting is When Not at Column Top. This setting tells Ventura not to add space above a line if it is the first line in a column. For example, Ventura considers the first line on a page or in a box the top of a column. If the word "DATE:" appeared as the first word on a page, you probably wouldn't want any extra space above the word. The top margin would supply all the blank space needed at the top of page. But in a text box, the top of the column is smack up against the top line of the box. In this case, you do want the Above space added to the column.

Point the mouse at the Always option and click the button. Now Ventura will add the space above the text, which will separate the text from the line at the top of the box. Note that Ventura does not allow you to create margins for boxed text. You must handle spacing problems from the Paragraph menu. But one question still needs to be addressed: How much space should be placed above the text? The current setting is for .23". Remember that the entire box is only .5" high. The text is 14 points in height, approximately .2", which means that there is about .3" of blank space to be divided above and below the text. Half of .3 is .15; thus, a good guess as to the correct height would be .15". Enter

[Esc]
.15
[return]

Now the text should be just about centered between the top and the bottom of the box.

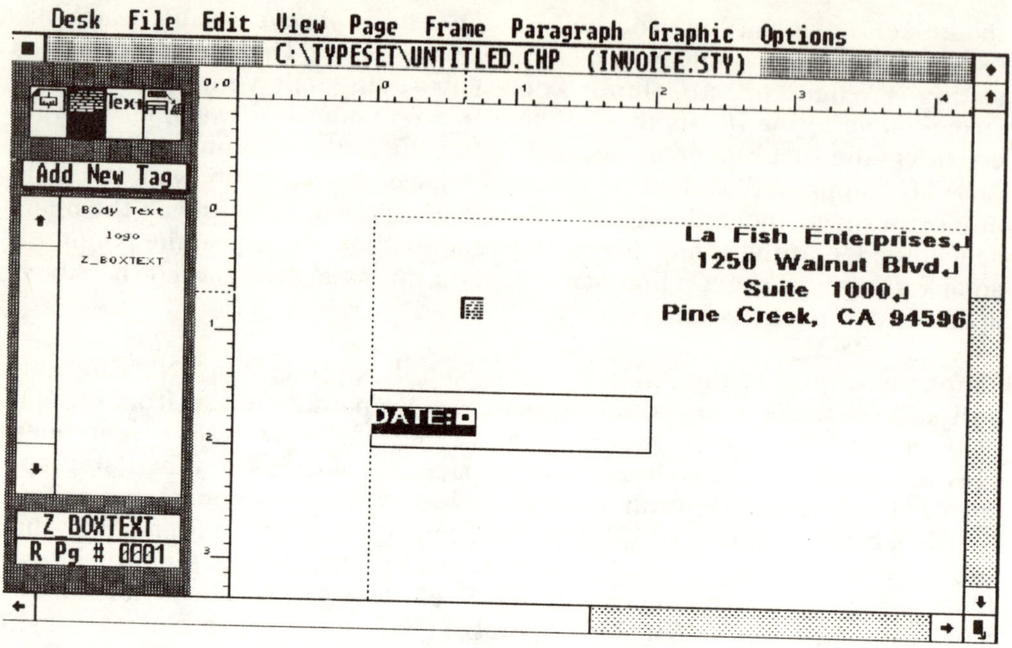

Figure 4.13

This process may seem like a lot of work for just one box, but because of the way Ventura uses style settings, you must set up the format for all the boxes on this form.

MAKING COPIES

The next task is to create a box for the PO number. Ventura allows you to copy text, frames, or graphics. Copying can be a shortcut when you want to slightly modify an existing item. Ventura can make copies when you press [Shift/Del] and [Ins]:

- **[Shift/Del]** copies the highlighted text, frame, or graphic into the computer's memory.
- **[Ins]** places the text, frame, or object that is in memory into the document.

To make a copy of the box, you must first highlight the box. Since the box is a graphic item, you must switch Ventura back into Graphics mode. Enter

[Ctrl/p]

You can select, or highlight, a graphic object by pointing the mouse at any part of the object and clicking the button. One simple way is to point at the text in the box, for example, point the mouse at "DATE:," and click the mouse button.

The box displays its buttons, indicating that you have selected that graphic object.

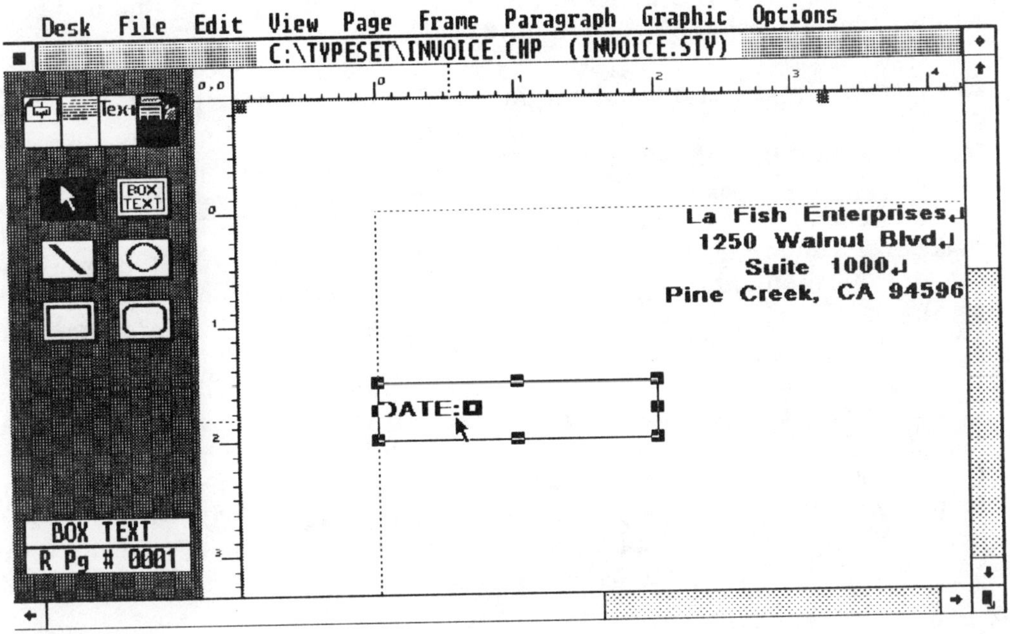

Figure 4.14

To copy this frame into memory, press

[Shift/Del]

Note that there is nothing on the screen that indicates you have performed this action. You are now ready to insert a copy of the box into the text; however, you first need to consider that your goal is to place the new box next to the existing box. And then you need to repeat the process throughout the entire form. But placing objects on the screen in correct alignment is not as easy as you might think. When you want to align objects exactly, you will often find the mouse very sensitive to slight movements, which will make it difficult to get an exact alignment.

You can control the sensitivity of the mouse by creating a grid that will control how far a graphic object will move each time the mouse is moved.

For example, you could use the mouse to move graphics in jumps of 1/4" or 1/2" at a time, which would make it simple to properly align items because Ventura would not allow you to move to an odd number, e.g., 7/32".

The movement of graphic objects is controlled from the Graphic menu. First, make sure you are in the Graphics mode, [Ctrl/p]. Then point the mouse at the Graphic menu heading. Ventura displays the Graphic menu (see Figure 4.15).

In this case, you are concerned with Grid Settings. Point the mouse at the Grid Settings selection and click the button. The GRID SETTINGS menu appears. The first option is Grid Snap, which is a useful feature that forces graphic objects to move only in evenly spaced increments. This limitation helps you align objects. The menu also allows you to specify the width and height of each increment of movement. In this case, you will set the Grid Snap to .5" in both directions. Enter

[Esc]
.5
[down arrow]
[Esc]
.5
[return]

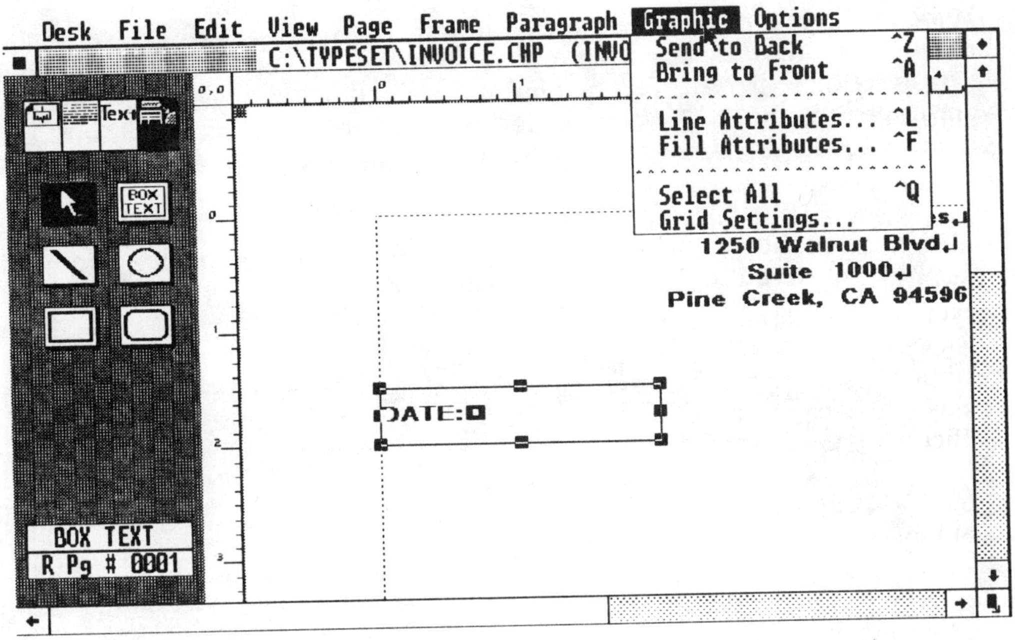

Figure 4.15

Now that you have set the grid, you can be sure that your boxes align properly.

Inserting Graphics

Even though some time has passed since you copied the box into memory, Ventura is ready at any time to insert the box into the text. Press

[Ins]

The screen clears and then repaints itself. If you look at the screen, you will see that it appears to be exactly as it was before. But here the screen is deceiving. There are really two boxes on the screen. You can't see them because Ventura places the copy in the exact same spot as the original. What you see on the screen is the copy you have just inserted. The original box can't be seen because the copy is hiding it. When you move the copy, then you will see the original box.

To move a graphic box, point the mouse at any part of the box except the box buttons and hold down the mouse button. The cursor will change to a four-directional arrow. This symbol indicates that the object will move as you move the mouse. Remember to hold the mouse button down until the graphics are in the correct position. This technique is called **dragging** the mouse.

You are now ready to move the box. Point the mouse at the box and hold down the mouse button. The cursor will change shape.

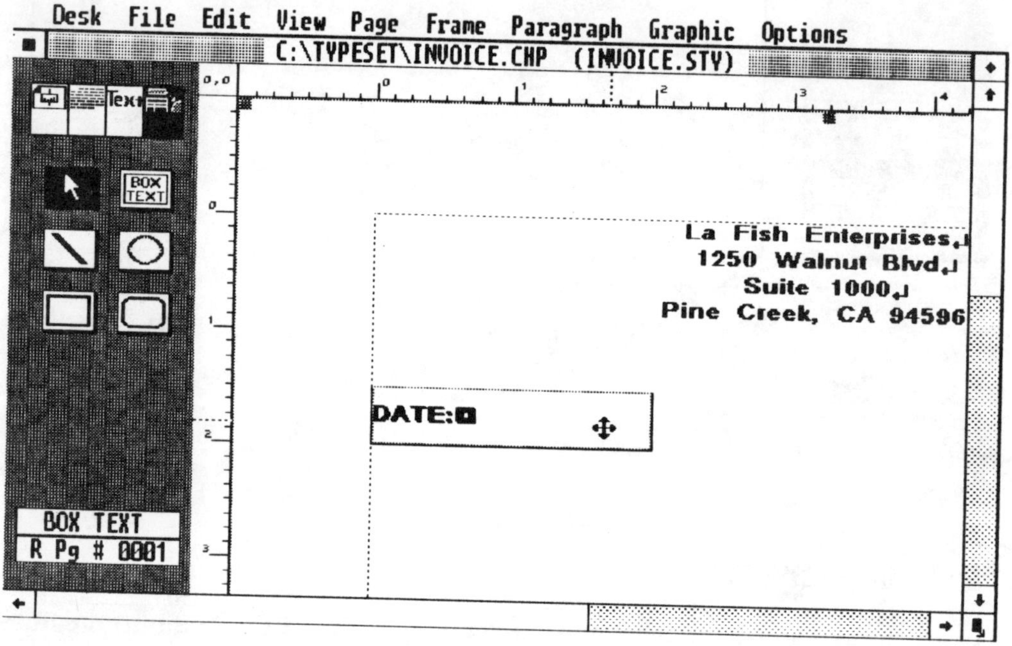

Figure 4.16

Now that you have selected the graphic for movement, drag the mouse to the right. Remember to keep holding down the mouse button. As you move, or drag, you will notice two things:

1. The box moves along with the mouse.

2. The box does not move smoothly; rather, it jumps in .5" increments, which is the result of the grid settings you selected.

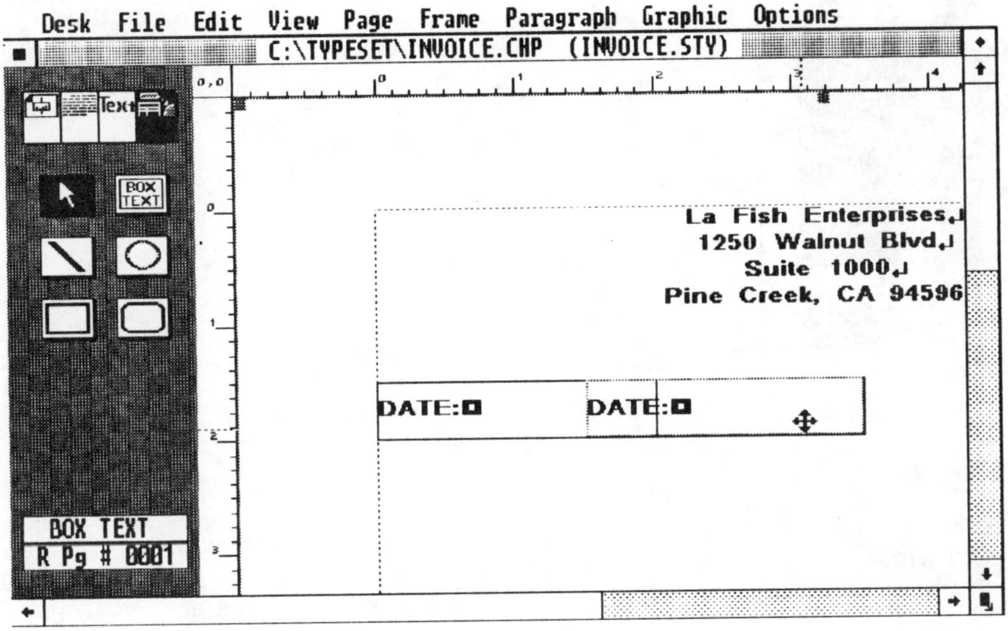

Figure 4.17

Keep moving the mouse to the right until you have positioned the boxes side by side. Then release the mouse button.

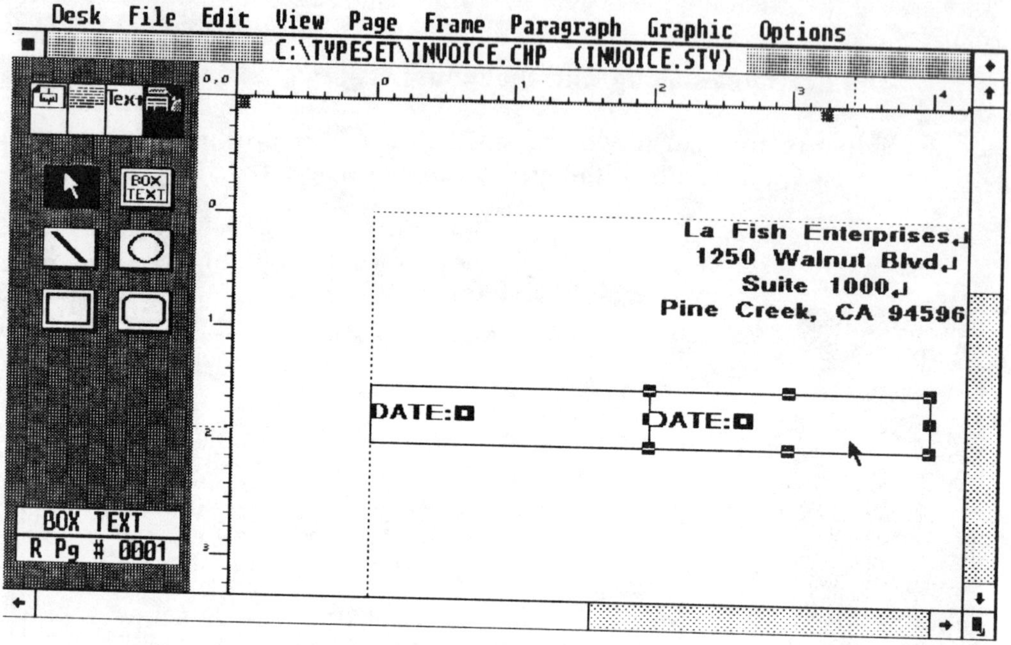

Figure 4.18

Note that the grid setting helps you maintain the alignment without much effort while you are moving an object. If you had not set the grid, you would find it much more difficult and tedious to make exact alignments.

Change the text in the box to read "PO #." First, return to the Text mode by entering

[Ctrl/o]

Point the mouse at the end-of-file symbol in the box and click the button.

Next, press the Backspace key to remove "DATE:" and enter

PO #

Changing Shapes

The boxes for DATE: and PO # are now exactly the same size. Suppose that you want to leave more room for the PO #. Ventura allows you to change the size and shape of a box after you have placed it in the text.

Before you do alter the box, move the document window to the right. Enter

[Ctrl/n]

The document window places the cursor toward the upper left corner of the window and displays more of the right side of the page.

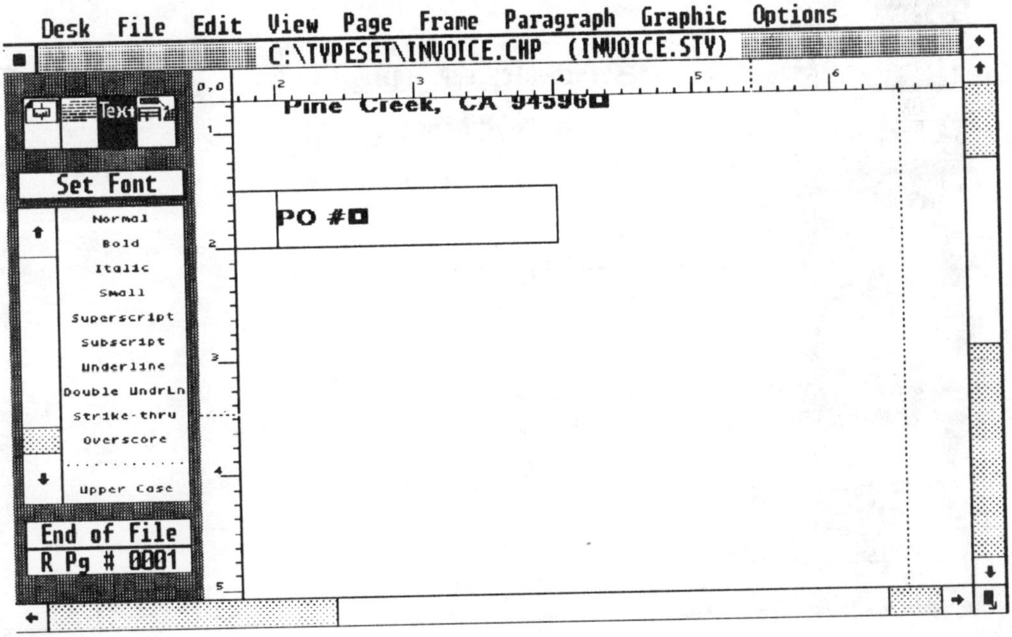

Figure 4.19

To change the shape of the box, switch to the Graphics mode by entering

[Ctrl/p]

Select the PO # by pointing the mouse at "PO #" and clicking the button. The buttons appear on the PO # box. The buttons are the key to changing the shape and size of a graphic. The buttons in the corners of the box allow you to expand or contract the box. To use a box button, point the mouse cursor at the button, and press and hold down the mouse button. The cursor's shape will change to a hand with a pointing finger. In this case, the box button you want to point at is in the upper right-hand corner. Point the mouse at the upper right box button and hold down the mouse button.

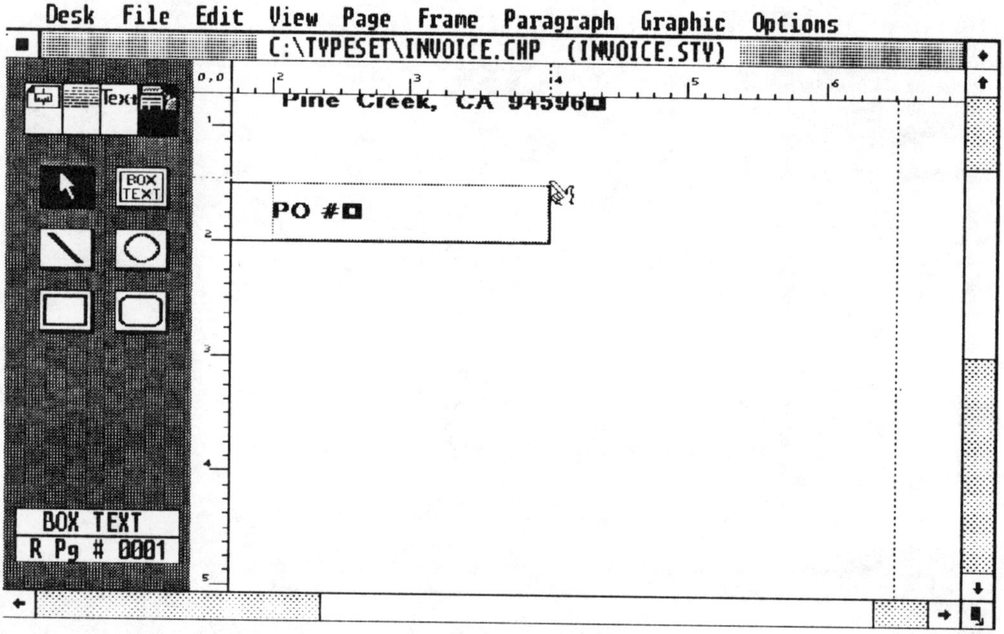

Figure 4.20

Move the mouse to the right. As you do so, the box stretches in that direction, .5" at a time. Stretch the box to the 5" mark on the ruler and release the button. You have expanded the size of the box.

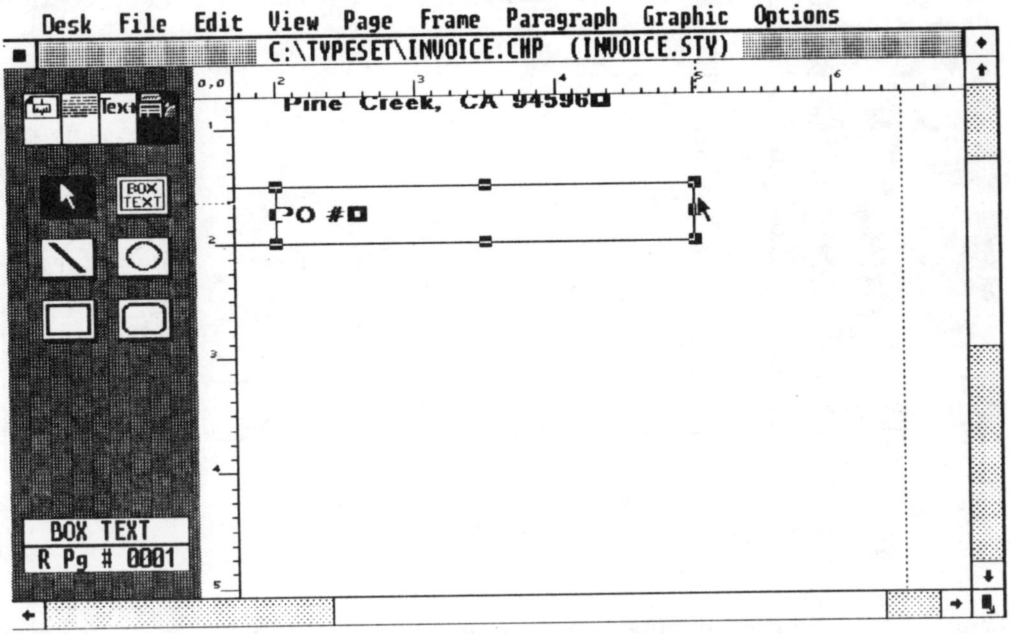

Figure 4.21

More Boxes

To begin to fill out the form with boxes, you might find it easier to work in the Reduced View mode. Enter

[Ctrl/r]

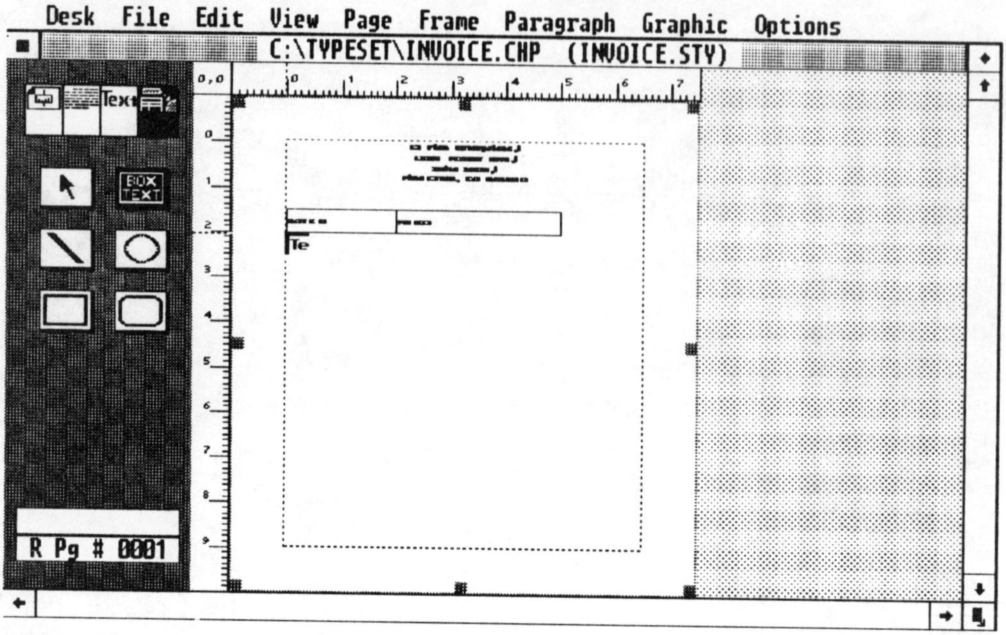

Figure 4.22

The next box will be for the company name. It will begin at the lower left corner of the DATE box and stretch across the entire page.

Point the mouse at the Box Text option in the Graphics side bar, and then click the mouse button.

Using the same method as before, press and hold the mouse button; then move the mouse so you can draw a half-inch box across the entire column. The result should resemble the following:

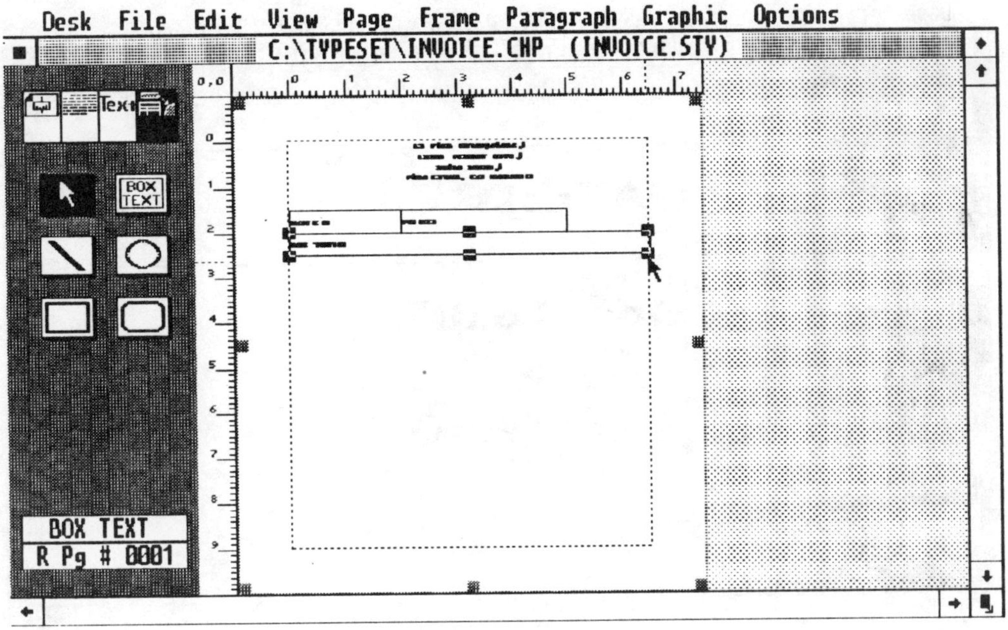

Figure 4.23

Draw another box with the upper left corner at 2.5" down on the column guide, stretching from 0" to 4" across and from 2.5" to 3.5" down. This box will hold the address.

Now that you have created the boxes, you need to edit them by placing the proper headings in the boxes. Change to the Enlarged View mode and then to Text mode. Point the mouse at "DATE:" and then enter

[Ctrl/e]
[Ctrl/o]

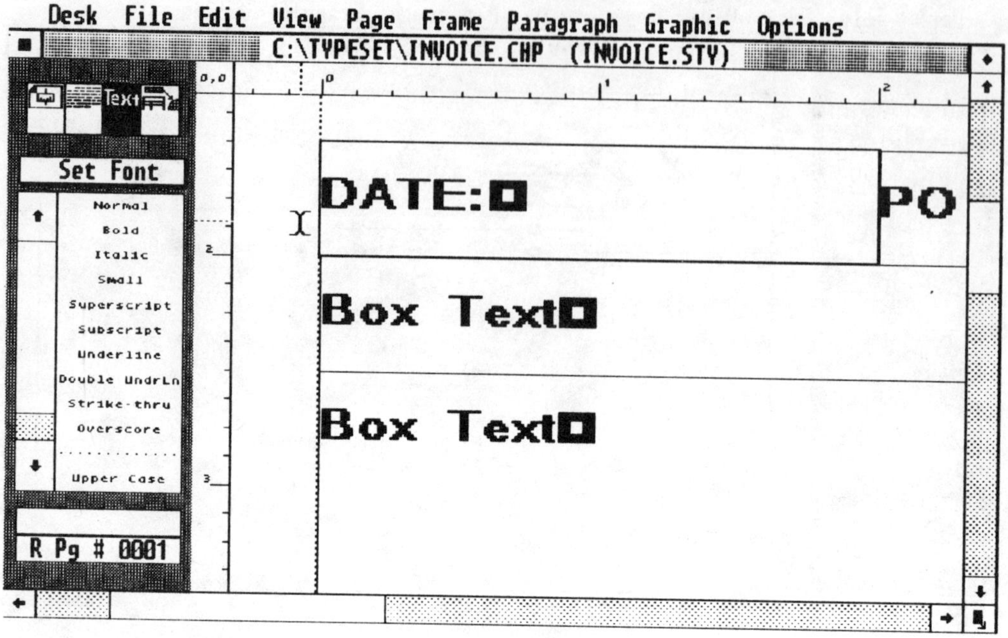

Figure 4.24

Change the Box Text to read "COMPANY" and "ADDRESS" respectively (see Figure 4.25).

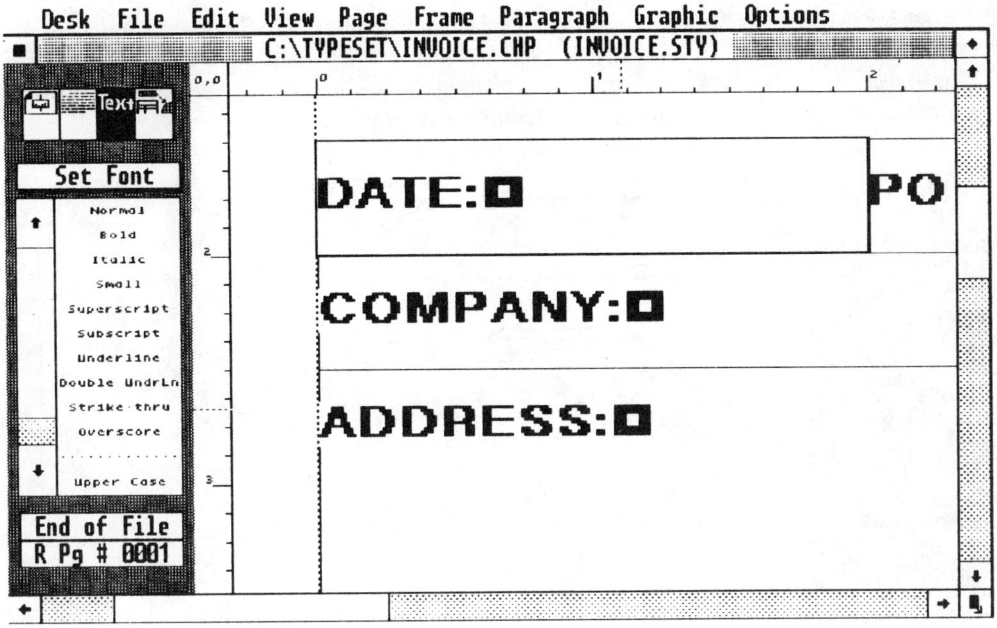

Figure 4.25

ADDING GRAPHIC LINES

You have completed the top portion of the invoice form. Before you move on and complete the bottom section, you may want to add a graphic that helps mark off the top section from the bottom section. Ventura allows you to draw straight lines. Change the display mode to Reduced. Enter

[Ctrl/r]

Place Ventura into the Graphic mode by entering

[Ctrl/p]

To draw a line, select Line Drawing from the graphics boxes shown on the side bar display. Point the mouse at the Line Draw option (a white back-slash mark) and click the button. Then point the mouse at the left column guide. The cursor should now appear as a pencil.

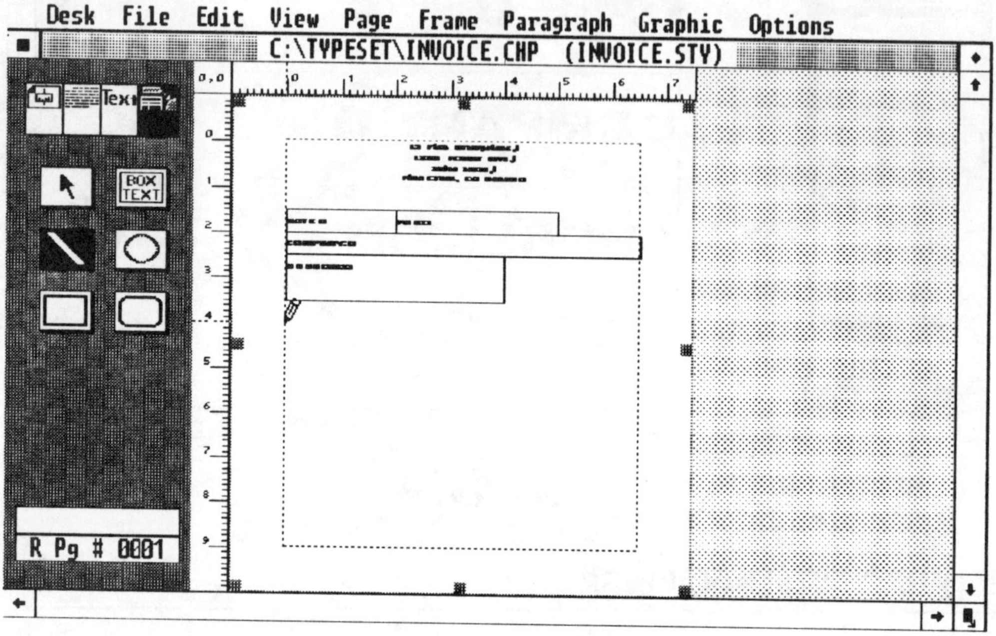

Figure 4.26

You can perform line drawing by holding down the mouse button and moving the mouse. Point the mouse at the column guide, about 4" down. Hold down the button and draw the line straight across the page to the right column guide. Release the mouse button. You have now drawn a line across the document.

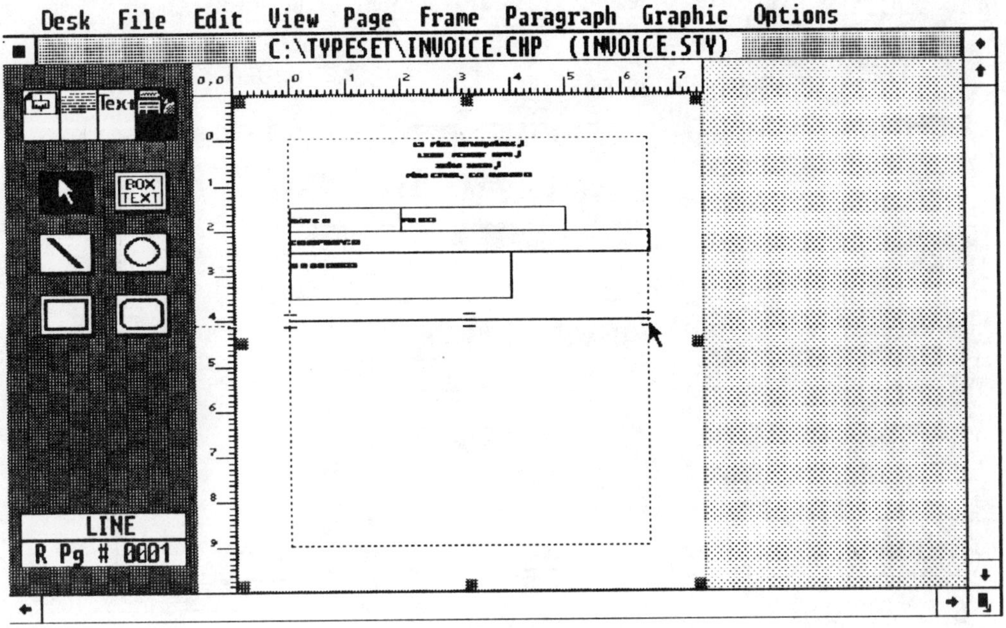

Figure 4.27

Line Options

Ventura allows you to change the thickness of lines. The Line Attributes menu can be displayed from the Graphic menu or by entering

[Ctrl/L]

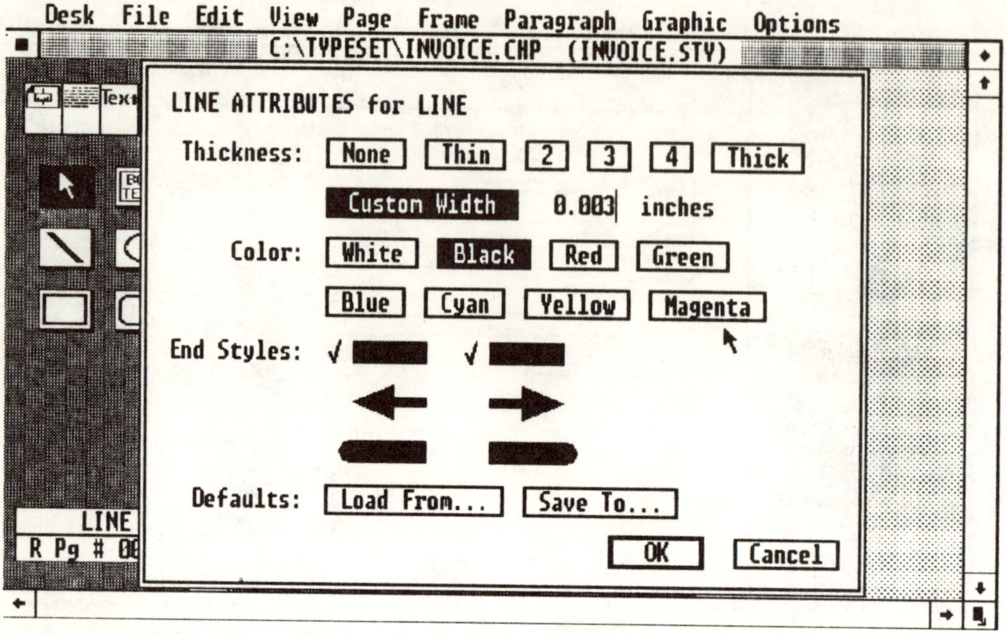

Figure 4.28

The menu reveals that the line thickness is currently set at .003". You can enter another thickness or select one of the preset thickness boxes. In addition, you can add arrow heads to the end of the line. In this case, choose thickness box #4 by pointing the mouse at 4 and clicking the button.

The box automatically inserts a line thickness of 1/8th (.125) of an inch. Complete the selection by entering

[return]

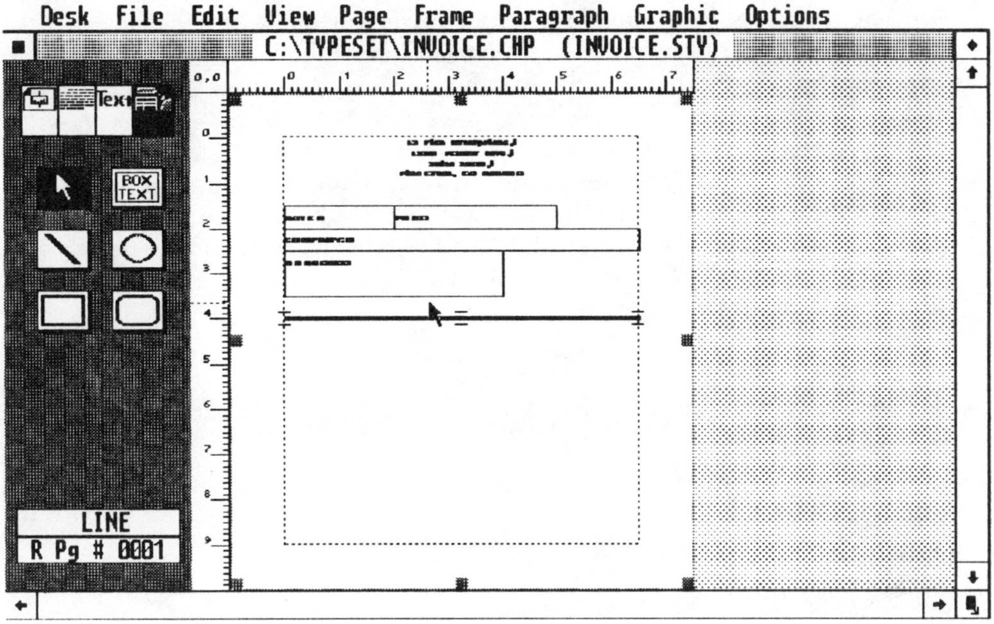

Figure 4.29

DRAWING SMALLER BOXES

The next section of the invoice will consist of a series of smaller boxes. The boxes contain the space on the invoice where the items or services purchased will be listed. These boxes do not need to be as large as the boxes you have been drawing. To keep the math simple, make the boxes 1/4" high. The best way to control this measurement is to change the grid setting to .25".

Point the mouse at the Graphic menu heading. Then, point the mouse at the Grid Settings selection and click the button.

Change the spacing to .25" vertically. Enter

[down arrow]
[Esc]
.25
[return]

Your next task is to create four small boxes on each line. There will be a box for the description of the item, price, quantity, and total cost. Select the Box Text option from the side bar by pointing the mouse at Box Text and clicking the button.

Beginning at the left column guide, draw a box 1/4" in height and 3" long. Next to that box, draw another box 1/4" in height between the 3" and 4.5" markers on the top column guide. Add two more boxes: one between 4.5" and 5.5" and one between 5.5" and 6.5". When you are done, the boxes should resemble the following:

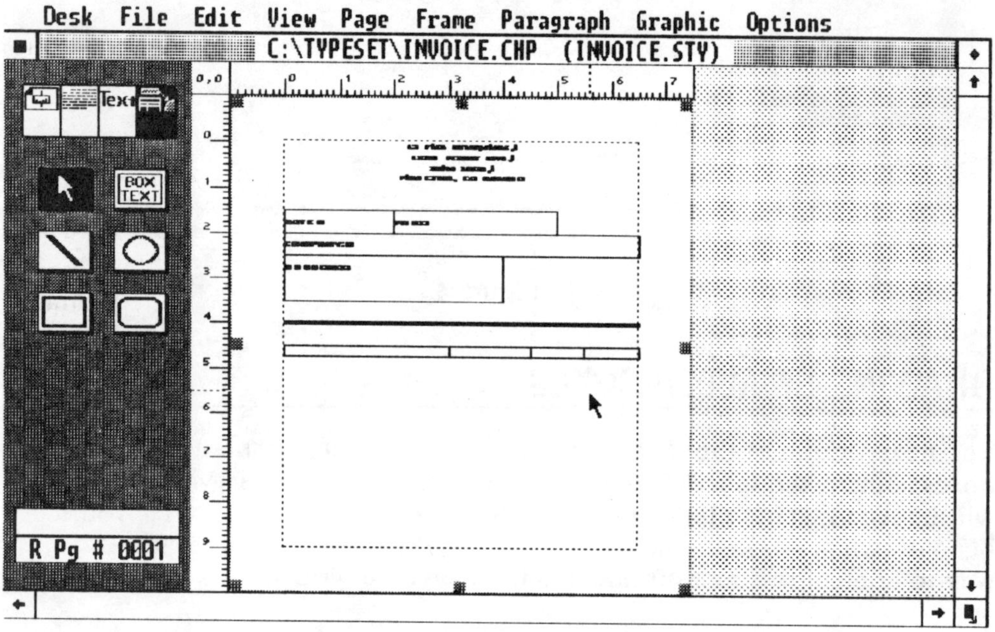

Figure 4.30

COPYING MULTIPLE GRAPHICS

You may have noticed that the words "Box Text" don't appear in the boxes you have just drawn because the spacing and font selections you made for the Z_BOXTEXT tag are too large for this 1/4" box. All you can see on the screen at this time is the blank space above the text in the box.

In this case, that screen display is actually quite handy. The bottom of the invoice form will consist of several rows of blank boxes. If the text had been small enough to be displayed, you would have to manually erase all the Box Text entries from each box.

Eventually, however, you will want to label the boxes as "Description," "Quantity," "Price," and "Cost." For now, you only need to make some copies of the boxes.

Ventura allows you to select more than one graphics object at a time, which means that you can copy and move all the selected items as if they were a single item.

The first step in performing this type of operation is to select all the objects at one time. Begin by selecting the left-most 1/4" box.

Point the mouse at the left box and click the button. The buttons appear, indicating that the box is selected (see Figure 4.31).

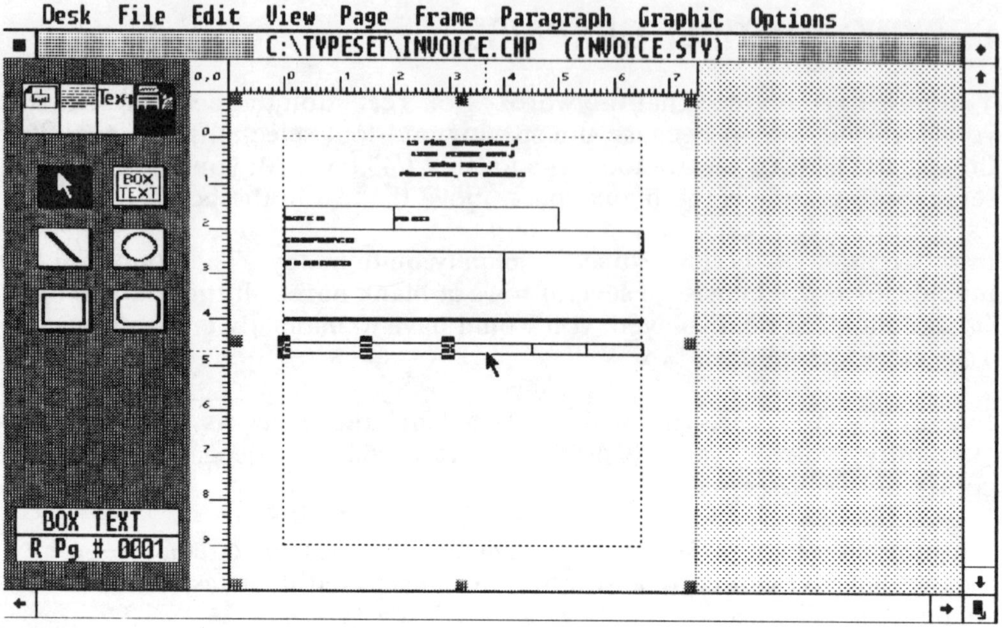

Figure 4.31

Point the mouse at the next box to the right. Instead of clicking the mouse button, hold down the Shift key and then click the mouse button.

Now the buttons appear on both boxes, indicating that you have two boxes selected.

Point the mouse at the next box on the line. Hold down the Shift key and click the mouse button. Repeat the process for the last box on the line, and you will see that all four boxes are selected.

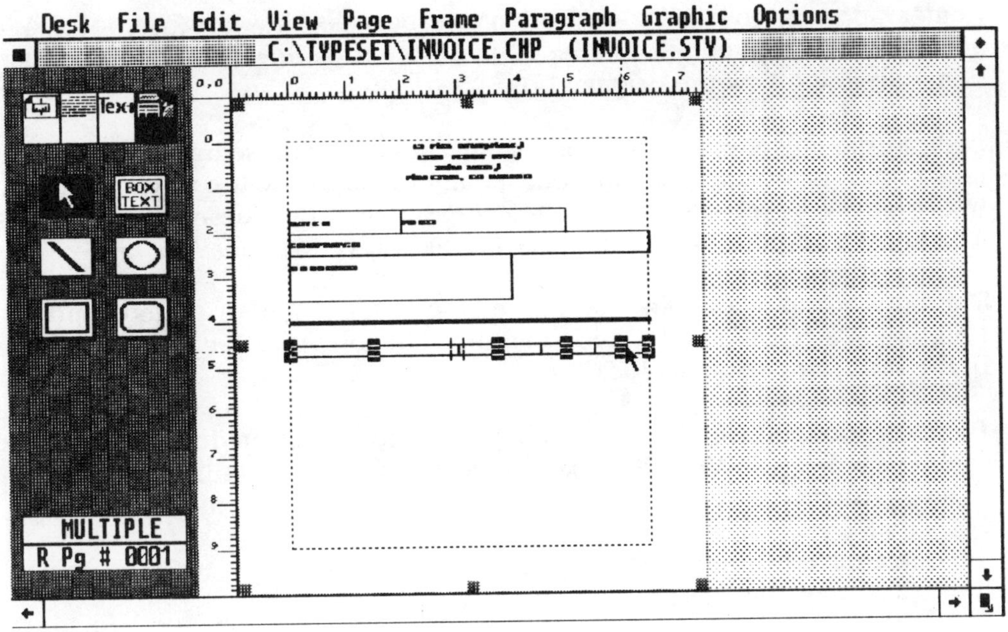

Figure 4.32

The [Shift]-click operation is used throughout Ventura to select multiple items. You might recall that you used it in Chapter 3 when you wanted to tag more than one paragraph.

Now that you have selected the boxes, you can place a copy of the graphic into memory by entering

[Shift/Del]

A copy of the four boxes has been placed in memory. Now insert a copy into the document. Press

[Ins]

Remember that you can't see both items because they are on top of one another at the moment. You need to move the copy down to its proper position, one line below the original box.

Point at the object you want to move and hold the mouse button down. To move the four boxes, you can point at any space inside the boxes. Ventura treats all the boxes selected as a single graphic, so it doesn't really matter which one you point at; all of the boxes will move together.

The only mistake you can make here is to point at any of the box buttons. Pointing at a graphic button tells Ventura that you want to change the shape of the box, *not* change its location.

Point the mouse inside any box and hold the mouse button down. Now move the mouse down so that the boxes move down to the next line. Release the mouse button.

You now have two lines of boxes.

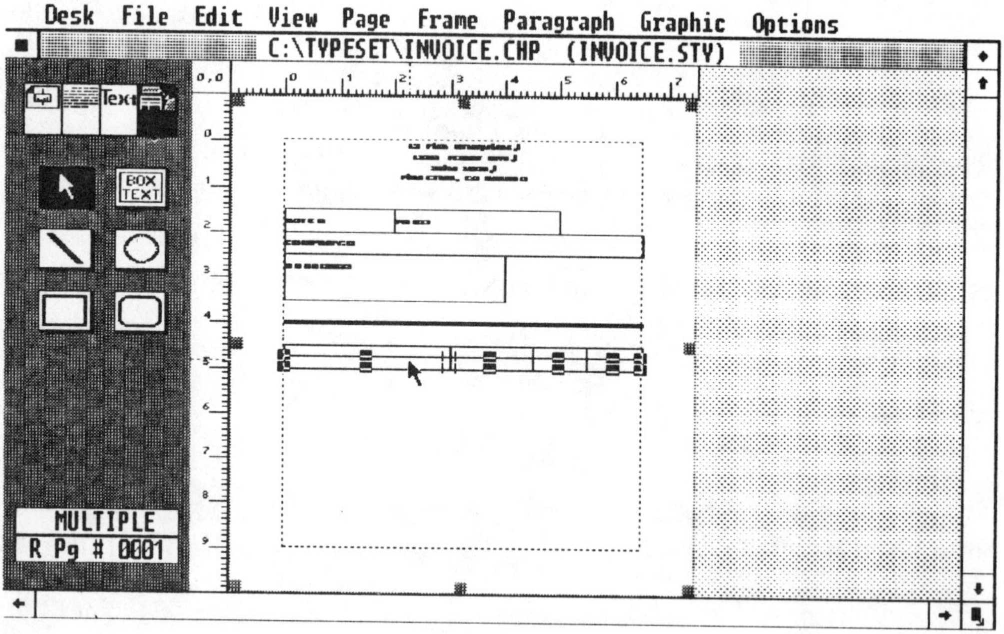

Figure 4.33

To make another line of boxes, insert another copy by pressing

[Ins]

Note that the copy is always inserted at the original location. Use the mouse to move this copy into place, below the two lines of boxes.

Repeat the process two more times, which will give you five lines of boxes.

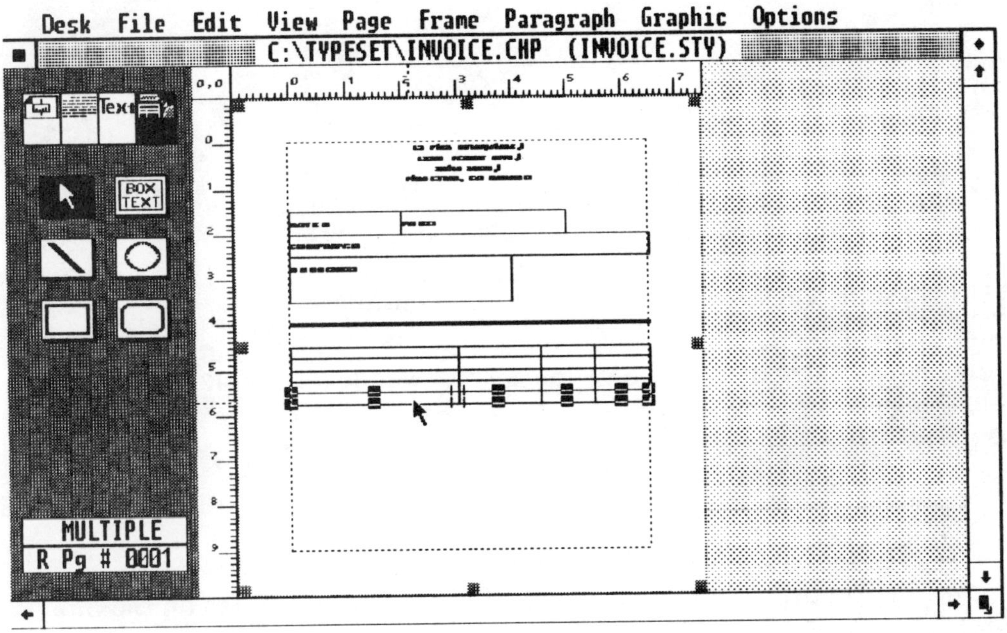

Figure 4.34

Note that the effect of placing the boxes together is to create a grid-like pattern of columns and rows. When the document is printed, you won't be able to tell that it was created by placing boxes next to each other. The lines from each box will overlap, forming a single grid pattern.

MOVING FASTER

Adding boxes doesn't take much effort, but you can get the job done even faster. Now that you have made more than one line of boxes, you can select several lines as a group. Copy that group into memory, and insert 2, 3, or more lines at a time into the text. As an example, extend the selection to include a line of boxes.

Since the boxes are fairly small in the Reduced View mode, it might be easier to select in the Normal View mode. Before you change modes, point the cursor at the left column guide on the current line. Then, change modes by entering

[Ctrl/n]

Use the [Shift]-click combination to add to the selected items the left-most box on the line above the currently selected box.

Using [Shift]-click, select the next box on that line.

You have reached the edge of the display window. Scroll the display by entering

[Ctrl/n]

Using the [Shift]-click combination, select the last two boxes on the line.

You now should have two lines worth of boxes selected. Copy them as a unit into memory by entering

[Shift/Del]

Return to the Reduced View mode by entering

[Ctrl/r]

Now insert two lines by pressing

[Ins]

Next, move the new line into position by pointing inside of any of the selected boxes, holding down the mouse button, and moving both lines as a unit.

When you are done, the screen should resemble the following:

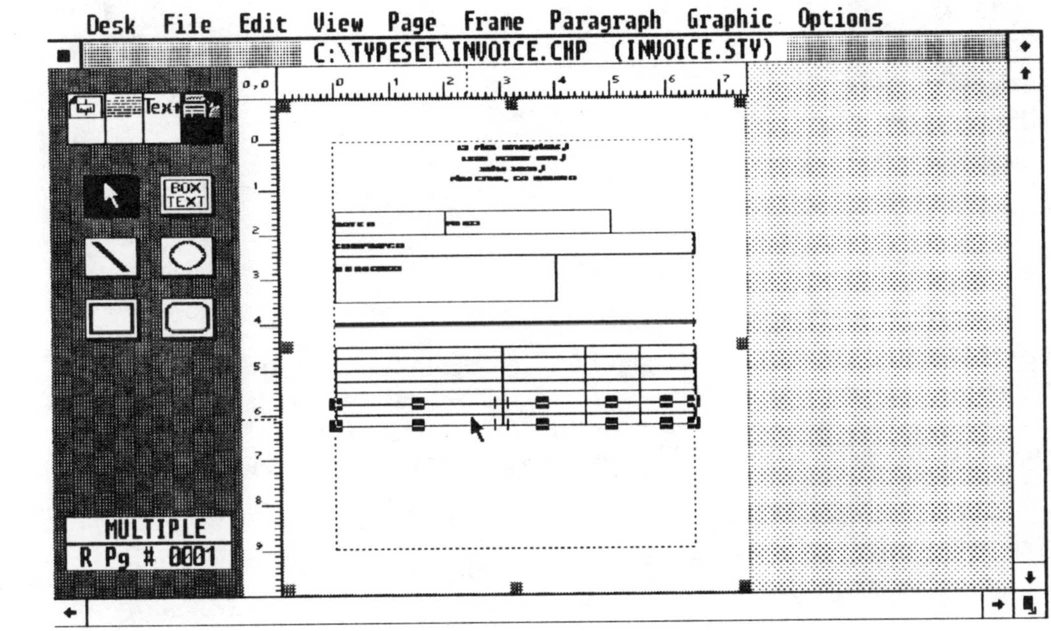

Figure 4.35

Continue the process until you have inserted six more lines. When you are done, you can remove the selection from the boxes by clicking any empty area on the screen. Your document should now resemble the following:

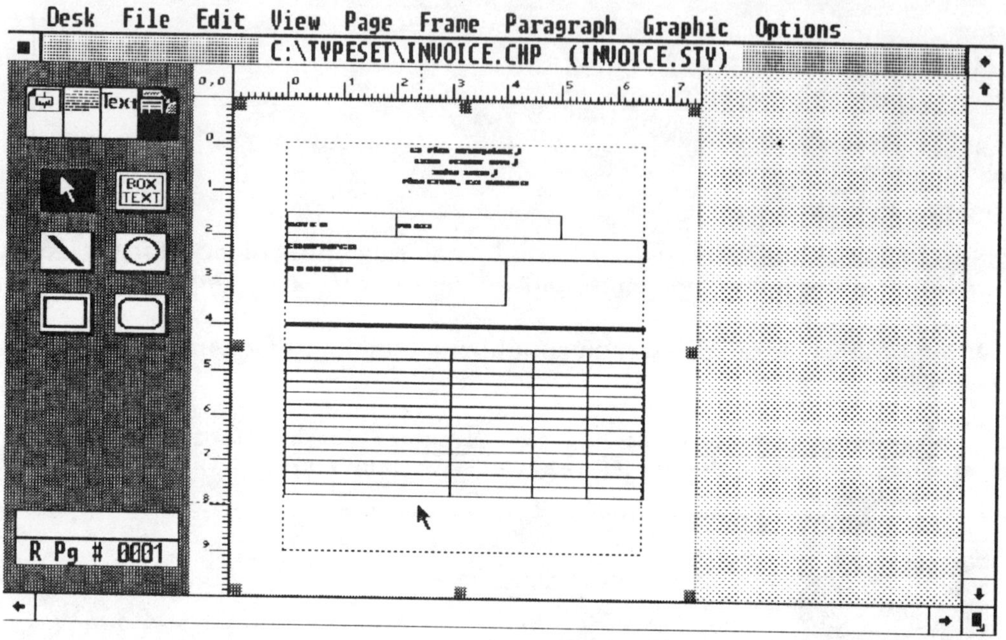

Figure 4.36

At this point, there is a 1/2" gap between the solid black line drawn across the middle of the form and the series of 1/4" boxes. Fill that area in by drawing four boxes, the same width as the 1/4" boxes, but make them 1/2" high to fill in the gap. Figure 4.37 shows what your document should look like.

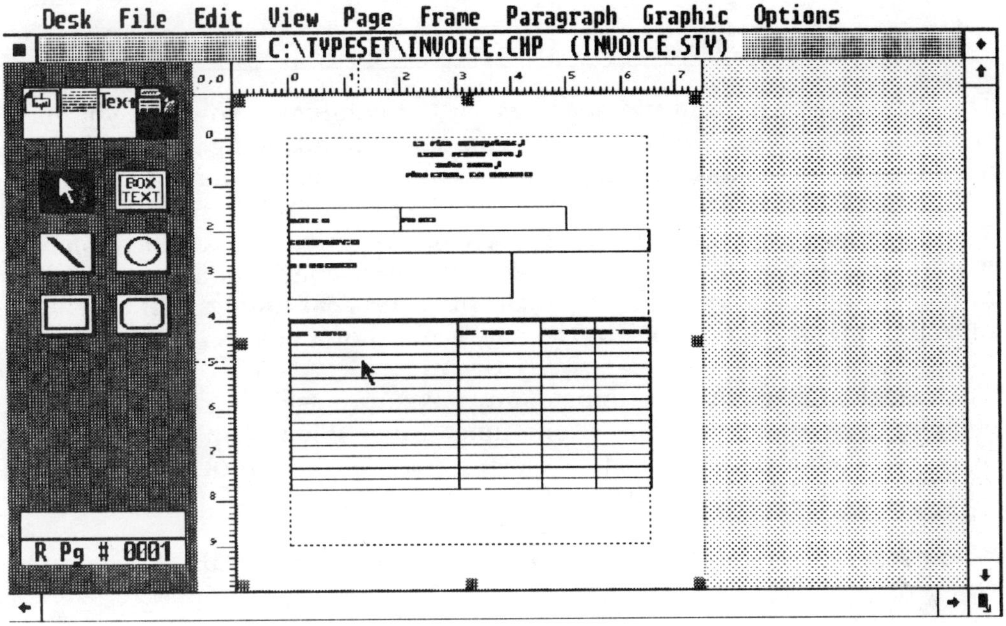

Figure 4.37

Change to the Text mode by entering

[Ctrl/o]

Delete all the Box Text entries so that the boxes are empty. You may want to change to the Normal View mode, [Ctrl/n], to get a better view while editing. When you are done, return to the Reduced View mode. Enter

[Ctrl/r]

Place Ventura back into the Graphics mode by entering

[Ctrl/p]

BOX BACKGROUNDS

The 1/2" boxes will hold the headings for the columns. Now that you have cleared the boxes of unwanted text, you can take advantage of another attribute of boxes to make the headings stand out from the empty lines.

Ventura allows you to select a background color for each box. Since the vast majority of printers only print in black, the colors consist of a variety of gray tones. The background shading is classified in Ventura as a **Fill Attribute**, meaning the gray tone that fills the background of a box.

You can change the Fill Attribute of any box, or, by selecting multiple boxes, you can change several boxes at one time. Since this example calls for four boxes to be changed, select the four 1/2" boxes at the top of the column by using the [Shift]-click combination.

When you have selected the boxes, display the FILL ATTRIBUTE menu by entering

[Ctrl/f]

Ventura displays the FILL ATTRIBUTE menu.

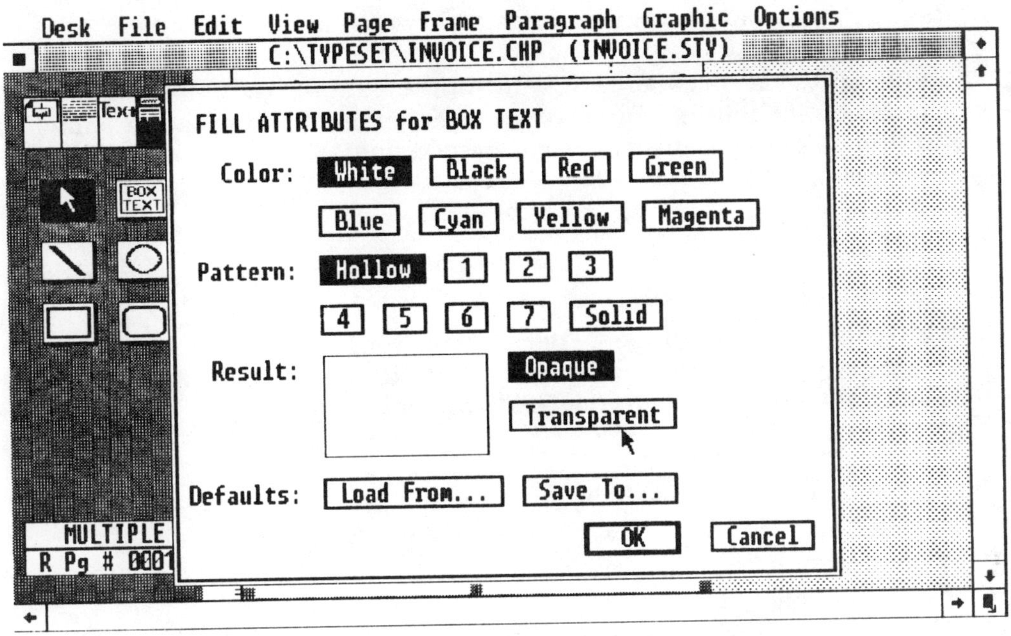

Figure 4.38

You now need to make three decisions:

1. **Color.** Unless you have a color printer, the color is always black or white. White would be selected if you wanted to put a white box on a background that was already black.

2. **Pattern.** Pattern selects the density of the gray tone. The patterns move from light gray, #1, to solid.

3. **See Thru.** You can choose to make the box opaque (no text shows through) or transparent (text appears on top of the background). Note that the actual effect of the gray tones will differ from the screen display to the printed page. Different laser printers will also produce a different quality of gray. In most cases, the screen display will look darker and harder to read than the printed page. The only way to make sure that the contrast between the text and the background is correct is to print the page and see how your laser printer actually draws the background.

In this case, you want a black pattern, #2, which is transparent.

Point the mouse at Black and click the mouse button. Then point the mouse at 2 and click the button. Finally, point the mouse at Transparent and click the button. Complete the command by pressing

[return]

The boxes are now gray-toned. Before you complete the boxes by typing in your heading text, you can make a copy of these boxes and put them at the bottom of the column where the totals will go. Enter

[Shift/Del]
[Ins]

Use the dragging method to move the copy to the bottom of the column.

To make the totals look a bit different from the heading, select a different fill attribute. Enter

[Ctrl/f]

Point the mouse at 1 and click the mouse button. Then press

[return]

The invoice form should now resemble the following:

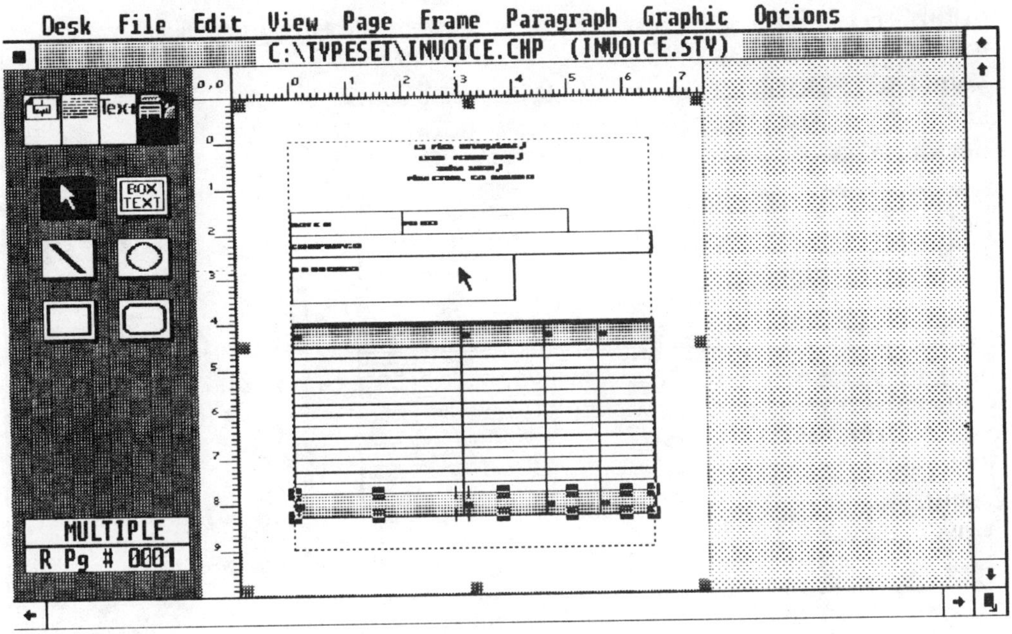

Figure 4.39

Only one last step remains. Place Ventura in the Text mode, [Ctrl/o], and enter the text into the shaded boxes. Type "Description," "Quantity," "Price," and "Cost" into column headings, and type "Total" into the left-most box at the bottom of the page. The final invoice should resemble Figure 4.40.

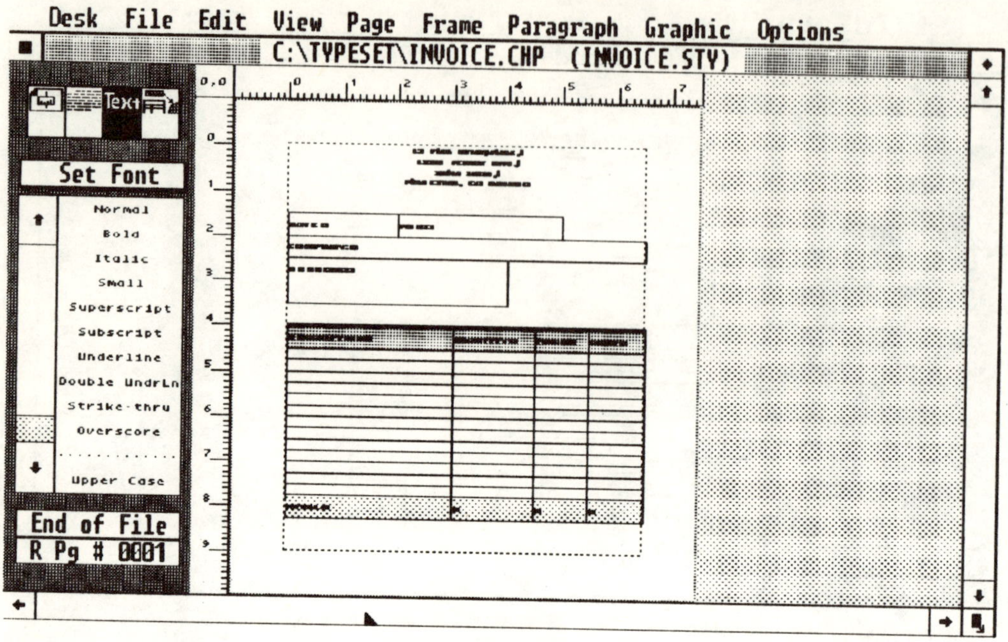

Figure 4.40

Note that the current font is set as a Swiss (or Helvetica) Bold. Swiss fonts, especially bold ones, are good fonts to use when you are placing text over a gray background. Swiss fonts use dark lines of even thickness, which tend to stand out when printed over a gray background. Dutch (Times-Roman) fonts tend to have thick and thin parts. These fonts are harder to see when printed against a gray background. If you want to use Dutch type, select a bold weight, if available.

You can now print the invoice to see what you have created.

Point the mouse at the File menu heading. Then point the mouse at the To Print option and click the button. When the PRINT INFORMATION menu appears, point the mouse at OK and click the button.

When printing is completed, save the invoice by pointing the mouse at the File menu heading. Then, point the mouse at the Save selection and click the button. When the Save menu appears, enter the name of the chapter:

invoice
[return]

If you are continuing on to the next lesson, clear the work area by using the New command. Point the mouse at the File menu heading. Then, point the mouse at the New selection and click the button.

SUMMARY

Rulers

Ventura can display rulers that mark off the page display with vertical and horizontal measurements. When you move the mouse cursor, Ventura displays a line in both rulers showing you the cursor's position. You can select the measurement format (inches, centimeters, or picas) and the starting location of the rulers, which allows you to compensate for any margins on the page.

Line Endings

When entering text that consists of short lines, Ventura provides an optional command to use for line endings. This command is entered with **[Ctrl/return]**. Line endings are different from paragraph endings, which you enter by pressing [return]. Text ended with line endings has the same spacing between lines as would text lines within a paragraph. Ending lines with [return] causes the Inter-Paragraph Above and Below Spacing to become active, so there is more space between lines. Also, lines ended with [Ctrl/return] function as a single paragraph when selected in the Paragraph mode.

Graphics

Ventura's Graphic mode allows you to add boxes, circles, ovals, lines, and text boxes to your documents.

Text Boxes

Text boxes are mini-frames. They allow you to place text at any location on the page. The box size defines it margins.

Graphic Selection

Graphic "selection" is roughly equivalent to highlighting text in the Text mode or tagging paragraphs in the Paragraph mode. When a graphic item is tagged, it displays small black squares on its border. These squares are called **buttons**. Buttons are used to change the size and shape of graphic objects. Selected graphic items can be deleted, copied, and moved on the page. You can select more than one graphic item at a time by using the **[Shift]-click** method.

Dragging Graphics

You can change the position of a selected graphic item by using the **drag** method. To drag an object, point the mouse cursor at any place in the object except at one of the buttons. Hold down the mouse button. The object enters a drag mode. Moving the mouse cursor will cause the object to move on the page.

Copying Graphics

You can copy a selected graphic item or items into memory by using **[Shift/Del]**. Entering **[Ins]** places a copy of the object in memory onto the page. You can then use the dragging method to move the graphic.

Changing Size

The size and shape of graphic items can be altered by pointing the mouse cursor at one of the object's buttons. Hold down the mouse button and move the mouse cursor. The graphic will stretch in the direction of the movement.

Grid Spacing

In order to make creating, dragging, and changing graphics more consistent, Ventura allows you to select size increments for movements and changes. These increments—horizontal and vertical—cause the graphic to change or move in jumps rather than in smooth movements. Setting a grid can make it simple to align graphics consistently on a page.

Line Attributes

Graphic lines can be displayed with a variety of thicknesses. **[Ctrl/l]** displays the Line Attribute menu.

Fill Attributes

Graphic boxes, ovals, circles, and text boxes can have white, gray, or black backgrounds. **[Ctrl/f]** displays the Fill Attribute menu.

Generated Tags

Ventura automatically generates special style tags when you select special features such as headers, footers, footnotes, and boxed text. **Generated tags** are used to format incidental text that is stored in footnotes, heads, and boxed text. Ventura normally does not display the names of these tags in the side bar display. You can choose to display these tags by changing the setting on the Set Preferences menu.

CHAPTER 5

MULTIPLE-FRAME LAYOUTS

The first four chapters of this book explore many of Ventura's features. Each chapter builds on concepts from the previous chapter and adds a layer of complexity to the document layout process.

This chapter covers one of the most significant aspects of learning to use Ventura: using more than one frame in a single document.

In Chapter 4, you learned that using boxed text allows you to place information at specific locations on a page. Boxed text frees you from the need to enter text into the master frame; instead, you paste boxes wherever you want on the page.

The use of boxed text, however, is limited. Ventura supplies other techniques that allow you to create additional frames on the page. Each frame is capable of all operations that can be performed within the master frame. For example, you can load text from a text file into a frame. If you create multiple frames on the same page, you can load text from several different files into a single document.

The goal of this chapter is to create an advertising layout. The layout will require that you extract information from three separate files and combine that information on the same page. Two of these files will be text, but the third file will be a picture—in this example, a Lotus 1-2-3 graph.

PREPARING THE FILES

The first step in putting together an advertising layout is to prepare the files—text *and* pictures—to be used in the document.

In this example, the document will be a direct-mail flier advertising a computer named the XL6000. Following is the text of a document named XL6000.WP created in WordPerfect. Prepare the file as shown in Figure 5.1. Note that the arrows mark the locations of hard returns (i.e., the ends of paragraphs).

A lot! - If you are using Microchamp's PC-XL6000 computer. The PC-XL6000 puts everything you need to perform any of today's most popular computer applications at your finger tips without turning your whole office upside down. Microchamp has taken the best features of today's most popular computers added some clever features of their own, and produced a gem of a computer that can fit onto the corner of the most crowded desk. ←
The PC-XL6000 has the power for word processing, spreadsheets, databases, graphics and even desktop publishing but won't east up your entire desk. ←
Microchamp provides more standard features than any computer in its price range. ←
But size isn't the only thing small about the PC-XL6000! Because of the popularity of this machine, your Microchamp dealer can now offer this computer at prices that make it silly to have three or four people waiting in line to use the office computer. ←

Figure 5.1

The XL6000.WP document contains a general description of the XL6000 computer and reasons why consumers should purchase it.

Figure 5.2 displays a second document named FEATURES.WP that contains a list of the XL6000's main features:

For only $3450.00 you get -←
1 Megabyte of internal memory.←
Dual speed processor - 8 and 10 MHz, switch selectable 80286. ←
Built in clock/calendar←
2 - 360K floppy drives←
14" built in monitor 640 by 350 resolution. ←
Full graphics capabilities (displays colors in 14 shades of green)←
30 Megabyte Hardcard for mass storage. ←
Full 84 character keyboard. ←
Parallel and serial ports for printers, modems or mice. ←
Color graphics adapter built in for color monitor (color monitor optional)←
MS DOS and BASIC included. ←
WORKTOOL spreadsheet, database and word processing software. ←
FINDIT software for file and hard disk management. ←
Options: ←
Internal 1200 baud modem only $225.00←
Second 30 Megabyte hardcard for a total of 60 megabytes of storage space $925.00. ←
←

Figure 5.2

Create and save the two text files as shown in Figures 5.1 and 5.2.

PREPARING A PICTURE

Ventura allows you to include high-resolution images in your documents. These images come from two sources:

1. A large number of graphics programs available for the IBM PC create images that can be imported into Ventura. Ventura can also read Lotus 1-2-3 graph files and drawings prepared with PC Paintbrush and GEM Draw. The current version of GEM software uses a different system of text fonts than Ventura, which means that if you prepare a GEM drawing that includes text, the alignment of the text will be distorted when you load it into Ventura. A new version of GEM (released in early 1988) will use fonts compatible with Ventura. For owners of older systems, it is recommended that you omit any text in your drawings and annotate text with the boxed text feature after importing the image into Ventura.

2. Image scanners can create bit-mapped graphics from images accepted by each particular model.

In this example, use a Lotus 1-2-3 graph file, which is probably the most common graphics image available. If you do not have access to 1-2-3 or do not know how to create and save a graph file, substitute any other image from a Ventura-compatible graphics program. If you don't have access to any such images, you can still complete the lesson, but the picture frame will be empty in the final document.

To create the graph image for this lesson, load 1-2-3 and create the following worksheet:

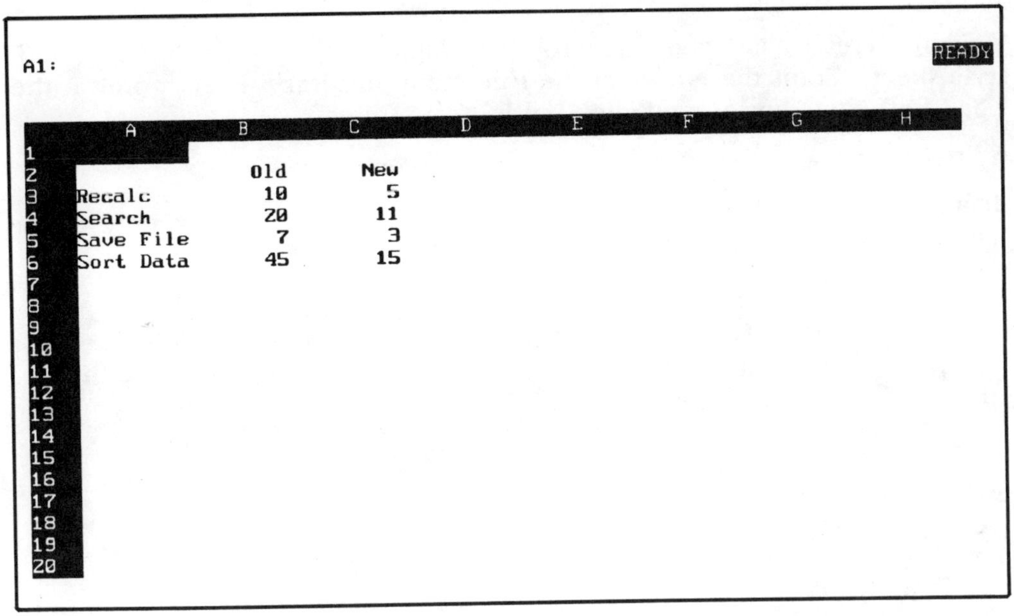

Figure 5.3

The worksheet illustrates how much faster the new XL6000 is than previous models.

Create the graph by making the A range B3..B6, the B range C3..C6, and the X range A3..A6. Enter the graph legends A=Old and B=New. Select a BAR graph to produce the graph.

Save the graph and name it COMPARE, which will create a file—COMPARE.PIC—on disk. After completing these steps, you are ready to assemble all the elements into a single document. Load Ventura in the usual manner.

CREATING A NEW STYLE SHEET

The style sheet created in Chapter 4—INVOICE.STY—is automatically loaded when you start Ventura.

You must create a new style sheet for this chapter. First, load the DEFAULT style sheet. Point the mouse at the File menu heading. Then, point at the Load Diff. Style option and click the button. Enter

default
[return]

Create a new style sheet named ADD. Point the mouse at the File menu heading. Then, point at the Save As New Style option and click the button. Enter

add
[return]

ADDING A FRAME

This document requires several frames. Multiple-frame documents have several advantages. Primarily, they allow you to treat different parts of a document as independent items. Each frame can contain a different set of margins and columns. You can quickly change the arrangement of a page by moving the location of one or more frames, which is quicker and easier than cutting and pasting. When you move or copy text, you do not move the margins and other settings along with the text; the text conforms to the margins at its new location. When you move a frame, the text inside the frame is unchanged; only its location on the page is altered.

The first frame you create will serve as the letterhead address block. Place Ventura into the Frame mode. Enter

[Ctrl/u]

The master frame is selected. You can determine that a frame is selected because Ventura displays **buttons** on the frame. Remember, Ventura displays buttons on graphic objects to indicate that they are currently selected.

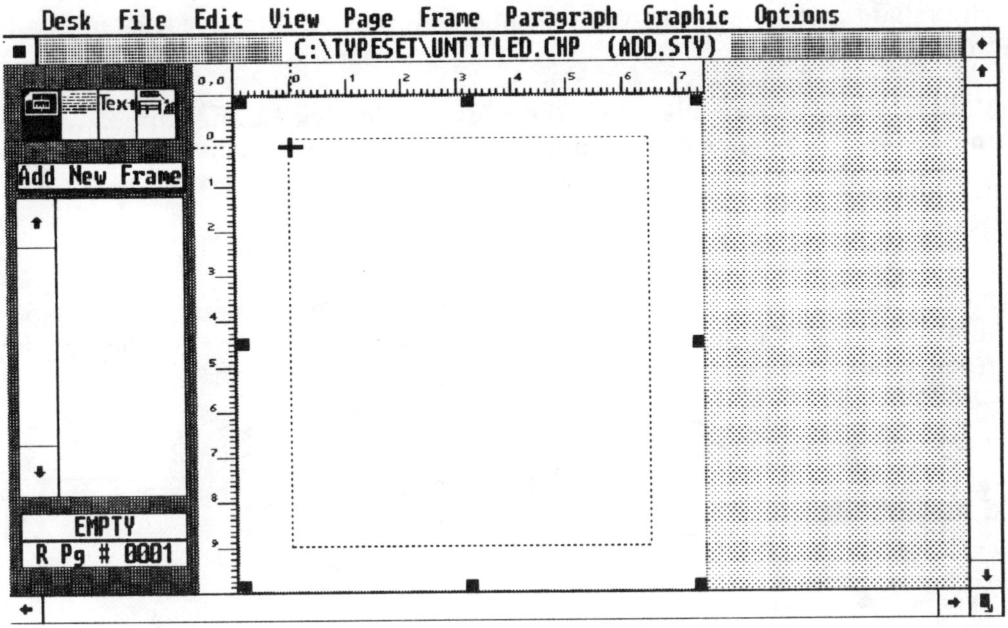

Figure 5.4

Ventura requires at least one frame – the master frame – in every document. Up to this point, all your work has taken place in the master frame. Now, you must create additional frames.

There are four reasons to use additional frames:

1. Each frame can hold text from only one document source. In this document, you must combine text from several files.

2. Frames include individual settings for margins and columns, which allow you to combine different layout styles on the same page.

3. When you create graphics, they are attached to a frame. If you attach a graphic to the master frame, it will repeat on all pages. If you create another frame, the graphic will appear only on the page including that particular frame.

4. You can quickly move frames to new locations without reformatting text inside the frame. You can change the size of frames to accommodate smaller or larger text files.

Note that there is only one master frame. All other frames are treated as additional frames.

When the Frame mode is active, the words "Add New Frame" appear above the side bar. To create a new frame, point the mouse at the Add New Frame box and click the button.

The Add New Frame box is highlighted.

Next, point the mouse at the upper left corner of the column guides. Note that the cursor is now a right angle containing the letters "FR," which is the frame cursor.

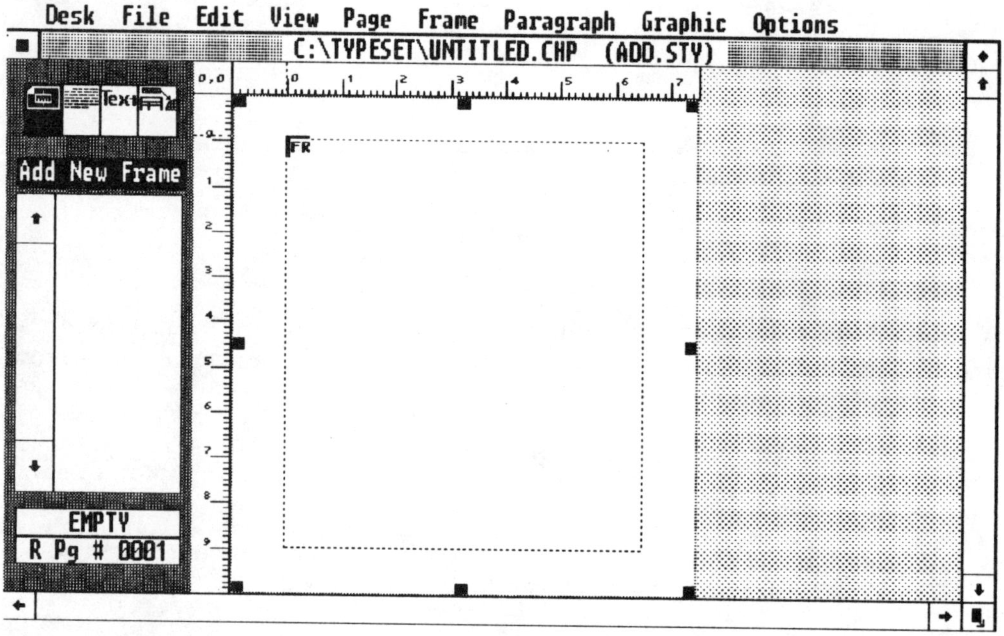

Figure 5.5

You can draw frames using the same basic techniques for creating boxed text:

1. Point the mouse cursor at the position in which you want the upper left corner of the frame to be placed.

2. Press and hold down the mouse button.

3. Move the mouse to the position in which you want the lower right corner of the frame. Ventura draws the frame as you move.

4. Complete the frame by releasing the mouse button.

As with boxed text, Ventura allows you to create a frame of the proper size without moving the mouse to the exact location. Ventura includes two settings on the Options menu that affect frame drawing.

Point the mouse at the Options menu heading. In the third section of the menu you will see two settings – Turn Column Snap Off and Turn Line Snap Off. "Off" informs you that these features are currently active. The features are called Snap because they cause Ventura to align your frame on an existing marker. When you drew boxed text in Chapter 4, you were able to control mouse movements with the Grid Settings option; however, this option affects only graphics and not frames. Frames are controlled by the Snap features, which work as follows:

- **Column Snap** aligns the left or right edge of a frame on the nearest column guide if the frame is drawn within .1" of the column guide.

- **Line Snap** causes the bottom and top of the frame to align on the next text line. The amount of space between line snaps is not always the same; it is determined by the amount of inter-line spacing entered for the Body Text tag. The default value is about .19".

Since both snaps are on, your frame will snap when drawn. To exit the menu without changing the setting, point the mouse at a blank area and click the button.

You are ready to draw the new frame.

Point the mouse at the upper left corner of the column guide. Press and hold down the mouse button. Drag the mouse to the right column guide and down about 1.5". Release the button.

You will now see a box at the top of the screen; this is your new frame. Note that Ventura displays buttons on this frame to indicate that it is active. The buttons on the master frame are no longer visible.

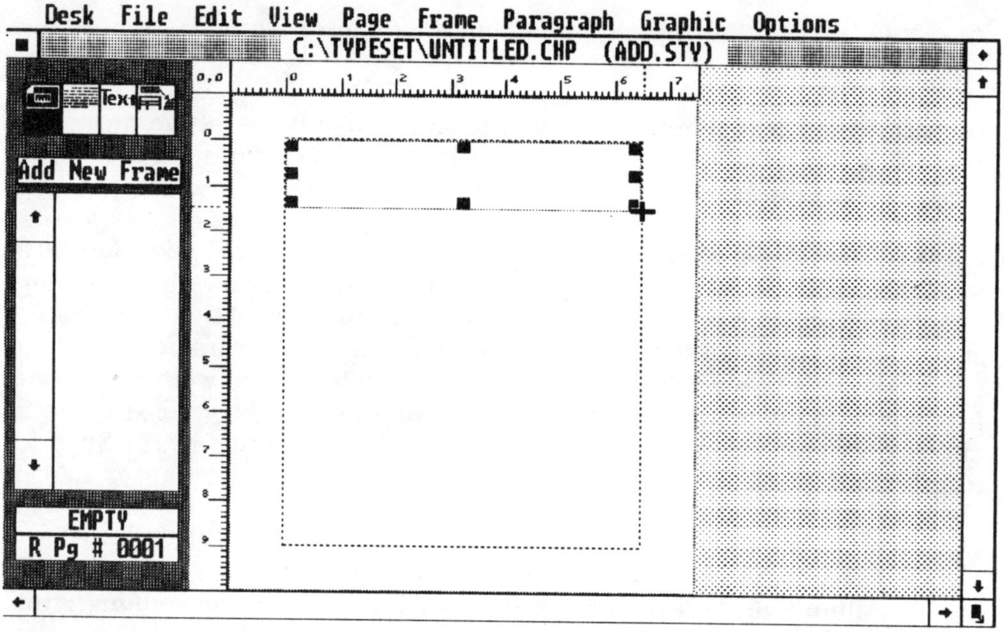

Figure 5.6

SELECTING FRAMES

Now that there is more than one frame on the page, you must learn to select the frame with which you want to work. Select a frame by pointing the mouse cursor anywhere in the frame and clicking the button. Then, point the mouse anywhere in the right margin and click the button. The buttons return to the master frame. Finally, point the mouse anywhere inside the new frame and click the button. The new frame is selected.

ADDING TEXT

After creating a new frame, you can enter the name and address of the company in one of two ways:

1. Activate the Text mode and manually enter text. Ventura will automatically store text entered into frames other than the master frame in files with CAP (for caption) extensions. These files use the same name as the corresponding chapter. For example, if a chapter file is named SAMPLE, the CAP file is named SAMPLE.CAP.

2. Load the text from a text file stored on disk.

In this case, you have not prepared a text file for the name and address, so you must enter it directly into the frame. Activate the Text mode by entering

[Ctrl/o]

Point the mouse cursor at the upper left corner of the new frame; make sure it is inside the new frame.

Click the mouse button, which positions the text cursor for text entry into the new frame. If Ventura displays the New File box, you have made a mistake; your cursor was pointed at the master frame and not the new frame just added to the document. If you have made this mistake, point and click on Cancel and reposition the cursor inside the new frame.

To simplify text entry, change to the Enlarged View mode by pressing

[Ctrl/e]

Enter the address information:

The Crummy Computer Company
[return]
1242B Partridge Avenue
[Ctrl/return]
Wilmington, Delaware 90300
[Ctrl/return]
210-777-3000

The next step is to format the text by creating appropriate style tags. Change to the Paragraph mode by pressing

[Ctrl/i]

You cannot create or modify a style unless you have selected at least one paragraph.

Point the mouse at "Wilmington" and click the button. Then, point the mouse at the Add New Tag box and click the button again. Enter the name of the new tag:

Address
[return]

Center the text by pointing the mouse at the Paragraph menu heading. Then, point at the Alignment option and click the button. Finally, point the mouse at Center and click the button again. Press

[return]

The paragraph is centered. To center the name of the company, point the mouse at "Crummy" and click the button. Then, point the mouse at the Address tag in the side bar and click the button again.

Change to Normal View mode by pressing

[Ctrl/n]

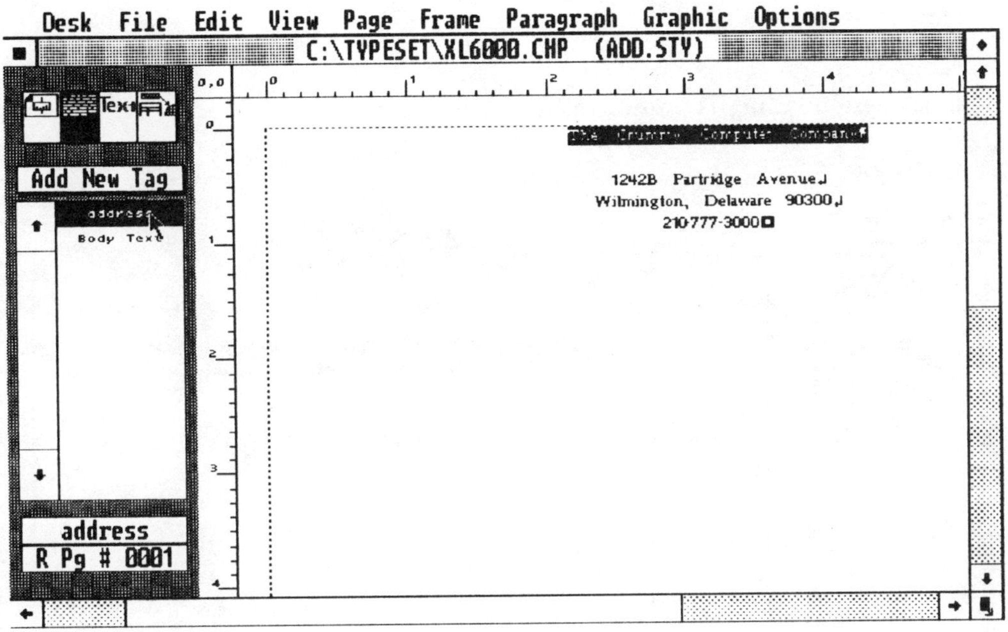

Figure 5.7

Since the company name is important, you might want to use a larger font to display it more prominently. Remember, you only want to change the company name—not the entire address. Create a new tag for the company name.

Point the mouse at the Add New Tag box and click the button. Enter

Company
[return]

Change the font for the new tag. Point the mouse at the Paragraph menu heading. Then, point at the Font option and click the button.

Select Swiss 18-point bold type. Point the mouse at Swiss and click the button. Then, point at 18 and click the button again. Finally, press

[return]

The address heading is entered into the frame.

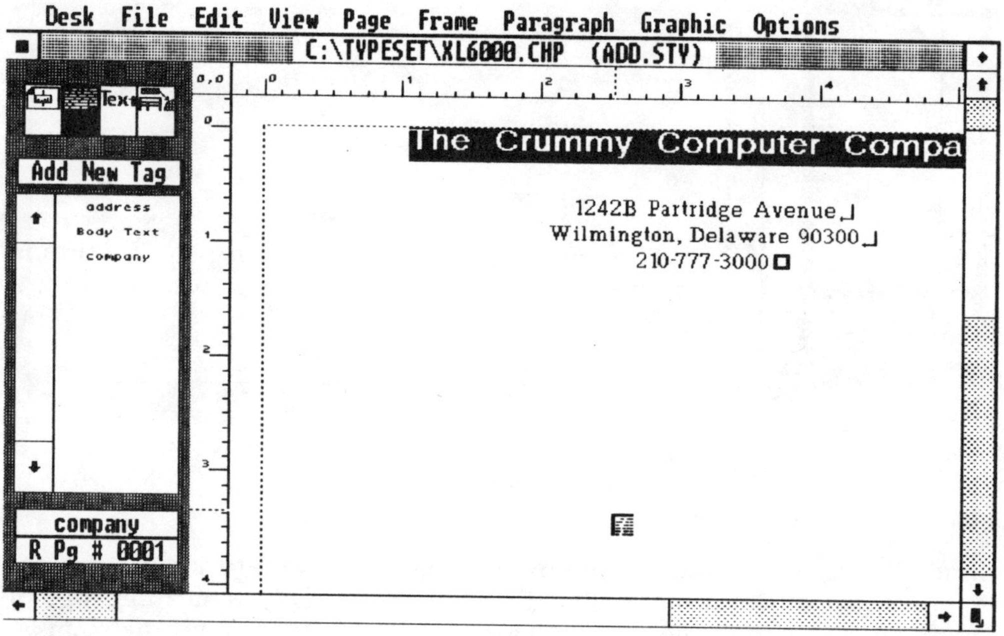

Figure 5.8

FRAME OPERATIONS

After establishing a separate frame for the address block, you can use commands from the Frame menu to enhance the display. To use Frame menu commands, you must activate the Frame mode. Press

[Ctrl/u]

Ventura displays the frame border lines. Buttons on a frame border serve the same purpose on a frame as on a graphics item. You can use buttons to enlarge or contract the size of the frame, and they also indicate the currently selected frame.

The box over the page number reads "FRAME TEXT," which indicates that text in this frame is stored in the document's CAP file instead of in a separate word processing file.

To make the address section stand out from the rest of the document, you might want to enclose the frame in a box. Point the mouse at the Frame menu heading. Ventura displays the Frame menu. In this case, you want to add a box around the frame. Point the mouse at the Ruling Box Around option and click the button.

Ventura displays the RULING BOX AROUND menu (Figure 5.9).

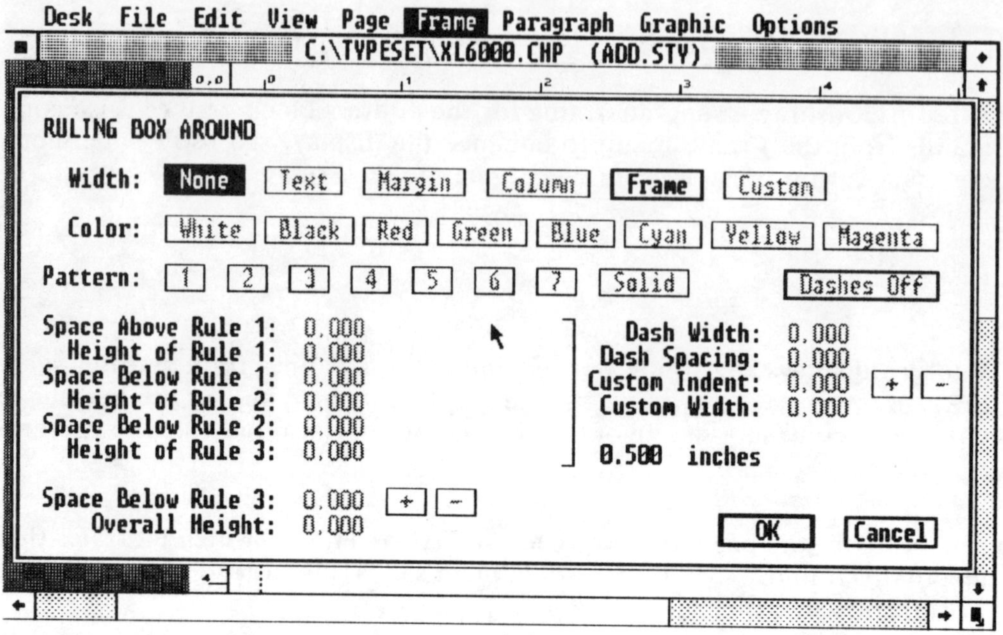

Figure 5.9

To draw the box around the entire frame, select Frame as the box's width. Point the mouse at Frame and click the button.

The bottom part of the display is now active; here you enter specifications for the line around the frame. You can define up to three lines at a time, which allows you to draw boxes within boxes for a framed effect.

Begin by placing a 3/100" line around the frame. Enter

[down arrow]
[Esc]
.03

Add another box with a line width of 1/100" inside the first box. You must decide the amount of space to leave between the boxes. In this case, make the space between the boxes equal to the line width of the first box (3/100"); then, enter the line width of the second box (1/100"). Enter

[down arrow]
[Esc]
.03
[down arrow]
[Esc]
.01

Ventura displays a model of the lines as you enter specifications:

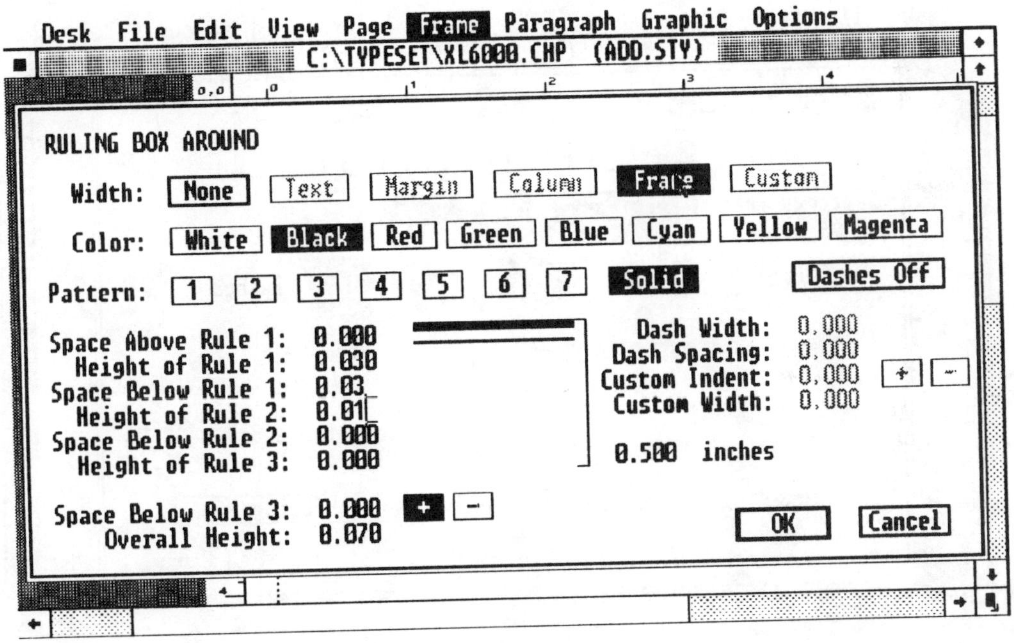

Figure 5.10

Complete the box by pressing

[return]

The double-lined box is drawn around the frame, but there is a problem. The company name is too near the top of the frame, and the boxes surrounding the frame overlap it. This problem can be solved by setting a top margin, which, in this case, applies to this frame only. The margins for the master frame remain separate.

Point the mouse at the Frame menu heading. Then, point at the Margins & Columns selection and click the button.

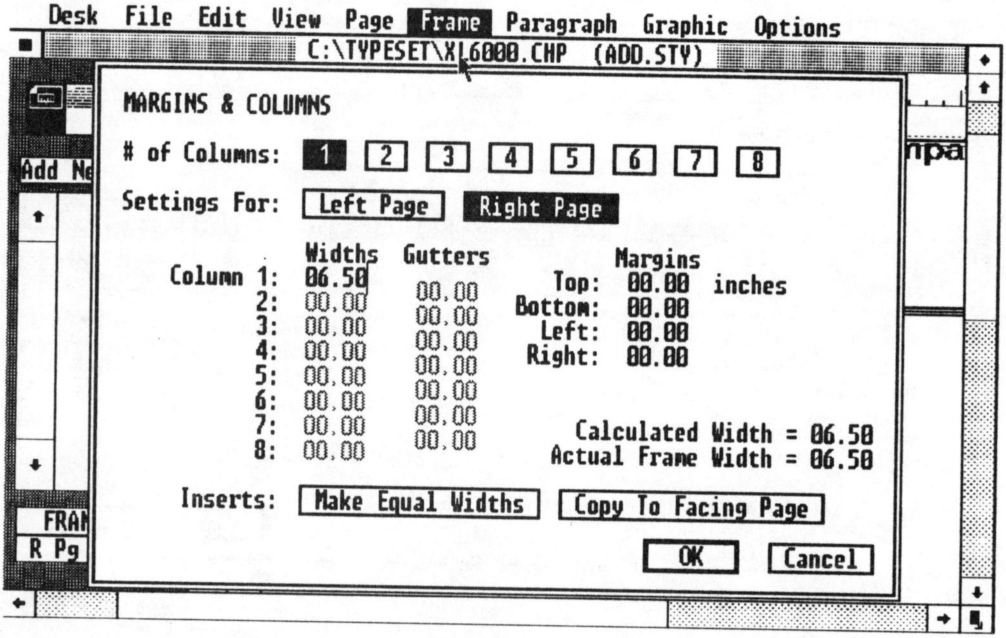

Figure 5.11

Ventura displays the MARGINS & COLUMNS menu, which allows you to set margins – left, right, top, and bottom – and create up to eight columns for each frame. In Ventura, each frame can maintain a different set of margins and columns.

In this case, you must create a top margin to lower the text so that it is not overwritten by the boxes. Point the mouse at "0" at the end of the Top option line and click the button. This action moves the text cursor to the position in which you enter a value for the top margin. The proper size of the margin can be calculated from the size of the boxes and the space between them. The boxes and the space between them total 7/100" (.03" + .03" + .01"); you should create a top margin of at least .8" and probably include additional space to separate the text from the boxes. Enter

[Esc]
.12
[return]

The top margin separates the boxes and the text.

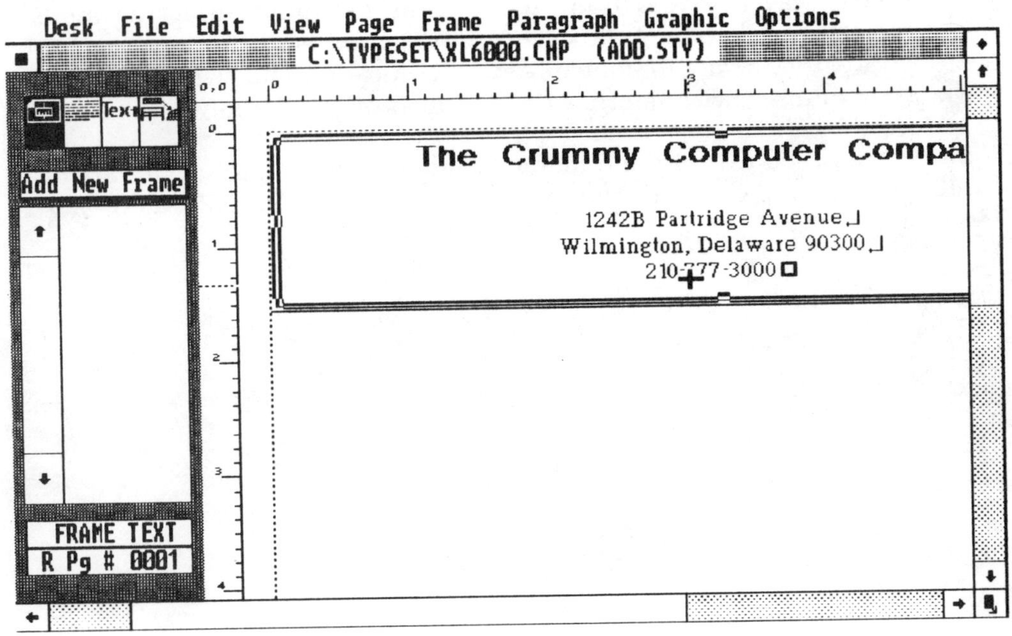

Figure 5.12

You have now completed the first frame on the page. The next step is to create a headline for the flyer. To place a frame on the page, you must activate the Reduced View mode. Press

[Ctrl/r]

Point the mouse at the Add New Frame box and click the button. Then, point the mouse cursor as close as possible to the lower left corner of the first frame.

Draw a frame across the width of the master frame so that the lower right corner of the new frame is approximately 2-3/4" down the page. Don't be too concerned about the exact length of the frame; just get as close as you can.

SIZING FRAMES

The simplest way to size a frame is by using the mouse-dragging method demonstrated in Chapter 4; however, this method isn't the most accurate. Ventura provides a way to control the exact location and size of a frame by having you enter exact numeric values instead of use the mouse.

Point the mouse at the Frame menu heading. Then, point at the Sizing & Scaling option and click the button. Ventura displays the SIZING & SCALING menu:

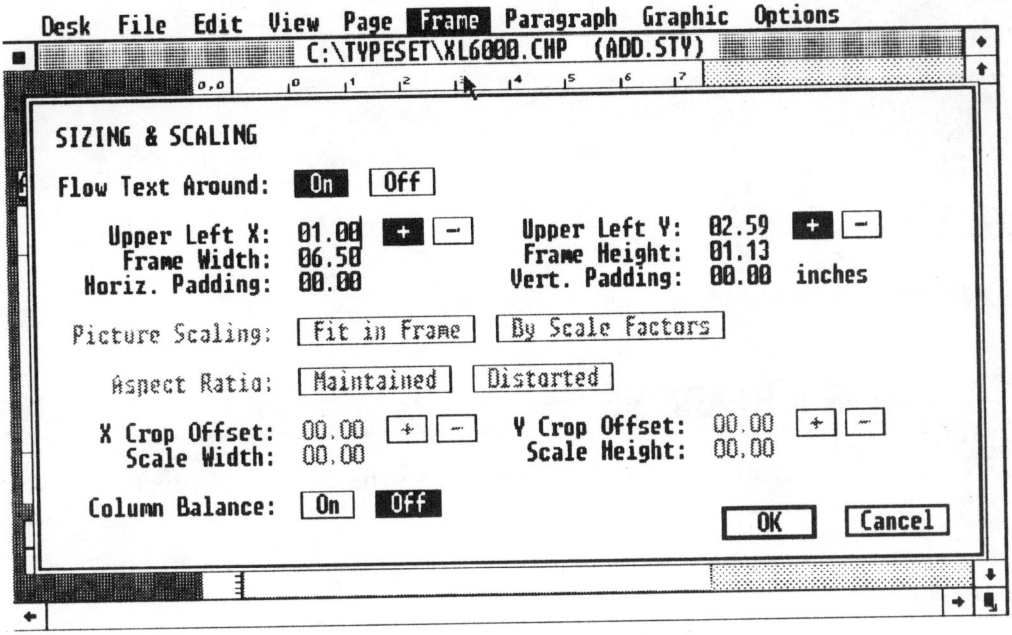

Figure 5.13

This menu displays an exact numerical description of the frame you just created by dragging the mouse. Because mouse-dragging is imprecise, the values may deviate from those originally intended.

The location of the frame is determined by two values: Upper Left X and Upper Left Y. The Upper Left X value is currently 1.00. X refers to the horizontal position of the frame. The value of 1.00 is no surprise because you began the frame at the left column guide of the master frame, which is set 1" from the edge of the page. Y refers to the vertical position on the page. In this case, the Y value is 2.59, indicating that the frame is positioned a little more than 2-1/2" down from the top of the page.

The size of the frame is shown in the Frame Width and Frame Height values. The frame height is currently 1.13". In this case, you want to specify a frame height of exactly 1". Move the text cursor to the Frame Height line by pressing

[down arrow] (3 times)

Then, enter

[Esc]
01.00
[return]

The frame's height is adjusted to exactly 1".

CREATING A HEADLINE

The next task is to add the headline text to the frame. Activate the Text mode by pressing

[Ctrl/o]

Point the mouse cursor at the upper left corner of the new frame and click the button. Change to the Normal View mode by pressing

[Ctrl/n]

Enter the headline text:

How much Computer can you fit in 1.5 Sq. Ft?

WHITE-ON-BLACK LETTERING

Since the flier's headline is intended to attract attention, you will want it to stand out from the rest of the document. One way to do this is to reverse the color to white letters on a black background.

The first step is to create a new style tag for the headline. The primary feature of this tag will be white lettering instead of black. Place Ventura in the Paragraph mode by pressing

[Ctrl/i]

Point the mouse at "How" and click the button. Then, point at the Add New Tag box and click the button.

Enter the name of the new tag, and specify that it should be copied from the Company tag and not the Body Text tag. By copying from the Company tag, the new tag will automatically center a paragraph and enlarge the font to 18-point. Enter

headline
[down arrow]
[Esc]
company
[return]

The next step is to change the color of the text to white. Point the mouse at the Paragraph menu heading. Then, point the mouse at the Font option and click the button. Point the mouse at White and click the button. Point at OK and click the button again.

The text seems to disappear; only a black block remains on the screen because the text now has the same color attribute as the background of the frame – white.

One way to resolve this problem is to change the background color to black or gray. Place Ventura into the Frame mode by pressing

[Ctrl/u]

Point the mouse at the Frame menu heading. Then, point at the Frame Background option and click the button. The FRAME BACKGROUND menu appears.

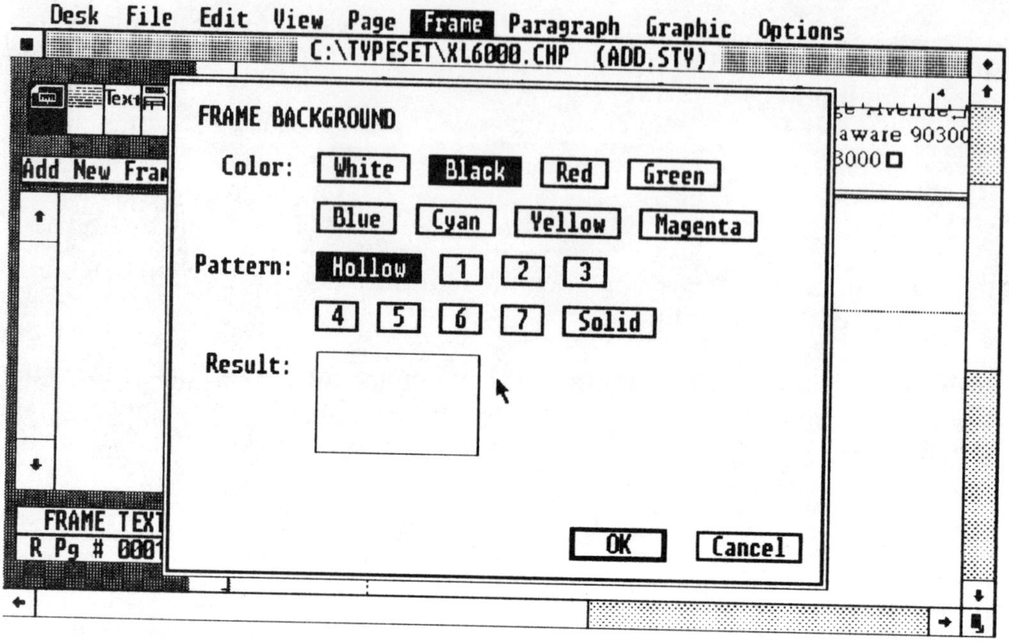

Figure 5.14

The color is already set to Black, but the Pattern setting is set to Hollow. You can choose gray tone levels from 1 to 7 or solid black.

Point the mouse at Solid and click the button. Point the mouse at OK and click the button again. You can now see the white letters against the blank background (see Figure 5.15).

If you decide the headline would look better if it were positioned closer to the vertical center of the frame, you can move the text down in the frame by changing the top margin value.

Point the mouse at the Frame menu heading. Then, point at the Margins & Columns option and click the button.

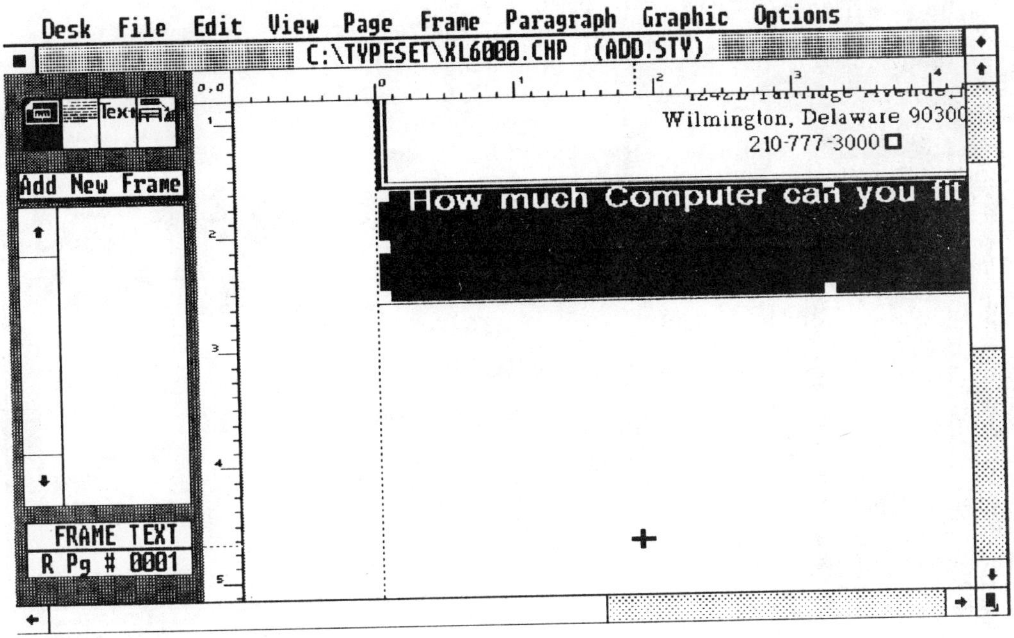

Figure 5.15

To determine the correct value for the top margin, review the numbers involved. First, the frame is exactly 1" in height. The text is 18-point (18/72"), which reduces to 1/4". This leaves 3/4" of blank space. Half of 3/4" is 3/8" or, in decimal notation rounded off to the nearest hundredth, .38"; therefore, the top margin should be .38". Enter

[down arrow]
[Esc]
.38
[return]

The text is now positioned in the center of the frame (horizontally and vertically).

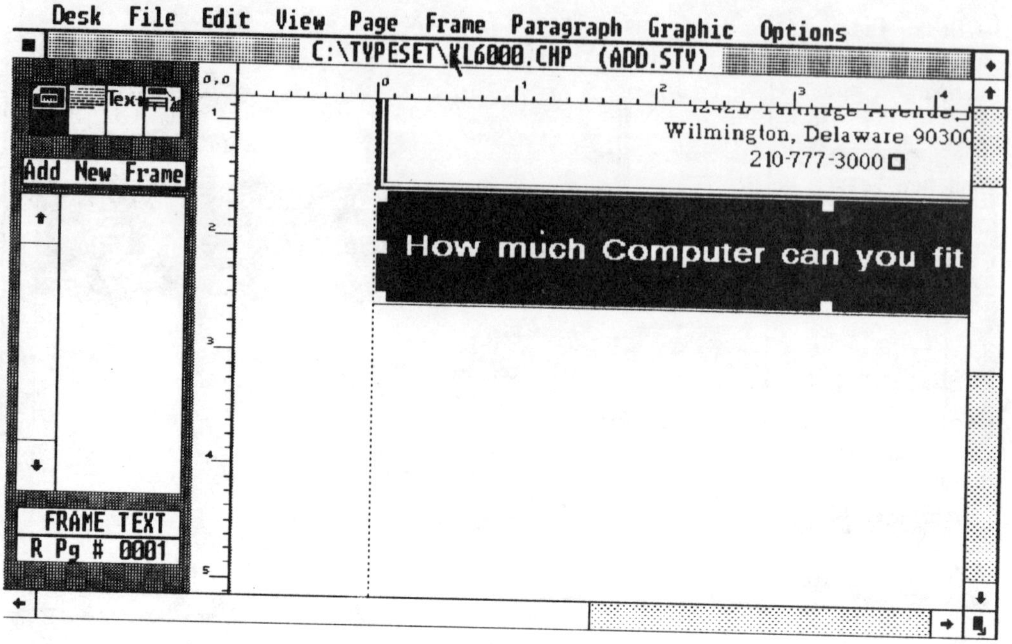

Figure 5.16

WHITE RULING BOXES

When you make the entire frame background solid black, you might create more black space around the text than you intended. For example, the text is approximately 1/4" high, but the black space above and below the text is 3/8" high. It might look better if you reduce the amount of black space.

One way to do this is to make the frame smaller; another way is to leave the frame the same size but draw a white line around it in the same way you placed a black line around the address box.

Point the mouse at the Frame menu heading. Then, point at the Ruling Box Around option and click the button.

Select a width by pointing the mouse at Frame and clicking the button. Change the color to white by pointing the mouse at White and clicking the button.

Finally, specify the line thickness. In this case, a little less than 1/4" will reduce the amount of black space to properly fit around the 18-point text. Enter

[down arrow]
[Esc]
.23
[return]

To see the entire document, press

[Ctrl/r]

The headline stands out on the page:

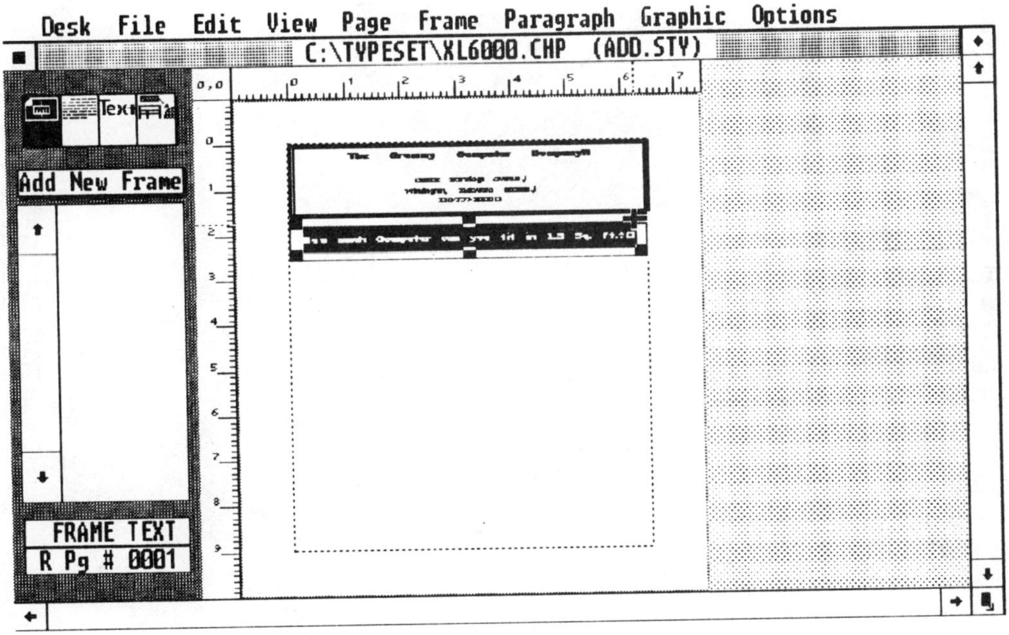

Figure 5.17

FILLING A FRAME WITH TEXT

There remain approximately six vertical inches of the page to fill with specific information about the XL6000 computer. The information has already been entered into text files; your task is to create frames and insert the text into them. Place Ventura into the Frame mode, [Ctrl/u]. Point the mouse at the Add New Frame box and click the button.

Draw a frame below the headline frame, across the master frame width, and down to approximately 6" vertically. The following figure displays the size and location of the frame:

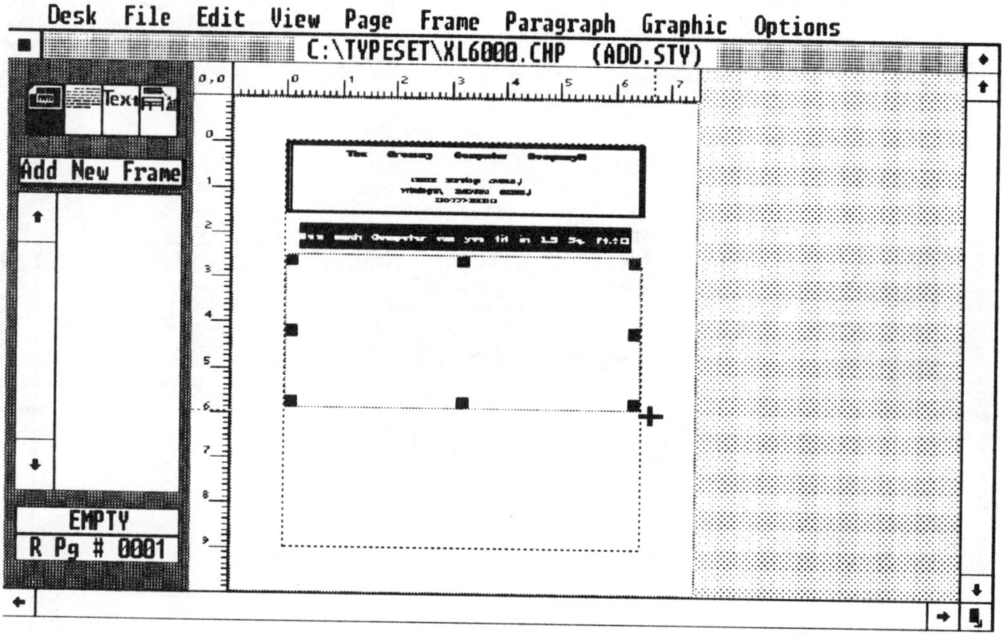

Figure 5.18

LOADING A TEXT FILE INTO A FRAME

Because you have already entered the text into a word processing document, you can load the file into the frame by using the File menu. Point the mouse at the File menu heading. Use the Load Text/Picture option to load text or graphics from other Ventura-compatible programs.

Point the mouse at the Load Text/Picture option and click the button. The LOAD TEXT/PICTURE menu appears. The file type should be Text, and the Text Format should be set for your word processor—in this example, WordPerfect. Recall, however, that two text files will be used with this flier: XL6000.WP and FEATURES.WP. At this point, you only need XL6000.WP, but you can save yourself later effort if you simultaneously load the FEATURES.WP file.

To load more than one file at a time, point the mouse at Several and click the button. Press

[return]

Ventura displays the ITEM SELECTOR menu:

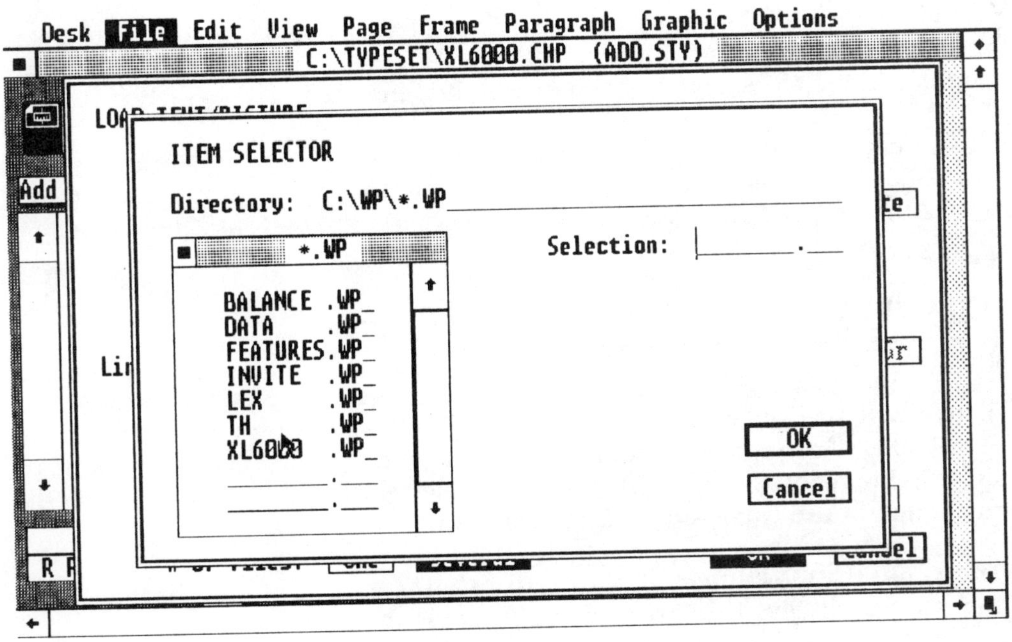

Figure 5.19

Ventura will return you to the last directory and selection wild card used – in this case, the directory \WP and files with WP extensions. If your display is not set to the correct directory, you or someone else using the same computer worked in a different directory the last time Ventura was used.

Point the mouse at the XL6000.WP file listing and *quickly* click the button *twice*. Ventura loads the text but does not return to the text display. Because you selected Several, the ITEM SELECTOR remains on the screen until you specifically exit the file-loading mode.

Point the mouse at FEATURES.WP and quickly click the button twice again. The two necessary files are now loaded. Exit the file-loading mode by pressing

[return]

Note that the side bar contains the names of the two loaded files; however, none of the text appears on the screen because Ventura waits until you indicate the frame to receive the text before it is inserted.

First, make sure that the frame is selected; again, buttons displayed on the frame border indicate that it is selected. Point the mouse at the XL6000.WP file listing and click the button. Ventura inserts the text into the frame.

COLUMNS

One major advantage of using multiple frames is that each frame can be formatted with a specific set of margin and column values that are independent of any other frame in the document. The new frame just created contains a single column of text and no margins. The text flows from the left to the right edge of the frame without interruption.

This is not the most effective way to display the text, however. Suppose that you want to display the text in three columns instead of one.

The new frame is still selected, as indicated by buttons displayed along the frame border. Point the mouse at the Frame menu heading. Then, point at the Margins & Columns option and click the button.

The MARGINS & COLUMNS menu box appears. The first item in the box is the number of columns. Ventura allows you to divide a frame into 1 to 8 columns. In this case, you want three columns. Point the mouse at 3 and click the button.

When you select more than one column, Ventura automatically calculates the width of each column. You can determine the values for each column by examining the Widths column. The columns are assumed to be of the same width—in this case, 2.17".

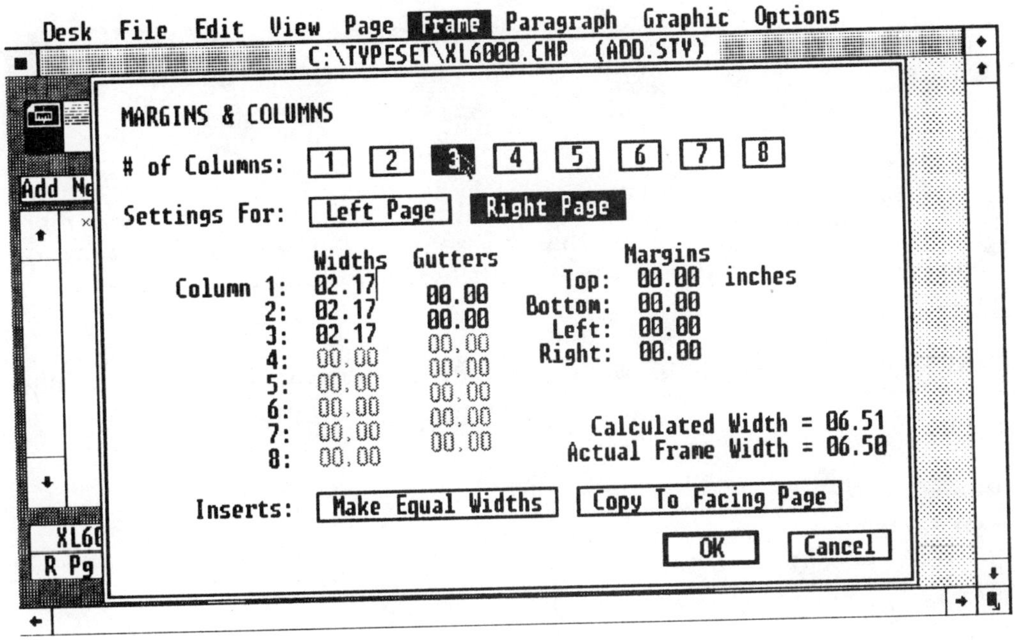

Figure 5.20

Next to the Widths display, Ventura displays a column labeled "Gutters." A **gutter** refers to the space between columns. When you indicate three columns, you encounter two gutter settings.

Ventura does not automatically insert gutter space; however, if you do not specify gutter spacing, the columns will be directly adjacent to each other.

The gutter spacing between columns 1 and 2 is set on line 2. Move the cursor to the gutter line for column 2 by pressing

[down arrow] (3 times)

Create gutters of 1/10" for both columns by entering

[Esc]
.1
[down arrow]
[Esc]
.1

Before you leave this menu, you might also want to consider creating margins for the frame itself. It is usually a good idea to establish margins for frames so that there will be some space between the edges of the frames and the text within them.

Since you have chosen 1/10" as the column gutter spacing, use the same value for the margins. Enter the following sequence four times:

[down arrow]
[Esc]
.1

Following is a summary of changes made in this menu:

1. Three columns of text are specified.
2. Gutter space between columns is set to 1/10".
3. Top, bottom, left, and right margins are set to 1/10".

To implement these settings and examine how they affect the text, press

[Ctrl/return]

The text in the selected frame is reformatted in three columns with gutter and margin settings of 1/10".

You can see that the third column is only about half as long as the other two columns. The square box (end-of-file symbol) at the end indicates that all text from the XL6000.WP document file is displayed.

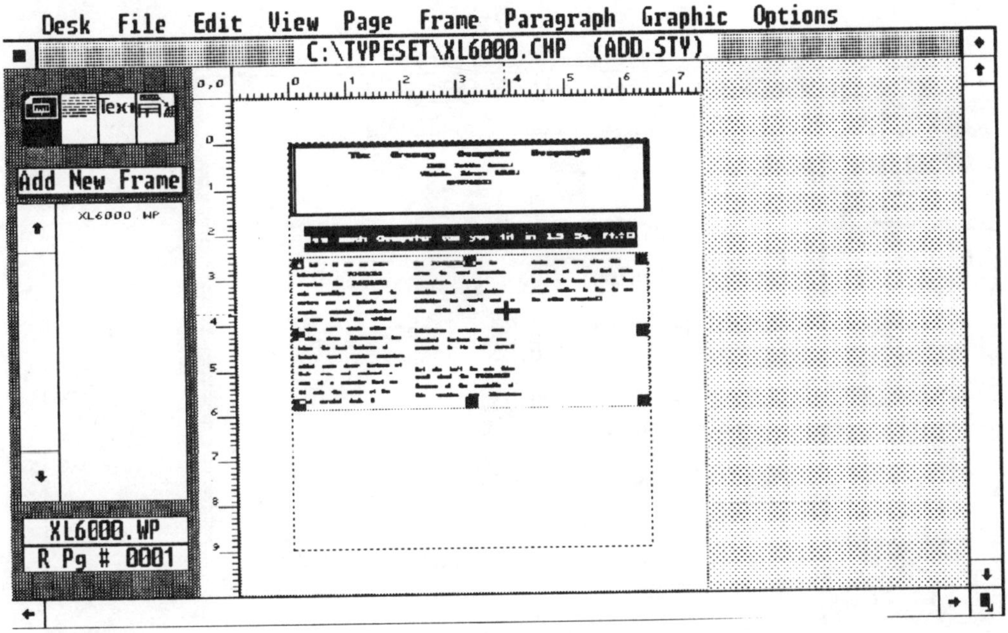

Figure 5.21

VERTICAL LINES

Now that the text is divided into columns, you have the option to add vertical lines between the columns. Vertical lines are set as frame attributes; when vertical ruling lines are added to a frame, Ventura automatically inserts the lines between each column. If you change the number of columns specified for a frame, Ventura will increase or decrease the number of vertical ruling lines to match the number of columns. Vertical ruling lines will also lengthen automatically if you change a frame's length.

To add vertical lines to a frame, point the mouse at the Frame menu heading. Then, point at the Vertical Rules option and click the button. Ventura displays the VERTICAL RULES menu box:

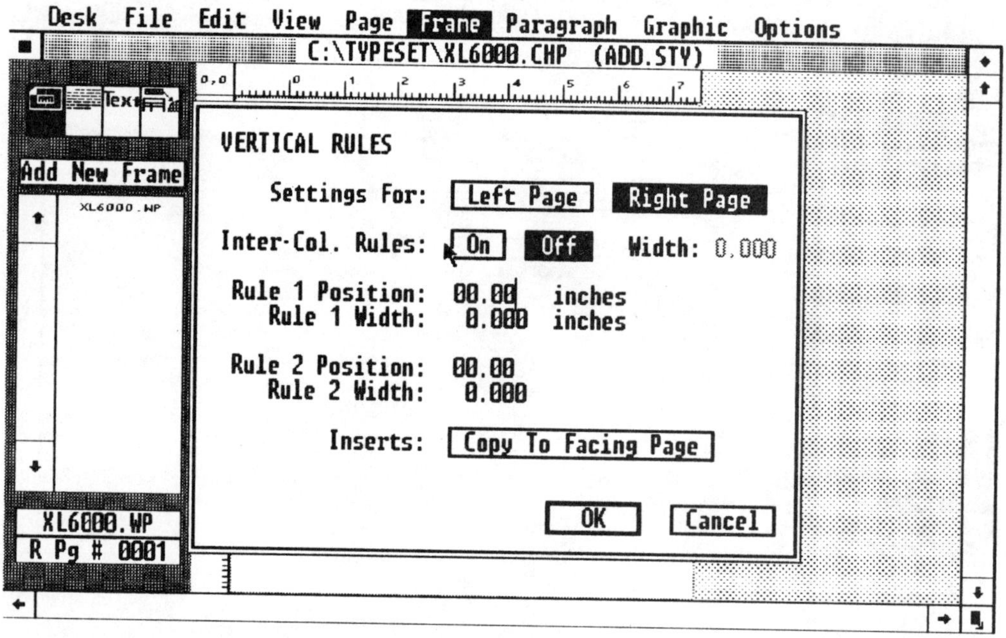

Figure 5.22

Ventura allows you to create two types of vertical lines within a frame.

The first type is referred to as **Inter-Col**(umn) Rules, which are lines automatically positioned between columns. The other ruling line selections – **Rule 1** and **Rule 2** – allow you to choose the exact locations of ruling lines. These vertical lines can be placed at any horizontal position on the page; they are measured from the left edge of the page – *not* the left edge of the frame. For example, if you specify 4.25" as the position, Ventura draws a line down the middle of the page within the frame. Ventura will not check to determine if that position is empty or filled with text when it draws the line. Use this option only when you want to manually control exact locations of vertical lines. The Rule 2 setting functions in much the same way and allows you to specify the location of a second vertical line.

In this case, choose the Inter-Col. lines. Point the mouse at On and click the button. Ventura automatically enters a line width of 3/100". Complete the entry by pointing the mouse at OK and clicking the button. Ventura adds vertical lines to the text in the frame.

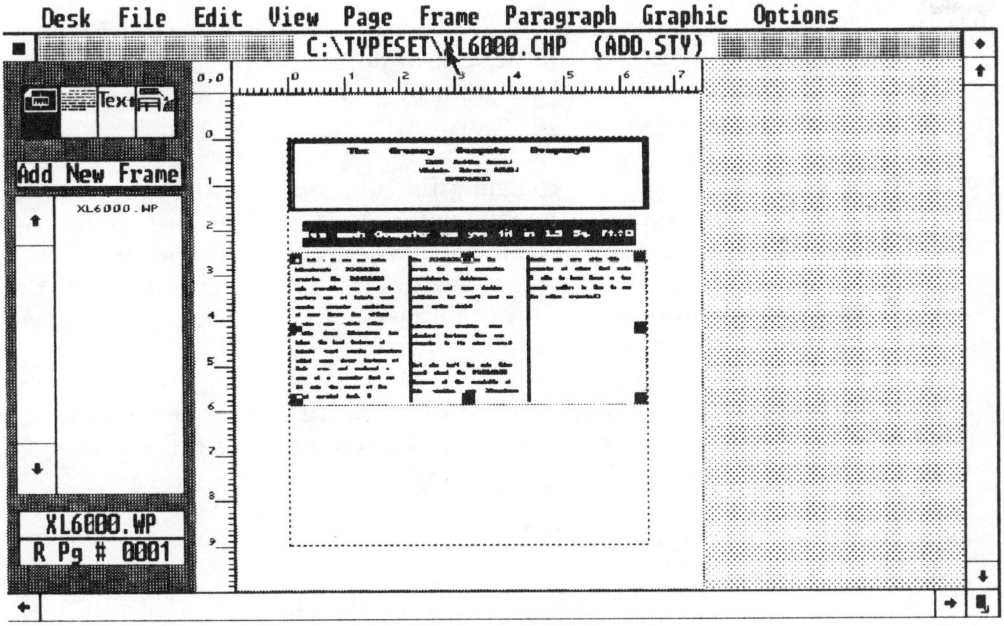

Figure 5.23

Before the lines were drawn, the white space at the ends of the lines in columns 2 and 3 made the gutter spaces between columns appear larger. Adding vertical lines emphasizes the real gutter space, which might be smaller than you thought. In this case, the text would look better with a wider gutter. To change the gutter value, return to the MARGINS & COLUMNS menu box.

Point the mouse at the Frame menu heading. Then, point at the Margins & Columns option and click the button. Change the gutter from .1" to .2" by entering

[down arrow] (3 times)
[Esc]
.2
[down arrow]
[Esc]
.2
[return]

The space between the lines and the text to their right has been increased a small amount – 1/10". Note that the length of column 3 has increased. By increasing the gutter size, you left less room in each column for text and increased the amount of space needed to display text.

When working with a document, you may find that you must often change settings to find the best combination by trial and error. The proper use of Ventura is a mixture of direct numeric calculation and trial and error. In this book, you have seen that whenever possible, it is best to calculate the distances instead of relying on estimates. Occasionally, you can better judge by trying a combination and examining the results.

For example, consider what this frame would look like with four columns. Point the mouse at the Frame menu heading. Then, point at the Margins & Columns option and click the button.

Select four columns. Point the mouse at 4 and click the button.

Ventura performs two calculations. First, it divides the text area into four columns. It also determines that the last gutter space was set at .2" and adds another gutter to the list. To see the effect of adding another column, press

[return]

The frame is now divided into four columns of text; Ventura automatically adds another vertical line:

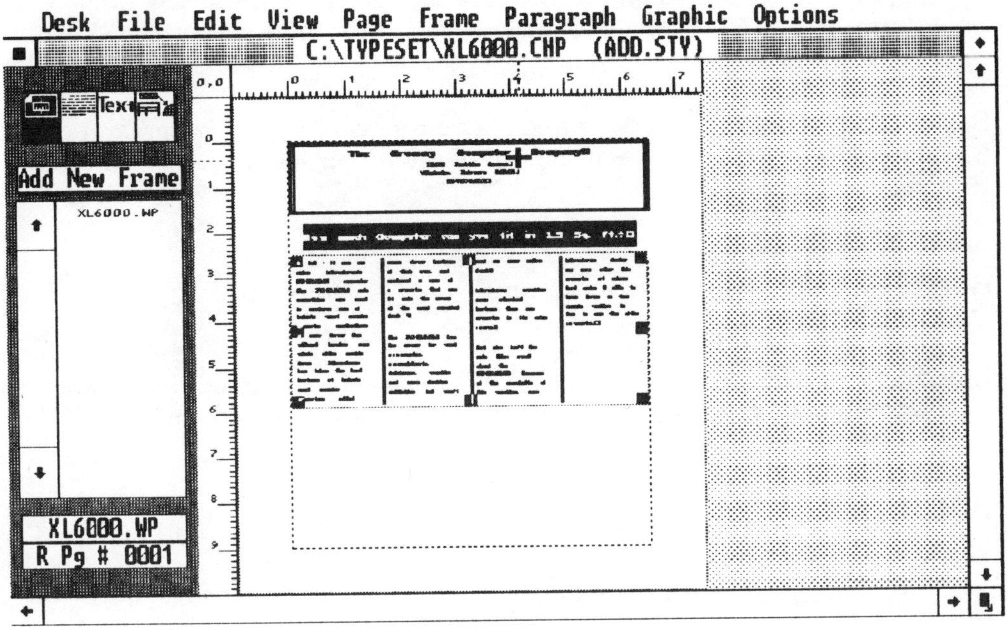

Figure 5.24

EMPHASIZING PARAGRAPHS

When text is arranged in columns, special effects are often used to add emphasis to various elements. In this example, you will add two common effects to the text in this frame:

1. **Big First Letter**. This effect is most often used with the first paragraph of a section or chapter. The first letter of the first word is printed in a much larger font than the rest of the text. The effect dates back to the Middle Ages, when large first letters were used to embellish handwritten manuscripts.

2. **Lifts.** The term **Lift** refers to a part of the text that is printed in enlarged, bold print and marked off from the other paragraphs by ruling lines. This effect is often used in magazines to display paragraphs of special interest that can be spotted quickly on a page.

Begin with the Big First Letter effect. Zoom in on the first paragraph of the frame by pointing the mouse at the top of the upper left corner of the frame. Enter

[Ctrl/e]

The first letter in the text is "A." The Big First Letter effect is included in a paragraph style tag. Activate the Paragraph mode by entering

[Ctrl/i]

Point the mouse at "A" and click the button.

You must create a new tag for this effect. Point the mouse at the Add New Tag box and click the button. Enter the name of the new tag:

First Para
[return]

To create the special effect, point the mouse at the Paragraph menu heading. Then, point at the Special Effects option and click the button. Ventura displays the SPECIAL EFFECTS menu box:

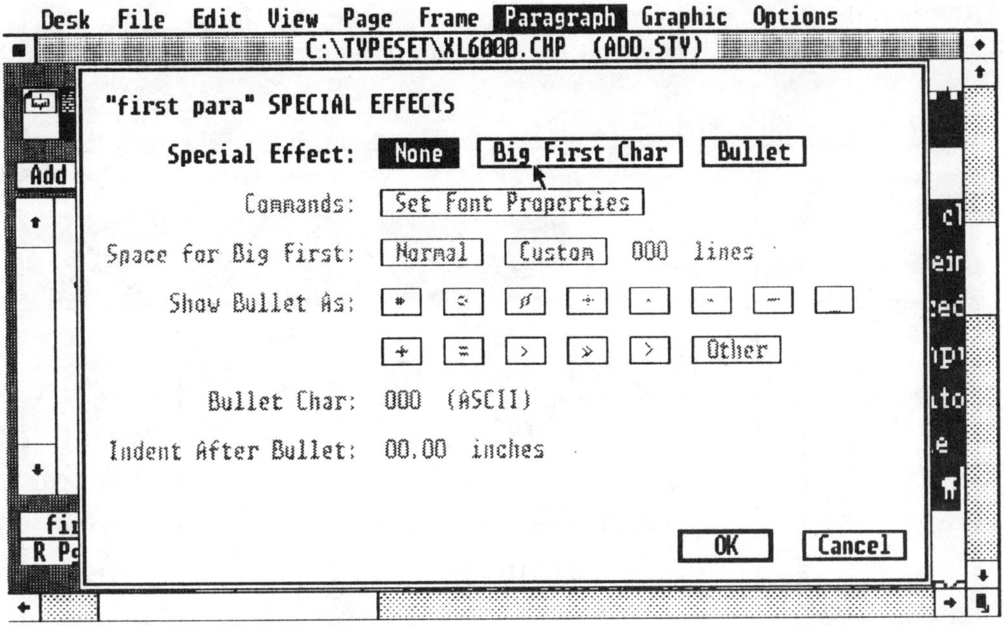

Figure 5.25

To create the Big First Letter effect, point the mouse at Big First Char and click the button.

The next step is to select a font for the big first letter. Point the mouse at Big Font Properties and click the button. The FONTS menu appears. Select a Dutch 24-point bold font.

Point the mouse at Dutch and click the button. Point the mouse at 24 and click the button again. Complete the tag by by pressing

[return]

Remove the highlight from the paragraph. Point the mouse at the margin and click the button. The first letter of the paragraph is enlarged:

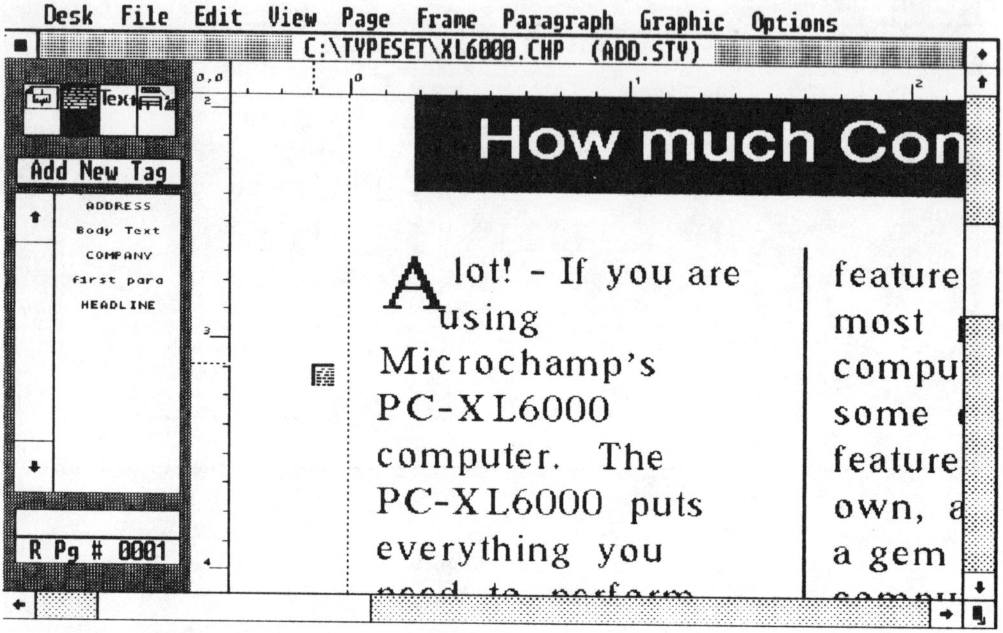

Figure 5.26

The next special effect is the lifted paragraph. You will work with the third paragraph. Zoom back to the Reduced View mode by entering

[Ctrl/r]

The third paragraph is located midway in the third column. Point the mouse at the beginning of that paragraph. Return to the Enlarged View mode by entering

[Ctrl/e]

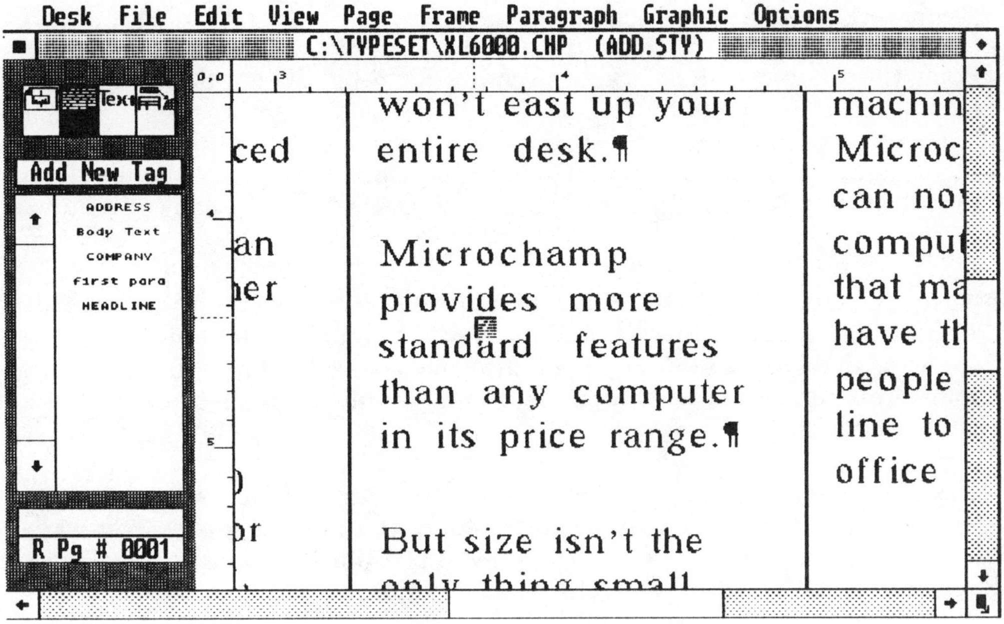

Figure 5.27

The paragraph you want to lift begins "Microchamp provides." Point the mouse at "Microchamp" and click the button.

Create a new tag named "Lift." Point the mouse at the Add New Tag box and click the button. Enter

Lift
[return]

To create a lift, you must make three changes in the paragraph format:

1. Change the text font to a larger and bolder font.
2. Add a ruling line above the text.
3. Add a ruling line below the text.

Begin with the first step—changing the font.

Point the mouse at the Paragraph menu heading. Then, point at the Font selection and click the button.

Select a Swiss 14-point bold font. Point the mouse at Swiss and click the button. Point at 14 and click the button. Point at OK and click the button a final time.

Next, add the ruling lines. Point the mouse at the Paragraph menu heading. Then, point at the Ruling Line Above option and click the button. The first choice is the width of the line to be drawn across the frame. In this case, you want the line only as wide as the column. Point the mouse at Column and click the button.

Next, enter spacing requirements for the line. Ventura allows you to specify the amount of space above and below a ruling line. Suppose you want to draw a line .05" high. To separate the line from the paragraphs, you must add space (e.g., .1") above and below the line.

Enter the space above the line:

[Esc]
.1
[down arrow]

Enter the height of the line:

[Esc]
.5
[down arrow]

Finally, enter the amount of space to be inserted below the line:

[Esc]
.1
[return]

The ruling lines separate the lifted paragraph from the rest of the text. To insert a ruling line below the paragraph, point the mouse at the Paragraph menu heading. Then, point at the Ruling Line Below option and click the button.

To select Column width, point the mouse at Column and click the button. Enter the height of the spaces and the line:

[Esc]
.1
[down arrow]
[Esc]
.05
[down arrow]
[Esc]
.1
[return]

To see the overall effect of the changes, zoom back to the Reduced View mode by entering

[Ctrl/r]

See Figure 5.28.

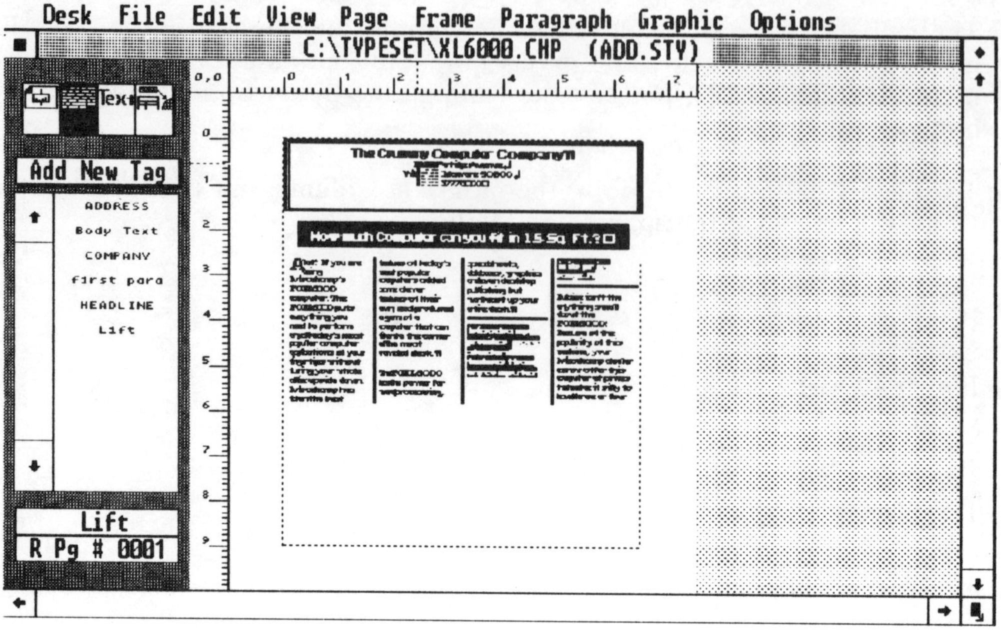

Figure 5.28

Note that adding the lifted paragraph causes the text to lengthen so that the end-of-file marker is not displayed at the bottom of the fourth column. Place Ventura into the Frame mode by entering

[Ctrl/u]

Reduce the number of columns to 3 again. Point the mouse at the Frame menu heading. Then, point at the Margins & Columns option and click the button.

Select three columns. Point the mouse at 3 and click the button. Press

[return]

The text is now formatted in three columns. The end-of-file marker appears at the bottom of the third column, indicating that all of the file's text is now displayed.

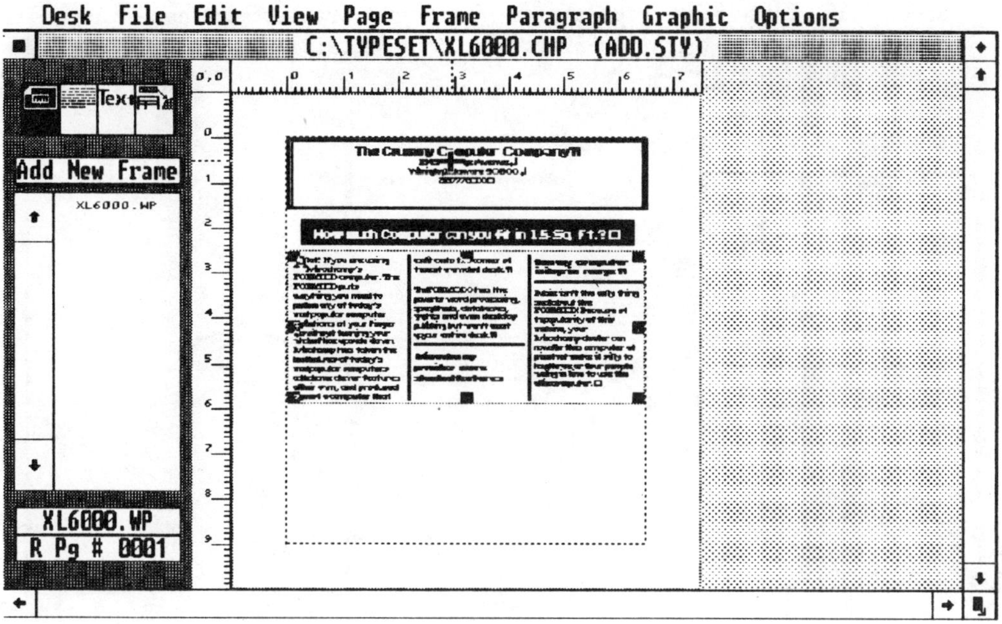

Figure 5.29

THE FEATURES FRAME

The next step in the layout of the flier is to add another frame and insert into it the text of the FEATURES.WP document. Point the mouse at the Add New Frame box and click the button.

Draw a frame below the last frame and cover the bottom part of the page. Make sure that you don't begin the new frame so close to the bottom of the previous frame that the two frames overlap. Start the new frame one line below the previous frame. Note that the Line Snap feature will snap the frame into the next line position as you position the cursor (see Figure 5.30).

In this frame, you want to place text entered in the FEATURES.WP document. Point the mouse at the File menu heading. Then, point at the Load Text/Picture option and click the button. Ventura displays the same settings used the last time a file was loaded. Accept the settings by pressing

[return]

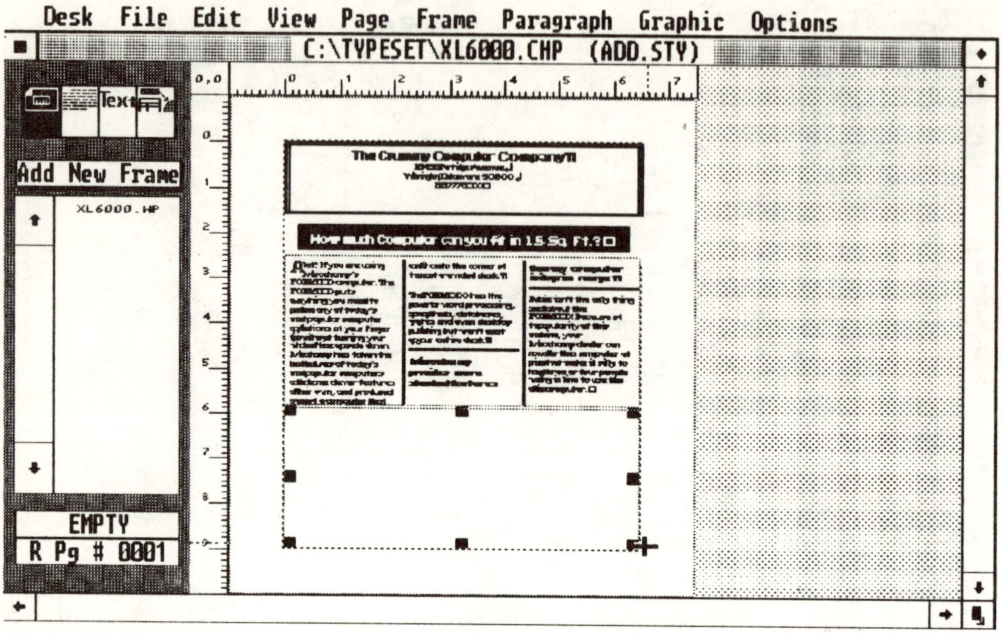

Figure 5.30

Point the mouse at the FEATURES.WP file listing and quickly click the mouse twice. Ventura adds the text to the frame. You can see that FEATURES.WP contains more text than will currently fit into the frame. You must make adjustments such as the following to display the entire text in the flyer:

- reduce the font size
- reduce the space between paragraphs
- create multiple columns

For a closer look at the text, change the display mode to Normal View again. Point the mouse at the upper left corner of the new frame and enter

[Ctrl/n]

BULLET TAGS

The next task is to create a new paragraph format for the text in the FEATURES.WP file. Remember, the text of this file is not organized into paragraphs; it is a list of the product's features. Such lists are referred to as **bullet** lists. Ventura has a special format for bullet text that can be combined with any font and spacing setting.

To create a bullet format for this text, begin by placing Ventura into the Paragraph mode. Enter

[Ctrl/i]

Point the mouse at "Megabyte" and click the button. Before you select a formatting change, you must create a new tag.

Point the mouse at the Add New Tag box and click the button. Enter the name of the new tag:

Feature
[return]

Select the bullet format from the SPECIAL EFFECTS menu. Point the mouse at the Paragraph menu heading. Then, point at the Special Effects option and click the button.

The SPECIAL EFFECTS menu box appears. Select the bullet effect by pointing the mouse at Bullet and clicking the button.

When you select Bullet, you can then select the bullet character—the character to be printed at the beginning of every Bullet paragraph. The default character is a dot, but you can select any of the other characters shown on the menu or enter a character of your choice. Characters are selected by entering the ASCII value of the character. The actual printed character depends on the current font's character for that ASCII value, which may differ from font to font. In this case, accept the default bullet character by pressing

[return]

The paragraph is formatted with a bullet:

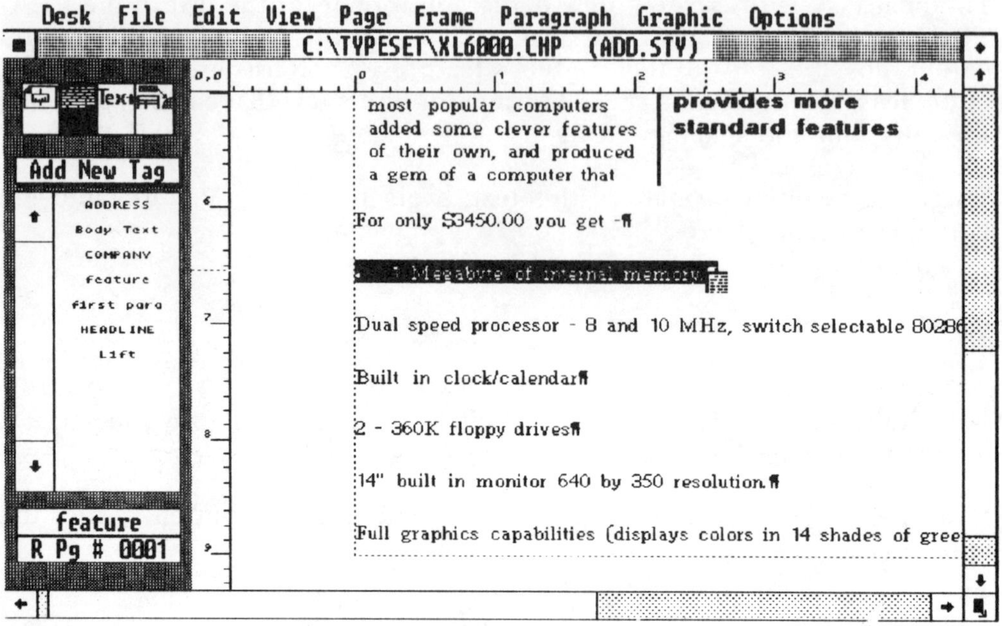

Figure 5.31

Select a new font for the bulleted text. Point the mouse at the Paragraph menu heading. Then, point at the Fonts option and click the button.

In this case, select an 8-point Swiss typeface to distinguish bulleted text from the normal Dutch typeface. Point the mouse at Swiss and click the button. Point at 8 and click the button again. Point at Normal and click the button a third time. Complete the font setting by pressing

[return]

Next, reduce the amount of space between bulleted paragraphs, which allows more text into the frame.

Point the mouse at the Paragraph menu heading. Then, point at the Spacing option and click the button.

Before you enter values for the spacing, you might want to calculate the minimum values. The text font selected is 8-point Swiss. Ventura uses an interline value of 9.36 fractional points, which is approximately .13". Use that value as a starting point for the Above and Below spacing. Enter

[Esc]
.13
[down arrow]
[Esc]
.13
[down arrow]
[down arrow]
[Esc]
[return]

Tag the next four paragraphs as Feature. The changes will reduce the amount of space used by each bullet, which makes the display more compact.

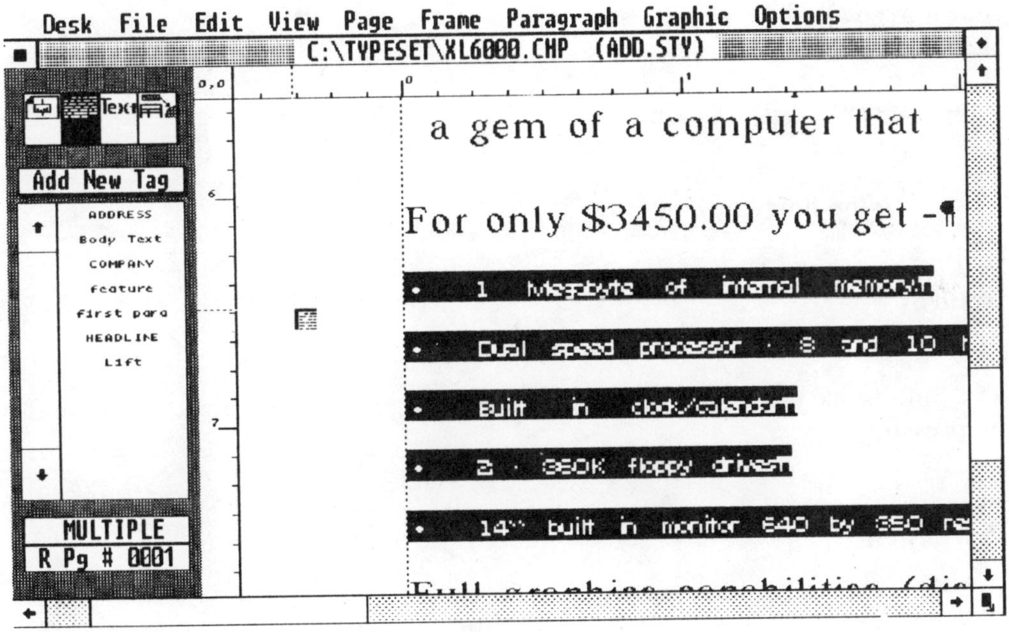

Figure 5.32

The next step is to tag all bulleted paragraphs with the Feature tag. You cannot, however, see all the text because it does not fit into the frame.

This problem can be solved by creating a multiple-column setup. Note that each bullet consists of short lines. With multiple columns, you can fit more text into the frame. Change to the Frame mode by entering

[Ctrl/u]

Make sure the frame is selected (i.e., buttons appear in the border). Change the layout of the frame to 4 columns. Point the mouse at the Frame menu heading. Then, point at the Margins & Columns option and click the button.

Select a four-column layout. Point the mouse at 4 and click the button.

Enter a gutter of .1" for each column:

[down arrow]	(4 times)
[Esc]	
.1	
[down arrow]	(3 times)

Complete the entry by pressing

[return]

The bullets are organized into columns. Change to the Reduced View mode by pressing

[Ctrl/r]

Change to the Paragraph mode by pressing

[Ctrl/i]

Now use the [Shift]-click method to tag all visible paragraphs (except the first one) as Feature. The document layout will resemble the following:

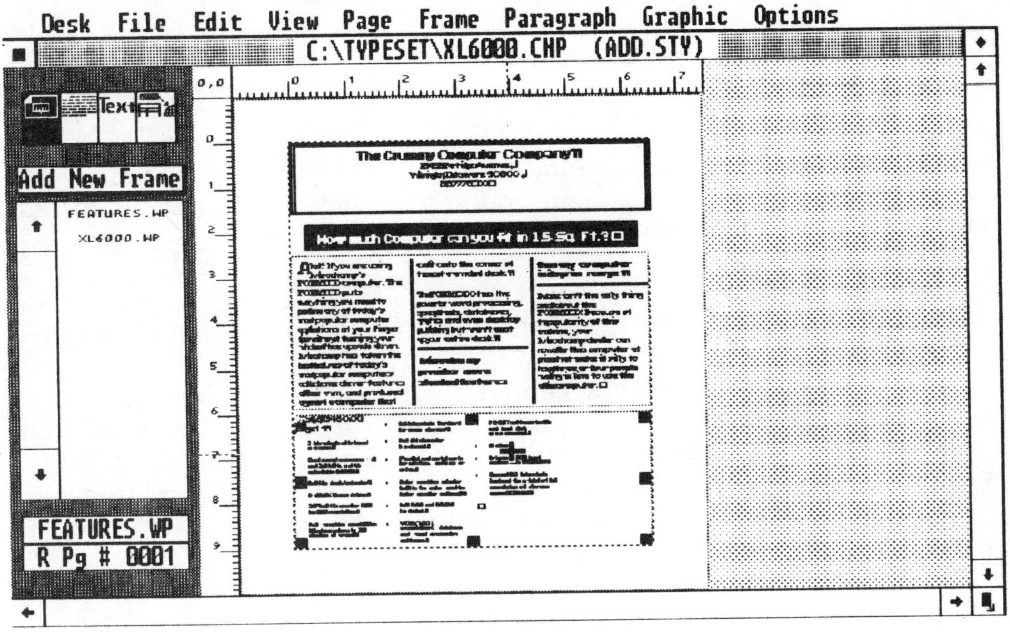

Figure 5.33

ALIGNMENT AND COLUMNS

The bottom frame now contains bulleted items, with the exception of the first line, which begins "For only $3450.00." That line is logically related to all the bulleted items. It might make more sense if that paragraph is not aligned as part of the first column but is centered over all the columns. Highlight the first paragraph in the frame by pointing the mouse at it and clicking the button.

If you examine the side bar display, you will see that this paragraph is currently formatted as Body Text. Create a new tag for this paragraph.

Point the mouse at the Add New Tag box and click the button. Enter the name for the new tag:

Col head
[return]

To change this tag's alignment, point the mouse at the Paragraph menu heading. Then, point at the Alignment option and click the button. Point the mouse at Center and click the button again.

The fourth selection on the menu is Overall Width, in which you choose alignment for a specific column or alignment for the entire frame's width.

Up to this point, you have only centered paragraphs in frames of a single column. In those cases, it wouldn't have mattered which setting you selected, but, when the frame contains more than one column, this item is significant. To center the paragraph between the frame margins and not the column margins, point the mouse at Frame-Wide and click the button. Complete the alignment by pressing

[return]

The paragraph is centered above the four columns. Note that to do this, Ventura starts all columns lower in the frame to accommodate the centered heading:

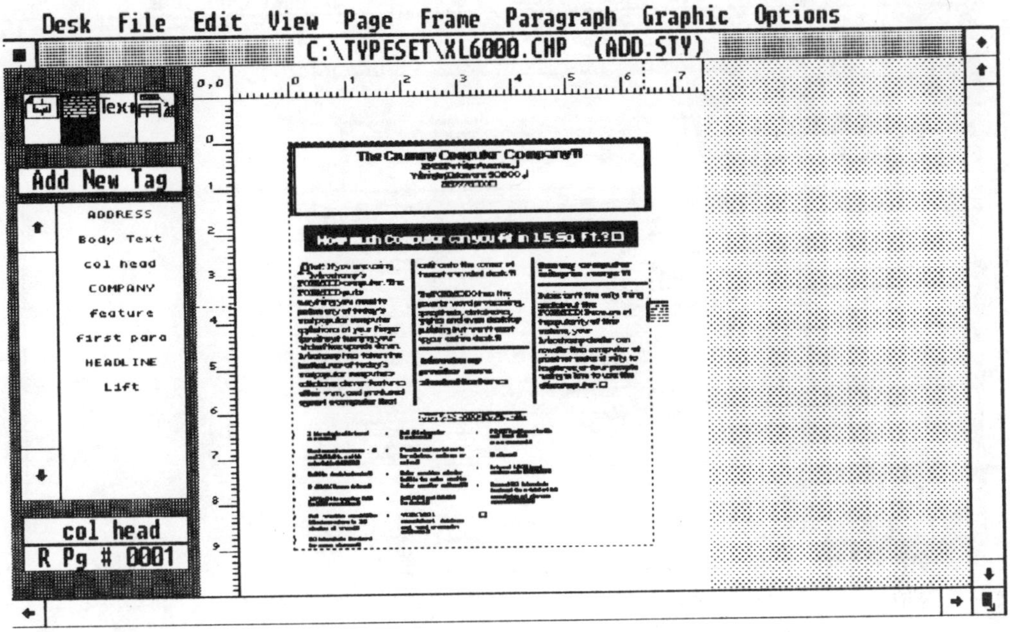

Figure 5.34

FLOW-AROUND TEXT

The final task in creating this flier is to add a graphic to the display. In this example, the graphic is a 1-2-3 graph file. Pictures and graphics created by Ventura-compatible programs are added to a document in the same way as text prepared in word processing programs – by creating a new frame and loading the picture file into it.

Note, however, that all space on the page is covered by existing frames. Ventura allows frames to be inserted into any part of the page. Ventura automatically **flows** the text around the frame.

Examine the following illustration, which displays a frame added inside the last frame on the page. The text in the previous frame flows around the new frame. Because the text of the FEATURES.WP file does not fill all four columns, there is room in column 4 for the text that flowed from columns 2 and 3.

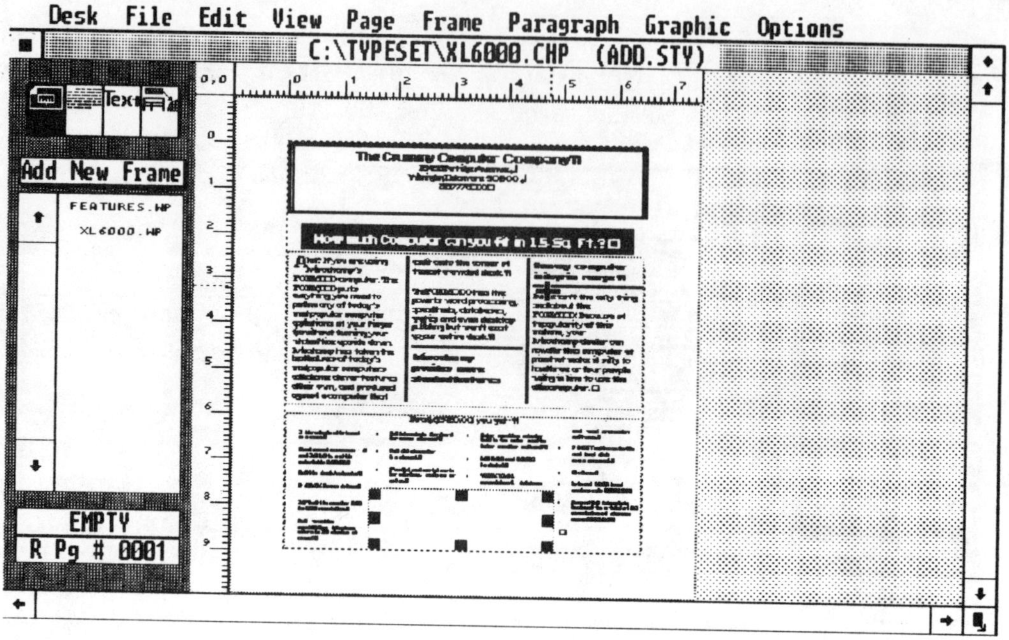

Figure 5.35

Your task is to draw that frame. Place Ventura into Frame mode by entering

[Ctrl/u]

Draw a frame at approximately the location shown in Figure 5.35. Don't worry about the exact location; you will learn to position your frame in the exact position later. When drawing the frame, remember that if you place a frame in the middle of a column, the text flow may create odd-looking columns.

SIZE AND SCALE

Now that you have drawn the frame, you can adjust the frame's size and location to precisely match the example. Point the mouse at the Frame menu heading. Then, point the mouse at the Sizing & Scaling option and click the button.

The menu in Figure 5.36 shows the exact location of the frame drawn for this example. The upper left corner of the frame is 2.5" in and 8.6" down. The frame is 3.4" wide and 1.4" high. If your screen shows different values, adjust the size and location by typing in the correct values. Use the arrow keys or the mouse cursor to change your position within the menu.

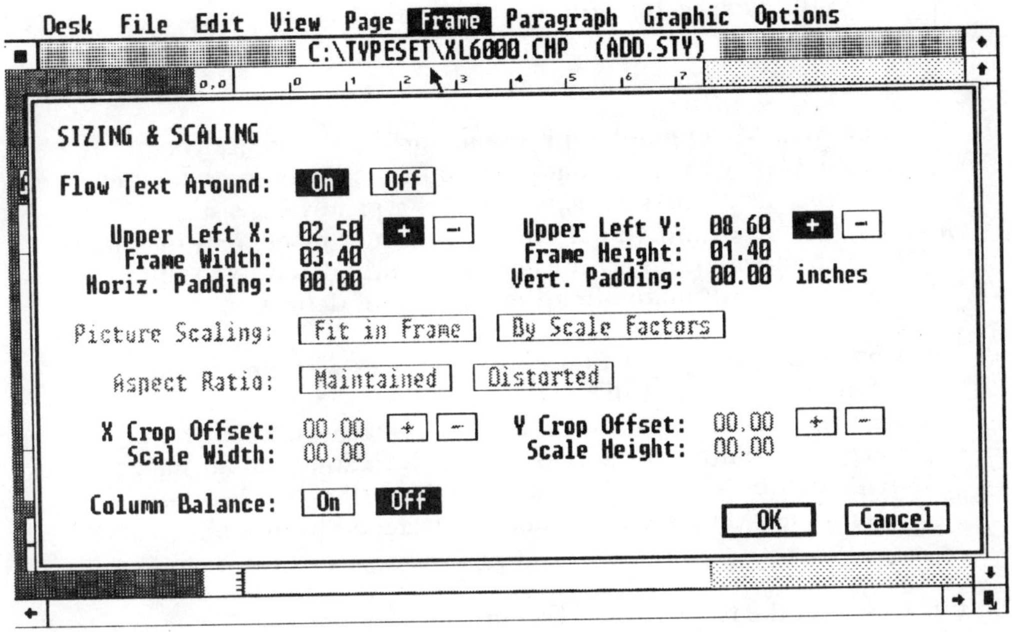

Figure 5.36

After making the necessary adjustments, complete sizing and scaling the frame by pressing

[return]

LOADING A PICTURE FILE

Now that you have created a frame, you can load the picture. Point the mouse at the File menu heading. Point at the Load Text/Picture option and click the button.

Until now, you have loaded only text files into a document. This time, you must change the type of file you want to load. Ventura allows you to load two types of graphics:

1. **Line Art.** Many graphic programs for the PC create vector graphics, which means that graphic files contain mathematical descriptions of images. Line art files typically consist of descriptions of individual objects and their placement in relation to each other. Line art files can be manipulated to fit different frames and still maintain a high degree of definition.

2. **Image Art.** Image art files contain images with one-to-one relationships to dots displayed on the computer screen. If a scanner is used to capture a printed image, it is usually stored in an image file. Since image files contain a facsimile of an image – not mathematical descriptions as in line art – they tend to lose definition if they are expanded or stretched to fit a new frame.

In this example, the file type is a line art file produced by Lotus 1-2-3. The file is a Lotus 1-2-3 picture file with a .PIC extension and is of the type produced when you use the /Graph Save command. Ventura does not read 1-2-3 worksheet files (WKS, WK1, etc.).

Point the mouse at Line Art and click the button. Ventura displays the line art formats it supports. Point the mouse at Lotus .PIC and click the button. Press

[return]

Ventura displays the ITEM SELECTOR box. The file extension .PIC is automatically selected. You must inform Ventura of the directory containing the picture file. In this example, it is assumed that the picture file is stored in a directory named \123. Ventura currently displays the TYPESET directory.

To move up one level to the root directory, point the mouse at the black box in the upper left corner of the ITEM SELECTOR box. Click the button. The other directories are displayed. A diamond symbol appears before each directory listing.

Point the mouse at the diamond next to 123 and click the button, which will display all the PIC files in the \123 directory. The file prepared for this document—COMPARE.PIC—will be displayed.

Point the mouse at the COMPARE.PIC file listing and quickly click the mouse twice. Ventura loads the file and displays the picture within the new frame.

To get a closer look at the picture, point the mouse at the upper left corner of the picture's frame. Enter

[Ctrl/n]

(see Figure 5.37)

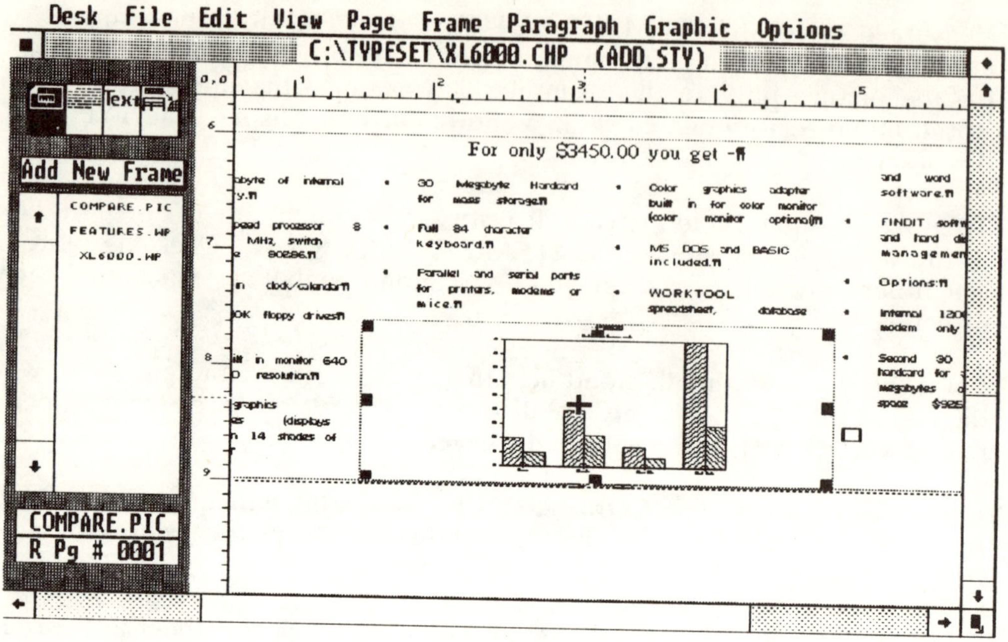

Figure 5.37

SCALING A PICTURE

The picture displayed in the frame is the entire 1-2-3 graphic. Ventura attempts to place the image inside the frame and maintain the original scale and height-to-width ratio.

Ventura includes many ways in which you can change the size and scale of an image. For example, the frame you created for the picture is a rectangle that is more than twice as wide as it is high. When Ventura attempts to maintain the original height-to-width ratio, it must reduce the size of the image. In this case, you might want to distort the original image to better fit the space you have created in this document for the image.

Point the mouse at the Frame menu heading. Then, point the mouse at the Sizing and Scaling option and click the button. The SIZING & SCALING menu appears:

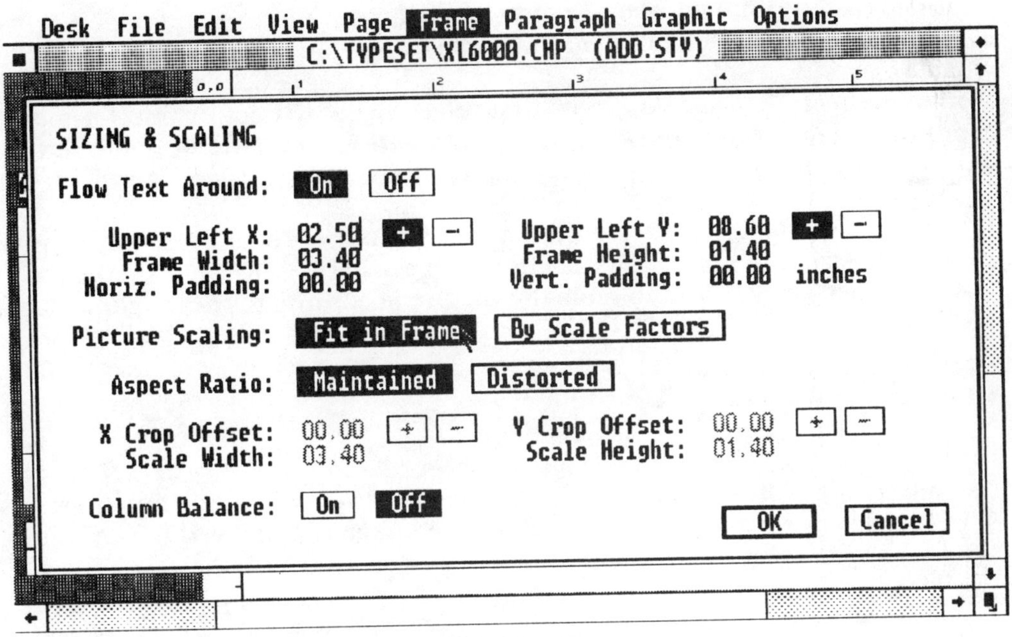

Figure 5.38

In the center of the display are two important options:

1. **Picture Scaling**. This option can be set for Fit to Frame or Scale by Factors. Fit to Frame instructs Ventura to use the current shape of the frame as a guide to how the picture should be scaled. When selected, this option calculates a scale that will allow the entire image to appear in the frame. Scale by Factors allows you to select an area of the overall picture to display in the frame, which is called **cropping**—a term borrowed from the field of photography.

2. **Aspect Ratio**. **Aspect** refers to the relative weight assigned to the width and the height factors used to scale the picture. Ventura has two options. **Maintained** instructs Ventura to maintain the original values for height-to-width ratio, even if the image is cropped. **Distorted** allows you to enter your own values for the height and width scaling. Because you can control the height and width factors separately, you can push, pull, stretch, and compress the image as needed.

For example, you might need to change the aspect ratio of an image so that it is horizontally stretched to fill empty space on the sides of the frame.

To make these changes, you must first select Scale by Factors and Distorted from the menu. Point the mouse at Scale by Factors and click the button. Point the mouse at Distorted and click the button.

You now have access to the settings at the bottom of the screen that control the image size and scale. The Scale Width setting is 3.40" and the height is 1.4". To instruct Ventura to scale the picture according to these values, press

[return]

Ventura recalculates the scale of the image and displays a much larger graph. The graph is now so large that not all of the image is displayed in the frame.

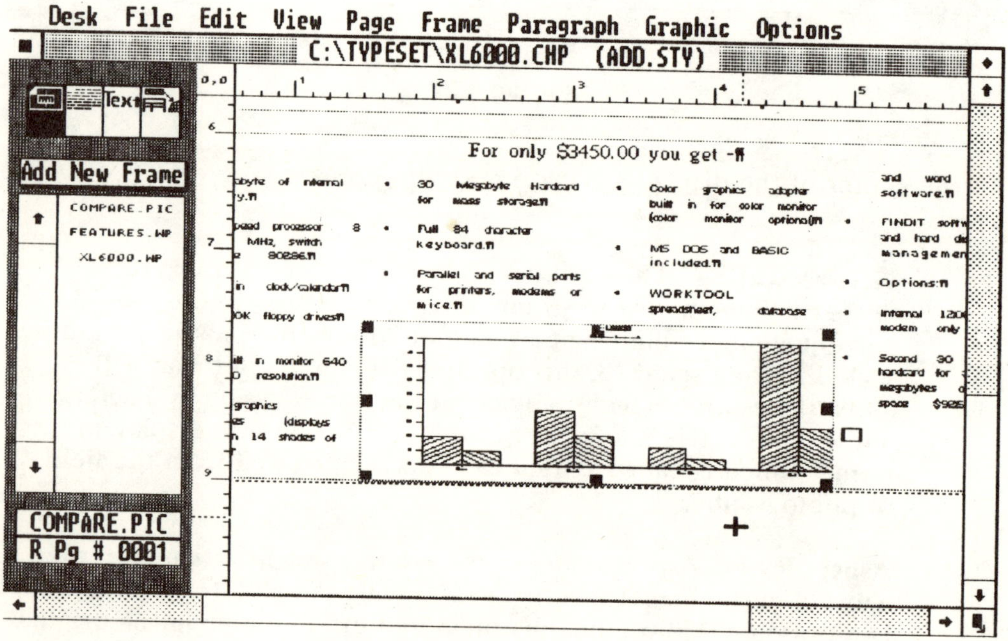

Figure 5.39

DISTORTING THE IMAGE

Ventura allows you to distort the height-to-width ratio of the picture. Point the mouse at the Frame menu heading. Then, point at the Sizing and Scaling option and click the button.

In this example, you might notice that the width of the graph is too large for the frame. You can reduce the width by changing the scaling factor for width. Currently, that value is 3.40".

Point the mouse at the "0" in 3.40" and click the button. Change the value to 3.20" by entering

[backspace]
[backspace]
20
[return]

The graph fits the frame because its width is scaled down:

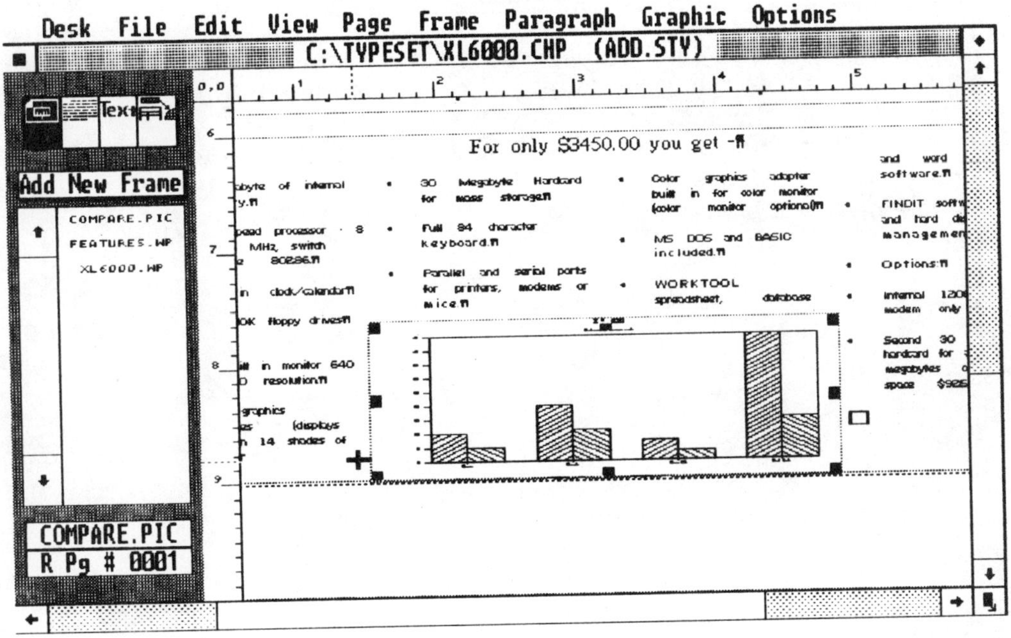

Figure 5.40

You can distort the image as much as necessary. In the current display, most of the bars are small because a single bar is much larger than the others. Suppose you want to enlarge the bottom portion of the graph to show more detail of the small bars. Point the mouse at the Frame menu heading. Then, point at the Sizing and Scaling option and click the button. In this case, you want to increase the value for Scale Height, which is currently 1.40".

Point the mouse at the "0" in 1.40" and click the button. Change the value by entering

[Esc]
02.25
[return]

Ventura recalculates the picture and displays the expanded graph, but the effect is not quite what you intended; the expanded graph displays only the top part without the small bars.

CROPPING WITH THE MOUSE

When an image is scaled so that only part of it can be viewed in the frame, you can crop it by using the mouse in combination with the [Alt] key.

Point the mouse inside the graph's frame. Press and hold the Alt key. While depressing the Alt key, press and hold the mouse button. The mouse cursor will change to a hand.

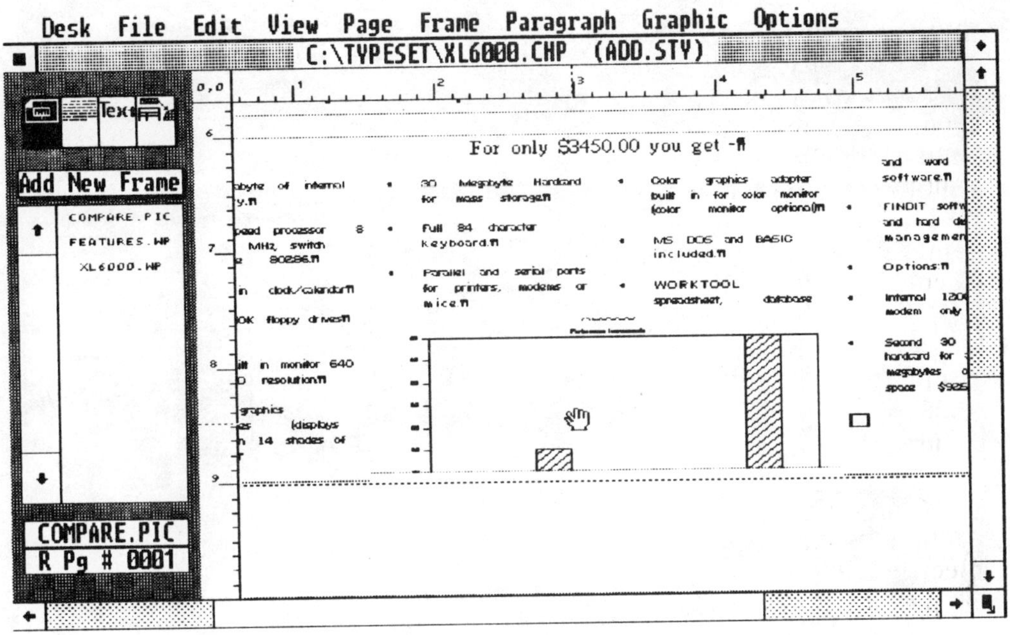

Figure 5.41

With the Alt key and mouse button still depressed, move the mouse up approximately 1". As you do so, the picture will scroll with the mouse.

Release the mouse button and the Alt key. Ventura redraws the graph to include the bottom portion of the image.

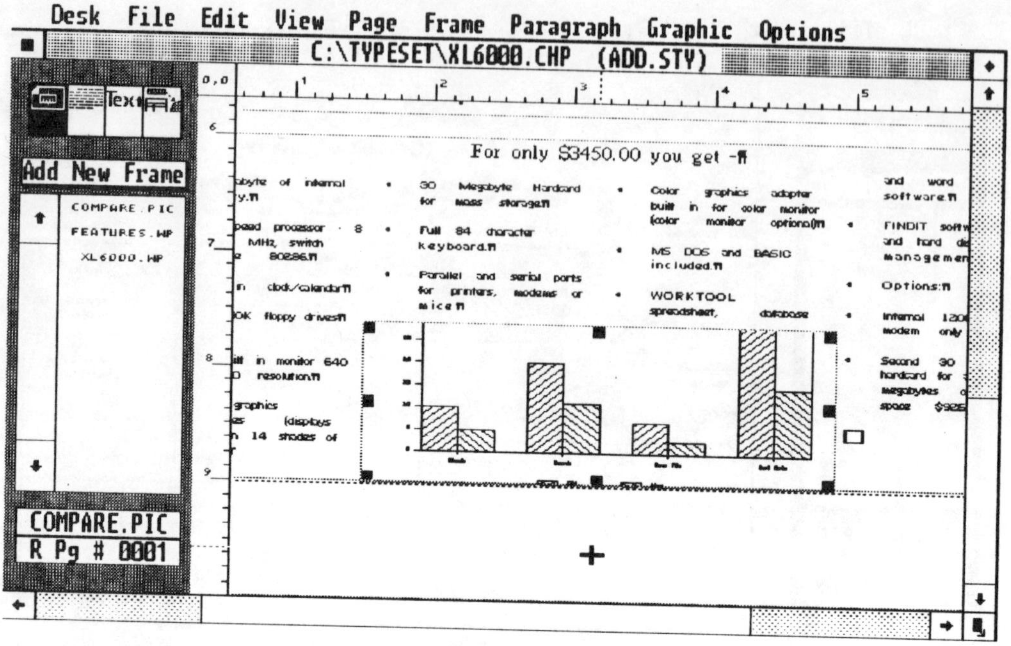

Figure 5.42

Cropping can also be performed with actual numerical values. Point the mouse at the Frame menu heading. Then, point at the Sizing and Scaling option and click the button.

If you examine the value for Y Crop Offset, you will see that it has changed from 0.00" to another value – probably .75" or .85". The Y Crop value indicates the amount of space (up or down) that the image has been cropped. The + or - symbols indicate the direction of the crop.

The X Crop value indicates horizontal cropping. This value is the number of inches the image has been cropped. If you want to, you can enter a specific value for X or Y cropping.

Point the mouse at the Y Crop Offset value and click the button. Enter a new value:

[Esc]
.80
[return]

The image is adjusted to the new cropping position. To see the final document you have created, return to the Reduced View mode. Enter

[Ctrl/r]

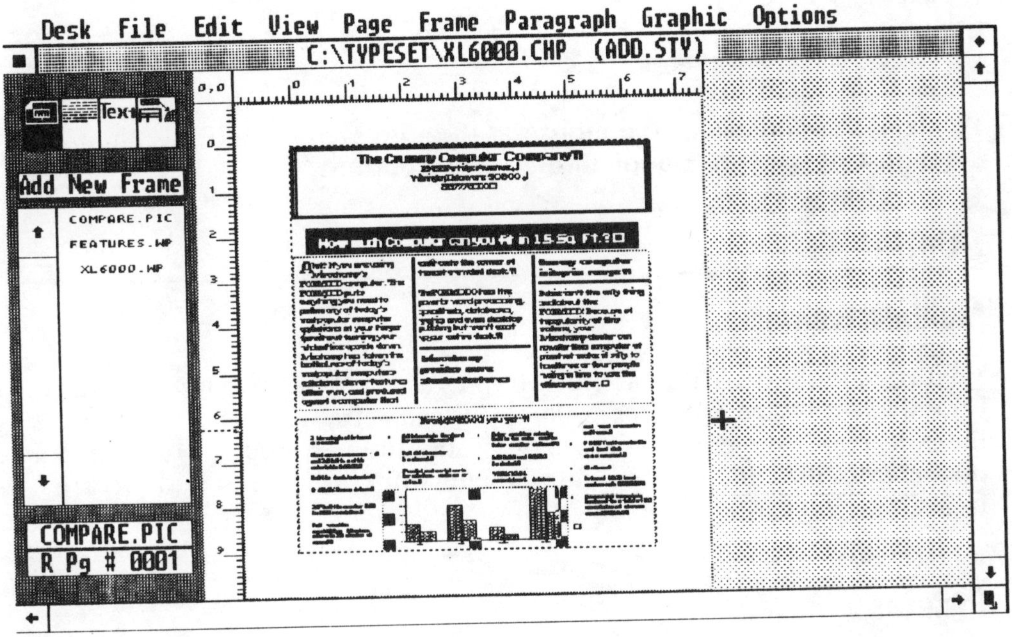

Figure 5.43

This document is the result of several different files inserted into a number of different frames on a single page. Multiple frames allow you to create different formats at different positions on the page. Each frame's layout is independent of the other frames; however, when frames are layered in the same position, Ventura flows text from the underlying frame around the new frame.

Print your document by pointing the mouse at the File menu heading. Then, point at the To Print option and click the button. Point the mouse at OK and click the button again. Save the chapter by entering

[Ctrl/s]
xl6000
[return]

To clear Ventura, point the mouse at the File menu heading. Then, point the mouse at the New option and click the button.

SUMMARY

Multiple Frames

Ventura allows you to add as many frames as necessary to a document. Ventura always creates a master frame. All other frames are created by using the Add New Frame option available in the Frames mode. Multiple- frame documents allow you to combine elements from several text and picture files in a single Ventura document.

Pictures

Ventura is compatible with a variety of programs that produce graphic or picture files. The most common ones are graph files with PIC extensions from Lotus 1-2-3.

Drawing Frames

When Add New Frame is selected, you can draw a frame on the current page. The mouse cursor changes to a special symbol indicating that the frame-drawing mode is active. Frames can be of any size (up to a full page). Frame-drawing is aided by Line and Column Snap features, but it is not affected by grid settings, which affect only graphics in the Graphic mode.

Sizing Frames

The size of frames can be specified by numeric values through the Sizing and Scaling Option in the Frame menu.

Reverse Lettering

You can achieve white-on-black printing by changing the font color to white and the frame background to black.

Columns

A frame can be divided into as many as eight columns. You can select columns from the Margins & Columns option in the Frame menu. Ventura allows you to specify a gutter between columns to separate text.

Vertical Lines

Ventura automatically draws vertical lines between columns in a frame. The Vertical Rules option in the Frame menu allows you select inter-column lines. You can also specify 1 or 2 vertical lines to be drawn at specific horizontal positions within a frame.

Special Effects

Ventura allows you to create two special effects for paragraph formats. The first – Big First Character – allows you to select a large font and point size for the first letter in a paragraph. The second is a bullet format. The bullet automatically indents a paragraph and places a character (e.g., a black dot) in front of each paragraph.

CHAPTER 6

MULTIPLE-PAGE LAYOUTS

Until now, all documents you have prepared have been single-page layouts, which in business is the most common use for programs like Ventura, but Ventura also has the power to format multiple-page documents from letters, reports, or even an entire book.

Multiple-page documents combine many features and techniques already discussed in the chapters on single-page layouts. In addition, multiple-page documents include page headers, footers, page numbers, tables of contents, and page indexes.

Unlike the small documents you have worked with, multiple-page documents usually consist of one large text file, perhaps supported by small files containing charts, tables, or illustrations. A book might consist of one large text file for each chapter, with illustration files inserted into frames throughout the text. Chapter summaries might be separate text files inserted into frames at the ends of chapters.

When creating large documents, you need to use different strategies from those used in the earlier chapters. In each previous example document, you prepared the text for the document in a word processor, but you didn't format the paragraphs until you loaded the text into a Ventura frame. You then used paragraph tagging to format different paragraphs. While large documents can be handled in the same way, Ventura provides a more efficient way of tagging paragraphs, which is important because large documents contain many more paragraphs than small, single-page text files.

The key to this technique is to insert codes into the text of the document as you type it in your word processor. Ventura usually recognizes simple formatting, such as bold and underlined text, performed in compatible word processor files, which means that if you use the bold command ([F6] in WordPerfect) or the underline command ([F8] in WordPerfect), Ventura recognizes the text attributes and formats and implements those effects when the file is loaded into Ventura. Bold text requires that the selected font include a bold font. If only a normal typeface is available, Ventura displays all text as normal; however, the bold code will remain in the document. If you change the font to one that includes a bold version, the bold will then appear. Formatting codes that affect margins, font styles, point size, or other sophisticated attributes implemented in your word processor, however, will not be translated into Ventura when the file is loaded.

In some ways, this aspect of Ventura is unfortunate. In large documents, the best time to add many of these attributes is as the text is initially being prepared. Word processors generally work more quickly than Ventura for entering and editing text, but Ventura does allow you to enter formatting instructions into a document's text. These instructions follow a special format that Ventura recognizes and converts into Ventura format features. The codes are entered as regular text. To learn how these codes are entered, you must load your word processing program. Then, you are ready to learn about text formatting codes.

TEXT FORMATTING CODES

To understand how Ventura works with text formatting codes, begin by loading the file prepared in Chapter 5–FEATURES.WP. When you load the document, you will see that Ventura has altered the document to include special text codes indicating the formatting tags used for each paragraph.

```
@COL HEAD = For only $3450.00 you get -←
@FEATURE = 1 Megabyte of internal memory.←
@FEATURE = Dual speed processor - 8 and 10 MHz, switch selectable
80286.←
@FEATURE = Built in clock/calendar←
@FEATURE = 2 - 360K floppy drives←
@FEATURE = 14" built in monitor 640 by 350 resolution.←
@FEATURE = Full graphics capabilities (displays colors in 14
shades of green)←
@FEATURE = 30 Megabyte Hardcard for mass storage.←
@FEATURE = Full 84 character keyboard.←
@FEATURE = Parallel and serial ports for printers, modems or
mice.←
@FEATURE = Color graphics adapter built in for color monitor
(color monitor optional)←
@FEATURE = MS DOS and BASIC included.←
@FEATURE = WORKTOOL spreadsheet, database and word processing
software.←
@FEATURE = FINDIT software for file and hard disk management.←
@FEATURE = Options:←
@FEATURE = Internal 1200 baud modem only $225.00←
@FEATURE = Second 30 Megabyte hardcard for a total of 60
megabytes of storage space $925.00.←
←
C:\WP\FEATURES.WP                         Doc 1  Pg 1  Ln 1     Pos 10
```

Figure 6.1

Ventura uses a special format to assign tags to paragraphs. The @ sign must be the first character in the paragraph, followed by the name of the style tag, a space, an = sign, another space, and then the text of the paragraph.

When paragraphs are tagged in Ventura, Ventura modifies your text file to include text codes corresponding to formatting tags assigned in Ventura. The relationship between Ventura and text files has several important implications:

1. When a file is loaded into a Ventura chapter, the text of the file is modified to reflect editing changes and style formats applied to the paragraphs, which means that your original document will not remain the same after it has been loaded into Ventura. In addition to adding Ventura formats, all nonconverted word processing formats, such as margin changes, will be eliminated from the text file.

2. If you want to preserve your text file in its original word processor format, including margin and pitch settings, make a separate copy of the file before you import it into Ventura.

3. You can add or change Ventura formats and style tags by typing appropriate text codes into your word processor document, which means that you can style a document you are creating or revise the tags in a document previously loaded into Ventura. This capability enables you to use features such as Search and Replace to quickly change style tags in a large document.

4. If you do not enter a style tag code at the beginning of a paragraph, Ventura assigns the Body Text tag to that paragraph.

In addition to style tags, you can insert text formatting codes to control Ventura features such as font and point size, footnotes, and index entries. Codes such as these are nested in angle brackets (< >). For example, to change the point size of a word from the standard size specified in the style tag, type

This is <P014>14 Point<P255> text.

The <P014> command instructs Ventura to change the point size to 14, and the <P255> command instructs Ventura to return to the normal point size for that style tag. You must take special care if you want to include the <, >, or @ characters in your text. The @ is only a problem if it is the first character in a paragraph, which is unusual in most documents but may come up in writing on technical topics, such as computer software, in which @ is often used as part of a computer command or function. In such cases, use @@ at the beginning of the paragraph. Ventura will recognize that the text is not a tag code, and the Ventura document will include only a single @. Angle brackets (< >) are considered to be part of a code whenever they appear. If you want to include them in you text (e.g., <return> or greater than or less than signs), nest the text inside a pair of angle brackets (<<return>> appears in Ventura as <return>). If possible, avoid this problem by using [] or {} brackets, which Ventura treats as text characters instead of codes.

By entering style tags directly into your text, you pre-format the document with the desired style codes; you needn't go through a long document and manually tag each paragraph. This procedure can save you time and effort, since it will generally take longer to format in Ventura then to enter the codes in your word processor document.

CREATING A TAGGED TEXT FILE

Begin with a new document. If you are using WordPerfect, press

[F7]
n
n

to clear the text window.

You are to prepare a report on the world's smallest country – Andorra. Instead of merely entering the text, you will also directly insert style tags and formatting commands into the document. When Ventura loads the text file, these codes will have the same effects as if you entered them from Ventura menus.

One way to determine the tags to use is to enter names of style tags used in a previously created style sheet file, but you are not limited to this method. You can begin a document and create style tag names that have not previously been used.

When Ventura encounters a unknown style tag in the text, it automatically creates a style tag and places the name of the tag into the side bar style box. Of course, Ventura does not recognize characteristics you want to assign to the tag; it simply assigns the new tag the same formatting settings as the Body Text style.

You still must create settings to distinguish paragraph styles from each other, but all paragraphs to be formatted with a particular style are already designated as such. If you change the style of any one of the paragraphs, Ventura automatically updates all paragraphs of the same format throughout the entire document. This ability is the primary advantage of using Ventura.

For example, in the report you are about to create, you will enter a number of topic headings. By tagging each topic heading with a specific tag (for example, @SUB HEAD), you instruct Ventura to automatically format all @SUB HEAD lines as soon as you define the fonts and setting for any one of the paragraphs.

To begin, enter the major heading for the report. Take care to enter a space before and after the = sign. Enter

@MAJOR HEAD = THE WORLD'S SMALLEST NATION
[return]

The next line will be the first subheading in the document. Enter

@SUB HEAD = ABOUT ANDORRA

The next two paragraphs will be normal body text. Enter the following two paragraphs:

In a world of powers and super-powers that fight to be the largest and most powerful nations, somebody has to be at the bottom of the ladder. That nation is the tiny mountain land of Andorra.

The nation of Andorra is officially called the Valleys of Andorra. The nation is located in the heart of the Pyrenees Mountains between the better known nations of France and Spain. Andorra marks the beginning of the Iberian peninsula.

The document should resemble Figure 6.2.

```
@MAJOR HEAD = THE WORLD'S SMALLEST NATION←
@SUB HEAD = ABOUT ANDORRA←
In a world of powers and super-powers that fight to be the
largest and most powerful nations, somebody has to be at the
bottom of the ladder. That nation is the tiny mountain land of
Andorra.←
The nation of Andorra is officially called the Valleys of
Andorra.  The nation is located in the heart of the Pyrenees
Mountains between the better known nations of France and Spain.
Andorra marks the beginning of the Iberian peninsula.←

                                        Doc 2  Pg 1  Ln 11      Pos 10
```

Figure 6.2

ADDING FOOTNOTES

Ventura supports the inclusion of footnotes in the text of the document. You can create footnotes in Ventura, but by far the best way to enter footnotes is directly into the text file. Enter the next section heading in the document, but do *not* press [return] at the end of the line.

@SUB HEAD = VITAL STATISTICS

Suppose that you needed to footnote the information in this section. To create a footnote, you type the text of that footnote into a special code. The code is placed into the text document at the position in the text where you want the footnote reference to be placed. Ventura will automatically number the footnotes and place the footnote text at the bottom of the appropriate page. Footnotes are created by entering <$F *xxxxxxxxx*> where *xxxxxxxxxx* is the text of the footnote. Enter

<$FWorld Almanac, Enterprise Associates, 1985>
[return]

The text entered into the code will appear as a footnote. The next item on the list is a topic heading. Enter

@TOPIC = POPULATION
[return]

Enter the following paragraph, but do *not* press [return] at the end.

The 35,000 people of Andorra live on 188 square miles of land. That is a population density of about 180.85 people per square mile. The United States has an average population of about 65 people per square mile, the Soviet Union 30 people per square mile, and China 278 people per square mile.

ANCHORING FRAMES

Suppose that you intended to create a graph using Lotus 1-2-3 to compare population densities among the countries mentioned in the text. In small, single-page layouts, the position of frames is determined visually; however, in multiple-page documents, the position of frames within the text is determined by the text itself. For example, the graph of population densities should always follow the paragraph about population. Ventura allows you to insert **anchors** into the text. Anchors are markers that indicate where in the text frames should be positioned. Anchors are important in large documents because they can be used to rearrange frames automatically, based on the position of the text in the document. This feature helps maintain the correct layout even when the text is altered.

An anchor is a special code that contains the name of the frame. As with the names of the style tags, it is not necessary to have created the frame. You can merely anticipate that you will eventually create such a frame and that it should be located at this position in the text. Enter

<$&pop density[V]>

The [V] tells Ventura that the frame should be placed below the anchor. If you had entered [^], Ventura would place the frame above the anchor in the text.

INDEX ENTRIES

Another type of entry that can be added directly to the text of your document is an **index reference**. These references will not appear in the text of your document but are used to generate an index of topics. Ventura uses the location of the index items to determine the page numbers for the index items. As with footnotes, you can also enter index codes in Ventura using the Ventura menu options; however, it is usually easier and faster to enter the index items in your word processor.

For example, suppose you want to generate an index for this report. You can insert codes into the text that will create those index references. Keep in mind that you do not have to generate an index even though you enter index codes. Entering the codes simply gives you that option should you later decide to produce the index.

Suppose that you wanted to create an index entry for population density. The code symbol for an index entry is $I. A simple index entry would resemble the following:

<$Ipopulation density>

Ventura also allows you to create major headings and subheadings for the index. For example, if you had several entries for "population," you could enter "population" as the main heading and the particular topic as a subheading. A semicolon is used to separate the major heading from the subheading, for example,

<$Ipopulation;density>
<$Ipopulation;totals>

The result would be an entry in the index that looks like the following:

Population
    density, 2
    totals, 3

Note that Ventura permits you to add a **sort order key** to index entries. A sort order key is used to determine the placement of an item in the index if you do not want Ventura to sort strictly according to alphabetical order. For example, an index entry might read, "The Second World War." You can insert a sort order for either the major entry or the subentry. For example,

<$IThe Second World War[War]>

In this case, create a simple entry for population density. Enter

<$Ipopulation;density>
[return]

You now know how to create special text codes that will save you time in formatting a document in Ventura. Following is the completed report on Andorra. Enter the rest of the text. The arrows indicate when to press [return].

```
@MAJOR HEAD = THE WORLD'S SMALLEST NATION←
@SUB HEAD = ABOUT ANDORRA←
In a world of powers and super-powers that fight to be the
largest and most powerful nations, somebody has to be at the
bottom of the ladder. That nation is the tiny mountain land of
Andorra.←
The nation of Andorra is officially called the Valleys of
Andorra.  The nation is located in the heart of the Pyrenees
Mountains between the better known nations of France and Spain.
Andorra marks the beginning of the Iberian peninsula.←
@SUB HEAD = VITAL STATISTICS<$FWorld Almanac, Enterprise
Association, 1985>←
@TOPIC = POPULATION←
The 35,000 people of Andorra live on 188 square miles of land.
That is a population density of about 180.85 people per square
mile.  The United States has an average population of about 65
people per square mile, the Soviet Union 30 people per square
mile, and China 278 people per square mile.<$&pop
density[V]><$Ipopulation density>←
@TOPIC = ETHNIC GROUPS←
Andorra is populated by three major ethnic grouping. Despite
Andorra's long history these groups live in rather separate
lives. The majority of the Andorrans are Spanish while the native
Andorran population is minority of about
30%.<$&enthic[V]><$Iethnic groups>←
@SUB TOPIC = HEALTH RATES←
Andorra has an annual birth rate of 16.5 per thousand. The death
rate is 5.0 per thousand anually. The population shows a natural
increase rate of 1.2%.←
@SUB HEAD = COMMUNICATIONS IN ANDORRA←
Andorra has rather limited communication in comparison to its
neighbor to the north, France. Andorra has about 10,000
telephones currently install, about 6,000 radios and some 3,000
televisions sets and a single big screen set located in the
capital city, Andorra la Vella.<$&comminications[V]>←
@SUB HEAD = GOVERNMENT←
@TOPIC = HEAD OF STATE←
Andorra is ruled by two princes.  One is usually the head of
state in France and the other is the Bishop of Urgel in Spain.
This joint sovereignty has been in effect since 1278. The current
co-princes are Francois Mitterrand, President of France and teh
current Roman Catholic Bishop of Urgel, Spain, Joan Marti y
Alanis.←
@TOPIC = DIVISIONS←
Andorra is divided in seven parishes.←
@TOPIC = HEAD OF GOVERNMENT←
Andorra is ruled by a local governor who is appointed by the
local council. The current head is Syndic Estanislao Sangra Font,
elected in January of 1971.←
@SUB HEAD = ECONOMICS←
@TOPIC = INDUSTRY←
The main economic activity is tourism and some goat herding.
Sheep were introduced from Spain in 1856 but mirgated back over
the Pyrenees to the warmer climate of Spain.←
@TOPIC = LABOR←
Some 20% of the population is engaged in agricultural activities.
The remained of the population is employed in government
services.←
The mainstay of the economy is tourism. Andorra is a major ski
center for southern France. Unfortunately the Spanish don't ski.
Andorra is a duty free country that attracts some 7 million
tourists a year.←
@TOPIC = CURRENCY←
Andorrans use two types of currency.←
@LIST = The French franc.←
@LIST = The Spanish peseta.←
```

When you have completed the text, save it as ANDORRA.WP. You can exit your word processing program once you have completed this task.

LOTUS DATA

In addition to the text entered into the file ANDORRA.WP, your report will include two other types of data: spreadsheet tables and graphics. The following figure shows a 1-2-3 spreadsheet that contains statistical data about Andorra:

```
A1: [W14]                                                        READY

         A              B        C        D        E        F        G
1
2                    Pop. Density
3   Andorra              180
4   China                278
5   USA                   65
6   USSR                  30
7
8
9                    In Use
10  Telephone         10,000
11  Radio              6,600
12  Television         3,000
13
14                   Ethnic
15  Spanish               60
16  Andorran              30
17  French                 6
18  Other                  4
19
20
19-Oct-87   12:41 AM
```

Figure 6.3

You can use this data to create graphs. Following are three graphs created from this data. If you have 1-2-3, you can create these graphs for use in your report. Remember to use the / G(raph) S(ave) command to create the PIC files needed for Ventura.

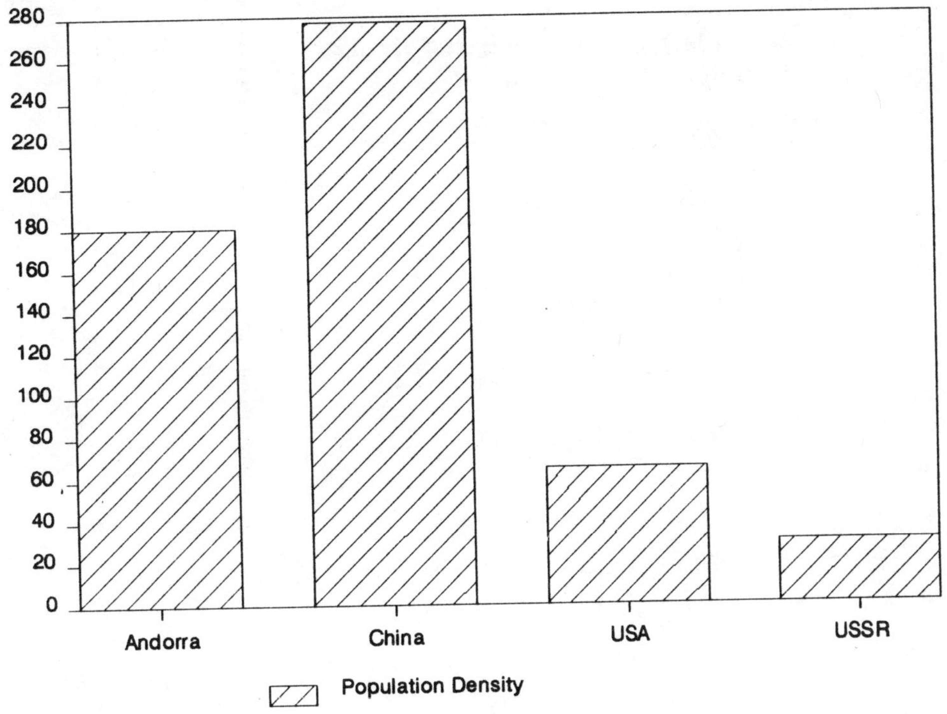
280
260
240
220
200
180
160
140
120
100
80
60
40
20
0
Andorra
China
USA
USSR
Population Density

POPDEN.PIC

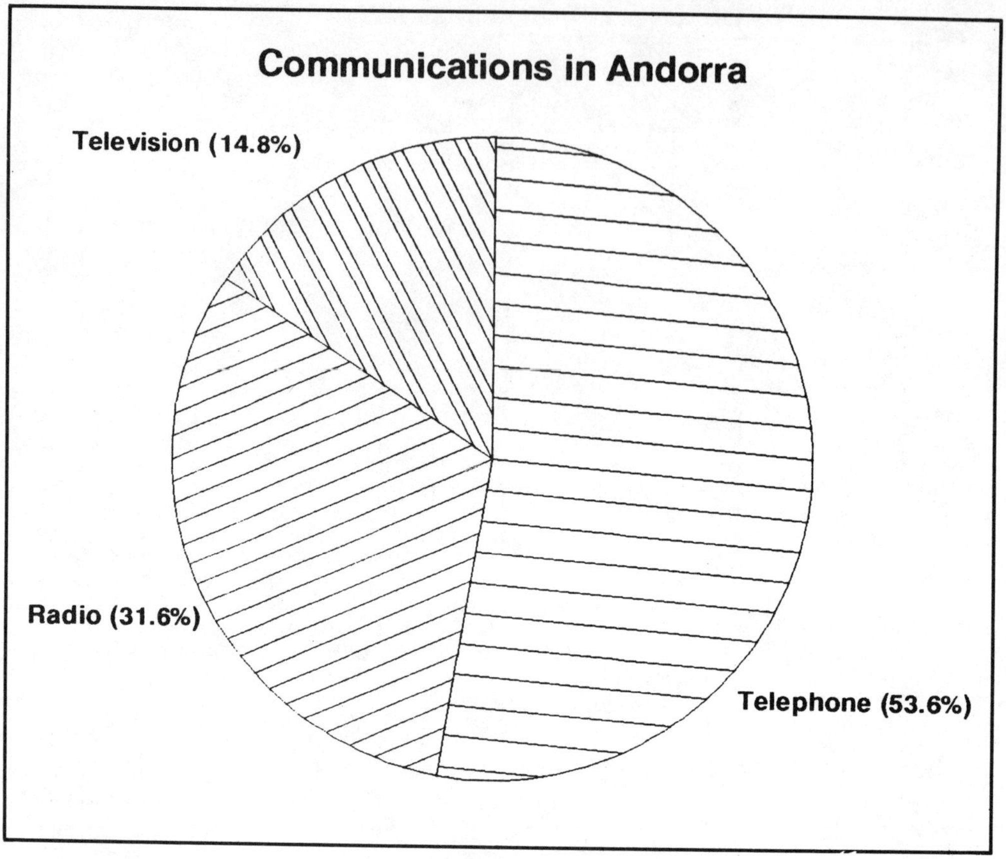
Communications in Andorra
Television (14.8%)
Radio (31.6%)
Telephone (53.6%)

COMM.PIC

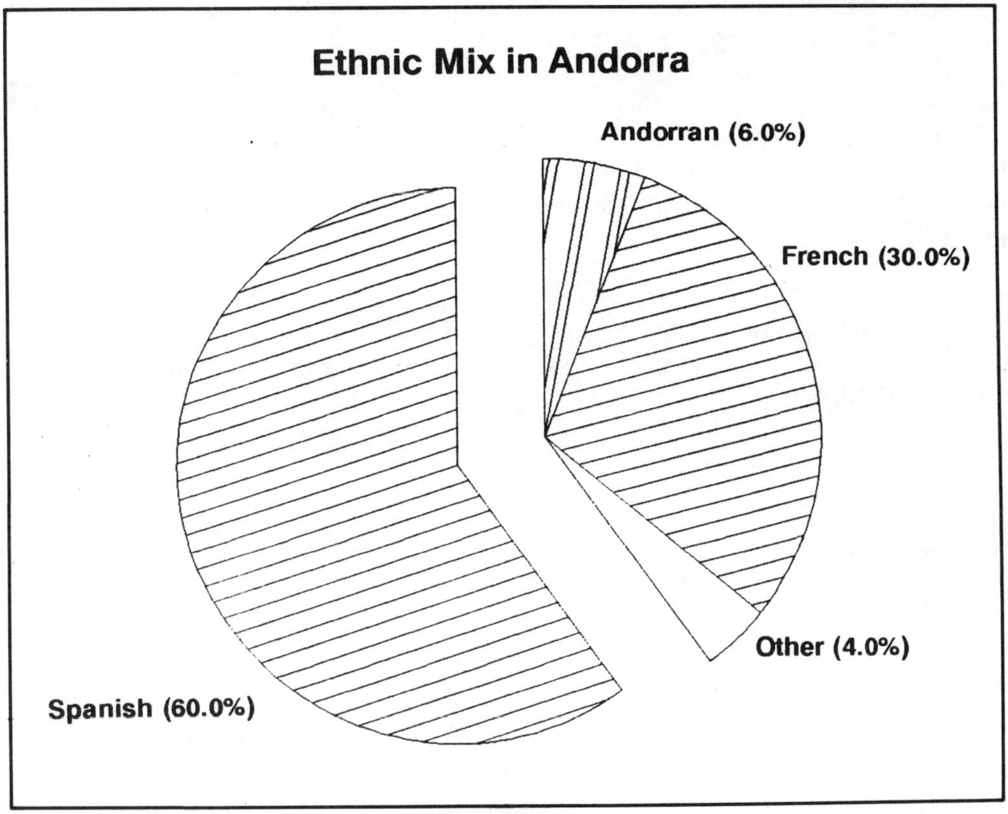
Ethnic Mix in Andorra
Andorran (6.0%)
French (30.0%)
Other (4.0%)
Spanish (60.0%)

ETHNIC.PIC

Transferring Text from 1-2-3

You can also create text files from 1-2-3 data. For example, suppose you wanted to insert the text of one of the statistical tables into your Ventura report. 1-2-3 files are not compatible with Ventura. But it is possible to create a text file that Ventura can load in the same way that it can load word processing files.

To create a text file with 1-2-3, you use the / <P>rint <F>ile command. For example, suppose in A9 through B12 of the worksheet, you have entered a table of communications information. To create a text file with that data, enter the following:

/pf
comm
[return]
r
a9.b12
[return]
oouq
gq

You have created a text file called COMM.PRN. 1-2-3 automatically attaches the PRN extension to the text file. (Note that the Option Other Unformatted command was used during the Print File to eliminate any margins or page breaks that 1-2-3 would normally insert into the text file. Because Ventura handles its own margins and page breaks, you want to eliminate any formatting done by 1-2-3.)

You now have all the text and graphic files you will need to create the Andorra report. Those files are as follows:

- ANDORRA.WP made with WordPerfect.
- POPDEN.PIC, COMM.PIC, and ETHNIC.PIC created with 1-2-3.
- COMM.PRN, a 1-2-3 text file.

You can now exit 1-2-3 and return to Ventura.

A REPORT STYLE SHEET

As with the other Ventura documents you have created, you will want to create a new style sheet for this report. In this case, the style tags will not be created manually but will automatically be generated by the special codes entered into the ANDORRA.WP text file. Place Ventura into the Reduced View mode and then into the Paragraph mode. Enter

[Ctrl/r]
[Ctrl/i]

To begin, load the DEFAULT style sheet. Point the mouse at the File menu heading. Then point the mouse at the Load Diff. Style selection and click the button. Enter

default
[return]

You are now ready to load the text of the ANDORRA.WP file into the master frame of this Ventura document. Note how Ventura automatically displays in the side bar the names of the style tags you entered into the text of the document, just as if you had created each tag in Ventura.

Point the mouse at the File menu heading. Then, point the mouse at the Load Text/Picture selection and click the button. Next, point the mouse at the Text option in the Type of File section and click the button. Point the mouse at the WordPerfect option in the Text Format section and click the button. Finally, point the mouse at OK and click the button.

You should now see a list of your word processor files. To load ANDORRA.WP, if necessary, point the mouse in the up or down arrow box and click the button until ANDORRA.WP appears in the list. Then, point the mouse at ANDORRA.WP, and click the button twice in rapid succession. Ventura loads the ANDORRA.WP file.

Note that in the Reduced View mode, the text may be illegible because the point size is too small. Change to the Paragraph mode by pressing

[Ctrl/i]

The side bar display shows the names of the style tags you entered into your document.

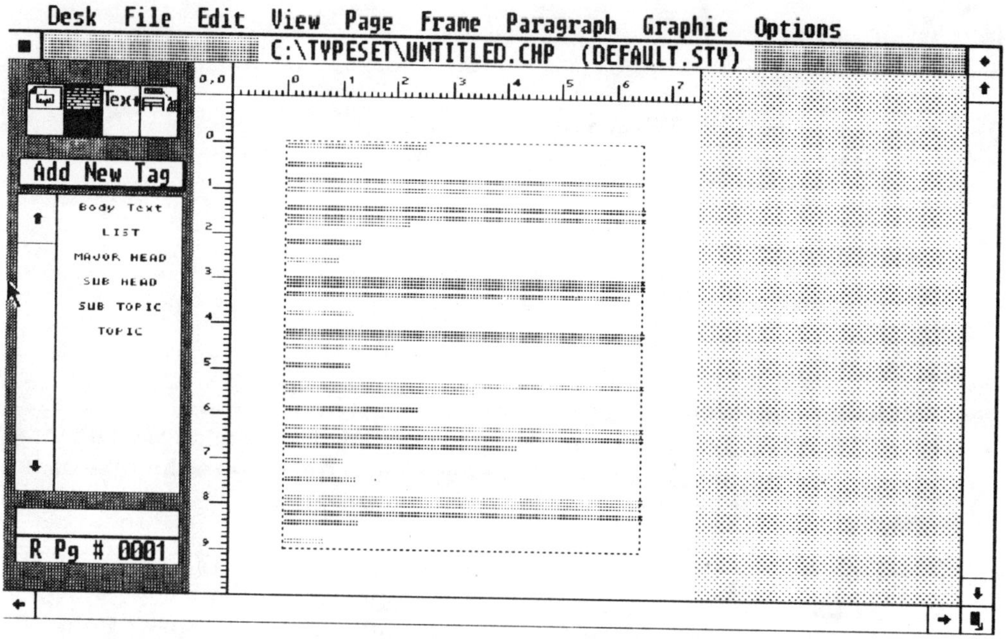

Figure 6.4

Your task is now much simpler than if you had loaded an unformatted document. You need only define the settings for each tab, and the style will flow through the entire document because each paragraph is already assigned its correct style tag.

To begin the processing of styling the document, you will want to change to the normal display mode. Point the mouse at upper left corner of the frame. Enter

[Ctrl/n]

HEADING STYLES

You are now ready to begin defining styles for the tags that you entered into the text file. First, you will want to assign style settings to the headings you have inserted into the document. At this point, all of the text looks the same. The style tags you entered into the ANDORRA.WP file were not defined in Ventura. When Ventura encountered a previously undefined tag name in the text, it automatically created a tag and assigned the tag the same settings as the Body Text tag.

Before you begin to differentiate the styles, create a new style sheet file. Point the mouse at the File menu heading. Then, point the mouse at the Save as New Style selection and click the button. Enter the name of the new style file:

report
[return]

You should now define the major heading of the report. To do so, point the mouse at the word "WORLD'S" and click the button.

The first paragraph should now be highlighted. Note that the name MAJOR HEAD appears in the box above the page number. The first choice is the font of the text. In this case, you will want to use a large typeface.

To choose a larger typeface, point the mouse at the Paragraph menu heading. Then, point the mouse at the Font selection and click the button. For this example, choose Swiss 24-Point bold. Point the mouse at the Swiss option and click the button. Then, point the mouse at the number 24 and click the button. Complete the entry by pressing

[return]

The major heading now stands out because of its new font.

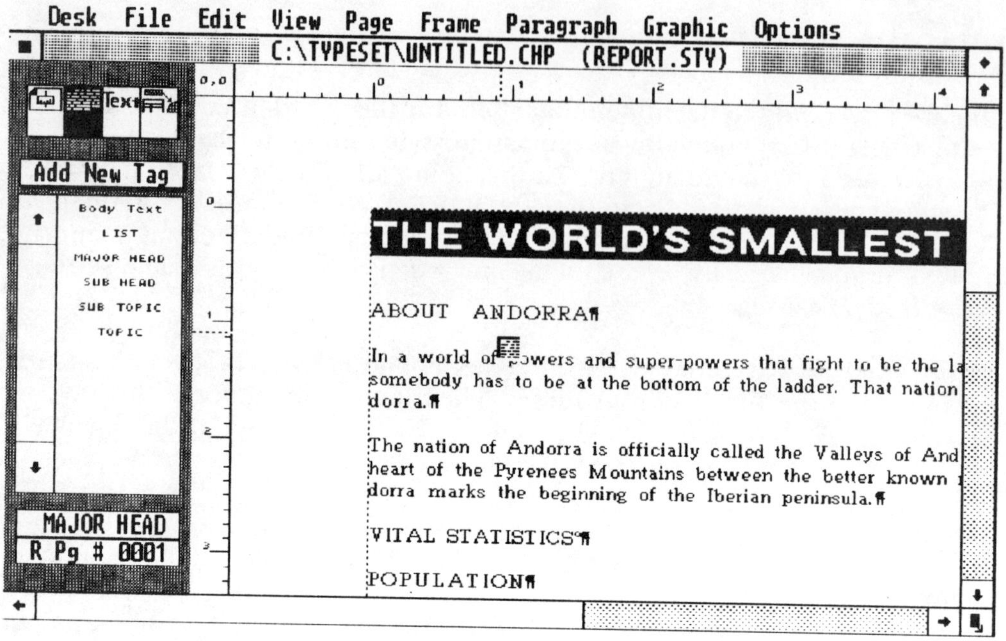

Figure 6.5

Spacing for Major Headings

While changing the font is useful for making headings stand out, it is not the only tool available for creating a more dramatic layout. A major heading, such as the title of a chapter in a book, can have spacing settings to increase its effect.

In this case, you might want to place several inches of blank space above the heading so that it will begin about 1/3 of the way down the page. This type of spacing is often used in books to mark off chapters. Point the mouse at the Paragraph menu heading. Then, point the mouse at the Spacing selection and click the button. Enter a new value for the space above the paragraph:

[Esc]
02.5
[return]

Notice that the heading appears in exactly the same place as it was before you entered the new value. The problem has to do with a special setting on the SPACING menu. Return to the SPACING menu by pointing the mouse at the Paragraph menu heading and then pointing the mouse at the Spacing selection and clicking the button.

In the center of the box, you will see the Add in Above setting. The currently selected option is When Not at Column Top. This setting is used to avoid placing blank space at the top of a page. But in this case, you want the space to be placed above the heading because it is at the top of the page.

Point the mouse at the Always option and click the button. Then, press

[return]

With this change, the spacing is inserted above the major heading.

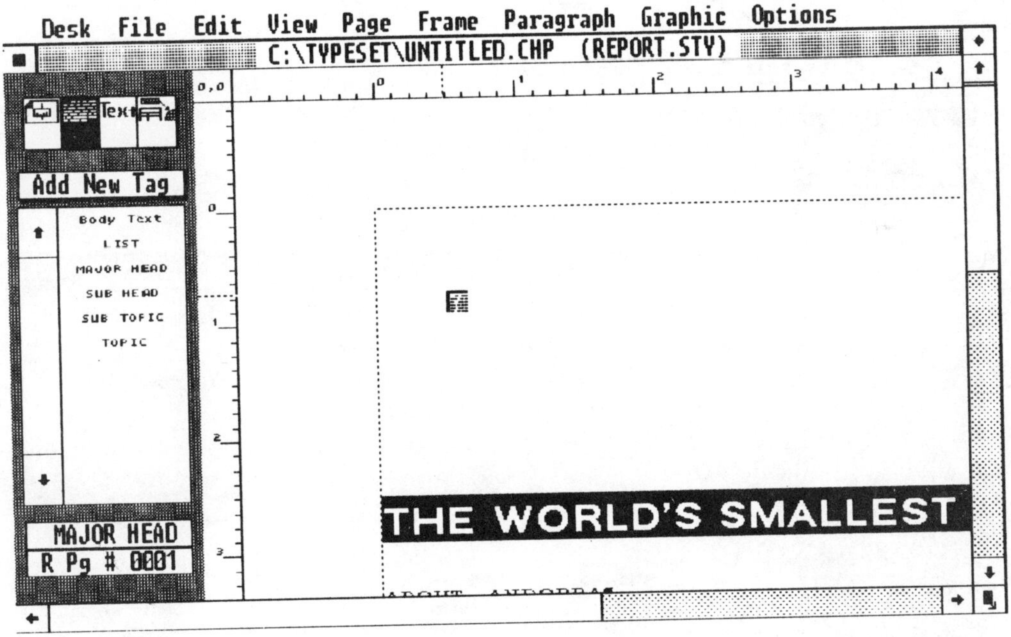

Figure 6.6

In addition to space above, you will want to create additional space below the major heading. Point the mouse at the Paragraph menu heading. Then, point the mouse at the Spacing selection and click the button.

The general rule about spacing is that you should have half as much space below a line as you do above the line. If the space above a line is 2.5", the space below should be 1.25". Enter

[down arrow]
[Esc]
01.25

The rest of the text probably extends beyond the display window. To change the window, point the mouse at the word "THE," and press

[Ctrl/n]

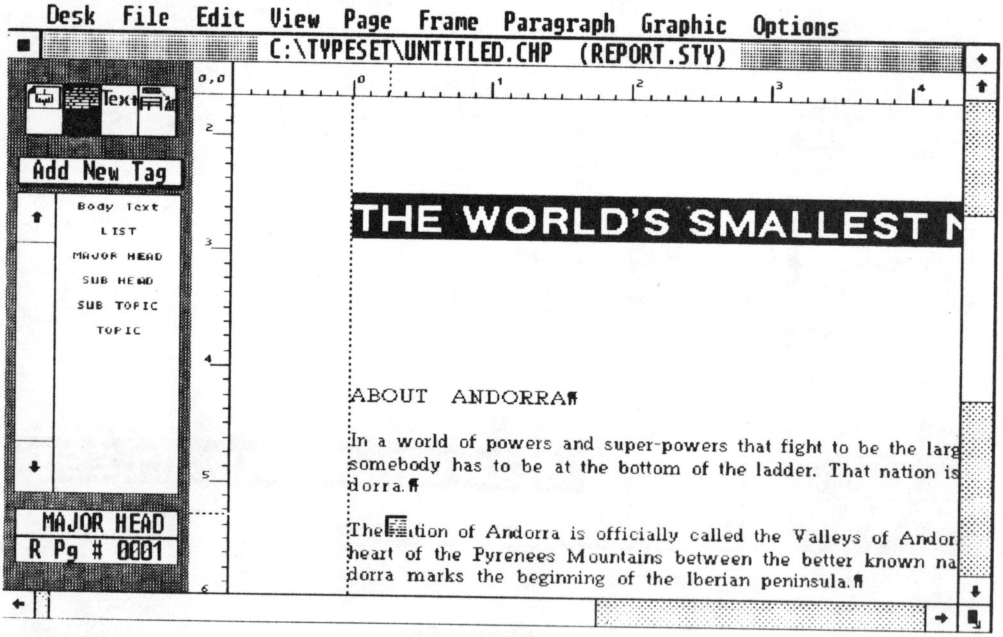

Figure 6.7

Ruling Lines

Another common way to emphasize a heading is to use ruling lines.

Point the mouse at the Paragraph menu heading. Then, point the mouse at the Rule Line Below selection and click the button. For this example, select a frame-wide line. Point the mouse at the Frame option and click the button.

Now enter the amount of space between the text and the line:

[Esc]
.2
[down arrow]

Next, enter the thickness of the line. A good guide is to make the line about half as thick as the space you left between the text and the line. Enter

[Esc]
.1
[return]

The line is drawn beneath the text (see Figure 6.8).

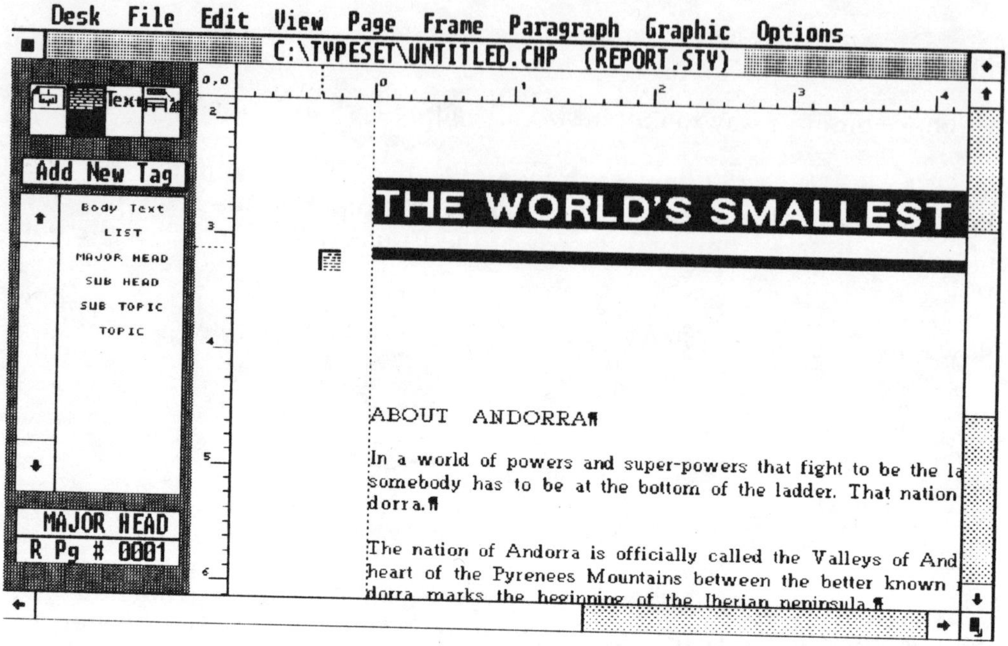

Figure 6.8

Subheadings

Now that you have created the major heading for the report, you will want to set the style for the subheadings.

In setting the style for the subheadings, take into consideration their function. In this document, the subheadings mark off specific sections, which means that you will want the subheadings to be easily identified by people who are skimming through your report.

To make your subheadings easy to identify, use a variation on the concept of ruling lines. In this case, the ruling line will be manipulated so that it appears as a shaded background for the text.

Because all the subheading paragraphs are already tagged, any change that you make to one subhead paragraph will ripple though all the subheadings in the document. To highlight the first subheading, point the mouse at the word "ABOUT" and click the button.

If you intend to shade the background, pick a font that will stand out against a gray background. Point the mouse at the Paragraph menu option. Then, point the mouse at the Font selection and click the button. For this example, select Swiss 18-point bold.

Point the mouse at the Swiss option and click the button. Then, point the mouse at the number 18 and click the button. Finally, execute these settings by pressing

[return]

The subheading's typeface is changed.

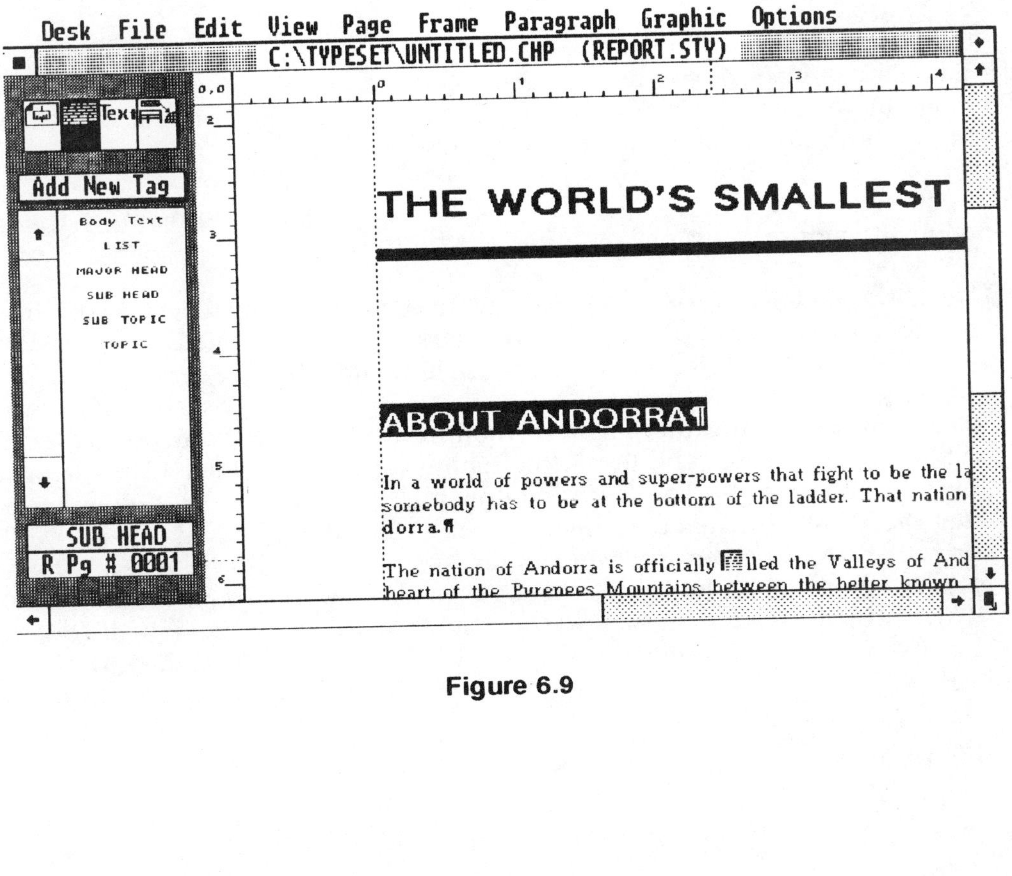

Figure 6.9

Gray Backgrounds

Changing the background of a specific paragraph tag is a bit tricky. In Chapter 5, you changed the background color of a small frame to black and displayed white text on top of it. But, in this case, you cannot use the same method because you want the majority of the frame to maintain a white background. Only the text tagged as SUB HEAD should have a gray background.

The answer to this problem may seem odd. Ventura uses its ruling line feature to implement this effect. Recall that when you set a ruling line, Ventura allows you to enter the amount of space left between the ruling line and the text. In most cases, you enter a positive value for this distance. A positive value is one that adds space to the text. But Ventura will accept a negative value. When spacing is entered as negative, it is subtracted from the text. The effect is that the ruling line and the text will overlap. Essentially, the text prints over the ruling line, making it appear that background shading is being used.

To create this effect, you must use the Ruling Line Above option. Point the mouse at the Paragraph menu heading. Then, point the mouse at the Ruling Line Above option and click the button.

First, select the width. To select a width equal to the width of the frame, point the mouse at Frame and click the button.

Next, select the pattern. The pattern determines the darkness of the line. Number 1 is the lightest gray and 7 the darkest. Solid produces a solid black line. For this example, point the mouse at 2 and click the button.

Next, you must enter the height of the line. In this case, you want to enter a line that will cover the text. Remember that you selected 18-point print for the subheadings. To determine how high 18 point type is, remembering that there are 72 points to an inch, which means that 18-point text is 18/72", or 1/4", high. In order to cover the text, your line should be at least 1/4" in height. You might, however, choose to make the line larger than the text, which would create a gray background that could show above or below the text itself. In this example, the gray will be the same height as the text. Enter

[down arrow]
[Esc]
.25

The next step is the tricky one. At this point, the 1/4" gray line would appear just above the text. To force Ventura to overlap the line and the text, you must subtract space from the layout, which is done by entering a value for Space Below Rule 3. In this case, the value will be .25", which will create a gray line the same height as the typeface. Enter

[down arrow] (5 times)
[Esc]
.25

The next step is crucial for the effect you are trying to achieve. You must change the setting to negative space. The negative setting will cause the ruling line and the text to overlap. By setting the positive and negative spacing values both at .25", the overlap will be 100%. Note the two boxes, plus (+) and minus (-) next to Space Below Rule 3. Point the mouse at the minus box and click the button. To complete the entry, press

[return]

The subheading now appears against a gray background.

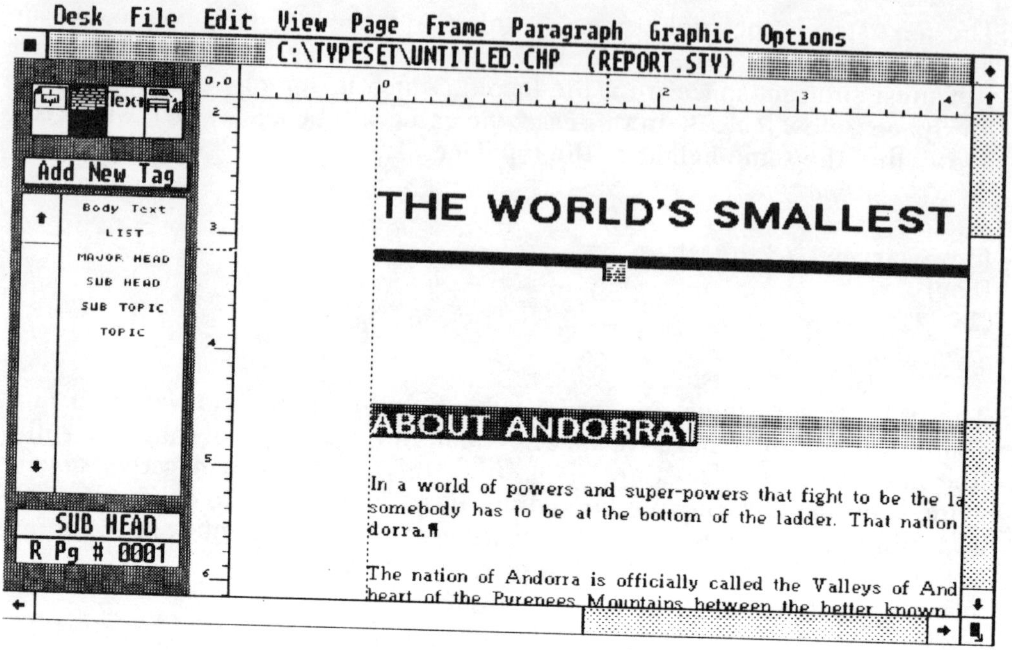

Figure 6.10

The changes you made for this subheading should affect all of the paragraphs tagged as SUB HEAD. Switch to the Reduced View mode to examine the entire page (see Figure 6.11). Press

[Ctrl/r]

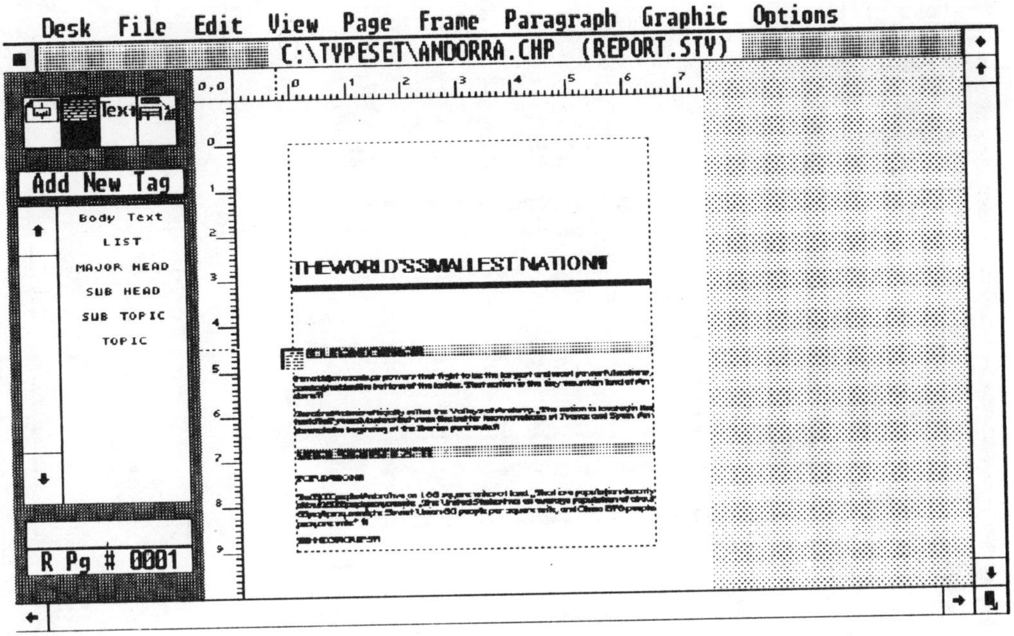

Figure 6.11

MOVING BETWEEN PAGES

You can see that there are two subheadings on this page that have been formatted against the gray background. Display page 2 of the document by pressing

[Pg Dn]

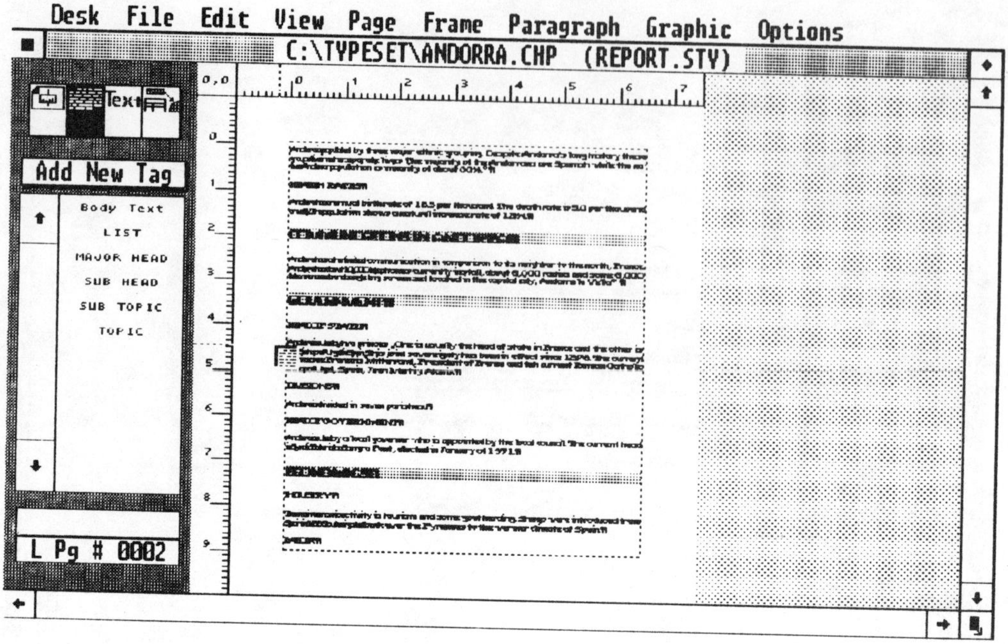

Figure 6.12

In a multiple-page document, you can use the following keys to change pages.

[Home]	Moves to the first page of the chapter.
[End]	Moves to the last page of the chapter.
[Pg Dn]	Moves to the next page of the chapter.
[Pg Up]	Moves to the previous page of the chapter.

You can also move to specific pages by using the Goto command. Press

[Ctrl/g]

The screen displays the GO TO PAGE menu box.

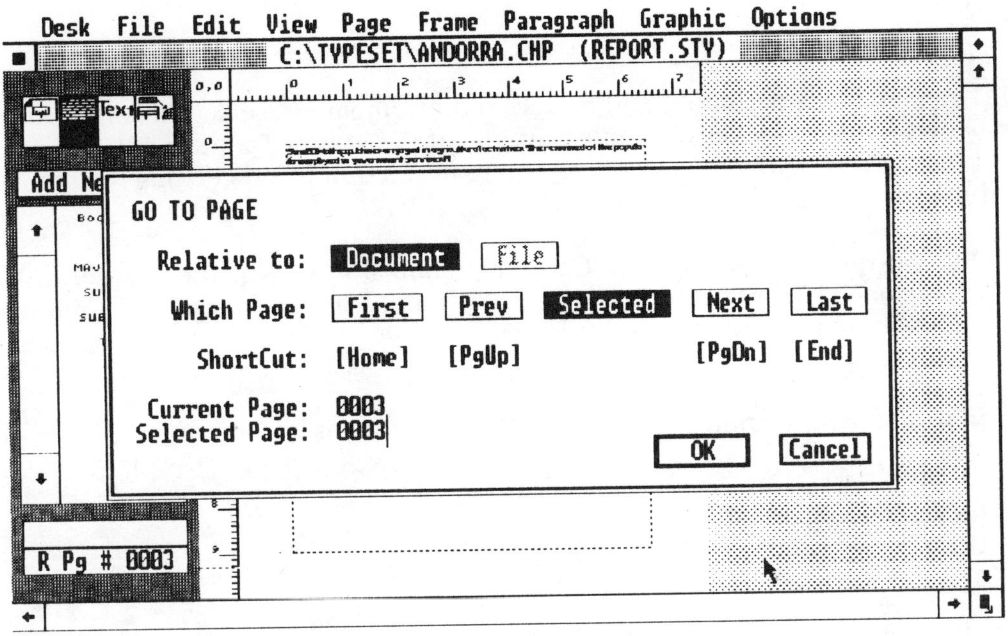

Figure 6.13

The menu presents the same options available with the keyboard commands except for the Selected option. This option allows you to type in the number of a specific page. Point the mouse at Selected in the Which Page selection and click the button. For this example, to select page 1, enter the following:

[backspace]
1
[return]

Page 1 is now displayed.

CHANGING MARGINS

The pages you have been looking at so far use the default margins, 1" all around. In a report or book format, you might want to narrow the margins, making the lines a bit shorter. To change the margins, place Ventura into the Frame mode. Press

[Ctrl/u]

The master frame should still be selected. Remember, selection is indicated by the appearance of the frame buttons. If the master frame is not selected, select it by pointing the mouse anywhere in the frame and clicking the mouse button.

Next, display the Margins & Columns menu box. Point the mouse at the Frame menu heading. Then, point the mouse at the Margins & Columns selection and click the button. Enter

[down arrow] (3 times)
[Esc]
01.25
[down arrow]
[Esc]
01.25
[return]

The frame margins narrow the width of the text.

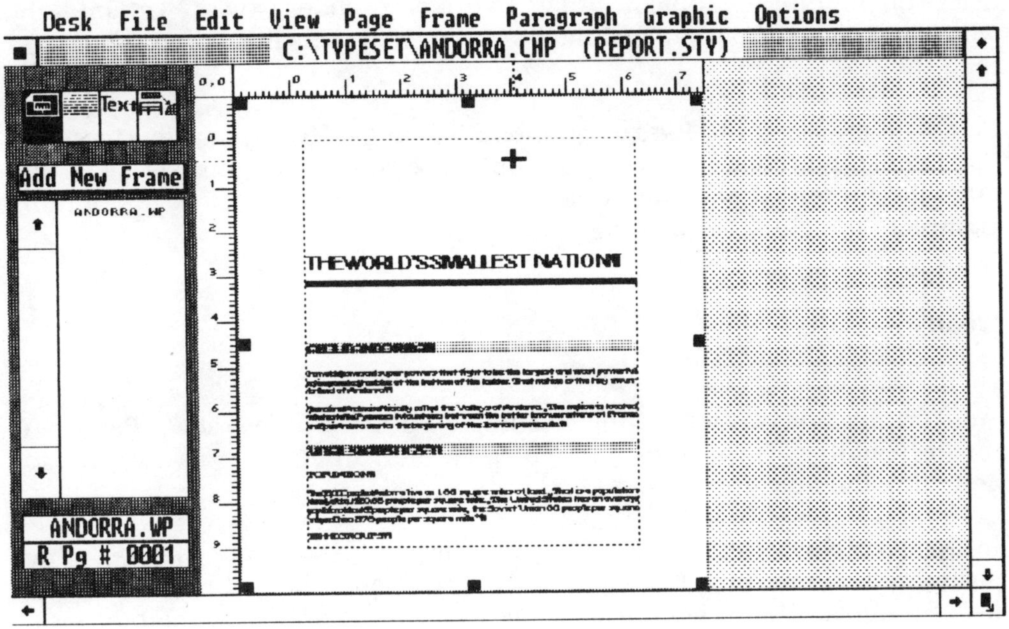

Figure 6.14

TOPIC HEADINGS

The next step in formatting this document is to define the type of format you want to use for the topic headings in the text. Place Ventura in the Paragraph mode by entering

[Ctrl/i]

Change to the normal display mode by pointing the mouse at lower left corner of the page and pressing

[Ctrl/n]

The first topic heading is POPULATION. Point the mouse at the word POPULATION and click the button.

Select the font for the topic heading. In this case, choose Swiss 14-point bold, which will make the topic headings smaller than the subheadings but larger than the text.

Point the mouse at the Paragraph menu heading. Then, point the mouse at the Font selection and click the button. Next, point the mouse at Swiss and click the button. Point the mouse at the number 14 and click the button. Complete the entry by pressing

[return]

Add a ruling line below the topic headings. Point the mouse at the Paragraph menu heading. Then, point the mouse at the Ruling Line Below selection and click the button.

In this case, you want to limit the ruling line to the width of the text, which gives you the same effect as underlining because the line will extend only as far as the text. Point the mouse at the Text option and click the button.

When drawing a line beneath text, you will want to add some space to separate the line from the text. The 14-point text is about .20" high. As a rough estimate of spacing, leave about 1/4 of that height, or .05" of space, below the text. Enter

[Esc]
.05
[down arrow]

Make the ruling line half the size of the space. Enter

[Esc]
.025
[return]

The topic headings are underlined. Now, examine page 2. Change to the Reduced View mode by pressing

[Ctrl/r]

Display page 2 by entering

[Pg Dn]

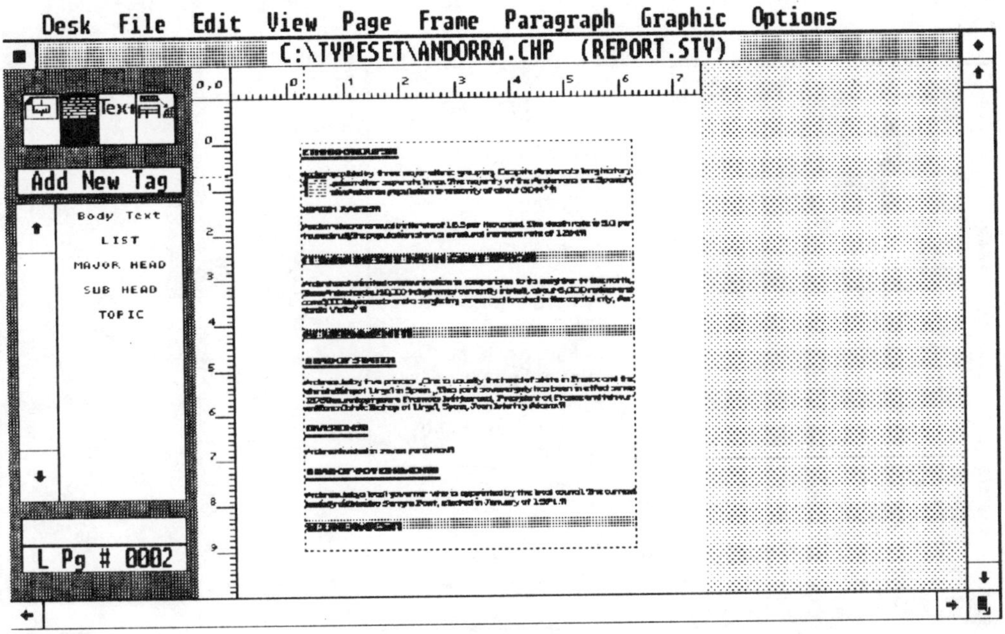

Figure 6.15

The subheading and topic headings are all formatted because they were already tagged in the text file.

HEADERS AND FOOTERS

In documents such as this one, you will usually want to add page headers and/or footers. Headers are used to designate information about the chapter, including chapter and page numbers.

To create headers or footers in Ventura, use the Page menu. Point the mouse at the Page menu heading.

Ventura displays the page operation menu. Most of these options can be displayed no matter what page or mode you are in at the time because most of the settings in this menu equally affect all the pages in your document.

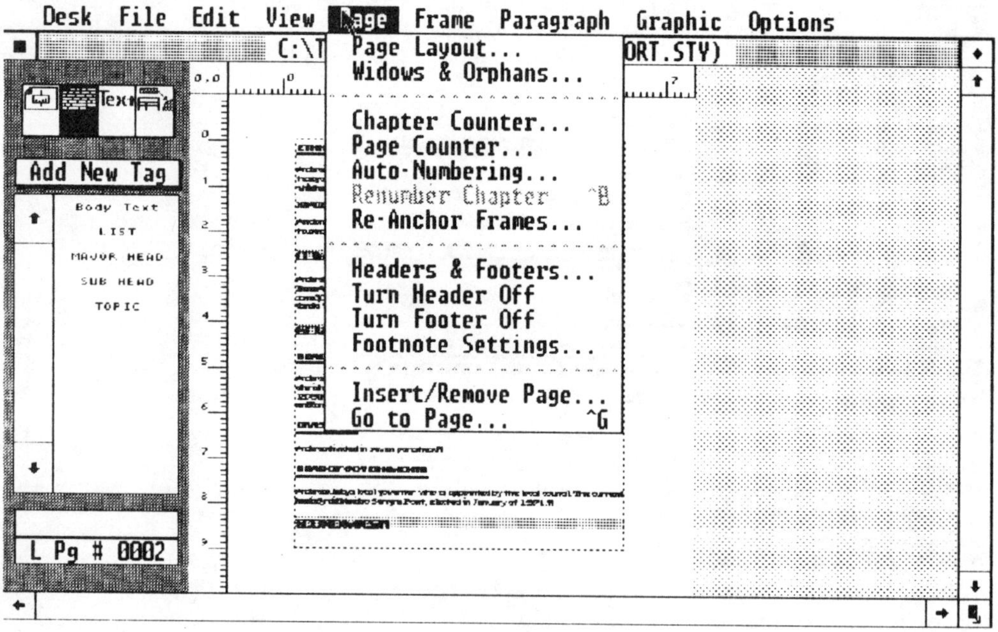

Figure 6.16

Point the mouse at the Headers & Footers selection and click the button. The HEADERS & FOOTERS menu box is displayed.

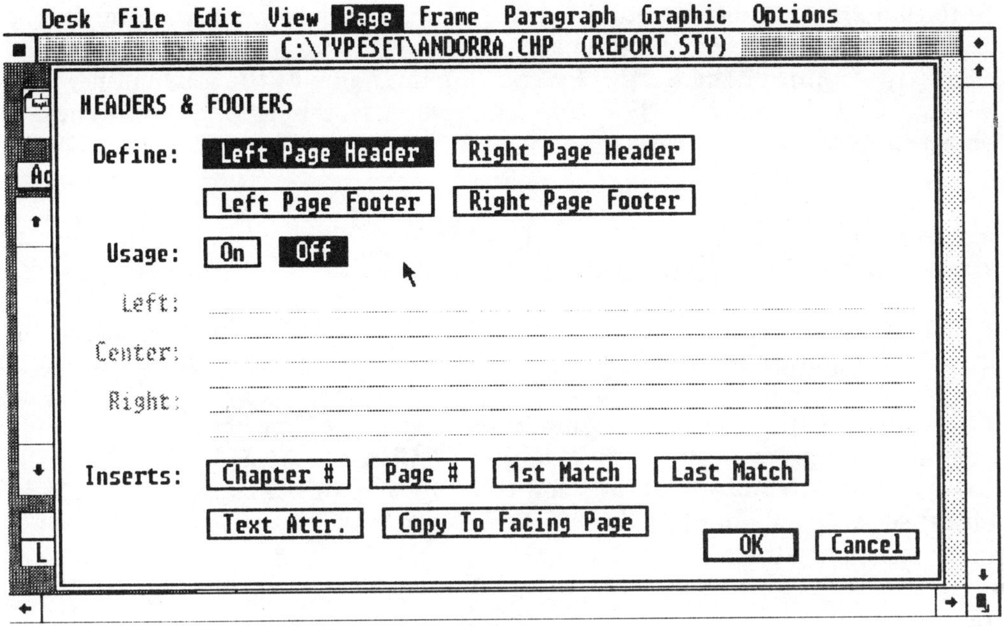

Figure 6.17

Ventura allows you to define a header and/or a footer for both the left and right pages. The left and right page distinction is important when you intend to reproduce your document by printing on both sides of the paper. In this chapter, the assumption is made that you intend to have left and right pages.

The first step in defining a header is to turn the header or footer on. The Left Page Header setting is currently selected, so point the mouse at On and click the button. The lines Left, Center, and Right are now open for entry.

Left page headers usually begin at the left margin. The first step will be to insert the page number, which is done by using one of the special symbols at the bottom of the box. Point the mouse at the Page # option and click the button.

Ventura inserts [P#] onto the header line. The [P#] will be automatically replaced with the actual page number on each page of the document.

Note that you could have obtained the same results by simply typing in the characters [P #]. The special boxes at the bottom are a convenience – not a necessity. Continue the header by entering the name of the journal in which the report will appear. For this example, use the title, "The Krummy Geographic Journal." Enter

[space bar] (5 times)
The Krummy Geographic Journal
[space bar]

You can also add a chapter number. Suppose the Andorra report is only one part of a larger project. The chapter number can be used to identify the section. Point the mouse at the Chapter # option and click the button. Ventura inserts the symbol [C #] onto the header line.

Text Attributes

Headers and footers are by nature different from the regular text that appears in the frames. You can see that in this case, the actual text is entered into the menu selections. Ventura does not allow you to change text attributes or change fonts by using Text mode commands implemented by highlighting.

You can, however, enhance the text in your headers and footers by entering text attribute codes into the header or footer.

For example, suppose you want the page number to stand out. You could use 14-point print for the number and a smaller print – 10- or 8-point – for the remainder of the header. To make the page number an exception, you will need to insert special codes.

Use the Left Arrow key to move the cursor back to the beginning of the header.

Insert a text attribute code. Point the mouse at the Text Attr. selection in the HEADERS AND FOOTERS menu, and click the button.

Ventura inserts a code into the header. The code is the instruction to resume normal printing. In this case, you want to change the point size of the page number. To do this, you must insert the letter "P" for point size, followed by a three-digit number indicating the size of typeface you want to use. Enter

[left arrow]
[backspace]
P014

These commands instruct Ventura to switch to 14-point type before the page number is printed. You must insert an instruction to set the point size back to normal after the page number is printed. Press

[right arrow] (5 times)

Point the mouse at the Text Attr. selection and click the button. Enter

[left arrow]
[backspace]
P255

P255 always instructs Ventura to use the point size indicated in the style tag for the header and footer text. This tag is automatically generated by Ventura when you create a header or footer. Like other automatically generated tags (boxed text for example), you can use the Paragraph mode to change the default values.

The header definition resembles Figure 6.18.

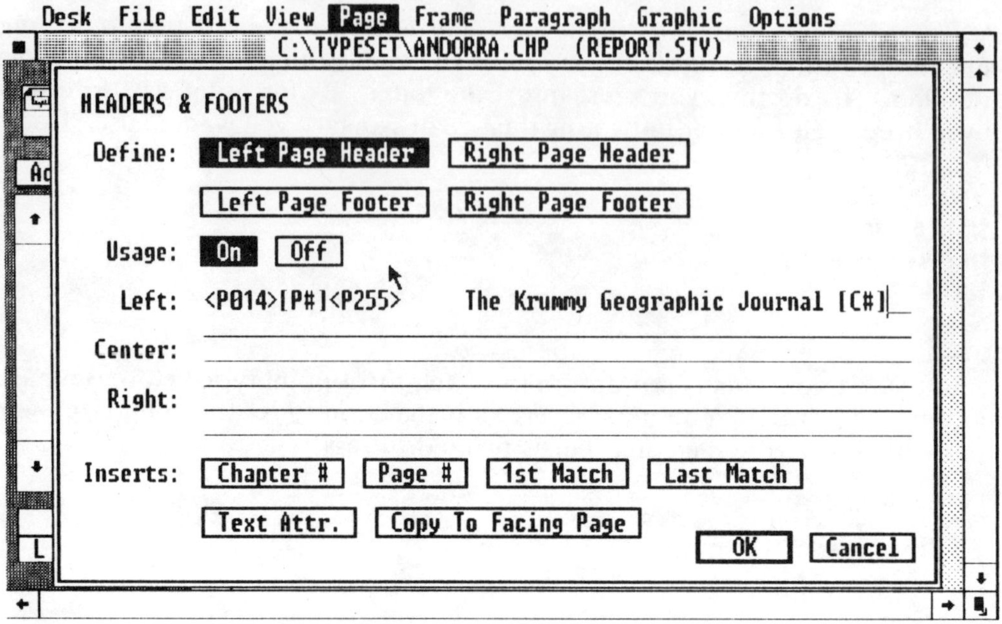

Figure 6.18

Create the header by pressing

[return]

At the top of the page, the header line appears. For a closer look at the header, point the mouse at the header and then press

[Ctrl/n]

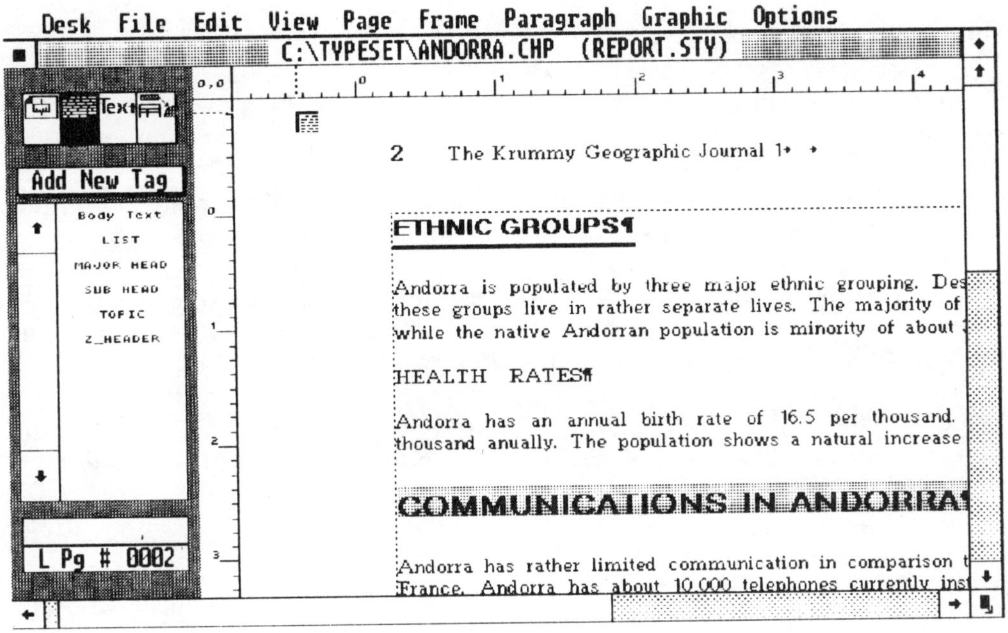

Figure 6.19

You can see that Ventura automatically inserts the page and chapter numbers into the header. Also note that the side bar display will show the tag Z_HEADER. In the previous chapter, you set your preferences to display generated tags. If you do not see the tag appear in the side bar display, it is because the generated tag setting has been turned off. The tag will function in exactly the same way whether it is displayed or not. Since the header has its own style tag, you can style the header text by using the Paragraph menu.

Point the mouse at the word "Krummy" and click the button. Then, point the mouse at the Paragraph menu heading. Point the mouse at the Font selection and click the button.

Make the text of the header small by selecting an 8-point typeface. Point the mouse at the number 8 and click the button. Point the mouse at the OK option and click the button.

Note that the page number (2) is not affected by the change in font size because you specified the point size for that character in the header text itself.

Special Header Features

The header that you created for the left pages is a standard header. Ventura has an interesting feature that allows the header to reflect the subject of the text on the page. For example, you can tell Ventura to include in the header the text of any subheadings that appear on the page. With this feature, the header will change depending on the headings used in the text.

To see how this works, create a right page header that uses this special feature. Point the mouse at the Page menu heading. Then, point the mouse at the Headers & Footers selection and click the button.

Select a right page header. Point the mouse at the Right Page Header option and click the button. Then, point the mouse at the On option and click the button. Next, place the cursor on the Right side entry lines. Press

[down arrow] (4 times)

You can instruct Ventura to insert either the next available (1st match) or the last previous (Last Match) text that is tagged with a particular style tag. For example, if you selected the SUB HEAD tag, Ventura would insert the text of the closest subheading into the header. In this example, you will use the Last Match option to insert the last previous subheading.

Point the mouse at Last Match and click the button.

Ventura inserts [> tag name] onto the header line. This symbol is incomplete. The > indicates that Last Match. A < would indicate 1st Match; however, you now must manually replace the words "tag name" with the name of an actual tag. In this case, you will use the SUB HEAD tag. Enter

[left arrow]
[backspace] (8 times)
SUB HEAD
[right arrow]

Complete the header by adding a page number. You will also want to change the point size to match the page number in the left page header. Enter

[space bar] (5 times)

Point the mouse at the Text Attr. option and click the button. Enter

[left arrow]
[backspace]
P014
[right arrow]

Point the mouse at the Page # option and click the button. Then, point the mouse at Text Attr. and click the button. Enter

[left arrow]
[backspace]
P255
[right arrow]

The right page header specification resembles Figure 6.20.

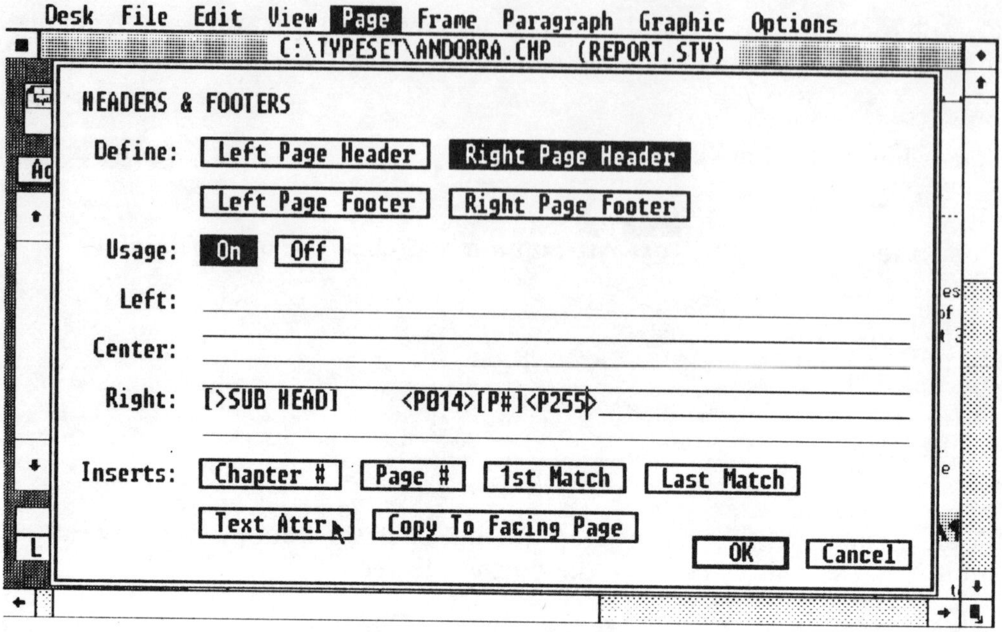

Figure 6.20

Complete the header by pressing

[return]

To see the header, move to the next page. Press

[Pg Dn]

Since the header is on the right side of the page, you will need to scroll the display window. Point the mouse at right edge of the window. Enter

[Ctrl/n]

The header on page 3 shows the word ECONOMICS, the last subheading in the text. Note that Ventura does not allow you to create multiple headers or footers for the same chapter. There can be only one definition for any of the four positions that headers and footers can occupy.

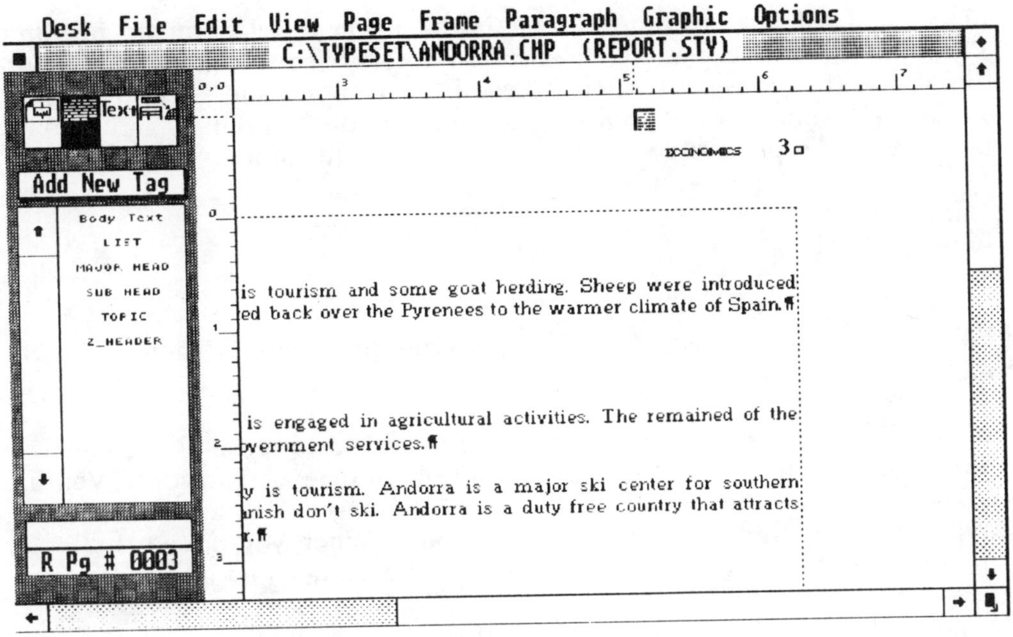

Figure 6.21

Suppressing Headers and Footers

In multiple-page documents, it is not unusual to display certain headers or footers on some pages and not on others. For example, in this document, headers are used to display page numbers; however, it is customary to suppress this header on the first page of a chapter and use a footer to show that page number. Ventura allows you to designate what pages should display headers or footers

To make these changes, return to the first page. Press

[Home]

Place Ventura into the Reduced View mode by pressing

[Ctrl/r]

Create a Right Page Footer. Point the mouse at the Page menu heading. Then, point the mouse at the Headers & Footers selection and click the button. Point the mouse at the Right Page Footer option and click the button. To turn the footer on by pointing the mouse at the On option and clicking the button. To place the page number in the center of the footer, press

[down arrow] (2 times)

Point the mouse at Page # option and click the button. Then, point the mouse at OK and click the button.

As you look at the page, you can make two observations. First, the page number is inserted in the footer at the bottom of the page; however, Ventura has also inserted the header at the top of the page. Ventura turns header and footer definitions on and off as a group. When you added the footer definition on page 1, Ventura also inserted the header for right pages.

Your goal is to have only the footer on this page, which means you must suppress the header on this page. You can suppress headers by again using the Page menu. Point the mouse at the Page menu heading. Then, point the mouse at the Turn Header Off selection and click the button.

The header is removed from this page. Press

[Pg Dn] (2 times)

The footer appears on the next left page—page 3. In this case, leave the header displayed, but suppress the footer.

To suppress the footer on this page, point the mouse at the Page menu heading. Then, point the mouse at the Turn Footer Off option and click the button.

The footer is removed from that page. Note that when new pages are added to an existing document, you should take care to check that the new pages at the end of the document display the proper header or footer. Ventura will turn on both headers and footers for new pages. You must manually suppress headers or footers you don't want to appear on new pages.

PAGE COUNTING

Ventura allows you to control the sequence and the style of automatic page and chapter numbers. For example, suppose that this Andorra document was really the fifth section in a larger document. You must adjust the page and chapter counters to show the correct page and chapter numbers.

You can set a new page number sequence on any page of the document. To start the sequence at the beginning of the document, move to page 1. Press

[Home]

To change the page counter, display the Page menu by pointing the mouse at the Page menu heading.

Page numbering is controlled from the PAGE COUNTER menu box, so point the mouse at the Page Counter selection and click the button. The PAGE COUNTER menu box appears.

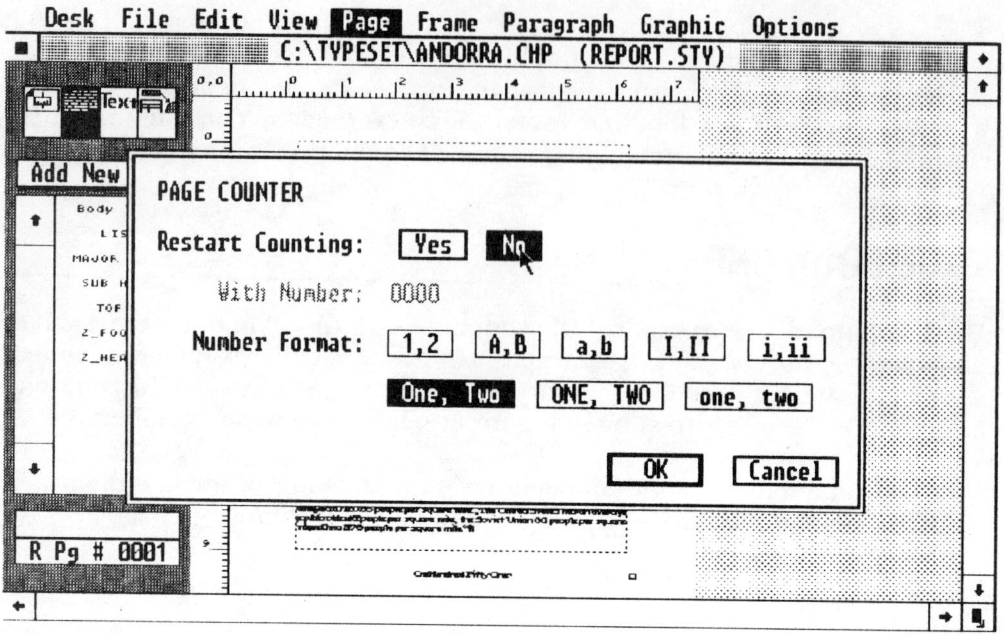

Figure 6.22

The menu allows you to choose a starting page number and a format for the page number. Ventura lets you choose between Arabic numbers, letters, or Roman numbers. The bottom row displays options for text numbering. For example, if you choose [One, Two], the number 21 would print as Twenty One.

In this example, begin the page numbering at 151. Remember, right-side pages will always be odd numbered. Point the mouse at Yes and click the button. Enter

[Esc]
0151

Point the mouse at the 1,2 option and click the button. Then, point the mouse at OK and click the button.

To check the results, point the mouse at page number and press

[Ctrl/e]

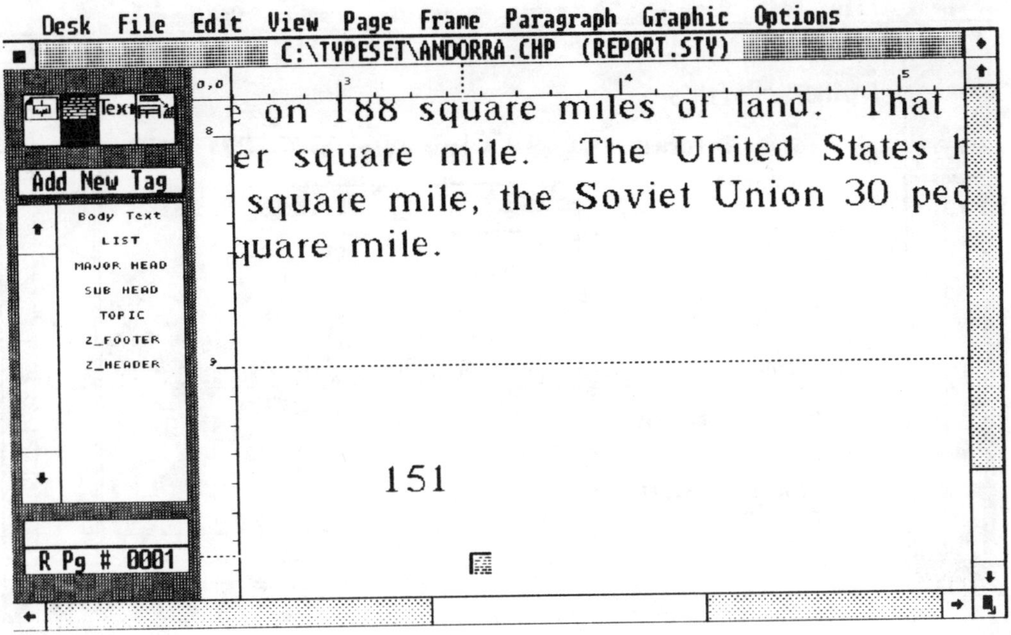

Figure 6.23

FOOTNOTES

You might remember that you created footnote text in the document ANDORRA.WP that has not appeared in the document so far. Ventura's default setting is to suppress footnote text. Footnote text is displayed by using the Footnote Settings option on the Page menu.

Point the mouse at the Page menu heading. Then, point the mouse at Footnote Settings and click the button. The FOOTNOTE SETTINGS menu box is displayed.

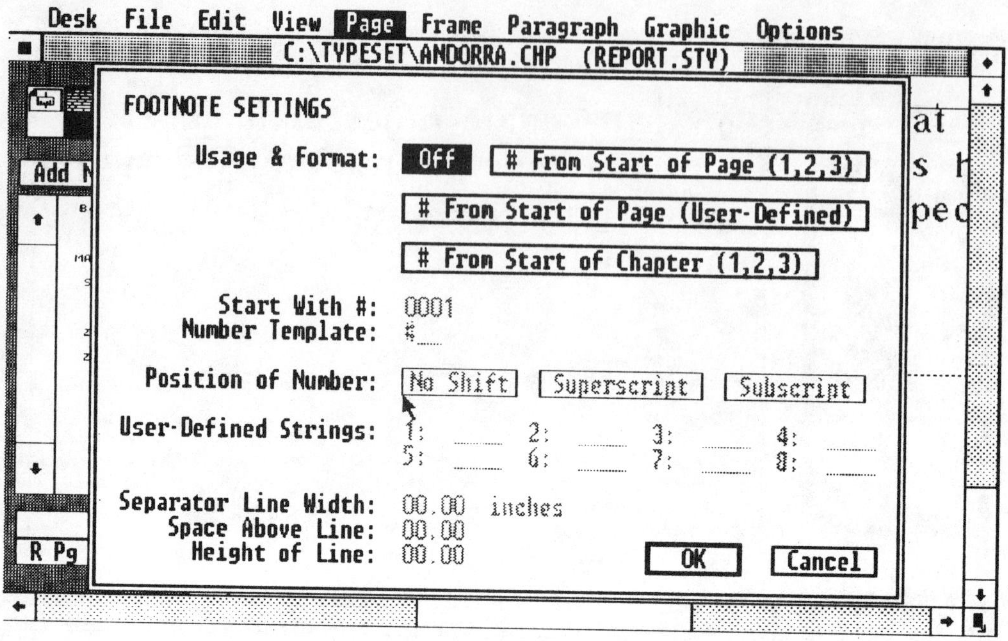

Figure 6.24

The first section of the menu deals with the general format used to create footnotes. The default setting is Off. The other three settings display footnotes at the bottom of each page that contains a footnote code. The three settings differ in the way they reference footnotes in the text.

The first option, # From Start of Page (1,2,3), places reference numbers on the page for each footnote. The numbering begins at 1 on each page. The second setting creates footnote references from symbols rather than numbers. The default value is *, which means that the first footnote on the page will be *, the second will be **, and so on. The final choice numbers the footnotes consecutively from the beginning of the document.

Point the mouse at # From Start of Chapter (1,2,3) and click the button.

The next section allows you to select the starting number for the footnotes and a template for the footnote reference. The default value is 1. (Use this option to continue footnote numbering from the end of a previous chapter. In that way, you can make your footnotes consecutive throughout the entire document.) The # indicates that the number itself will be used as the footnote reference. You can also add characters to the template to create footnote references with additional characters. For example, a template of (#) would create footnote references such as (1), (2), (3), etc.

If you want superscript or subscript references, you can select that option from the Position of Number option. Point the mouse at Superscript and click the button.

The bottom of the display allows you to create a ruling line that will separate the text from the footnotes. To create a line, enter

[down arrow]
[down arrow]
[Esc]
06.5
[down arrow]
[down arrow]
[Esc]
.02

The menu setting should now resemble Figure 6.25.

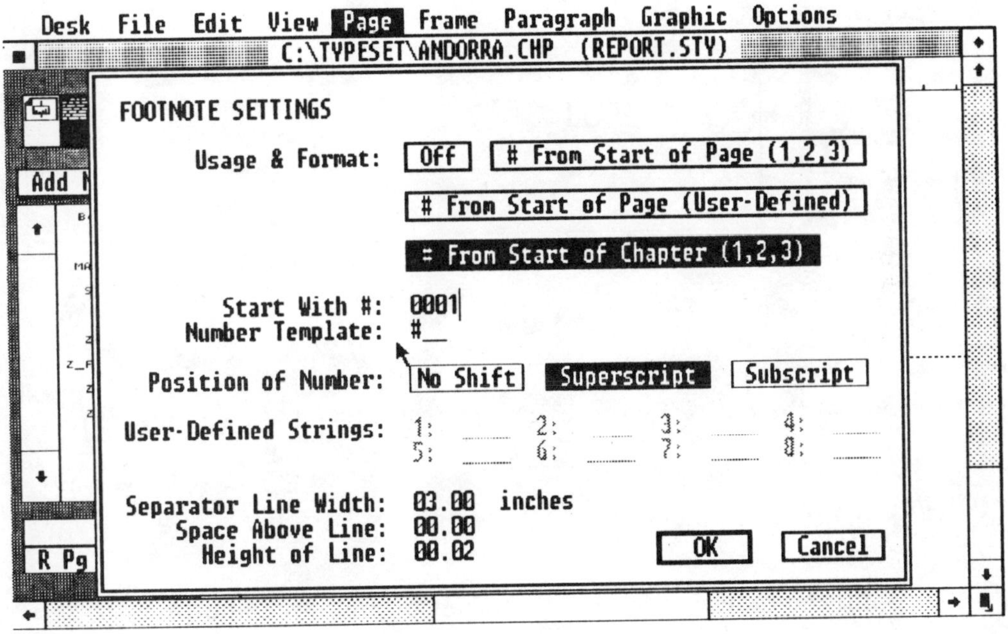

Figure 6.25

Complete the menu by pressing

[return]

The end of the footnote text appears in the window.

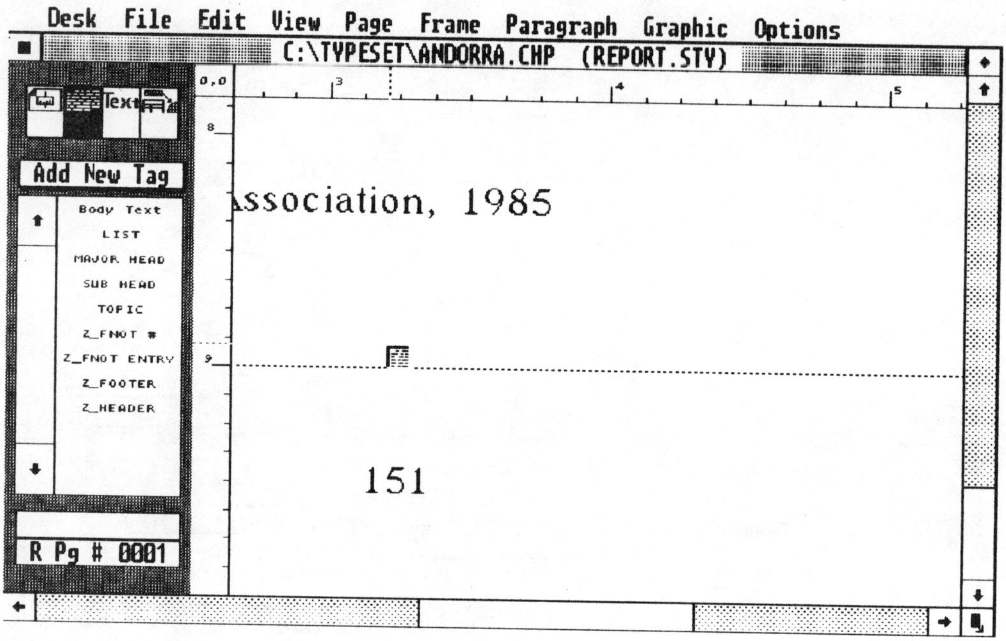

Figure 6.26

For a look at the entire footnote, change to Reduced View mode. Press

[Ctrl/r]

Then, point the mouse at lower left corner of the frame and press

[Ctrl/n]

You can now see the full text of the footnote. It has automatically been numbered as 1.

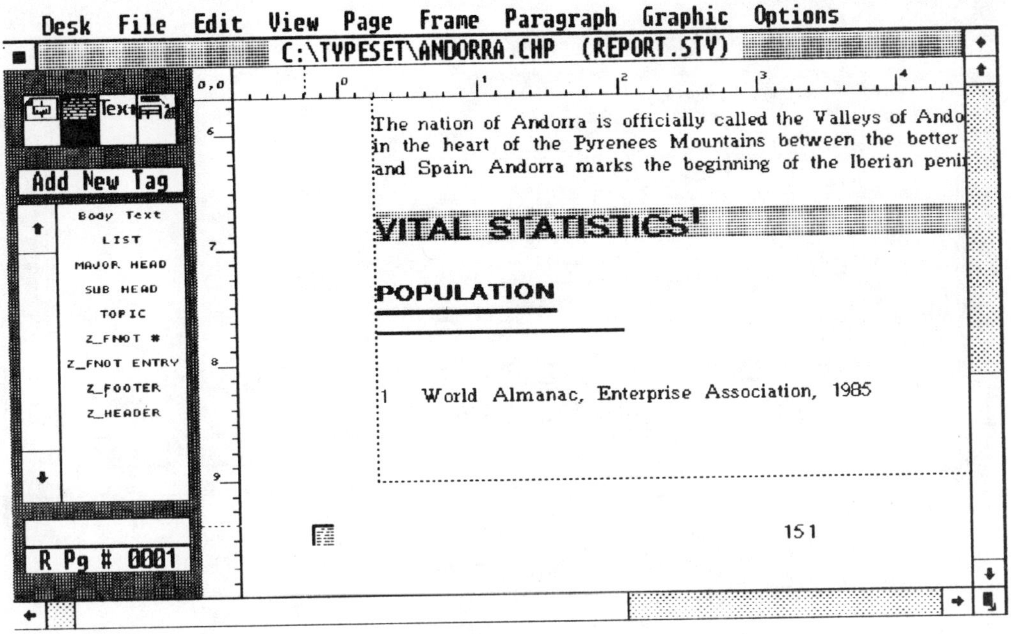

Figure 6.27

PARAGRAPH NUMBERING

Ventura has the ability to generate paragraph numbers, which means that you can automatically create outline-type headings. Ventura uses the tag names to locate the paragraphs that should be numbered in a document. For example, suppose that you want to number the subheadings and topic headings. Point the mouse at the Page menu heading.

Paragraph numbering is controlled by the Auto-Numbering option. Point the mouse at Auto-Numbering and click the button.

Ventura displays the AUTO-NUMBERING menu box.

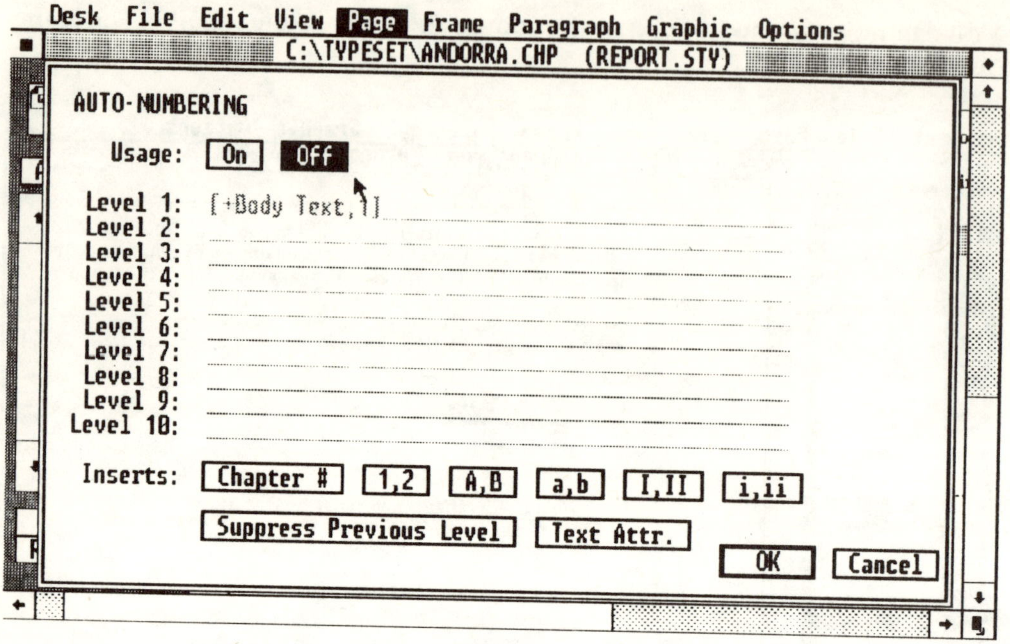

Figure 6.28

You can specify up to 10 levels of numbering. In this example, there are only two levels.

Point the mouse at the On option and click the button, which turns the Auto-Numbering option on and allows you to enter tag names on the level lines. Ventura places a Body Text tag on the first level. Clear that tag by pressing

[Esc]

To create a numbering sequence, select one of the numbering styles from the bottom of the menu. For example, suppose that you want to number the subheadings A, B, C, etc. Point the mouse at A,B and click the button.

Ventura inserts a code [*tag name,A] onto the Level 1 line. As with the header and footer codes, you must manually replace a tag name with the name of an existing style tag. The A indicates the style of numbering selected. To specify SUB HEAD tags, enter

[left arrow] (3 times)
[backspace] (8 times)
sub head

Keep in mind that these commands insert the number only. If you want punctuation, such as parentheses or periods, you must enter those characters specifically. Enter

[right arrow] (3 times)
. (a period)

Move down to the next level. Press

[down arrow]

Select Arabic numbering for this level by pointing the mouse at the 1,2 option and clicking the button.

Enter the topic style tag. Enter

[left arrow] (3 times)
[backspace] (8 times)
topic
[right arrow] (3 times)
. (a period)

The menu resembles Figure 6.29.

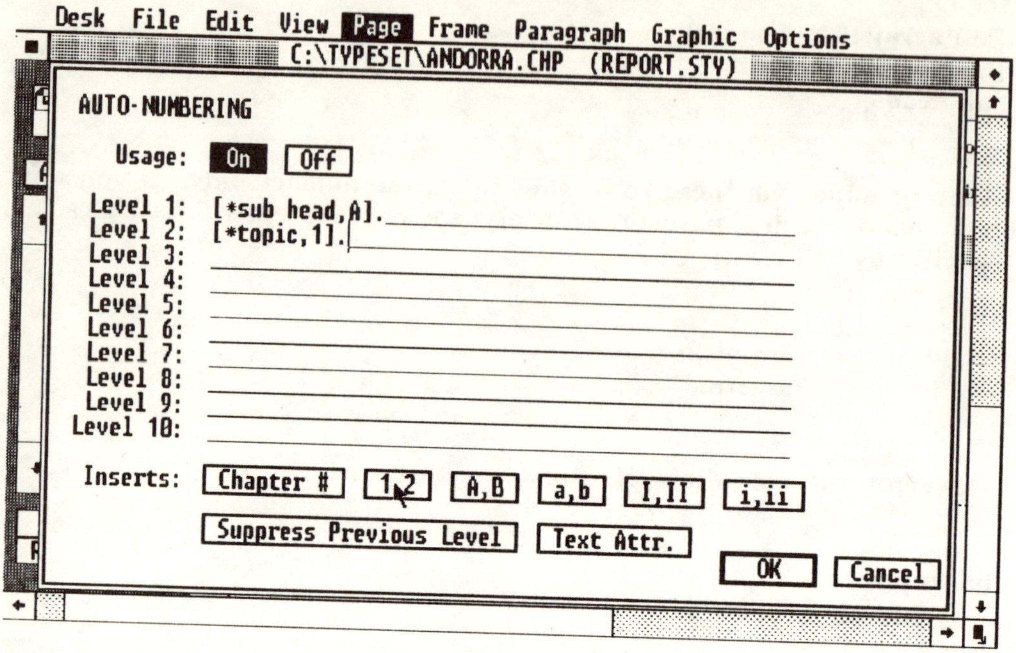

Figure 6.29

Complete the menu by pressing

[return]

Ventura automatically goes through the document and numbers the paragraphs. Note that the new style tags are automatically generated – Z_SEC1 for level 1 numbers and Z_SEC2 for level 2 numbers. The effect is probably not what you expected.

Instead of placing the numbers on the same line as the subheading and topic text, Ventura inserted the numbers as paragraphs in front of the subheadings and topic headings. Instead of the following display,

A. ABOUT ANDORRA

You see this display:

A.

ABOUT ANDORRA

However, Ventura can create the look you want by altering the paragraph format of the style tags you want to number.

You must change two characteristics. First, indent the heading paragraph to make room for the paragraph number on the left. Then, remove the line break before the heading, which will cause the line to print on the same line as the previous paragraph. The result will look like a single line of text combining the paragraph number with the heading that needs to be numbered.

To implement these changes, you must change the style of the subheading and topic tags. Place Ventura into the Reduced View mode and the Paragraph mode. Enter

[Ctrl/r]
[Ctrl/i]

Point the mouse at the words "ABOUT ANDORRA" and click the button.

The first step is to select a paragraph indent for the subheadings, which is done from the ALIGNMENT menu. Point the mouse at the Paragraph menu heading. Then, point the mouse at the Alignment selection and click the button.

The ALIGNMENT menu is displayed. In the bottom portion of the menu, you will see a setting for In/Outdent Width. This setting affects only a selected number of lines in a paragraph. The lines can be indented (moved in from the left) or outdented (released to the left). The default is to indent the first line of the paragraph. In this case, an indent of 1/2" will leave enough room for the paragraph number. Enter

[Esc]
.5
[return]

The next step is to suppress the line break. If you are accustomed to working with word processing programs, this concept may seem a bit strange. In word processors, it is almost always the case that a [return] in the text begins a new line. In that way, no two lines can ever print over each other. In Ventura, you can control the way [return] characters are treated. In this case, you want to instruct Ventura that even though the subheading and the paragraph number are two separate paragraphs separated by a [return], they ought to appear as a single line. For example, in the case of the SUB HEAD tag, Ventura ignores the new line that would normally occur when a [return] is encountered.

Point the mouse at the Paragraph menu heading. Then, point the mouse at the Breaks selection and click the button. The BREAKS menu appears.

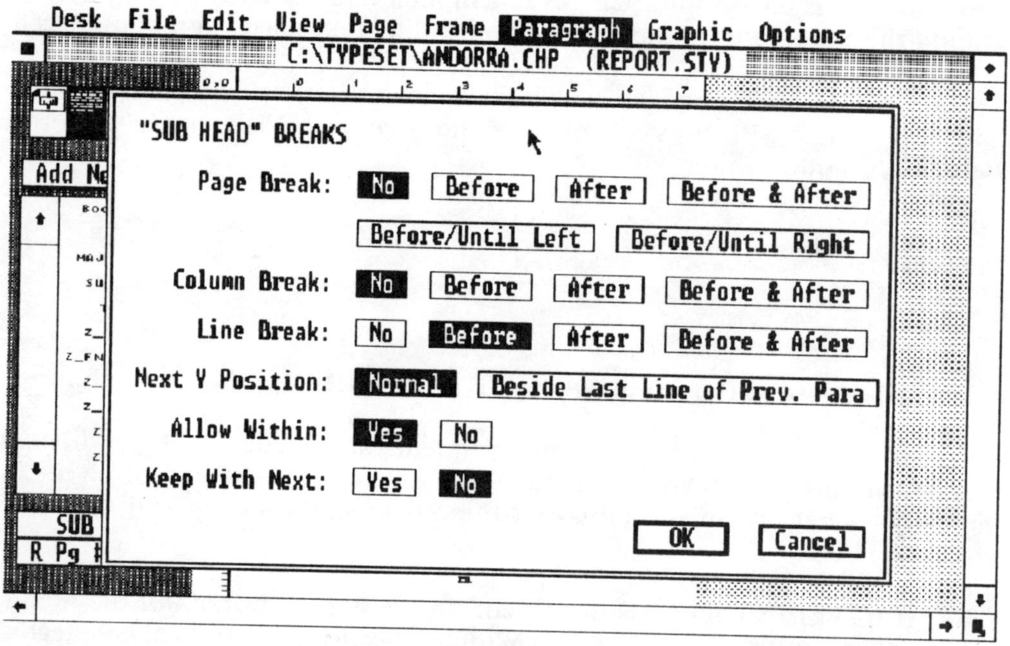

Figure 6.30

This menu allows you to control three types of breaks: pages, columns, and lines. In this case, you are interested in line breaks. Ventura automatically sets a paragraph for a line break Before. You might want to take a moment to consider what is meant by this setting. Ventura is instructing you to create a line break when a paragraph begins. Ventura defines the beginning of a paragraph as the first character following a [return] in the text.

With this in mind, if you select No break, the SUB HEAD paragraph will begin on the same line as the previous paragraph (the paragraph number), which is exactly the effect you want. Point the mouse at the No option for Line Break and click the button.

The SUB HEAD paragraphs are now combined with the paragraph numbers for level 1 headings. Note that the ruling line used to create the background for the SUB HEAD paragraphs also covers the paragraph numbers.

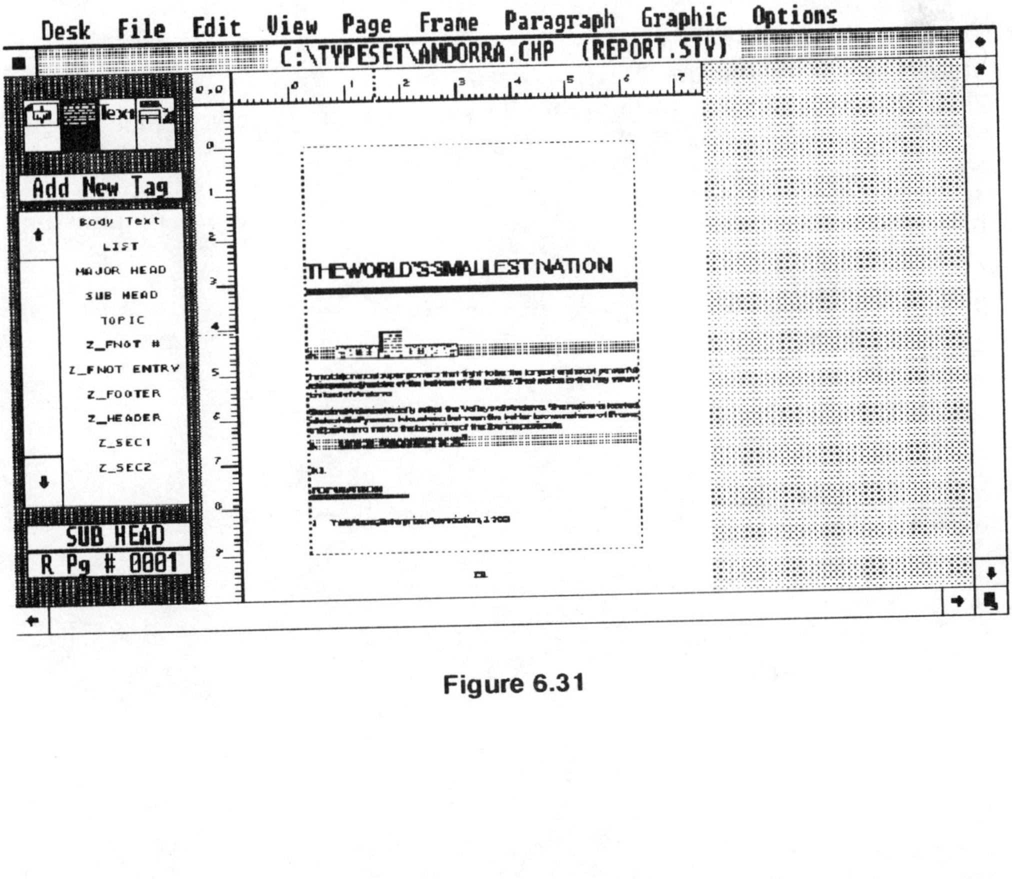

Figure 6.31

It is important to understand the role played by indenting the SUB HEAD. If you had not indented the paragraph, it would have printed on top of the paragraph number, making that number unreadable. By indenting the paragraph and suppressing the line break, you created two lines that resemble a single line with an indent. The difference between using one or two lines to achieve the same effect is significant. By fusing two lines together in one format, each part can retain its individual style tags. This ability to retain style tags allows you to change the font or other paragraph attribute of one of the elements without having to change the other.

For example, suppose you want to change the font of the paragraph number without changing the font of the SUB HEAD text. Point the mouse at [A.] and click the button.

The [A.] will be highlighted. You should also see the tag name – Z_SEC1 – appear above the page number in the side bar display. Change the font.

Point the mouse at the Paragraph menu heading. Then, point the mouse at Font and click the button. Next, point the mouse at Dutch and click the button. Point the mouse a the number 24 and click the button. Finally, point the mouse at OK and click the button.

The paragraph numbers are enlarged, but the SUB HEAD text remains unchanged.

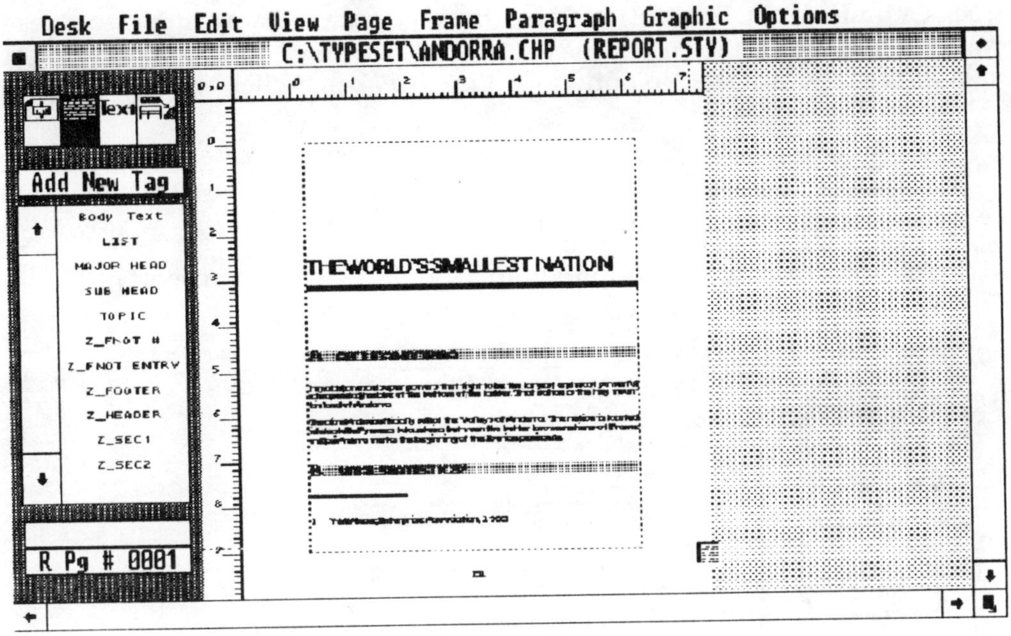

Figure 6.32

You must now perform the same operation on the topic paragraphs to align them with their paragraph numbers. Move to the second page. Press

[Pg Dn]

Point the mouse at the word "POPULATION" and click the button.

Change the paragraph indent to 1/2". Point the mouse at the Paragraph menu heading. Then, point the mouse at the Alignment selection and click the button. Enter

[Esc]
.5
[return]

Next, eliminate the line break. Point the mouse at the Paragraph menu heading. Then, point the mouse at the Breaks selection and click the button. Point the mouse at the No option for Line Break and click the button. Press

[return]

The topics and their paragraph numbers are also aligned properly.

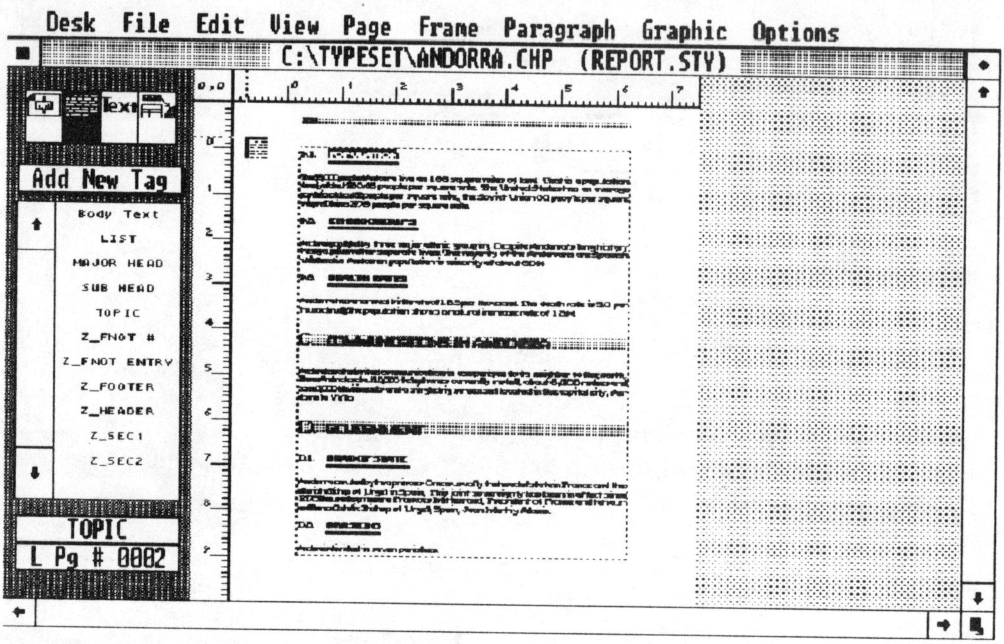

Figure 6.33

Suppressing Levels

Take a closer look at the topic paragraphs. Point the mouse at the upper left corner of the frame and press

[Ctrl/n]

You can see that the level 2 numbers are a combination of the previous level (A, B, C, etc.) and the topic numbers (1, 2, 3 etc.): B.1., B.2., etc.

Suppose that, in this case, you don't want Ventura to combine levels but simply to print the topic numbers. This can be done by modifying the Auto-Numbering specification. Point the mouse at the Page menu heading. Then, point the mouse at the Auto Numbering selection and click the button.

The AUTO-NUMBERING screen displays the two level settings you had previously entered. At the bottom of the screen, you will see a box labeled Suppress Previous Level. That box will insert a code into the heading specification that will tell Ventura not to print the previous SUB HEAD level in front of the topic number. You must insert that code in the proper place. Enter

[down arrow]
[left arrow] (11 times)

Your text cursor is now at the beginning of the level 2 line, which is where you want to insert the suppression instruction. Point the mouse at the Suppress Previous Level option and click the button.

Ventura inserts the code [-] into the level specification. Complete the entry by pressing

[return]

Ventura will automatically recalculate the paragraph numbers and display the modified results.

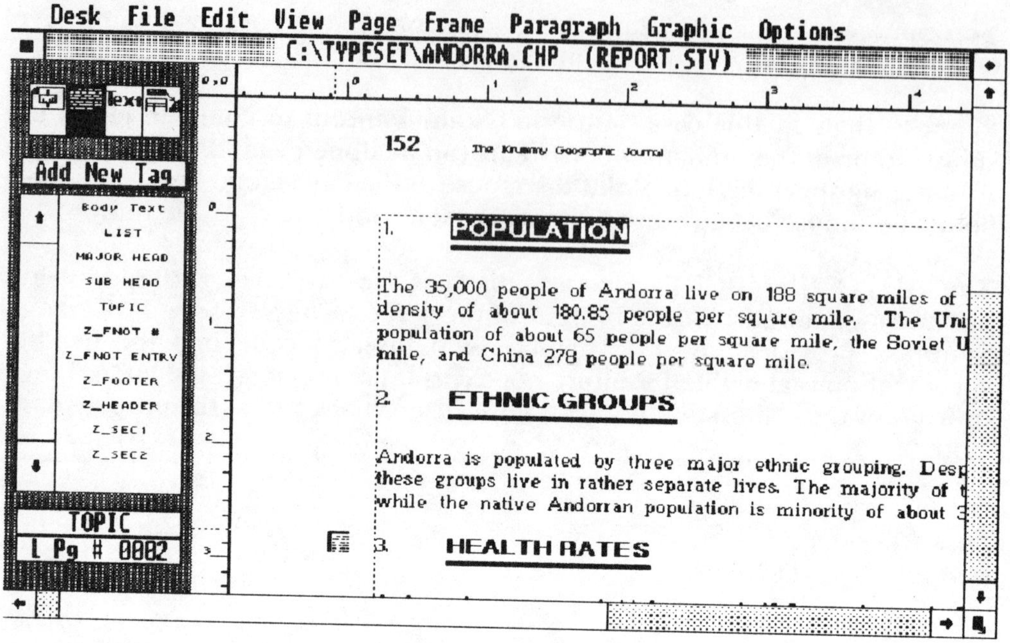

Figure 6.34

The topic headings no longer contain the SUB HEAD letters.

Before you continue to the next stage in this document, consider the following short review of what you have accomplished so far:

- Formatted heading and topic tags
- Created page headers and footers
- Selected a beginning page number
- Selected footnote format
- Created paragraph numbers
- Combined numbers with headings

ADDING PICTURES AND TABLES

The next stage in this document's development requires you to add the information stored in other files to the main document.

In this case, there are four files that should be added:

- Three graphs—POPDEN.PIC, COMM.PIC, and ETHNIC.PIC.
- A table of values—COMM.PRN.

In previous chapters, you carefully plotted the position of each frame as it was inserted, but that is not the case here. Remember, you created anchors for the three graphs in the text of the document. These anchors can be used to automatically position frames such as the graphs. If you use anchors, you can follow a different strategy for adding frames to a document.

For example, instead of trying to position frames manually, you can simply enter all frames at the end of the document. Then, let Ventura automatically place the frames at the proper place in the text, based on the position of the frame anchors.

To implement this technique, move to the end of the document. Press

[End]

Place Ventura in the Reduced View mode. Press

[Ctrl/r]

To create a new frame, place Ventura in the Frame mode. Press

[Ctrl/u]

Point the mouse at the Frame menu heading. Then, point the mouse at the Add New Frame option and click the button.

Draw a frame at the bottom of the page that is as wide as the master frame and about 2" high. Don't worry about the exact size of the frame; the size will be handled from the Sizing menu.

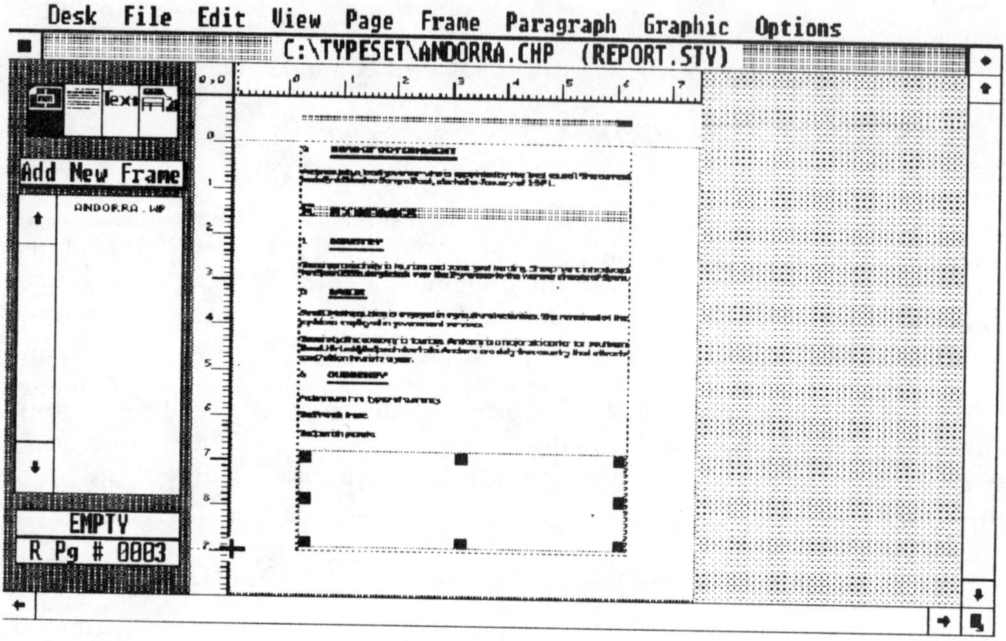

Figure 6.35

To make the size of the frame more exact, use the Sizing & Scaling menu. Point the mouse at the Frame menu heading. Then point the mouse at the Sizing & Scaling selection and click the button.

The Frame Width and Height settings control the size of the frame. The width should be exactly 6", but the height may vary. In this case, you can set the height to exactly 1.75". To set the height, enter

[down arrow] (3 times)
[Esc]
01.75
[return]

ANCHOR NAMES AND CAPTIONS

Now that you have created a frame, you must do the following:

- Give the frame an anchor name so that Ventura will know where in the text the frame should be positioned.
- Create a caption for the frame, if desired.
- Load the picture or text file into the frame.

You can perform these operations in almost any order. In this case, begin with the newest idea, creating a frame anchor name.

The anchor names of the frames should be exactly the same names that you used when you inserted location anchors into the document. You may not remember these names exactly, however. Ventura can display the anchor names if you instruct Ventura to anchor all frames in the text. This won't accomplish much, because you haven't created the anchor names for the frames, but it will cause Ventura to display each of the anchor names in the document for which there is not yet an anchor, thereby reminding you of the names you entered.

To instruct Ventura to anchor the frames (so that you can recall the anchor names), point the mouse at the Page menu heading. Then, point the mouse at the Re-Anchor Frames selection and click the button.

Ventura displays a box on the screen. In this case, you want to check all the anchors. Point the mouse at the All Pages option and click the button.

Ventura encounters the first anchor and displays the following (Figure 6.36):

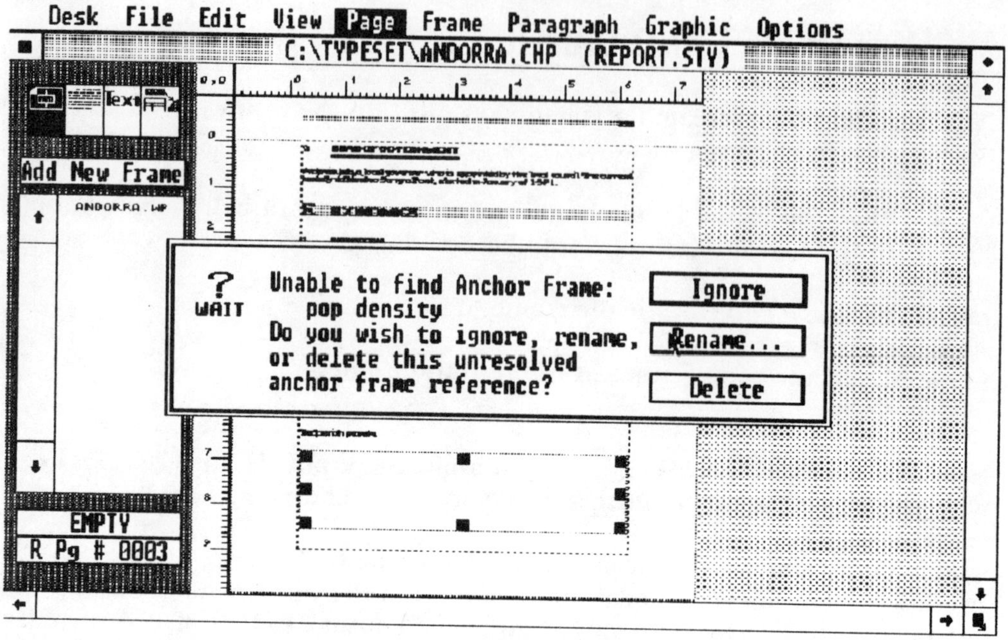

Figure 6.36

You can see that this display shows you the name of the anchor, "pop density," and asks you to decide on an action. Since you don't want to change anything, point the mouse at Ignore and click the button.

The next anchor name, "ethnic," appears. Again, point the mouse at Ignore and click the button.

The last anchor, "communications," is displayed. Point the mouse at Ignore and click the button.

You have now been able to review your anchor names. Your next task is to assign the anchor name to a frame. Begin with the "pop density" anchor. First, reselect the new frame. (Note that anchoring frames unselected the frame.) Point the mouse at the new frame and click the button.

Display the ANCHORS & CAPTIONS menu box by first pointing the mouse at the Frame menu heading, and then pointing the mouse at the Anchors & Captions selection and clicking the button. The Anchors & Captions menu box appears.

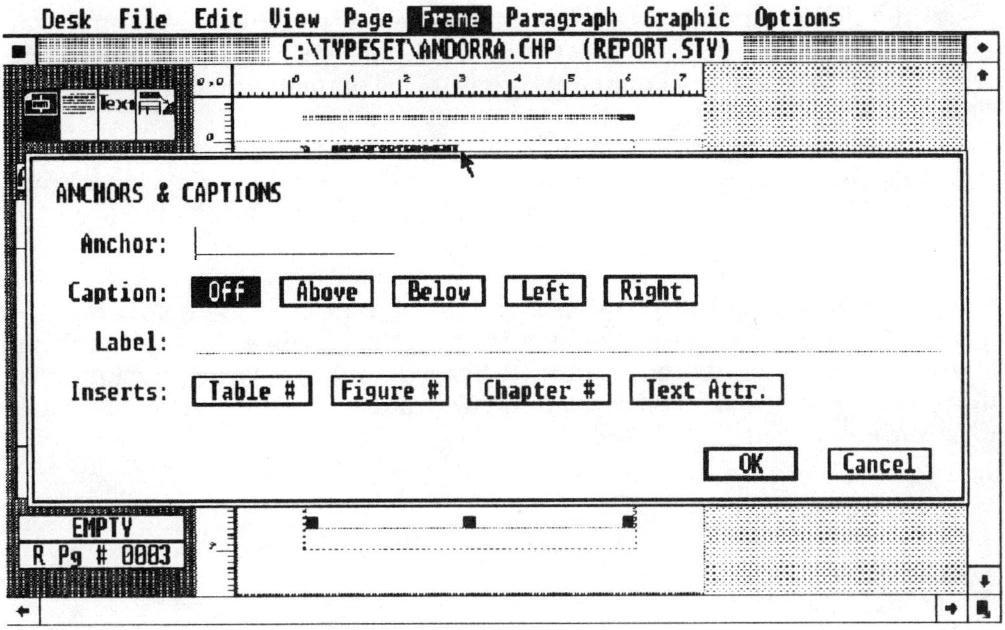

Figure 6.37

This menu has two purposes. You can create an anchor name for a frame and/or create a caption. In this example, you will do both. Begin by entering the anchor name of the frame. Enter

pop density

You also want to create a caption for the frame. A caption can contain any type of text and special codes for table, figure, and chapter numbers. Ventura keeps counters for tables and figures as well as for pages and chapters. You can create a caption that will automatically number the figures in the chapter.

First, select the location of the caption. For this example, point the mouse at the Below option and click the button. Next, enter the text of the caption:

Figure
[space bar]

Insert the figure number by pointing the mouse at the Figure # option and clicking the button. Ventura inserts the [F#] code. This symbol will be replaced by the value calculated by Ventura. Complete the menu by pressing

[return]

Ventura has automatically added a small frame (1/2" high) below the new frame. The words "Figure 1" appear in the frame. This is the caption frame automatically generated by Ventura when you chose to place a caption on the frame. The frame and its caption will move together when the frame location is changed.

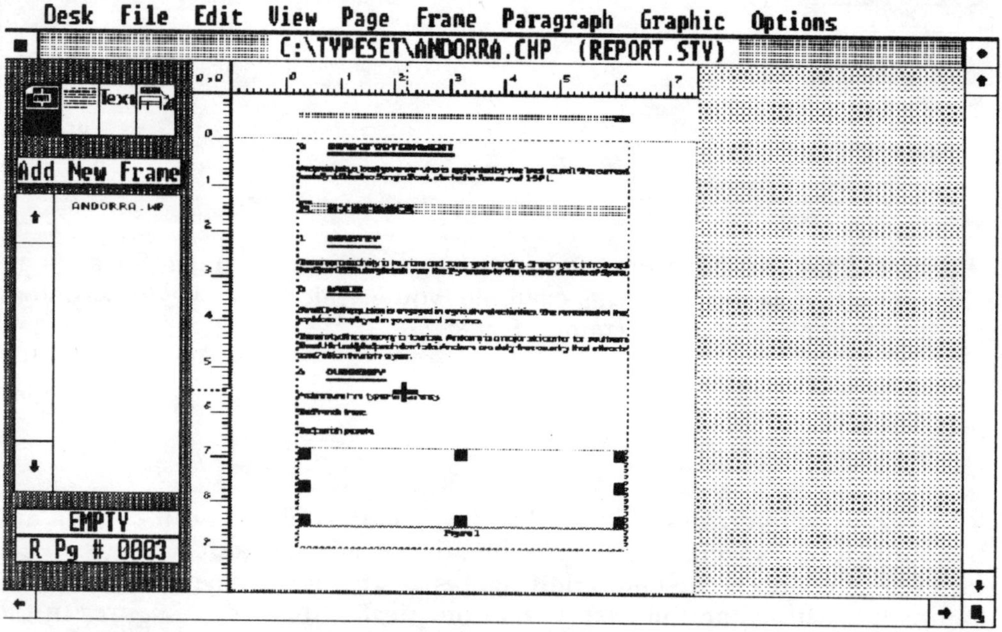

Figure 6.38

Before you complete the operation by loading the picture into the frame, you should copy the frame into memory. The other two graphs will fit into the exact same frame. All you must do is change the anchor name. By copying the frame into memory now, you can recall a copy of it when you want to add the next two graphs. Copy the frame into memory by pressing

[Shift/Del]

The next step is to load the graph file. Point the mouse at the File menu option. Point the mouse at the Load Text/Picture selection and click the button.

This time, you want to load line-art data. Point the mouse at the Line-Art option and click the button.

In the previous lesson, you selected Lotus .PIC files. That setting should still be active. If Lotus .PIC is not selected, select it by pointing the mouse at it and clicking the button. To save time, you might as well load all three graphs, so point the mouse at the Several option and click the button. Press

[return]

The item selector displays the last directory used for loading Lotus Graph files, which is C:\123 in this example (see Figure 6.39).

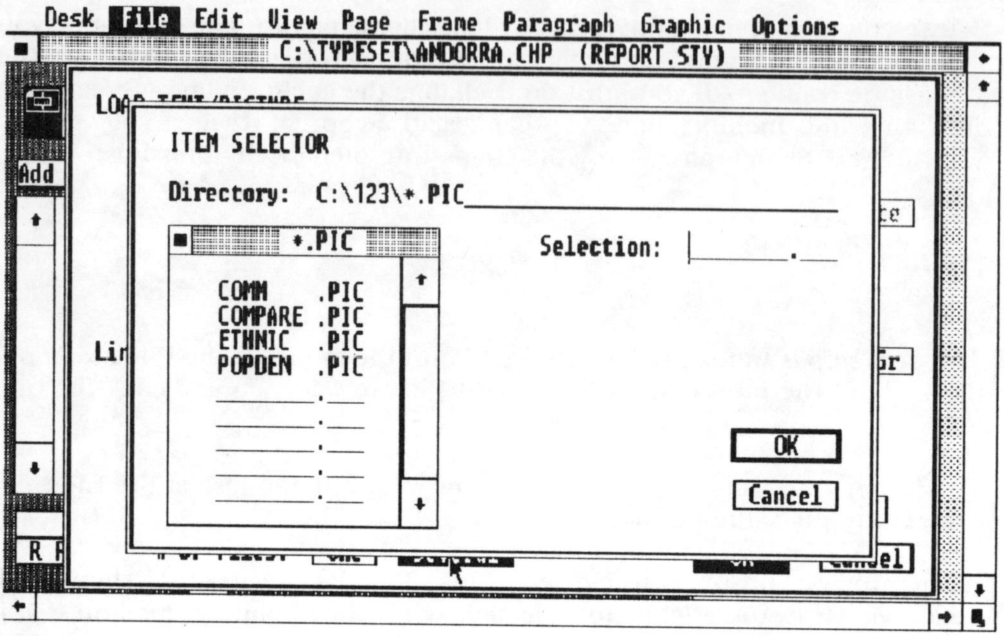

Figure 6.39

Load the three needed picture files. Point the mouse at COMM.PIC and click the button twice in rapid succession. Point the mouse at ETHNIC.PIC and click the button twice in rapid succession. Point the mouse at POPDEN.PIC and click the button twice in rapid succession. Then, point the mouse at OK and click the button once.

The three pictures are added to the list of files in the side bar display. To insert the POPDEN graph into this frame, point the mouse at POPDEN.PIC and click the button. The graph is displayed in the frame.

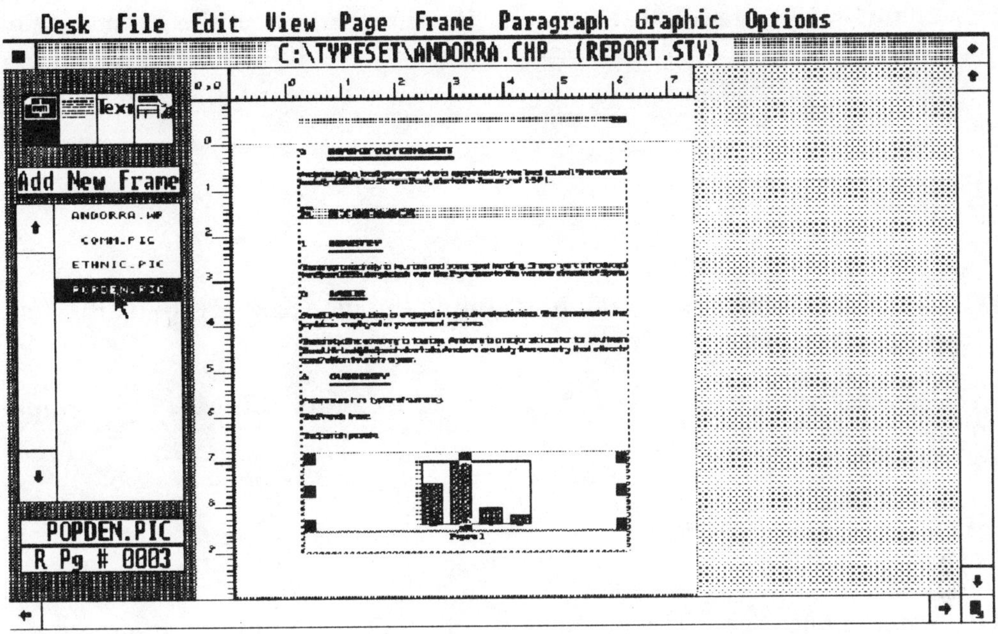

Figure 6.40

You can now save effort by recalling a copy of the frame from memory. Press

[Ins]

The new frame is laid precisely on top of the previous frame. Because the frames are transparent, the POP DENSITY frame shows through, making it appear as if there is only one frame on the page. If you look at the side bar, however, you will see "EMPTY" in the box above the page number, which indicates that the selected frame is empty. Normally, you would want to move the frames so that they would not overlap in this manner, but, in this case, it is just as easy to complete the loading and allow Ventura to automatically reposition the frames.

Enter the anchor name of the frame. Point the mouse at the Frame menu heading. Then, point the mouse at the Anchors & Captions option and click the button. Enter

ethnic
[return]

Load the graph into this frame by pointing the mouse at ETHNIC.PIC and clicking the button.

The process needs to be repeated for one more picture. Insert another empty frame. Press

[Ins]

Point the mouse at the Frame menu heading. Then, point the mouse at the Anchors & Captions selection and click the button. Enter

communications
[return]

Point the mouse at COMM.PIC and click the button. You have now set the stage for having Ventura automatically re-arrange the frames.

RE-ANCHORING FRAMES

Point the mouse at the Page menu heading. Then, point the mouse at the Re-Anchor Frames selection and click the button. Point the mouse at the All Pages option and click the button.

Ventura distributes the frames in the positions where the anchors have been entered into the text. Page 3 should resemble Figure 6.41.

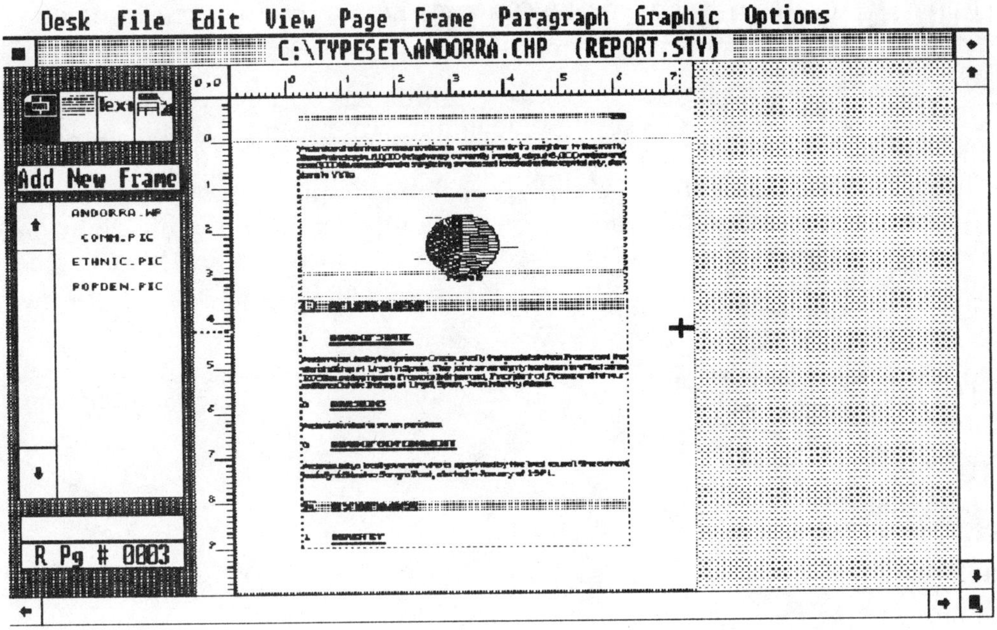

Figure 6.41

Review the entire document. Return to the first page by pressing

[Home]

Use the PgDn key to display each page. You will find that the document is now four pages long. Page 2 contains two graphs placed onto the page because of the anchors inserted in the text.

The system of frame anchors allows you to assemble a complex document with a minimum of manual frame manipulation. By planning ahead, you can assemble a document composed of a large number of frames without having to manually adjust each frame on the page, which is a clear example of how you can improve the operation of a program by taking advantage of automatic commands rather than manually carrying out each individual operation.

ADDING A NEW ANCHOR AND FRAME

The three anchored frames were easily positioned because you had already inserted the frame anchors into the document when you created it; however, there is still one frame that needs to be added to the report, but it is not yet either loaded or anchored. While it is desirable to place all the anchors into the text before the text is loaded, you can add anchors at any time by using the Edit menu. The frame that needs to be added is in the table of values imported from 1-2-3 in the form of a text file. The table shows the raw data used to create the communications graph.

Move to page 3 by entering

[Ctrl/g]
[backspace]
3
[return]

The table should be inserted between the "D. GOVERNMENT" subheading and the graph, which means that the anchor should be placed before the "D."

Anchors are inserted in the Text mode. Change to the Text mode by entering

[Ctrl/o]

Zoom in on the heading by pointing the mouse at "D" and entering

[Ctrl/e]

To add the anchor to the text, you will want to position the cursor before the "G" in "GOVERNMENT." Note that you cannot edit the paragraph number "D" because that number is text that is automatically generated by Ventura.

Point the mouse at "G" in "GOVERNMENT" and click the button. This action will place the text cursor on the line. The text cursor should be in front of the letter "G." Use the Left Arrow key to move the text cursor so that it is positioned at the beginning of the line. Here, you insert the anchor.

Point the mouse at the Edit menu heading. Then, point the mouse at the Insert/Edit Anchor selection and click the button. Ventura displays the INSERT/EDIT ANCHOR menu box.

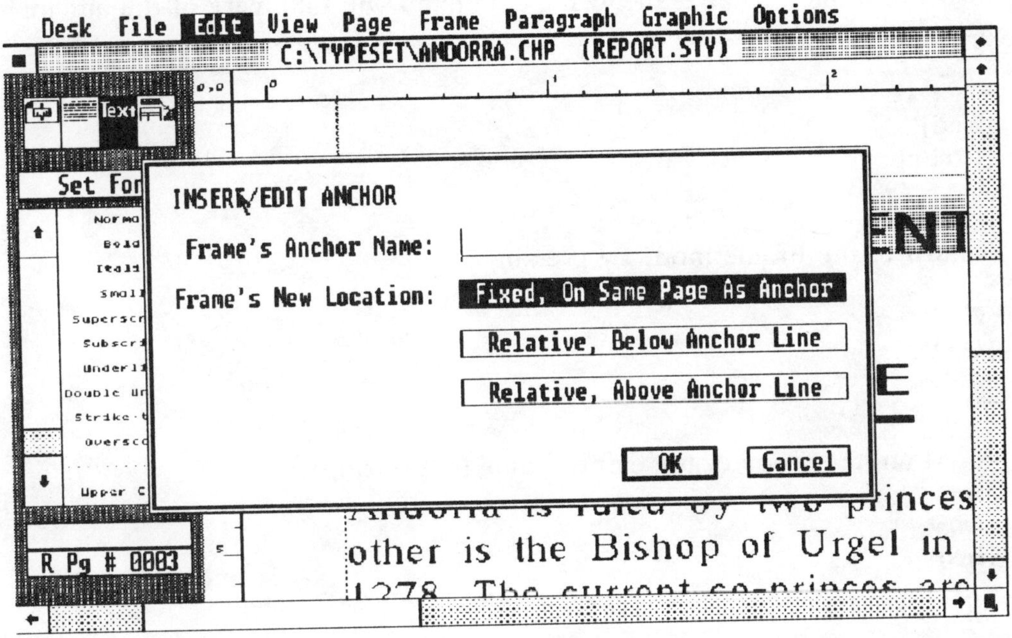

Figure 6.42

In this case, you want the frame to be positioned above the anchor location. Note that the Fixed option is used to make sure that the frame always appears at the same vertical position on the page. For example, if you placed a frame in the middle of the page, when it was re-anchored, it would be placed in the middle of whatever page the text anchor was located on. The position of the anchor on the page – top or bottom – would not affect the vertical placement of the frame.

Point the mouse at Relative, Above Anchor Line and click the button. Enter the name of the anchor:

comm text
[return]

With the anchor inserted, you can move to the last page of the document to load the frame. The re-anchoring command will take care of the anchor's actual placement. Enter

[End]
[Ctrl/r]

Return to the Frame mode by pressing

[Ctrl/u]

Insert another copy of the empty frame by pressing

[Ins]

The frame will remain in memory until you delete another frame or exit Ventura, which makes it possible to copy a frame from one document to another by copying a frame into memory, loading a different chapter, and inserting the frame into that chapter.

Give this frame an anchor name. Point the mouse at the Frame menu heading. Then, point the mouse at the Anchors & Captions selection and click the button. Enter the anchor name:

comm text
[down arrow]

Because this frame is a table, not a figure, you will want to change the caption. Enter

Table
[T #]
[return]

Next, you must load the text file into that frame. Point the mouse at the File menu heading. Then, point the mouse at the Load Text/Picture selection and click the button. This time, the file is text. Point the mouse at Text and click the button. The format of a Lotus text file is closest to WordStar. Note that the ASCII setting expects to enounter two [return] characters at the end of each line. If the text file has only one [return], such as in a Lotus PRN file, the WordStar format is the one that should be used.

Point the mouse at WordStar US and click the button. Then, press

[return]

The item selector attempts to find files with a WS extension in a directory called WS. In this instance, that specification is not what you are looking for. The file you want to load is a 1-2-3 file with a PRN extension. Enter

[up arrow]
[Esc]
c:\123*.prn
[return]

The selector box displays the PRN files. Point the mouse at COMM.PRN and click the button twice in rapid succession. The text is loaded into the new frame. For a closer look at the text, point the mouse at the upper left corner of the COMM.PRN frame and enter

[Ctrl/e]

The screen displays the text. You can see that the information is not properly aligned in columns. Also note that a special symbol appears between the text items. These symbols mark the location of "hard" space characters. The hard space characters and misaligned columns are related.

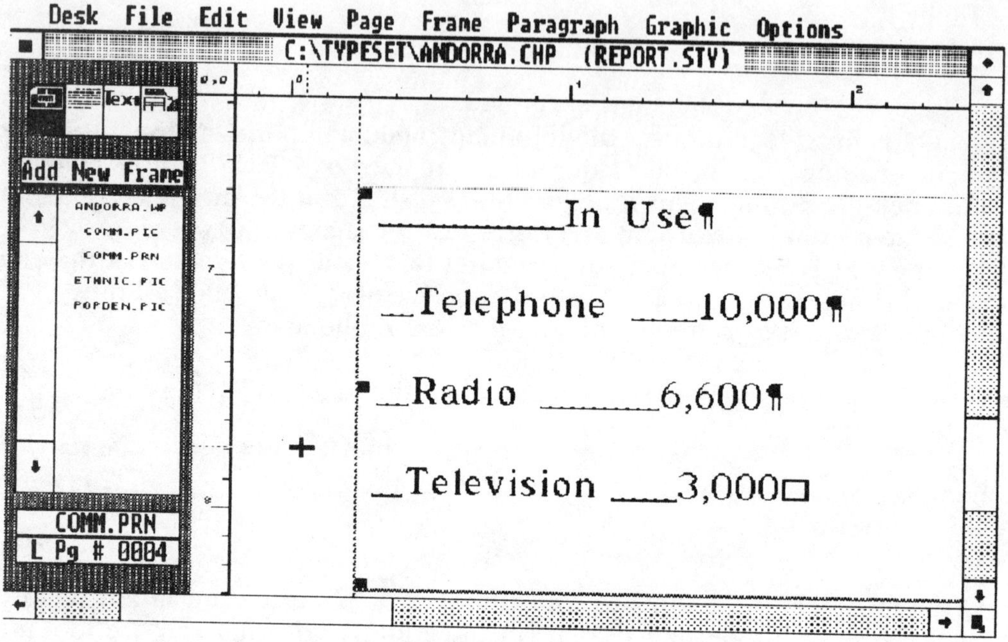

Figure 6.43

The characters and columns are a result of how Lotus 1-2-3 (and most text-oriented IBM PC programs) handle spacing. In these programs, all text printed is treated as **monospaced** text, in which the same amount of space is occupied by all printed characters, which means that a W (a wide character) will occupy the same width of space as an I (a narrow character). The advantage of this system is that getting text to align in columns is a simple matter of counting the number of characters. If there is a gap on a line, it can be filled with blank spaces since in a monospaced scheme, a space takes up the same amount of room as any other character.

Ventura, however, uses a more complicated system in which each character in each font is assigned a specific width. Spacing in Ventura is more than just a count of the number of characters; it matters which characters are actually entered (i.e., if they are wide or narrow). This system is called **proportional spacing** because space is assigned in proportion to the physical width of each character.

The file produced by 1-2-3 does not take into account this difference in formatting. The columns do not align properly in Ventura for this reason. There are two possible solutions:

1. The simplest is to format the text with a monospaced font such as Courier 10-point; however, this solution only applies to users who have such a font available on their systems.

2. Edit the text, which means that you must manually remove the spaces between items and replace them with [Tab] characters. The tabs can then be aligned using Ventura tab alignment features. While this solution takes longer, it is not font-dependent, so it can be implemented on any computer. (If you have a large file, however, you might want to edit it in your word processor.)

Place Ventura into the Text mode by pressing

[Ctrl/o]

Use the Delete key to remove all spaces, and replace each group with a single [Tab]. Figure 6.44 shows the tabs that replaced the spaces.

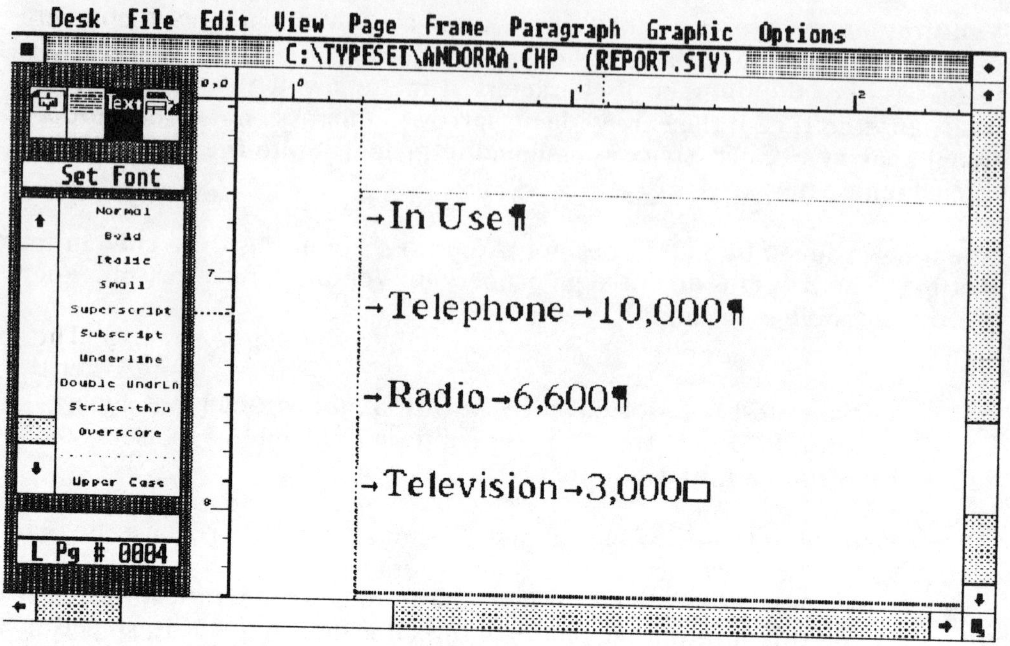

Figure 6.44

The next step is to create a new tag for the spreadsheet data. Place Ventura into the Paragraph mode by pressing

[Ctrl/i]

Point the mouse at "In Use" and click the button. Create a new tag by pointing the mouse at Add New Tag and clicking the button. Enter the name for the new tag:

spreadsheet
[return]

Before you set any tabs, you must change the alignment from justified to left-aligned. Ventura will not display tab-aligned text in justified paragraphs. Point the mouse at the Paragraph menu heading. Then, point the mouse at the Alignment selection and click the button. Point the mouse at Left and click the button. Complete these settings by pressing

[return]

Next, set the tabs. Point the mouse at the Paragraph menu heading. Then, point the mouse at the Tab Settings selection and click the button. Enter the first tab position:

[Esc]
01

Point the mouse at the number 2 and click the button. Enter the second tab stop by pointing the mouse at Decimal and clicking the button. Then, enter

[Esc]
03
[return]

Use the [Shift-click] method to tag the other three lines of text in the frame. Format them as SPREADSHEET by pointing the mouse at the Spreadsheet tag and clicking the button.

To complete the layout, change to the Reduced View and Frame modes. Enter

[Ctrl/r]
[Ctrl/u]

You can position the text in the frame by adding margins. Point the mouse at the Frame menu heading. Then, point the mouse at the Margins & Columns selection and click the button. Enter

[down arrow]
[Esc]
.15
[down arrow]
[down arrow]
[Esc]
01.5
[return]

You can also add a frame around the box to mark off the data from the rest of the text. Point the mouse at the Frame menu heading. Then, point the mouse at the Ruling Box Around selection and click the button. Select Frame by pointing the mouse at Frame and clicking the button. Enter

[Esc]
.05
[down arrow]
[Esc]
.02
[return]

You can now have Ventura re-anchor the frames and put this one in its proper position. Point the mouse at the Page menu heading. Then, point the mouse at the Re-Anchor Frames selection and click the button. Point the mouse at All Pages and click the button.

Save the completed document by entering

[Ctrl/s]
andorra
[return]

You can now print the document if you want to see the results of your work. In the next chapter, you will learn how to create a table of contents and index from this document.

SUMMARY

Text Files

Ventura alters the text in text files loaded into frames by inserting text codes that indicate style tags, font changes, text attributes, index entries, and footnotes. Conversely, adding text codes to document files in word processors will cause Ventura to automatically tag and format text, which means you can designate Ventura style tags as you create a text file.

Text Formatting Codes

Ventura style tags are entered into text files by using the format

@tag name =

Footnotes are created by entering

<$Ftext of footnote>

Index entries are created by entering

<$Ientry;sub entry>

Frame Anchors

Frame **anchors** are used to position frames at specific locations within a document. By inserting frame anchors into the document, you can have Ventura automatically position the frames within a document when you use the Re-anchor Frames command. A frame anchor is inserted into the text by entering

<$&anchor name[^]> (places frame above anchor)

<$&anchor name[V]> (places frame below anchor)

Gray Backgrounds

You can create the effect of printing text on a gray or black background for individual paragraph tags by using a special form of the Ruling Line Above command. The ruling line is set for a height that covers or exceeds the height of the typeface; for example, for 18-point type, set the line at a height of 18/72" or .25". The background effect is achieved by setting the Space Below Rule 3 to a negative value equal to or in excess of ruling line height. This setting causes the text of the paragraph and the ruling line to overlap, creating the background effect.

Headers and Footers

Ventura allows you to create page headers and footers. You can define separate headers and footers for the left and right pages. The header or footer will appear on all pages unless you use the Page menu to turn off the header or footer on specific pages.

In addition to text, headers and footers can include page and chapter numbers. The starting page and chapter numbers can be controlled from the Page menu. The default value for both is 1.

Text enhancements can be added to headers and footers by using text codes. For example, <P014> sets the text to 14-point type.

Headers and footers can also include text from the document. You can specify a tag name, usually a heading of some kind, which will be inserted into the header or footer on that page. In case no text with the specified tag appears on that specific page, you can tell Ventura to use the previous or next instance of that tag name.

Footnote Settings

Footnotes will not appear in the text unless the footnote settings are turned on. You can select the numbering style, sequence, and normal, super-, or subscripted footnote references. You can also create a line to separate footnotes from the rest of the text.

Paragraph Numbering

Ventura can automatically generate a paragraph numbering sequence in the text, based on tag names. Each tag is assigned a numbering level and sequence style. The paragraph numbers are separate paragraphs from the text of the tagged paragraphs they number, which means that they will appear on the line above the tagged text, not on the same line. To place the numbers on the same lines as the tagged text, you must alter the tagged text by indenting the paragraph and suppressing the line break before the paragraph.

Frame Anchor Names

Frames added to the main document can be assigned anchor names. These names are meant to match up with anchors placed into the text. The Re-anchor Frames command will reorganize the document, placing each frame above or below the anchors in the text. This system allows you to connect illustrations and text while you edit your document.

Captions

Frames can also have captions. A caption can be any text that you want to appear above, below, or to the right or left of a specific frame. Ventura will also consecutively number the captions. Ventura uses two caption counters: one for figures and the other for tables.

CHAPTER 7

MULTIPLE-DOCUMENT OPERATIONS

In Chapter 6, you created a multiple-page document that used Ventura to organize a document layout consisting of a major text file with additional text and picture files. Ventura created footnotes, page headers and footers, paragraphs, figures, and table numbers.

All of these features were implemented in a single document; however, there are operations that can only be performed using Ventura's multi-chapter commands. The term **multi-chapter** is a bit misleading. Many of the operations that fall under the heading of multi-chapter operations can apply to a single document or chapter. For example, the ANDORRA chapter (from Chapter 6) contains table of contents and index items. You can generate an index for that one document or combine other documents with that one to create a multi-chapter table of contents or index.

Perhaps a better name for the operations that Ventura calls multi-chapter would be reference tasks; however, it doesn't matter what name you use; these tasks have some important points in common. First, these tasks are performed on chapter files that have been saved; you cannot perform any of these operations on a document you are working on but have not saved. All the multi-chapter operations are conducted automatically. You do not have explicit manual control over what takes place. For example, when Ventura generates an index, it does so automatically, based on the codes inserted into the files you are indexing. You do not see the text of the documents or the generated index. The index is stored directly on disk in the form of a text file that must then be loaded into a chapter file to be viewed. Multi-chapter operations can be performed only on full chapters. You cannot index part of a chapter.

In this chapter, you will use the ANDORRA document prepared in Chapter 6 to generate an index, table of contents, and perform other multi-chapter tasks. To begin this chapter, load Ventura in the usual manner.

THE PUBLICATION FILE

All multi-file, or reference, operations begin with the creation of a **publication file**. Publication files are used for groups of related chapters so that operations such as indexing or table of contents generation can determine which files compose the entire document. As mentioned previously, a publication chapter can contain only a single chapter if that chapter is the only one with which you need to work.

The first step is to select multi-chapter operations by pointing the mouse at the Options menu heading. Ventura displays the Options menu.

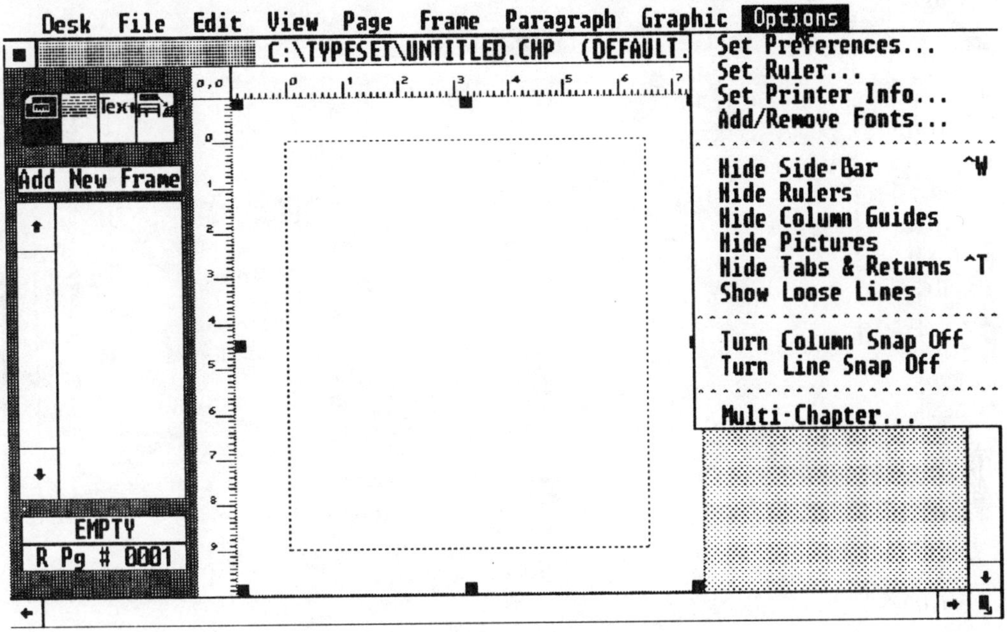

Figure 7.1

Point the mouse at the Multi-Chapter option and click the button. Ventura displays the MULTI-CHAPTER OPERATIONS menu box.

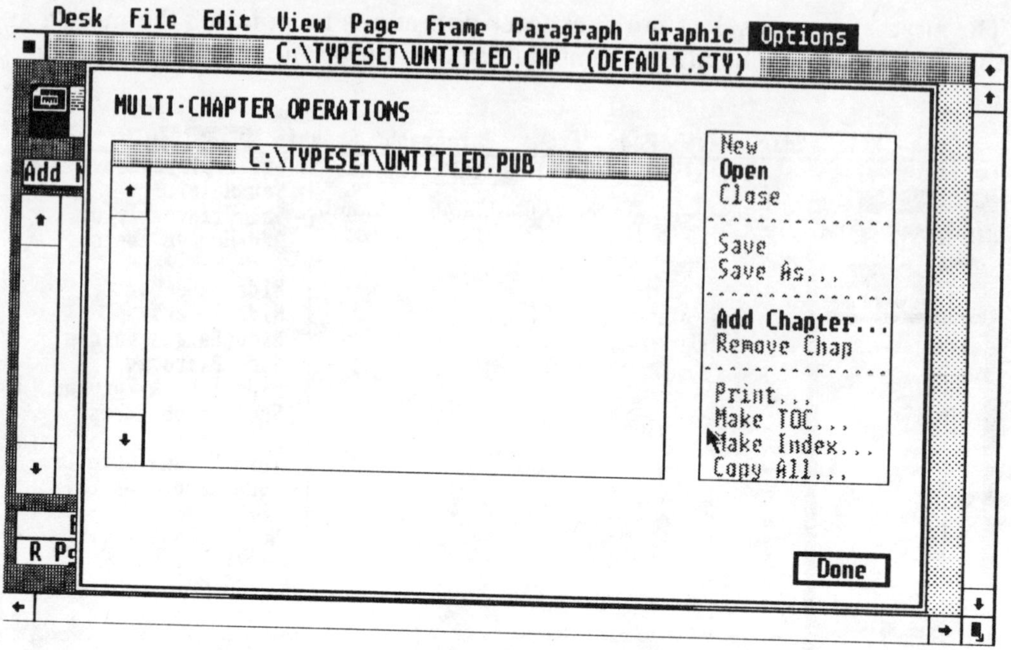

Figure 7.2

In the center of the menu box is a file selector box. Since multi-chapter operations work on entire files, the selector box is the focus of your operations. On the right side of the box is a list of command options. At this point, there are only two options available:

- **Open**: used to open an existing publication file.
- **Add Chapter**: used to add a chapter to the current publication file, if any.

In this case, you will begin to create a new publication file by adding a chapter.

Point the mouse at Add Chapter and click the button. Ventura overlays the Multi-Chapter box with a file selector display. You can use the display to locate the chapters you want added to the publication file.

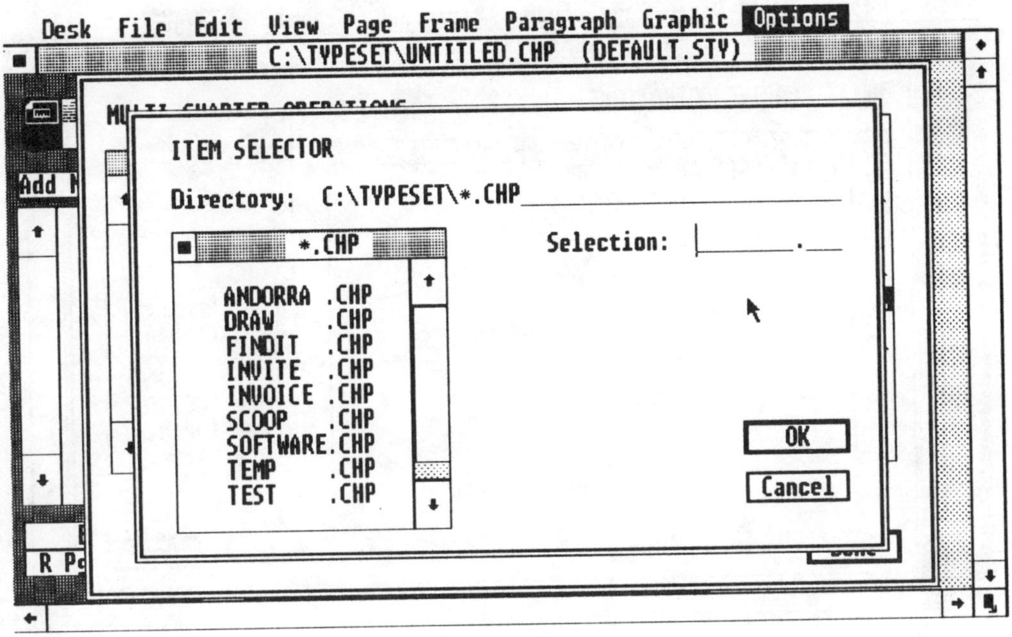

Figure 7.3

Select the ANDORRA chapter by pointing the mouse at ANDORRA.CHP and clicking the button twice in rapid succession. The chapter is then entered into the multi-chapter display.

In the case of the chapters in a publication file, Ventura displays the drive and the directory names as well as the chapter name because you can store chapters in different directories or drives as part of the same publication file.

Currently, the publication file is called UNTITLED. To create a publication file for the chapter, use the Save command. Point the mouse at the Save option and click the button. Then, enter the name of the publication file:

geograph
[return]

You have now established the name of this publication file.

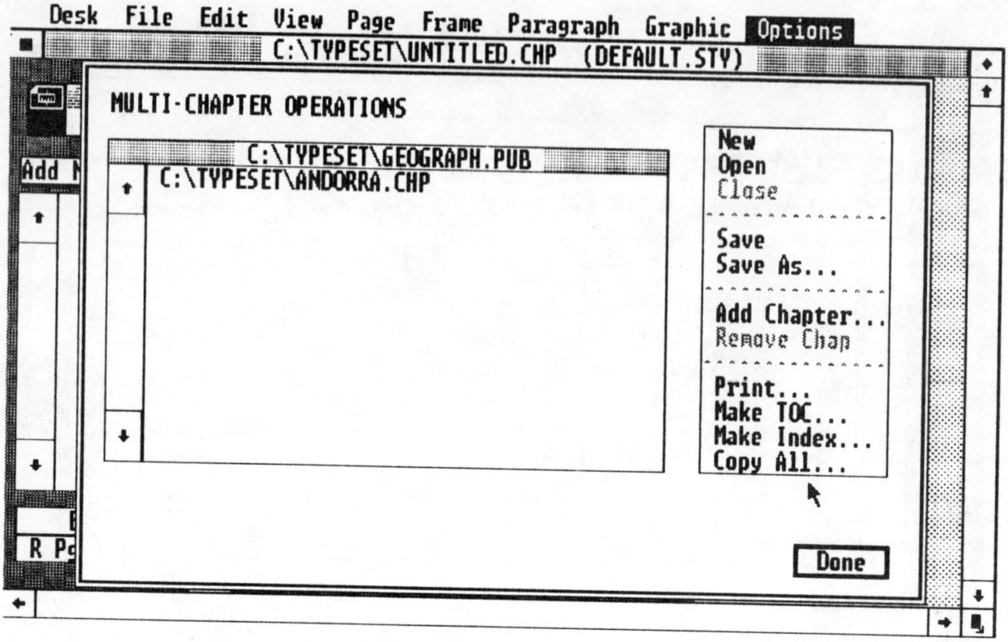

Figure 7.4

ADDING AND REMOVING CHAPTERS

You can add new chapters to the publication file in the same way that you added the first chapter. Point the mouse at Add Chapter and click the button. Next, add the invoice chapter. Point the mouse at INVOICE.CHP and click the button twice in rapid succession.

You now have two chapters in the publication file. Remember that the order in which the files are listed is significant for the table of contents operation. Ventura assumes that the order of the chapters in the publication file list is the order in which the chapters will appear in the final product and, therefore, the order in which the table of contents should be constructed.

Ventura always places the new file at the bottom of the list. If this order isn't correct, you can change the order of the files by dragging the names to new locations. In this example, the INVOICE chapter follows ANDORRA because you loaded it after the ANDORRA file. Suppose that the order of the files should be reversed. You can use the drag method to change the position.

Point the mouse at ANDORRA and hold down the mouse button. A hand symbol appears, indicating that you have activated the drag mode.

While holding down the mouse button, drag the highlighted text below the INVOICE chapter. Then release the button. The order of the chapters in the publication file is changed.

You can also remove a chapter from a publication. First, highlight the file you want to remove. Point the mouse at INVOICE.CHP and click the button. Then, point the mouse at Remove Chapter and click the button.

The name of the chapter is removed from the publication file list. Remember that you cannot delete a chapter from the disk; you can only delete its name from the list of chapters in the publication file.

OPENING A CHAPTER FILE

One of the options in the multi-chapter display is Open. You need to understand that Open in this instance has a very different meaning than it does when you are in the normal Ventura chapter mode. In this case, Open is used to display a list of all the files—text, picture, style, etc.—that are used by the chapter file. This list is quite handy because you may eventually find it difficult to sort out which files belong to which chapters.

To see the list for ANDORRA, make sure that the ANDORRA.CHP file is highlighted. Point the mouse at ANDORRA.CHP and click the button. Next, open the chapter file list by pointing the mouse at the Open option and clicking the button.

Ventura displays a box warning you that you are about to lose some data—the changes you made when you added and then removed that INVOICE chapter. In this case, you don't care about those changes, so point the mouse at Abandon and click the button.

Ventura lists the files that are used by ANDORRA.CHP.

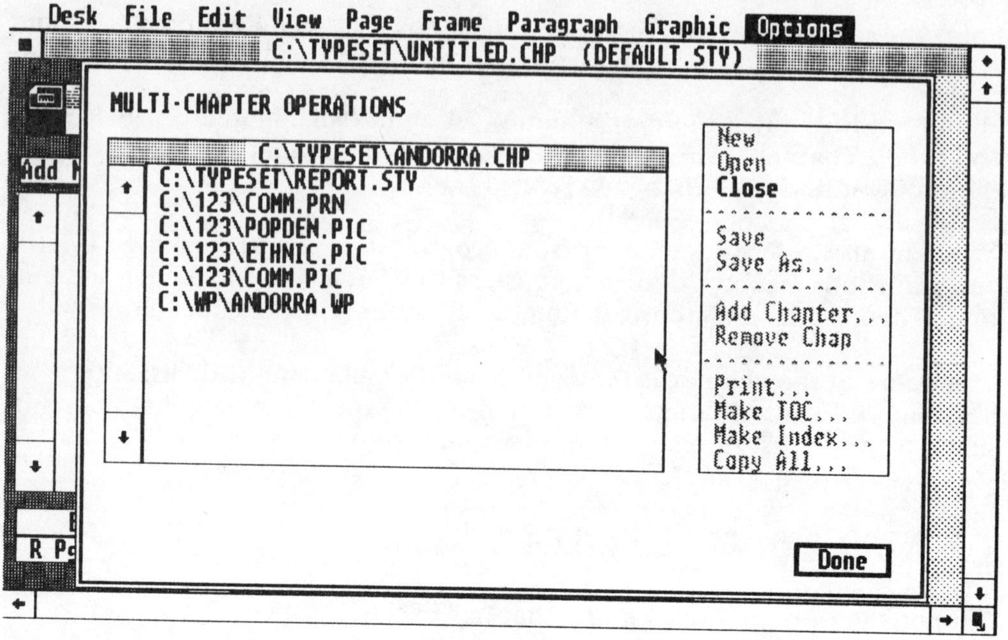

Figure 7.5

You can see that there are six files drawn from three different directories. To return to the publication display, select the Close command. Point the mouse at Close and click the button.

GENERATING A TABLE OF CONTENTS

Ventura can produce a table of contents from the chapter or chapters listed in the publication file. In this example, there is only one file. You can create a table of contents for this one chapter, or you can add other chapters. Ventura produces the table of contents by searching each chapter for specific style tags. The text from those tags is copied into a table of contents file. The text in the table of contents file reflects the order in which the tagged text appears in the chapter and the order in which the chapters are listed in the publication file.

To create a table of contents, select Make TOC from the Multi-Chapter option in the Options menu. Point the mouse at Make TOC and click the button. Ventura displays the GENERATE TABLE OF CONTENTS menu box.

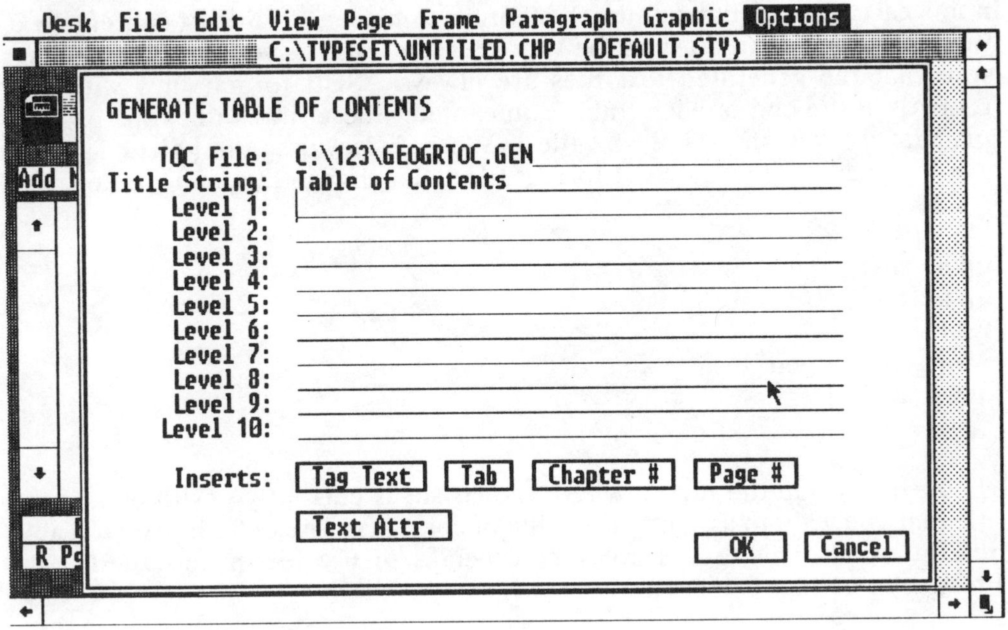

Figure 7.6

The menu box consists of three types of entries.

The first line is the name of the text file that Ventura will create. This file will contain the text copied from the chapter files. Ventura automatically creates a name for this file. It takes the first five characters of the publication file name, GEOGR, and adds TOC and an extension of .GEN (generated text) with a final result of GEOGRTOC.GEN; however, you might have noticed that the directory for the text file is assumed to be \123. If you do not want the text stored in the \123 directory, then change the file name to reflect the appropriate directory.

In this case, you might want to tell Ventura to place the table of contents text file into the same directory as the WordPerfect text files you have been using. Note that the generated text files are always ASCII format files with two [return]s at the end of each line. You can edit these files with word processors that work with ASCII text files. WordPerfect uses the [Ctrl/F5] command to load and save ASCII format files. To change the name, enter

[up arrow]
[up arrow
[Esc]
c:\wp\geogrtoc.gen
[down arrow]

The next item on the menu, where the cursor is currently positioned, is the title that you want to assign to the table of contents. The default text is "Table of Contents." This text is not very crucial because it can be edited later. Press

[down arrow]

The next ten lines are significant. They tell Ventura what information to draw from the file and place into the table of contents text file.

Ventura allows you to specify up to ten levels for the table of contents. In practice, however, most users will never include more than three or four levels since most publishers like to keep tables of contents to two or three levels.

A typical table of contents sets the first level as chapter headings, the second level as subheadings, and the third, if desired, as any topic headings within the subheadings.

Begin with the chapter heading level. Enter

Chapter
[space bar]

At this point, you might want to insert the chapter number. Point the mouse at Chapter # and click the button.

Separate the chapter number from the chapter heading by a tab. Point the mouse at Tab and click the button.

The next item on the line will tell Ventura what text should be used as the chapter heading. Ventura selects text based on the style tag used for a particular paragraph. In this example, the MAJOR HEAD tag was used for the main chapter title. To insert a tag name, select the Tag Name item by pointing the mouse at Tag Text and clicking the button.

Ventura inserts the symbol [*tag name] on the line. Remember that this symbol cannot be left as it is. You must change the words "tag name" to the name of an actual tag used in the document. Enter

[left arrow]
[backspace] (8 times)
major head

The final step is to add the number of the page on which the major heading is found. Enter

[right arrow]

Insert a tab between the heading text and the page number by pointing the mouse at Tab and clicking the button.

Now insert the code for the page number. Point the mouse at Page # and click the button. The menu box now resembles Figure 7.7.

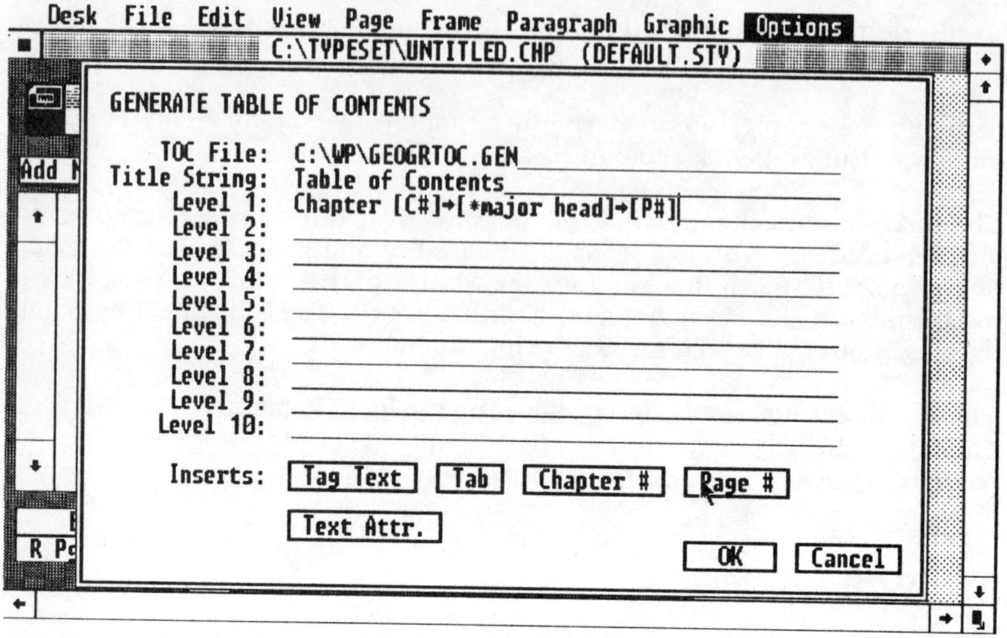

Figure 7.7

You are ready to create the next level of the table of contents. Press

[down arrow]

The second-level heading can begin without a title such as CHAPTER. You can enter the name of the text tag manually; you do not need to use the Tag Text box. Enter

[*sub head] (type in brackets here)

Next, add the page number. Point the mouse at Tab and click the button. Then, point the mouse at Page # and click the button.

The final entry will be the third-level heading and will be the TOPIC tag. Enter the name of the tag to be used for third-level headings:

[*topic] (type in brackets here)

Add the page number codes. Point the mouse at Tab and click the button. Then, point the mouse at Page # and click the button.

The specification is now complete.

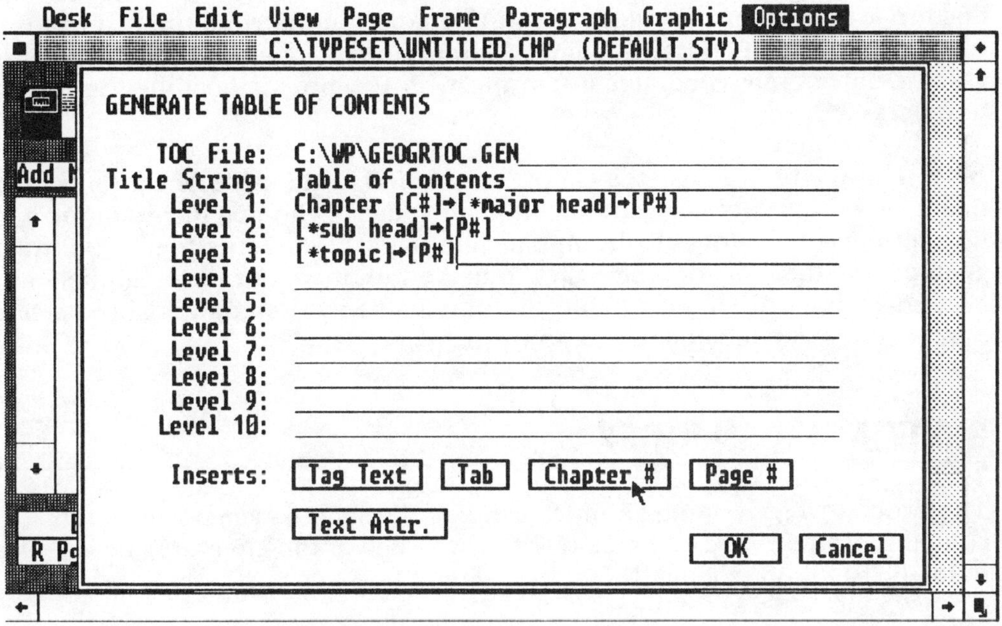

Figure 7.8

You are now ready to generate a table of contents file. Keep in mind that once you create a table of contents specification for a publication file, Ventura will store that setup so you can use it over again. You need only set up a specification from scratch when you start a new publication file, which means that as you add, remove, or rearrange chapters in the publication file, you can simply run the same table of contents specification and generate an updated table of contents.

To begin the generation process, point the mouse at OK and click the button. Ventura displays a box on the screen that shows the files it is loading and working with. When this process is complete, the GEOGRTOC.GEN file is written to disk. This file contains the table of contents text; however, it is not really a finished table of contents. To get the final product, you will need to load that text file into a Ventura chapter and format the text to look like a real table of contents. The table of contents operation you have just carried out merely generates a text file with the proper headings and page numbers.

Note: If you edit or revise the chapters included in the table of contents, you might, as a result, change the location of some of the headings. Ventura is not designed to automatically update the table of contents file. You must generate the table of contents again to make sure that your page numbers are accurate. For this reason, table of contents generation should be the last operation in the document creation process.

GENERATING AN INDEX

The process of generating an index is much the same as generating a table of contents. Indexes are not sensitive to the order of the chapters because the index is listed alphabetically.

Like table of contents generation, index generation produces a text file with the index entries and their page numbers. This text file still needs to be loaded into a Ventura chapter file and formatted before you can print out an index.

To begin the index generation, select Make Index from the Multi-Chapter option in the Options menu by pointing the mouse at the Make Index option and clicking the button. Ventura displays the GENERATE INDEX box.

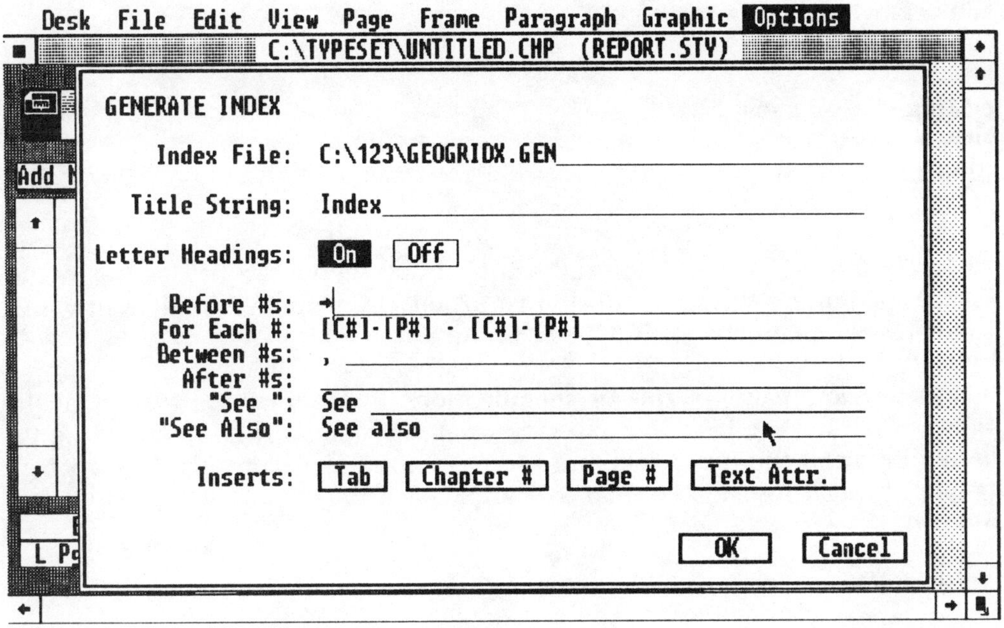

Figure 7.9

In some ways, indexes are less complicated than tables of contents. One reason is that Ventura already knows where to find the index text. Unlike tables of contents, which are drawn by tag name, the index text is entered into special index codes that do not appear in the text of the document. Ventura automatically knows that index generation is aimed at finding those specific items.

Ventura displays a default setup for the index file. This setup is the most commonly used type of index format, so you probably can accept the default.

Before you do, however, examine the settings to learn what they mean. The top line shows the name of the index text file. Note the drive and directory location to see if they agree with your specifications. In this case, you will want to change the location so you can place the file in your WP directory. Enter

[up arrow]
[up arrow]
[Esc]
c:\wp\geogrindx.gen
[down arrow]
[down arrow]

The title for the index is entered as "Index." Below the title is the Letter Headings option. When the option is turned On, which is the default value, it creates the headings A, B, C, etc. in the index.

The next section is a series of specifications that define the format of the index entries. The first lines specify what characters, if any, should be inserted between the index text and the page number. The default is a tab. It is more typical to use a comma and a space. Enter

[backspace]
, (a comma)
[space bar]

The next item determines the type of page numbering used. The default is to use both chapter and page numbers, e.g., 1-10. In this case, use only the page numbers. Enter

[Esc]
[P#]-[P#] (type in brackets here)

You can leave the rest of the defaults are they are. Generate the index text file by pointing the mouse at OK and clicking the button.

When the file has been created, you will be returned to the MULTI-CHAPTER OPERATIONS menu. Exit this menu by pointing the mouse at Done and clicking the button. Then, save your changes. Point the mouse at Save and click the button.

The next step is to load the text files and format them to look like tables of contents and indexes.

FORMATTING THE TABLE OF CONTENTS

The previous section of this chapter showed you how to generate text files that contain the basic information for the table of contents and the index, which means those files merely contain the text but are not formatted Ventura chapters that are ready to be printed. To get the table of contents and index ready for printing, you must create Ventura documents from the text files.

The only difference between normal text files and files created when a table of contents or index is generated is that for the latter, Ventura automatically tags the paragraphs with specially generated tags.

To format the table of contents, all you must do is define the paragraph format of the tags that you have already entered into the text.

Begin by loading the table of contents text file into the current document. Point the mouse at the File menu heading. Then, point the mouse at the Load Text/Picture selection and click the button.

The LOAD TEXT/PICTURE menu box appears. Remember that the text file was created automatically by Ventura, which means you should use the generated format.

Point the mouse at Generated and click the button. Press

[return]

Ventura displays the ITEM SELECTOR box. Ventura may not suggest the correct directory. You can use the cursor to change the selector or manually enter the selector specification. In this case, because you know the location and the names of the files needed, make a manual entry:

[up arrow]
[Esc]
c:\wp\geo*.wp
[return]

Point the mouse at GEOGRTOC.GEN and click the button twice in rapid succession. Ventura loads the text of the table of contents into the document window.

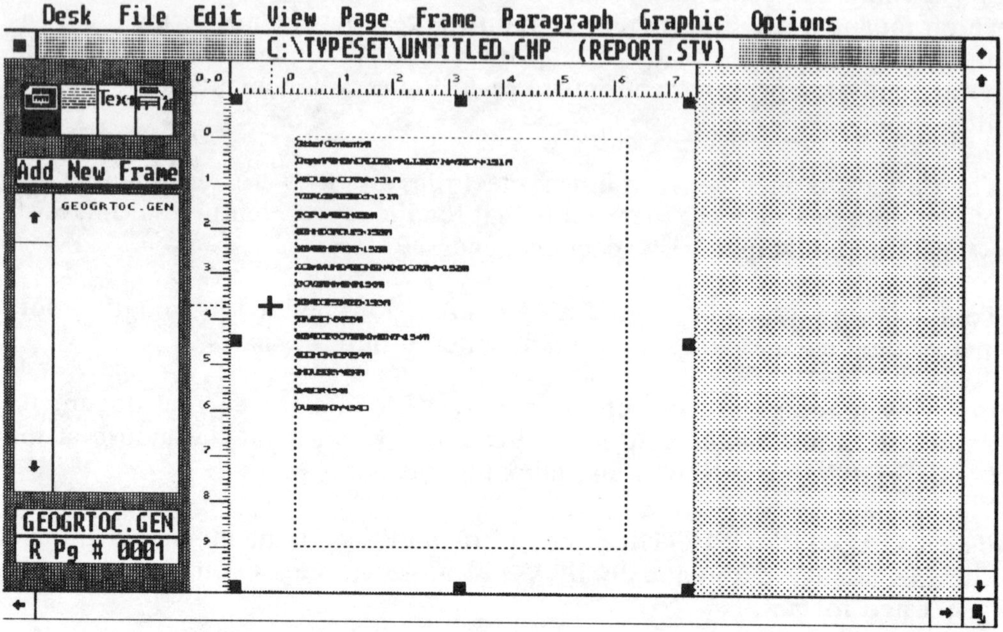

Figure 7.10

Note that it is common to enter headings in all uppercase letters in a document. When the table of contents is compiled, Ventura extracts the text exactly as it is entered into the document, which means that all items in the table of contents may be in uppercase. If you want to change the text, you can use the Capitalize function in the Text mode to change all uppercase text to first letter uppercase and remainder lowercase, without having to re-enter any text.

The top line of the text is the title of the table of contents. Place Ventura in the Paragraph mode. Enter

[Ctrl/i]

Then, change the display mode to Normal View. Point the mouse at the upper left corner of the frame and enter

[Ctrl/n]

Highlight the first line of the text by pointing the mouse at "Table of Contents" and clicking the button.

The box above the page number shows that the name of this tag is Z_TOC TITLE (table of contents title). This tag was automatically created during the table of contents generation. The text for the title was determined by the heading entered in the table of contents generation menu. Change this title to centered, Swiss 24-point Bold.

First, point the mouse at the Paragraph menu heading. Then, point the mouse at the Font selection and click the button. Point the mouse at Swiss and click the button. Point the mouse at 24 and click the button. Remember, Swiss 24-point is automatically bold. Execute these settings by pressing

[return]

Next, again point the mouse at the Paragraph menu heading. Then, point the mouse at the Alignment selection and click the button. Point the mouse at Center and click the button. Execute these settings by pressing

[return]

The next step is to format the first level of the table of contents, which is the chapter heading. Point the mouse at "Chapter" and click the button. The box on top of the page number shows the name of the tag, Z_TOC LVL 1. Ventura creates a separate tag for each level in the table of contents, Z_TOC LVL 2, Z_TOC LVL 3, etc. Change the font to 14-point Swiss Bold.

Point the mouse at the Paragraph menu heading. Then, point the mouse at the Font selection and click the button. Point the mouse at Swiss and click the button. Finally, point the mouse at 14 and click the button. Execute these settings by pressing

[return]

Next, create the tab stops that will align the text on that line. Point the mouse at the Paragraph menu heading. Then, point the mouse at the Tab Settings selection and click the button.

Set the first tab at 1.5". Enter

[Esc]
01.5

The second tab on the line should be set as a decimal tab at 5.5". Point the mouse at 2 and click the button. Then, point the mouse at Decimal and click the button. Enter

[Esc]
05.5
[return]

Ventura displays a box telling you that it will not show the tabs you just entered because the alignment value of the paragraph is set for justified text.

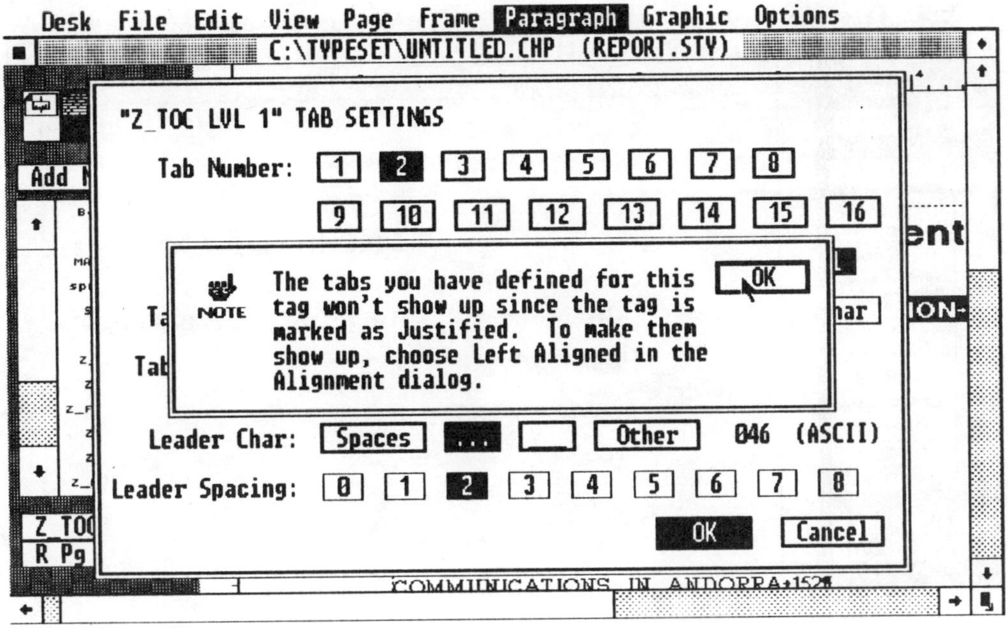

Figure 7.11

Point the mouse at OK and click the button. You need to change the alignment setting so the tabs can affect the text.

Point the mouse at the Paragraph menu heading. Then, point the mouse at the Alignment option and click the button. Point the mouse at Left and click the button. Finally, press

[return]

The first line is now formatted correctly.

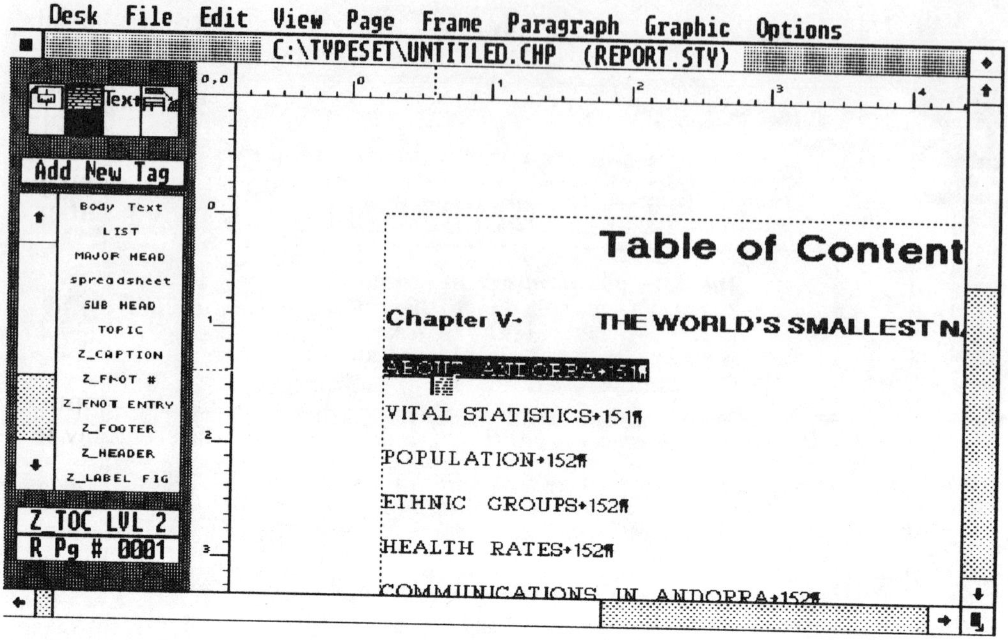

Figure 7.12

Now format the second-level paragraphs. Point the mouse at "ABOUT ANDORRA" and click the button.

In this case, you want to perform three steps:

1. Change the alignment from justified to left-aligned.
2. Create an indent of 1.5", matching the tab used for the first level.
3. Create a tab at 5.5" for the page number.

First, point the mouse at the Paragraph menu heading. Then, point the mouse at the Alignment selection and click the button. Select left alignment by pointing the mouse at Left and clicking the button. Enter

[Esc]
01.5
[return]

Note that not only did the line that was highlighted change, but all the subheadings in the table of contents changed because they all share the same style tag, Z__TOC LVL 2, which was inserted into the text file while the table of contents was generated.

Create the tab for the page number. In this case, you will also want to create a series of dot leaders that will run between the text and the page number.

Point the mouse at the Paragraph menu heading. Then, point the mouse at the Tab Settings selection and click the button. Next, point the mouse at Decimal and click the button.

To create a series of dot leaders, select the Shown as Leader Char. option. This setting changes the space between tabs from an open-space display to a line of dots. This format is commonly used in tables of contents.

Point the mouse at Shown as Leader Char. and click the button. Then, enter the value for the page number tab:

05.5
[return]

The second-level headings are formatted (see Figure 7.13).

The third-level headings should be treated exactly the same except that the indent should be set at 2 to show the headings in the proper outline format.

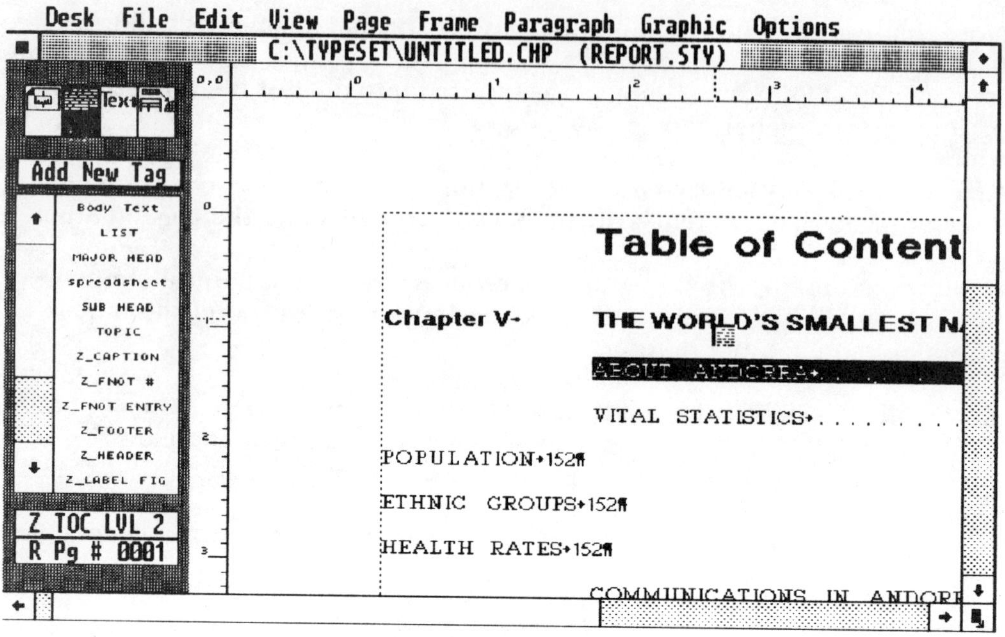

Figure 7.13

Point the mouse at "POPULATION" and click the button. Change the format to match the other headings by pointing the mouse at the Paragraph menu heading, pointing the mouse at the Alignment selection, and clicking the button. Then, point the mouse at Left and click the button. Enter

[Esc]
02
[return]

Next, again point the mouse at the Paragraph menu heading. Then, point the mouse at the Tab Settings selection and click the button. Point the mouse at Decimal and click the button. Finally, point the mouse at Shown as Leader Char. and click the button. Enter

05.5
[return]

The third-level headings are formatted.

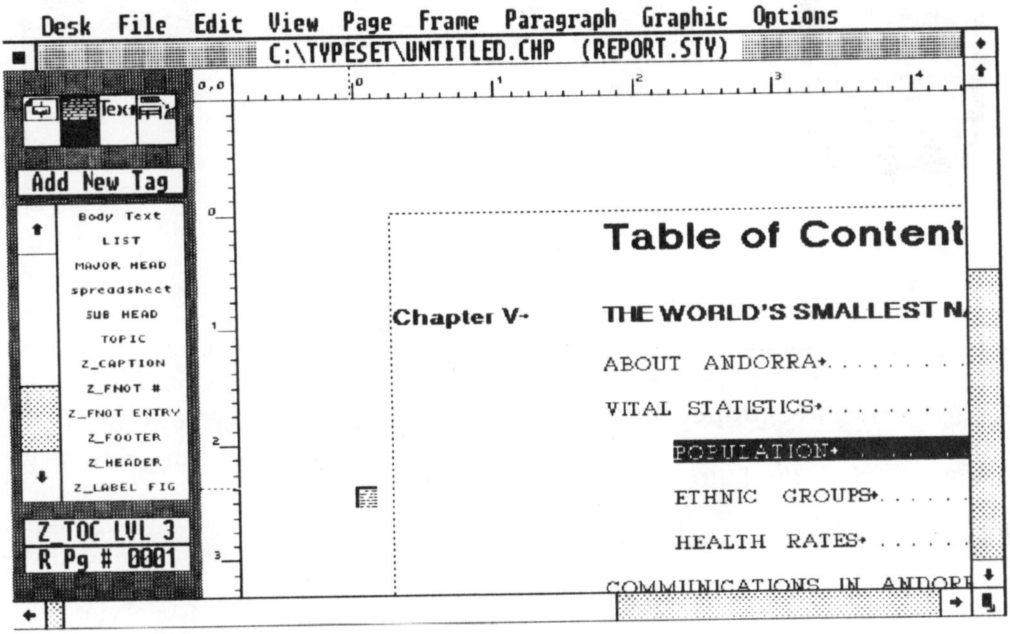

Figure 7.14

To see the entire display, change to the Reduced View mode. Enter

[Ctrl/r]

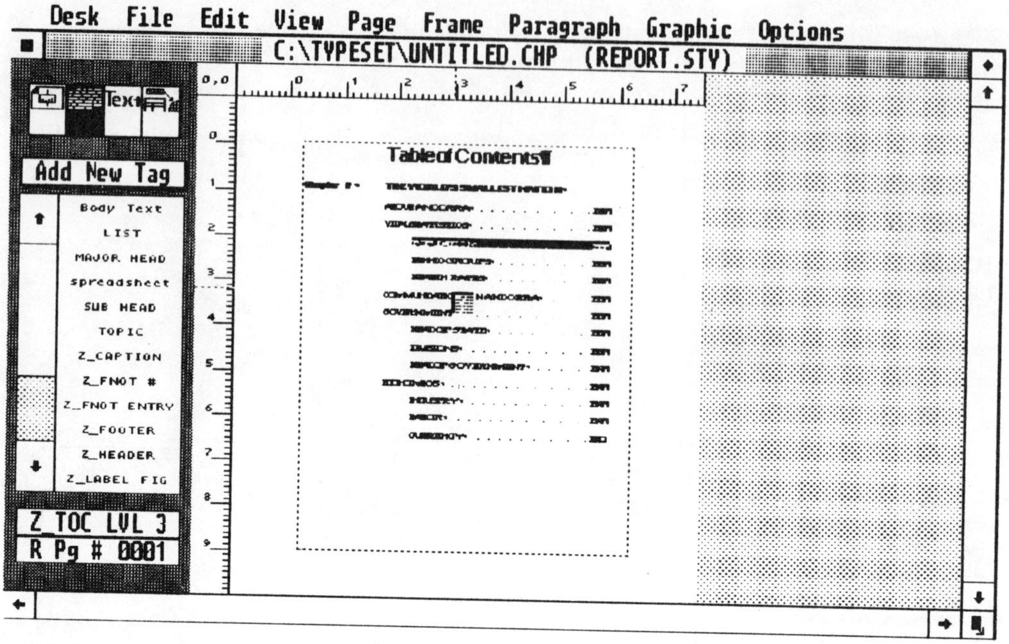

Figure 7.15

The table of contents is ready for printing.

When you have printed the text, clear the document area by pointing the mouse at the File menu heading. Then, point the mouse at the New selection and click the button.

Save the table of contents document by pointing the mouse at Save and clicking the button. Enter a name for the file:

ANDTOC
[return]

FORMATTING THE INDEX

To begin formatting the index, load the text of the index by pointing the mouse at the File menu heading. Then, point the mouse at the Load Text/Picture selection and click the button. Press

[return]

Next, point the mouse at GEOGRIDX.GEN and click the button twice in rapid succession. The index text should appear in the document frame.

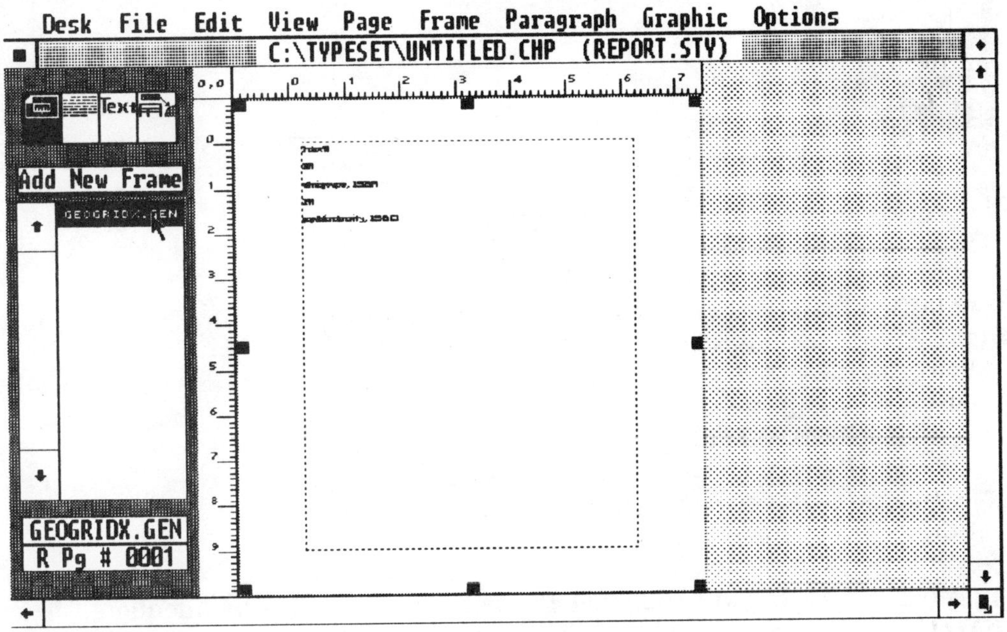

Figure 7.16

Enlarge the display mode by pointing the mouse at the upper left corner of the frame and pressing

[Ctrl/n]

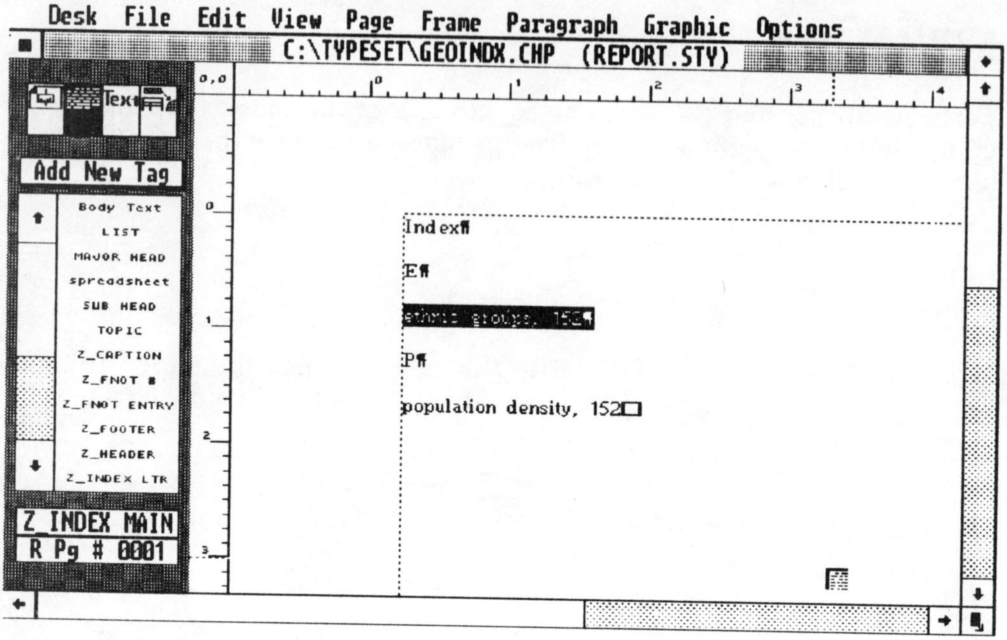

Figure 7.17

The index in this example is very small. Note that Ventura creates three types of tags for index text:

- **Z__INDEX TITLE** – the tag for the index title.
- **Z__INDEX LTR** – the tag for the letter headings.
- **Z__INDEX MAIN** – the tag for index text.

In most cases, you will find that the default layout will be adequate. The most common change made to index text is to format the page into two columns to save space.

In this example, you can leave the document as it is. Save the index file by entering

[Ctrl/s]
geoindx
[return]

You have now created the table of contents and index chapter files for your multi-page ANDORRA document.

ADDING TABLE AND INDEX FILES

The final step in this process is to add the newly created index and table of contents files to the publication file. Display the multi-chapter operations menu by pointing the mouse at the Options menu heading. Then, point the mouse at the Multi-Chapter selection and click the button. The GEOGRAPH publication file is displayed.

Now, add the table of contents file to the publication file. Point the mouse at the Add Chapter option and click the button. The ITEM SELECTOR box is displayed.

Point the mouse at ANDTOC.CHP and click the button twice in rapid succession. The file is added to the publication list.

As discussed previously, Ventura adds new files to the bottom of the list. In this case, you will want to place the table of contents file at the top of the list because it should print before the main chapter text.

You can change the position of the file by dragging it up. Remember, dragging refers to pointing and holding down the mouse button while you move the mouse. So point the mouse at ANDTOC.CHP, and drag it to the top of the list.

Now add the index file. Point the mouse at GEOINDX.CHP and click the button twice in rapid succession.

All three related chapters should now be in the same publication file.

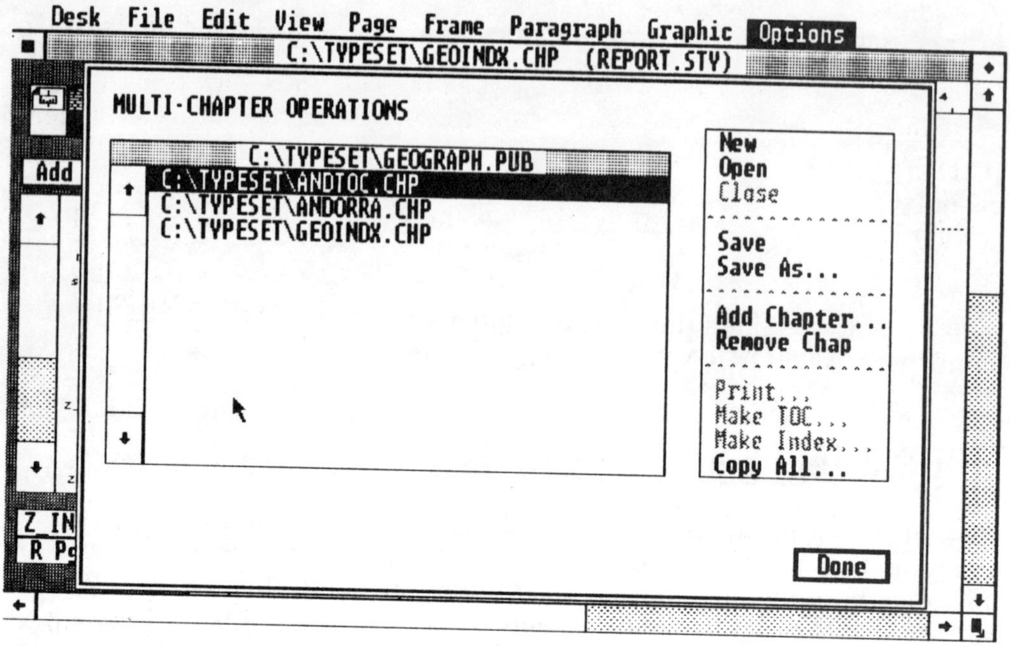

Figure 7.18

Save the modified file by pressing

[return]

Then, point the mouse at Save and click the button.

MOVING A CHAPTER

The ANDORRA multi-page document illustrates how many different computer files can go into making up a single printed document. This process is much different from the way most word processing programs operate. A word processing document is usually stored in a single computer file. You can transfer or copy a file easily by using DOS commands or, in the case of most word processing programs, using the built-in Copy command. For example, in WordPerfect, you can copy a file by using [F5/8].

But Ventura chapters and publication files consist of many different computer files. To copy the entire set of files needed to complete a printed document, you must know and keep track of all the computer files you'll need to include. Even with simple documents, such as the ANDORRA document, this task is quite formidable.

Ventura has a command in the Multi-Chapter menu that helps you copy all the files that belong to a particular publication. The best way to work with these groups of files is to take advantage of the DOS concept of a directory. You can create a new DOS directory and copy all of the files that make up a document into that directory. There are two reasons why this strategy is a good one:

1. When all the files related to a given publication are placed into a directory, it is easy to copy or move all the files. You also reduce the danger of deleting a necessary file because all of the relevant files will be grouped together.

2. You can use the DOS BACKUP command to back up all the files in a directory.

As an illustration, suppose you wanted to move the files that make up the GEOGRAPH publication file to a new directory. The first step is to create a DOS directory for the files, which can be done outside Ventura with the DOS command CD; however, Ventura also allows you to create a directory from within its menus.

Point the mouse at the File menu heading. The last item on the menu is DOS File Ops (DOS file operations). Point the mouse at the DOS File Ops selection and click the button. Ventura displays the DOS FILE OPERATIONS menu.

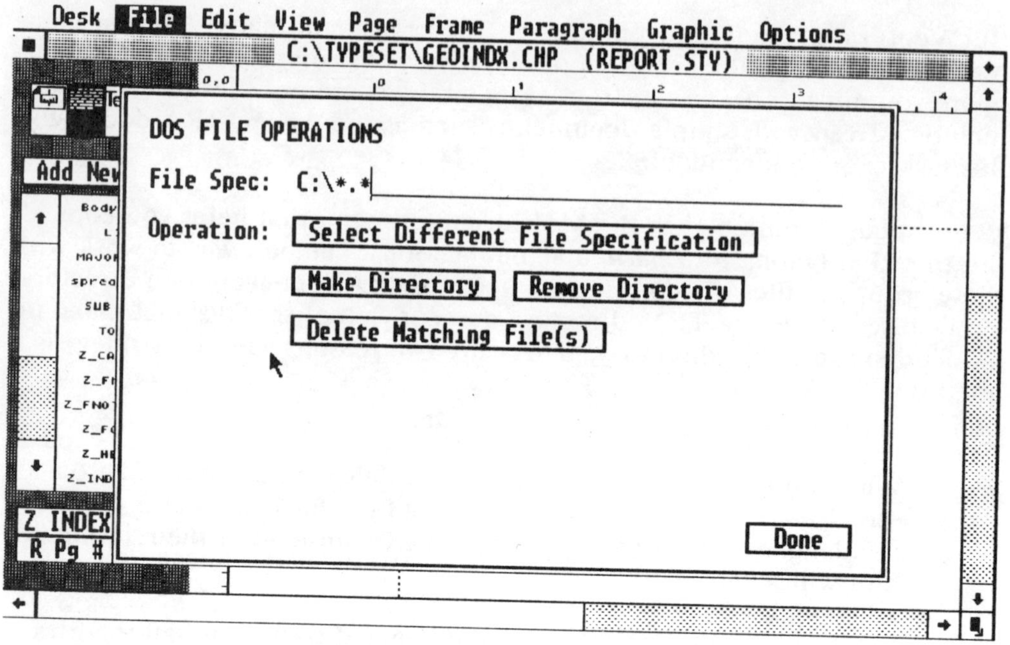

Figure 7.19

To create a new directory, enter the name of that directory on the file specification line:

[Esc]
c:\geograph

Then, point the mouse at Make Directory and click the button. Ventura creates a new directory on disk. Exit the menu by pointing the mouse at Done and clicking the button.

You can now use the Multi-Chapter menu to instruct Ventura to copy all the related files to the new directory. Point the mouse at the Options menu heading. Then, point the mouse at the Multi-Chapter selection and click the button.

The last option on this menu is Copy All. Point the mouse at Copy All and click the button. Ventura displays the COPY ALL menu box.

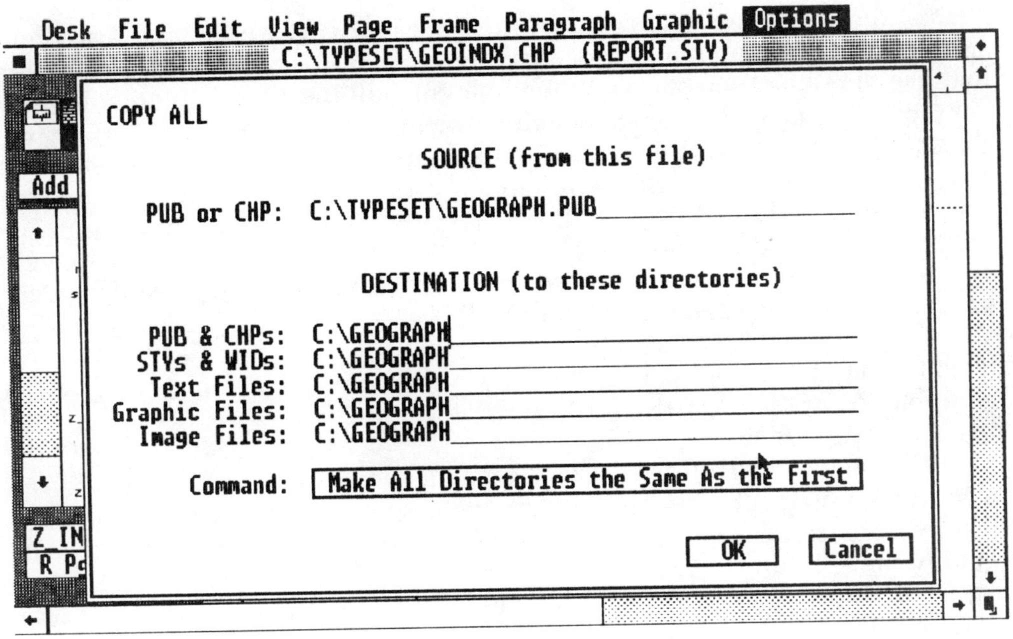

Figure 7.20

This menu box displays a list of the types of files used by Ventura and the directory to which these files will be copied. Because you have just created a new directory with the Make Directory command, Ventura has automatically filled in the name of the new directory, C:\GEOGRAPH, on each of the display lines.

You can change the directories or accept the layout. Note that Ventura provides a shortcut to changing the directory. If you enter the new directory in the first line, the one for PUB and CHP type files, you can use the option Make All Directories the Same as the First to copy that name into the other file specification lines.

In this case, the settings are correct; however, there is one significant decision you need to make at this time. It involves the files specified on the second line, STY and WID files.

STY refers to the style sheet or sheets used for the documents in the publication file. WID refers to the printer width table used by Ventura to match up its fonts with your specific printer.

These files deserve special consideration because you are likely to use them again for other documents. For example, you may create many documents that use the same style sheet. When you copy all the files, you create a new copy of the attached style sheet, which means that you now have two style sheets with the same name on disk. This duplication in itself is quite all right. But think for a moment what will happen if you modify the style sheet. The original style sheet will change and be updated, but the one copied with the publication file will remain the same. This result may in fact be exactly what you want to happen. On the other hand, you may want to have the document updâted when the style sheet changes.

If you want to keep just a single copy of the style sheet on disk, you can eliminate from the copy the files specified on line #2.

The WID file also falls into the same classification. In many cases, there will be only one WID file, the one Ventura creates when you install your printer. If you purchase additional fonts for your laser printer, you may need to modify the WID file to include these new fonts. If you have multiple copies of the WID file on the same disk, you will need to update all those copies individually.

For these reasons, it may be a good idea not to copy the STY and WID files along with the other files. To prevent these files from being copied, eliminate the directory name from the second line and replace it with the name of the current directory that holds the STY and WID files. Enter

[down arrow]
[Esc]
c:\typeset

Begin the processing by entering

[return]

Ventura copies all the files until it reaches the style sheet, REPORT.STY.

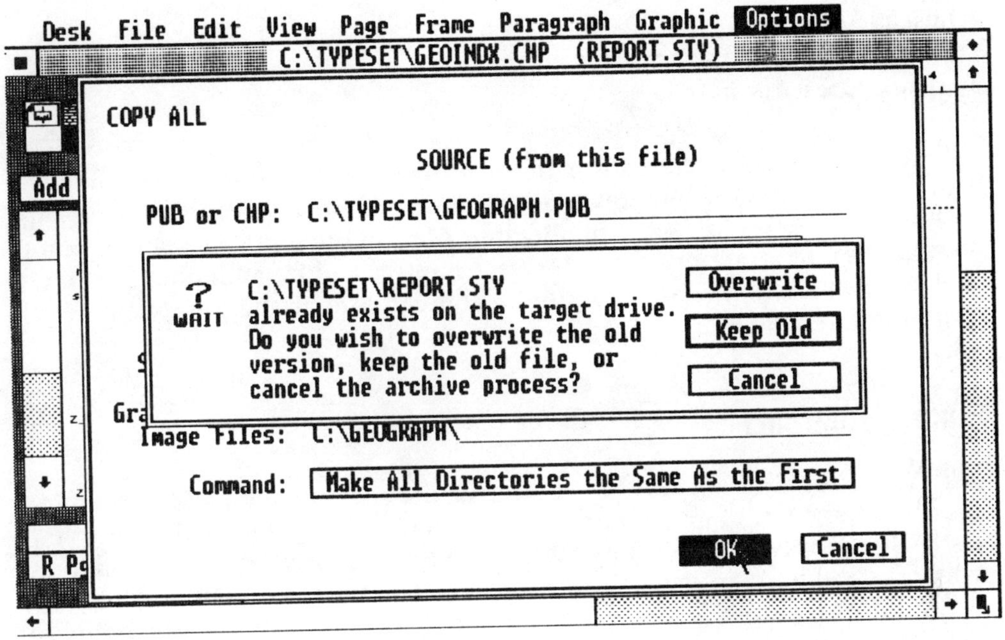

Figure 7.21

Your directory instructions have told Ventura to copy over an existing file. Skip this file by pointing the mouse at Keep Old and clicking the button. Select Keep Old for any duplicate files.

When Ventura is finished, you will have a duplicate of all the files included in the GEOGRAPH publication.

Exit from the Multi-Chapter menu by pointing the mouse at Done and clicking the button.

Exit from Ventura by pointing the mouse at the File menu heading, and then pointing the mouse at Quit and clicking the button.

SUMMARY

Publication Files

Ventura allows you to create a publication to include organizational and reference tasks that may involve one or more chapter files. Ventura uses the PUB extension to indicate a **publication file**. Publication files allow you to create tables of contents and indexes. Chapters can be added and removed from the publication file at any time. You can also create a publication file with only one chapter.

Table of Contents

Ventura will generate a table of contents from a publication file. The headings are selected as Ventura searches for specified style tags used in the chapters in the publication file. The table of contents is ordered according to the order of the chapters listed in the publication file. The table of contents generated by Ventura is a text file and is not ready to print. To be ready for printing, the text file must be loaded into a chapter file and formatted. Ventura automatically tags each heading with a style tag.

Indexes

Indexes are produced in the same manner as table of contents files. The index text is drawn from the data stored in the index codes inserted in the text files used in the publication file. Index entries are alphabetized. Ventura inserts letter headings into the index if you want them. Like table of contents files, the index output file is a text file that cannot be printed unless it is loaded into a chapter file.

Copying Files

Ventura allows you to copy all the files related to all the chapters in a publication file. The Copy All option on the Multi-Chapter menu is used for this purpose. The main reason for using this command is to isolate all the necessary files for a particular publication and copy them into a unique disk directory that you can use later for copying or backup purposes.

CHAPTER 8

NEWSLETTERS

The newsletter is one of the documents most commonly associated with desktop publishing programs like Ventura. Creating a newsletter involves some of the techniques used for creating multiple-frame and multiple-page documents in Chapters 5 and 6. Like those documents, newsletters contain multiple frames used to combine text from several document files into a single printed output.

In Ventura, what makes a newsletter different from other multiple-frame and multiple-page documents is the fact that frequently, at least one of the document files used in a newsletter is too large to fit into a single frame. In a newsletter layout, Ventura must divide a document into one or more frames on the same or different pages—exactly the type of layout you encounter in a newspaper.

To begin, you must prepare the text of the articles to be used in this newsletter. Any text files will do if you don't want to bother to create the document shown in this chapter. There will be four files: three articles and one file for the masthead of the newsletter. As with the rest of this book, the assumption made is that you are using WordPerfect as your word processing program.

Enter the following document. Save it as JAVELIN.WP.

JAVELIN PLUS ⟵
Javelin Plus adds database operations to the existing Javelin package. Javelin is a program designed for building financial models but it differs from standard spreadsheet programs in a number of significant respects. The most important difference between Javelin and spreadsheets like 1-2-3, SuperCalc, and Multiplan is that data is stored in time series blocks, not in spreadsheet cells. ⟵
A time series block is a list of dates with corresponding values. The entire block is assigned a variable name. For example, suppose that you have income and expense figures for four quarters. ⟵
The data is not assigned row and column locations as is the case in a standard spreadsheet. Instead, data is related by virtue of the time period for which it is entered. The advantage of this is that you can carry out a series of calculations by relating one time series to another. A good example would be the calculation of the net income for each quarter. In Javelin this is done by writing a formula using the variable names. Example: net = income-expenses. ⟵

continued...

...*from previous page*

You don't have to worry about copying formulas into the correct cells. Because each value is related to a specific period of time, Javelin can figure out which numbers should be subtracted. It then creates a new table called NET with the results of the calculation. Javelin can also display the relationship between variables as a diagram.←

Javelin has always had a strong database flavor. Each time series block can be viewed as a simple two-field database. Since all the variables have the same time periods, then all the variables have a field in common that can be used to relate each to a corresponding item: a sort of mini-relational database.←

In Javelin Plus this ability is enhanced to handle data lists that do not fit into a time series framework. These new features are smoothly integrated into the Javelin's financial modeling operations. To a great degree, Javelin Plus blurs the traditional distinctions between databases and modeling programs. ←

The implications and advantages of this are that you can create new spreadsheets that display part or all of the basic information stored in the database, in new ways. In addition, you can create new fields by writing formulas that relate data items.←

The challenging part of this formula is the multiplication. Javelin evaluates each record for the criterion ITEM TYPE = "Software." If it is false the value of the expression is zero; if it is true the value of the expression is 1. ←

Javelin handles sorting in an unconventional but useful manner. Sorting is the result of a function and is very different from the type of sorting done in most spreadsheets. 1-2-3 performs physical sorts, i.e., it actually rearranges the values and places them in new cells. Javelin uses a method closer to a dBASE index file because it does not actually change the order of the records in the database. Rather it copies the data into a new spreadsheet sequenced by a specific field. Javelin uses two functions, SORTA (ascending) and SORTD (descending).←

CONCLUSION←

continued...

...from previous page

Javelin remains one of the most innovative programs available in the spreadsheet market. While most spreadsheet programs maintain the same basic approach to designing financial models, Javelin provides a wide range of tools in a totally unique environment. To my way of thinking, Javelin provides a better environment for model building than 1-2-3 or the other major spreadsheets. ←

However, if you are used to working cell by cell, Javelin's approach may seem light years removed from you. In the long run, I cannot help but believe that the superior design of the program will win more and more users. Keep in mind that Javelin is not a general computing environment, something that many people feel that 1-2-3 is. It is strongly prejudiced toward modeling building tasks. ←

Javelin is a product of Javelin Software Corp., One Kendall Square, Building 200, Cambridge, MA 02139, list price $199.00.

Enter the following document. Save it as OS2.WP.

WHAT WILL OS/2 MEAN TO YOU ←

It is now more than 6 months since OS/2 was officially announced. The "new" operating system is still little more than a name to everyone except a handful of developers. Of course, the lack of actual software has not seemed to deter a lot of people from praising and damning the yet-to-appear product. I don't know anymore than any other average computer user about what OS/2 will be like and how the computing world will react to it. ←

One point made in the computer press is that most of the features that OS/2 is supposed to offer already can be implemented by existing software and hardware. Programs like DeskQ offer multitasking, and many applications that can already use extended memory and graphics interfaces (like Windows and Gem) are already available. But OS/2 is important, not so much because it will implement new ideas, but rather that it will create a standard way of implementing the type of features that have slowly been creeping into the IBM PC world over the past five years. ←

continued...

...from previous page

While multitasking and memory expansion get the most attention, I believe the graphics interface is the feature that will most immediately affect the user. Microsoft believes that the PC world should look more like the Mac world. In fact, the PC world has had software like this for some time. Digital Research's GEM Desktop and Windows from Microsoft show how you might implement a graphic interface on a PC. The Ventura desktop publishing program uses a form of GEM as its basic operating environment. ←

But it is programs like Ventura and GEM that illustrate exactly why OS/2 is significant. Today, most programs on the PC use the built-in set of 254 characters to display all the information on the screen. This system is fast and simple but it lacks the flexibility to show on the screen many of the effects implemented by today's sophisticated printers. As printer technology moves forward, the PC's display ability has remained almost at a standstill.←

One reason is that if you want to create a display in which there is a close correspondence between the printed page, with its font changes and high resolution graphics, and the screen display, where will you get the characters? The answer is that you need to create the characters. When HP introduced the LaserJet, people began to learn about font cartridges in order to implement fancy printing features. But if you want the screen to show those fonts, you have got to supply them, in the form of font files.←

For better or worse, OS/2 and Windows will set the standard for the way that information gets displayed and printed, and how the two images should correspond. This will free up the creative efforts of developers to concentrate on applications once again. In addition, it will give developers new tools with which to work. The use of more varied and dramatic screen displays will enable programmers to express ideas in new ways. ←

continued...

...from previous page

The Mac started with a new standard for the way information should be displayed on a computer. It seems obvious that Microsoft has wanted to bring that vision to the PC world. But history never repeats itself exactly. Progress seems to move in leaps and fits, rather than in smooth transitions from one phase to another. For example, when Japan rebuilt her industrial plant, following the Second World War, she used the latest technology. It wasn't necessary for Japan to go through the slow, intermediate transitions that America's industry, which survived the war intact, had to. In part, this allowed Japan to "leap frog" ahead in technology.←

For many software companies, the new OS/2 environment is a chance to start on a level playing field. They feel that in OS/2 there is no reason to assume that Lotus will automatically get 60% of the market. It certainly seems that Microsoft thinks it has a chance to out-flank Lotus. Since OS/2 is Microsoft's, they ought to be pretty embarrassed if they don't make a respectable showing. While desktop publishing gets most of the attention, I am looking forward to what will be developed in the order of frontline business software.

Enter the following document. Save it as PLANNER.WP.

VP PLANNER PLUS←

When Paperback Software released VP Planner a little more than a year ago, the program made headlines even in the non-computer press, not because of its functional parts but because it embroiled Paperback in a legal fight with the giant of the spreadsheet companies, Lotus Development Corporation.←

Lotus claimed that VP Planner had copied the "look and feel" of their 1-2-3 program, which they considered a violation of their copyrights. The controversy probably helped bring VP Planner to the attention of a lot of people who might not have otherwise thought about the program. It also raised a lot of questions concerning what copyrights mean in the computer industry, how innovation and creativity can be encouraged, and what role can be played by software standards.←

continued...

...from previous page

VP Planner Plus is really two products. One is a spreadsheet that accepts Lotus 1-2-3 commands and macros. The other program is a database. In VP Planner Plus the integration of the two programs has been greatly improved and the functional aspects of the database module built up substantially.←

VP Planner Plus remains a program with a dual character. On one hand it is a fully functional spreadsheet that performs keystroke for keystroke like 1-2-3. On the other hand VP Planner Plus provides two types of structured database files that can be used by themselves or integrated into spreadsheets. By emphasizing database operations, the designers of VP Planner Plus are placing stress on the need to integrate database information with spreadsheet analysis. The idea is that spreadsheets are usually based on the accumulation of historical data. The design of VP Planner Plus suggests that you can enter historical data into VP Planner Plus databases and then pull the information into spreadsheets for analysis and presentation. Taken at its best, VP Planner Plus offers many of the features of a database program plus all the spreadsheet and graphics operations found in 1-2-3.←

To get an idea of how VP Planner Plus puts this package of goodies together, let's look at each of the major components of the program. ←

THE VP PLANNER PLUS SPREADSHEET←

The most talked about feature of VP Planner was its spreadsheet module because it used the same keystroke commands as 1-2-3. VP Planner Plus retains the same structure. Gone is the menu that VP Planner once used to integrate its modules. ←

As far as memory is concerned, VP Planner Plus takes up a bit more memory than 1-2-3 Release 2. In a 640K computer, VP Planner Plus begins with about 355K of free memory as compared to about 425K for 1-2-3 Release 2. Keep in mind that VP Planner Plus prints graphs directly from the main program, while 1-2-3 uses a separate Printgraph program.←

VP Planner Plus also retains VP Planner's use of the function keys to make menu selections. Instead of entering /RFC, you could enter / [F3] [F2] [F4]. I have always felt that this feature was added just to show some sort of difference between their menus and 1-2-3's menus. ←

continued...

...from previous page

While the commands on the menus follow 1-2-3 Release 2 exactly, VP Planner Plus has some additional functions that are quite handy. The Tools option added to the main menu contains a simple text editing feature and the ability to draw lines and boxes. The text editing features are not quite full word processors, but they are adequate for adding text to your worksheets. You can set line widths and indents, center text, perform search and replace, and perform some copy and move operations. If you are a demanding spreadsheet user who feels the performance is critical, VP Planner Plus may not be for you. On the other hand, I cannot help but like boxed menus, text editing, and other small improvements made to the basic spreadsheet.

The final document is the text of the masthead for the newsletter. Enter

Technology Tid Bits
[return]
Volume 5
[Tab]
Number 12
[Tab]
Nov. 3, 1987

Save this text as MASTHEAD.WP.

You are now ready to use Ventura to combine these files into a newsletter. Load the Ventura program in the usual manner.

CREATING THE MASTHEAD

The masthead refers to the master heading showing the name and the issue of the newsletter. Since this heading appears at the top of every issue of your newsletter, it is the first item you will create.

Whenever you begin a chapter, you should perform some basic housekeeping tasks. First, place Ventura into the Frame mode and the Reduced View mode by pressing

[Ctrl/u]
[Ctrl/r]

Next, create a new style sheet for this document. Point the mouse at the File menu heading. Then, point the mouse at the Load Diff. Style selection and click the button. Type in the name of the new style sheet. Enter

default
[return]

Create the new style sheet. Point the mouse at the File menu heading. Then, point the mouse at the Save as New Style selection and click the button. Enter

newsltr
[return]

You are now ready to create the frame for the newsletter's masthead. Place Ventura into the frame-drawing mode. Activate the Frame mode, [Ctrl/u]. Then, point the mouse at the Add New Frame selection and click the button.

Beginning at the upper left corner of the master frame, draw a frame as wide as that frame and about 1" in height.

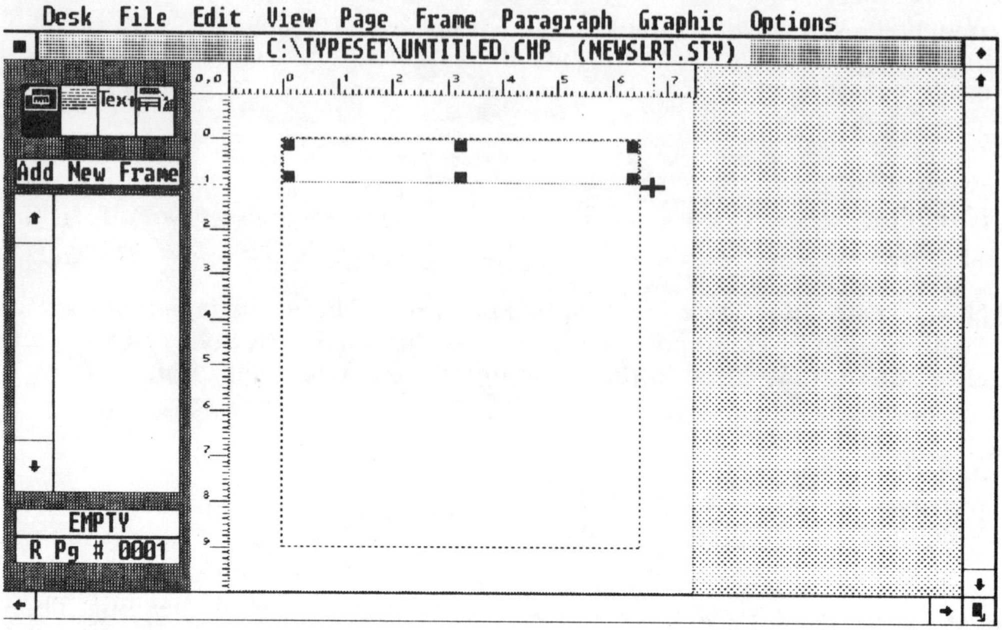

Figure 8.1

Place the text from the MASTHEAD.WP file into this frame. Point the mouse at the File menu heading. Then, point the mouse at the Load Text/Picture option and click the button. Point the mouse at OK and click the button.

If you have been following along in this book, you will find that the ITEM SELECTOR box is still set only for files that begin with GEO. Change the selection back to a more general wild card specification. Enter the following:

[up arrow]
[Esc]
c:\wp*.wp
[return]

Point the mouse at MASTHEAD.WP and click the button twice in rapid succession. The text is inserted into the frame. Zoom in to get a closer look at the text. Point the cursor at the upper left corner of the frame and press

[Ctrl/n]

Change Ventura to the Paragraph mode. Press

[Ctrl/i]

You will want to create a new tag for the masthead. Point the mouse at the word "Technology" and click the button. Then, point the mouse at the Add New Tag box and click the button. Enter

masthead
[return]

You should set the masthead as centered, with a bold, 18-point Swiss font. First, point the mouse at the Paragraph menu heading. Then, point the mouse at the Font selection and click the button. Point the mouse at Swiss and click the button. Next, point the mouse at 18 and click the button. Execute these settings by pressing

[return]

To center the masthead, point the mouse at the Paragraph menu heading. Then, point the mouse at the Alignment option and click the button. Point the mouse at Center and click the button. Execute these settings by pressing

[return]

Now format the date line, which also requires a new tag. Point the mouse at "Volume" and click the button. Then, point the mouse at the Add New Tag option and click the button. Enter

dateline
[return]

In this case, the text is divided into three parts by tabs. You will want to create tabs that align the three parts: left, center, and right. To do so, activate the Paragraph mode. Once you have done so, point the mouse at the Paragraph menu heading. Then, point the mouse at the Tab Settings option and click the button.

The first part of the text will automatically be aligned flush left, which means that tab #2 should be centered. To create this effect, you need to take the width of the frame, 6.5 ", and divide it in half, which results in a value of 3.25". Place a center-aligned tab at 3.25". Then, point the mouse at the Center option and click the button. Enter

[Esc]
03.25

The second tab on the line should be flush with the right edge, which can be accomplished by setting a right-aligned tab at the right edge of the frame, 6.5". Point the mouse at 2 and click the button. Then, point the mouse at Right and click the button. Enter

[Esc]
06.5
[return]

You are warned that this paragraph is still set for justified alignment and therefore does not display the tabs you just set. To eliminate this problem, point the mouse at OK and click the button. You can now correct the alignment.

Point the mouse at the Paragraph menu heading. Then, point the mouse at the Alignment option and click the button. Now, point the mouse at Left and click the button. Press

[return]

The tabs correctly separate the date elements. To make the masthead stand out, draw a ruling line beneath the frame. Place Ventura into the Frame mode. Enter

[Ctrl/u]

Point the mouse at the Frame menu option. Then, point the mouse at Ruling Line Below and click the button. To turn on the ruling line display, point the mouse at the Frame option and click the button.

Make the line fairly thick. Enter

[down arrow]
[Esc]
.1
[return]

The document should resemble Figure 8.2.

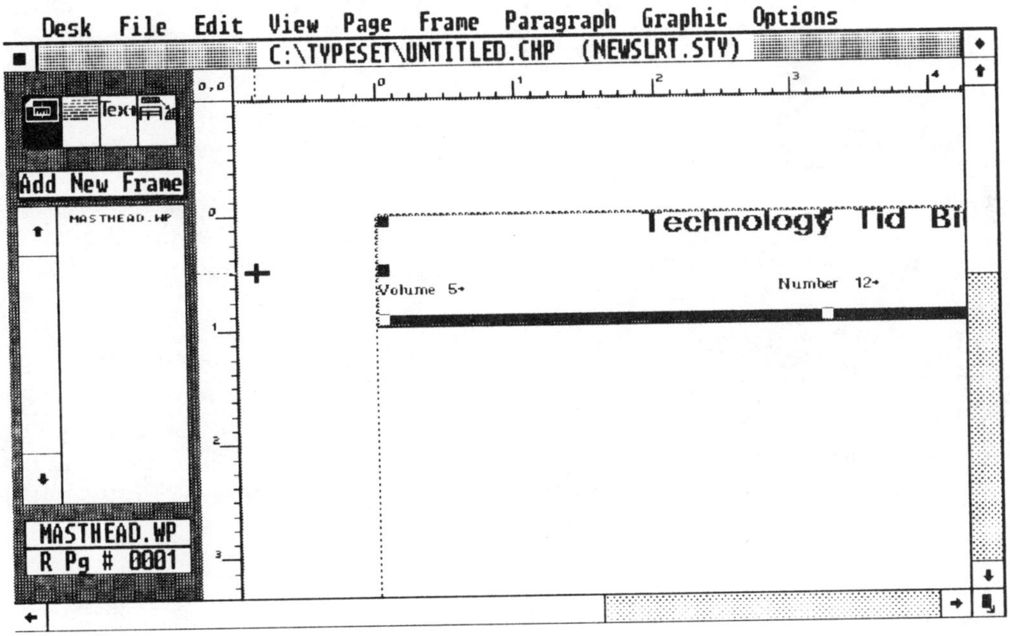

Figure 8.2

SAVING UNDER A NEW NAME

Instead of continuing with the newsletter layout, you will now save this text as a chapter file to maintain a copy of the masthead without also saving specific frames that contain actual articles. Doing so will enable you to start the layout of each issue of the newsletter with the masthead already set, rather than having to start from scratch. Enter

[Ctrl/s]
newsform
[return]

Executing these commands creates a file called NEWSFORM.CHP that can be used as the starting point for each issue. Before continuing to the next phase of the newsletter, be sure to change the name of this file so that you don't accidentally overwrite your Newsform chapter. Point the mouse at the File menu heading. Then, point the mouse at the Save As option and click the button.

Enter the name under which you want to store this particular issue of the newsletter. Use the name TTBNOV87 (Technology Tid Bits, November 1987). Enter

TTBNOV87
[return]

You are now ready to place the articles into the newsletter.

COLUMN GUIDES

When you create a newsletter, you will find that many of the frames you create do not extend to the full width of the master frame in which you are working. To achieve more consistent frame alignment, create columns in the master frame.

The column in the master frame will not be used to place text into a column format. In newsletters, the master frame is not used for text. Instead, the column guides in the master frame will be used to help you align the new frames properly.

Creating a column in the master frame allows you to use the column-snap feature to make sure that all the columns are aligned on the same vertical positions. Without using the master frame as a column guide, you will find it difficult to make uniform frame widths.

To create the column guide, you must first select the master frame. Point the mouse anywhere in the master frame and click the button. The frame is selected. Remember, you can tell a frame is selected by the buttons on the frame's border.

The next step is to divide the master frame into columns. A general rule of thumb is that a 6.5" frame should be divided into three columns if you use 12-point print or four columns if you use 10-point print. In this case, select four columns. Point the mouse at the Frame menu heading. Then, point the mouse at Margins & Columns and click the button. Finally, point the mouse at 4, click the button, and press

[return]

The column guides appear in the master frame (Figure 8.3).

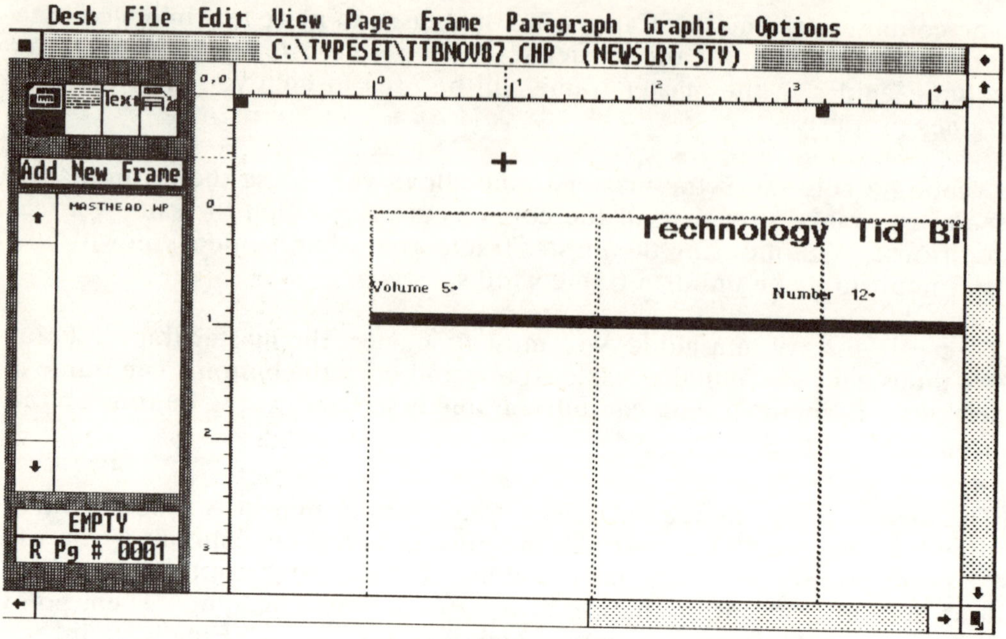

Figure 8.3

ADDING FRAMES

The next step in the layout of the newsletter is to set up the frames that will be used to contain the text of the articles. In this example, there are three articles. There are many ways to combine the frames on a page. For example, you might put two articles at the top of the page and one at the bottom, or vice versa.

In this case, you will divide the remainder of the page into three parts. The first articles will cover the full width of the page but will take up only half the page. The other two articles will be split between the left and right portions of the bottom half of the page.

Place Ventura into the Frame mode. Then, point the mouse at the Add New Frame box and click the button. Draw a frame starting just below the lower left corner of the Masthead frame, across the width of the master frame, and down to about 4.5". Allow the column-snap feature to align the right edge of the frame on the right column guide.

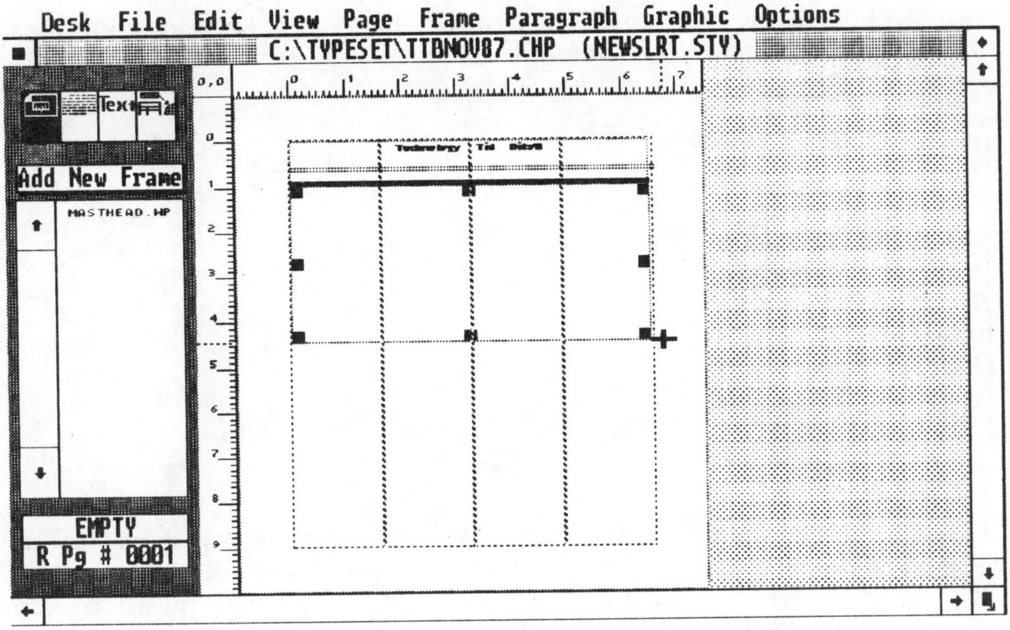

Figure 8.4

Next, divide this frame in four text columns. Point the mouse at the Frame menu heading. Then, point the mouse at Margins & Columns and click the button. To select four columns, point the mouse at 4, click the button, and press

[return]

Ventura creates the four columns. Insert a 1/10" gutter between columns to separate the text in the columns. Enter

[down arrow] (4 times)
[Esc]
.1
[down arrow]
[Esc]
.1
[down arrow]
[Esc]
.1
[return]

To save time creating the other frames, you can simply copy this frame and then move and change it. You have already defined the text columns and gutters, which you will want to be the same for the other frames. To copy the frame into memory, press

[Shift/Del]

Insert a copy of the frame into the window. Press

[Ins]

The frames do not appear to be separate because they are layered directly on top of one another.

MOVING AND SIZING THE FRAME

You can change the size and location of the frame by using the mouse. To move the frame, point the mouse cursor anywhere inside the frame. Press and hold down the mouse button. A symbol appears in the frame that indicates you have placed the frame in dragging mode (see Figure 8.5).

While holding down the button, drag the frame to the bottom of the master frame, and release the mouse button (see Figure 8.6).

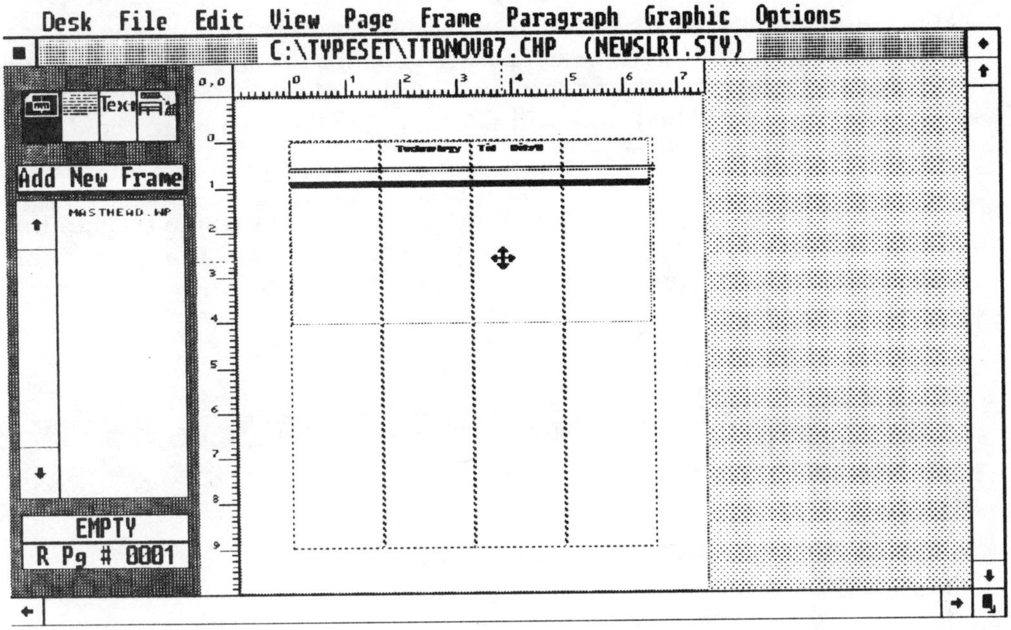

Figure 8.5

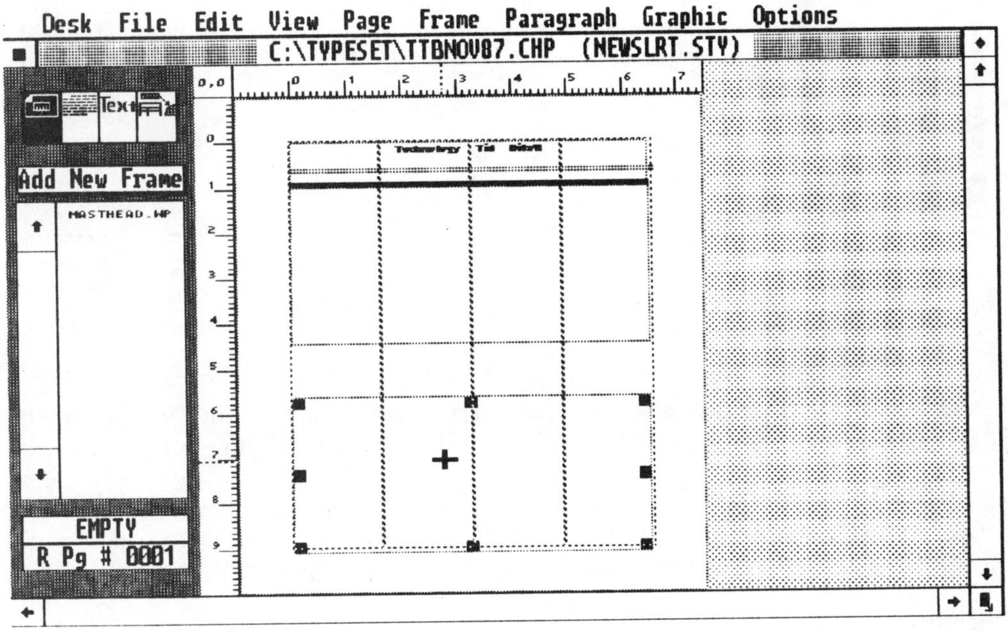

Figure 8.6

You must now change the size of the frame, which is done by using the square buttons that appear on the frame border. To change the size of a frame, you must point the mouse at one of the buttons, hold down the mouse button, and move the mouse. The frame will alter its shape according to the direction in which the mouse is moved.

In this case, you want to make sure that the top of the new frame reaches the bottom of the previous frame. Point the mouse at middle button on the top border of the frame. Press the mouse button and hold it down. Ventura changes the mouse cursor to a pointing hand.

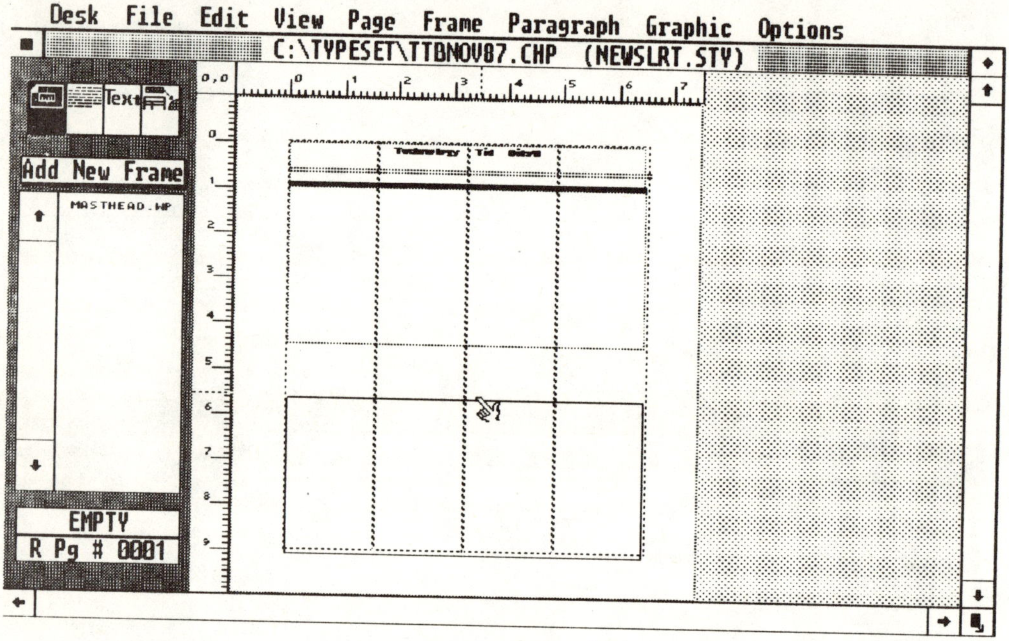

Figure 8.7

Drag the mouse until the top of the current frame meets the bottom of the previous frame. Then, release the mouse button (see Figure 8.8).

Use the same method to narrow the width of the frame to the two left columns. The column-snap feature will make sure that the right edge of the frame matches the column guides in the master frame. The layout should resemble Figure 8.9.

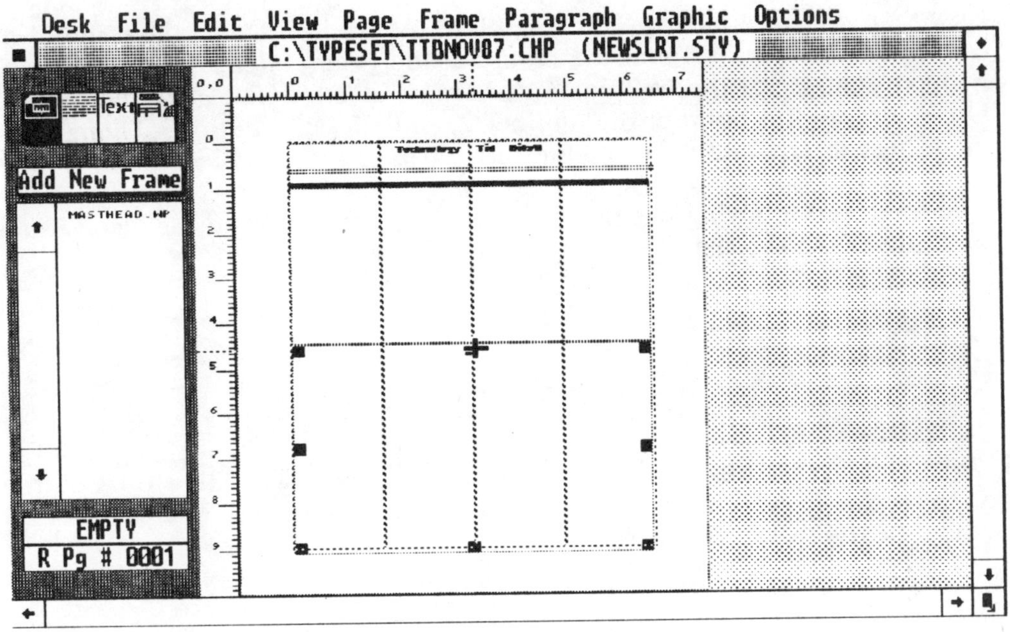

Figure 8.8

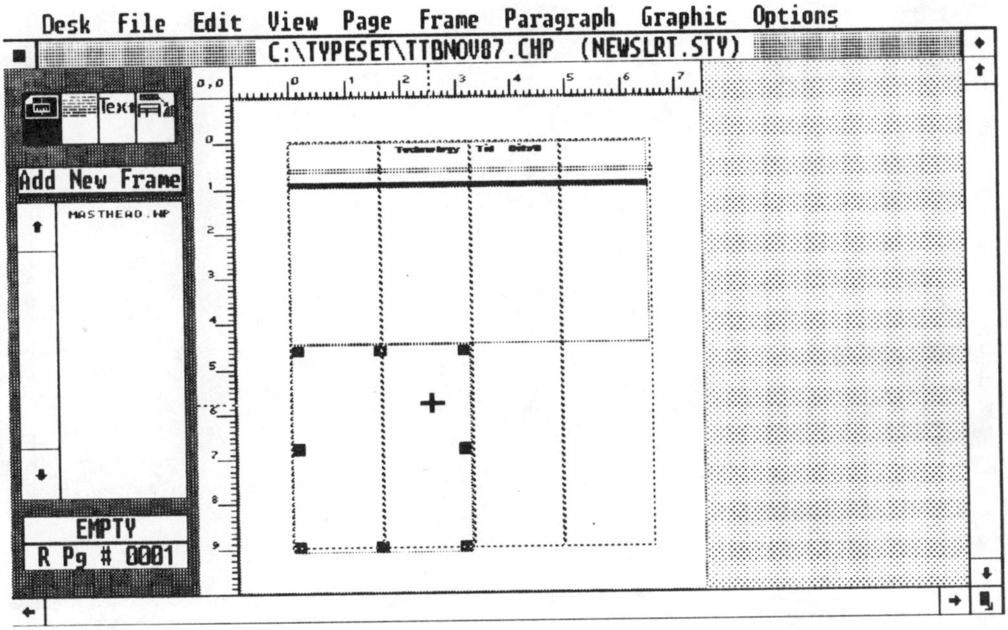

Figure 8.9

Now that you have narrowed the width of the frame, change the number of columns from 4 to 2. Point the mouse at the Frame menu heading. Then, point the mouse at the Margins & Columns selection and click the button. Use the mouse to point at the number 2, and click the button. Then, point the mouse at OK and click the button.

The final step in laying out this page is to copy the currently selected frame and move it to the right side of the page. Press

[Shift/Del]
[Ins]

Use the mouse to drag the frame to the right side of page. Allow the Column Snap feature to align the frame on the right column guide. The page is now ready for the text to be inserted.

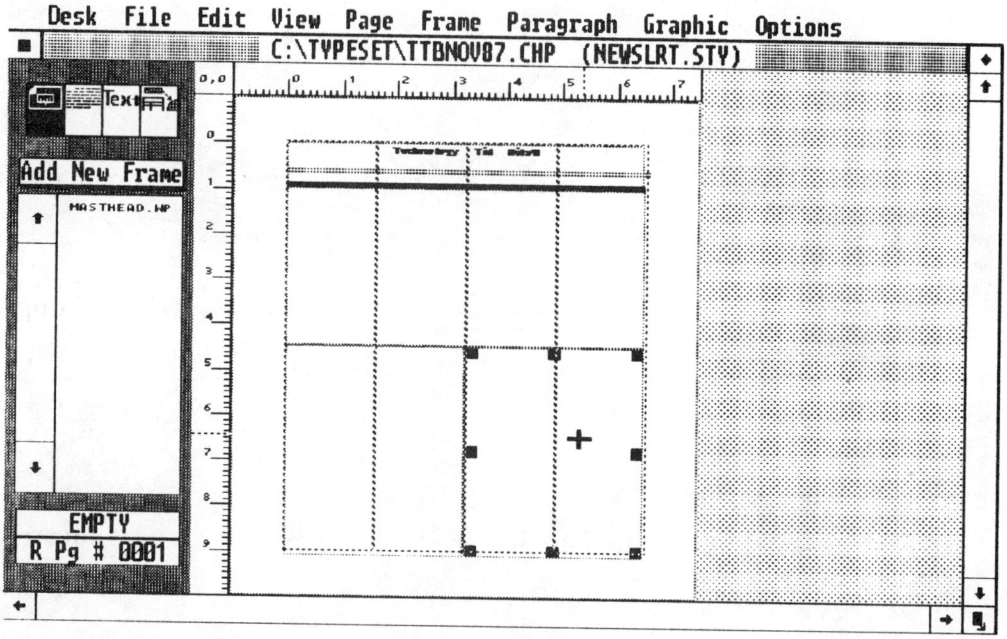

Figure 8.10

ADDING THE TEXT FILES

Now that the basic frames have been laid out, you can load the text frames into the chapter. Because you want to load several files, you will use the Several option on the Load Files menu.

Point the mouse at the File menu heading. Then, point the mouse at Load Text/Picture selection and click the button. Next, point the mouse at the Several option and click the button. Point the mouse at OK and click the button.

You want to load three files: JAVELIN.WP, OS2.WP, and PLANNER.WP. Point the mouse at JAVELIN.WP and click the button twice in rapid succession. Then, point the mouse at OS2.WP and again click the button twice in rapid succession. Next, point the mouse at PLANNER.WP and click the button twice in rapid succession. To complete the loading proces, press

[return]

The file names appear in the side bar display. The text of the files is not yet visible because you have not selected the frames that will hold them.

The currently selected frame is for the PLANNER article. To insert that text into this frame, use the mouse to select the file name. Point the mouse at PLANNER.WP and click the button.

To see the text better, zoom in on the frame. Point the mouse at the upper left corner of the frame. Enter

[Ctrl/n]

You can see that the text of the PLANNER article is arranged into two columns of text.

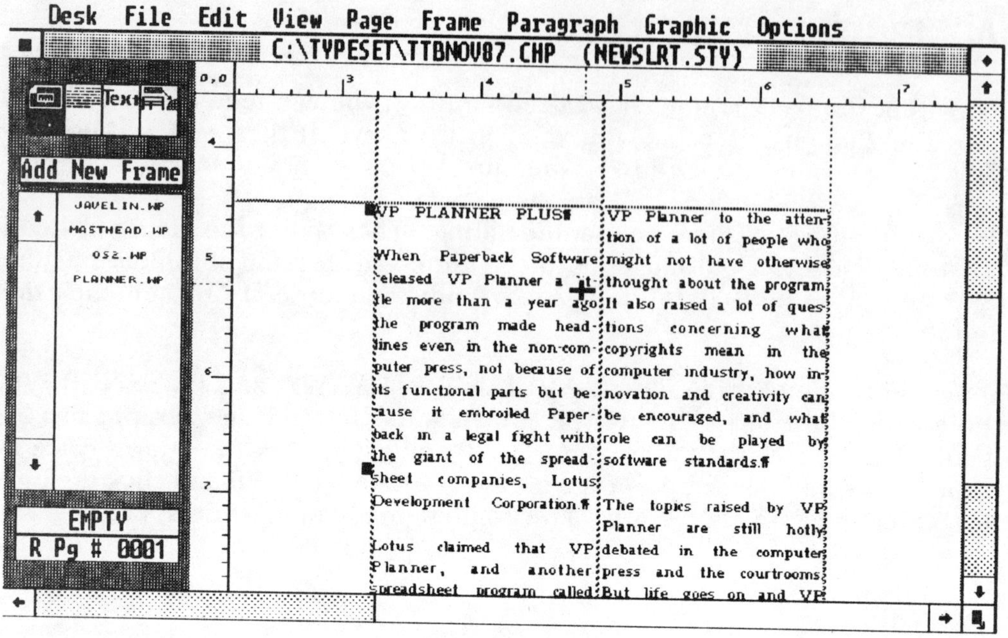

Figure 8.11

HEADLINES ACROSS THE FRAME

The headline of the Planner article is currently formatted to fit into the first column of the frame. In this type of layout, it is customary to format the headline so that it cuts across all columns. This effect can be achieved by creating a paragraph tag instructing Ventura to align the headline across the entire frame and not just across one column.

Place Ventura into the Paragraph mode. Enter

[Ctrl/i]

To highlight the headline of the article, point the mouse at VP PLANNER PLUS and click the button.

To create a new tag, point the mouse at Add New Tag and click the button. Enter the name of the new tag:

headline
[return]

The key to the way that the text is treated relative to columns is controlled from the Alignment menu.

Point the mouse at the Paragraph menu heading. Then, point the mouse at the Alignment selection and click the button. You can select left alignment by pointing the mouse at the Left option and clicking the button.

To create a headline that crosses all columns, select the Frame-Wide option for Overall Width, which instructs Ventura to ignore columns when formatting this paragraph. Point the mouse at Frame-Wide and click the button.

Complete the settings by entering

[return]

You can see that Ventura now begins the columns below the headline, which also gives you more room for the headline text because you now have space to use a larger font. Change the headline text to Swiss, 18-point bold. The screen should resemble Figure 8.12.

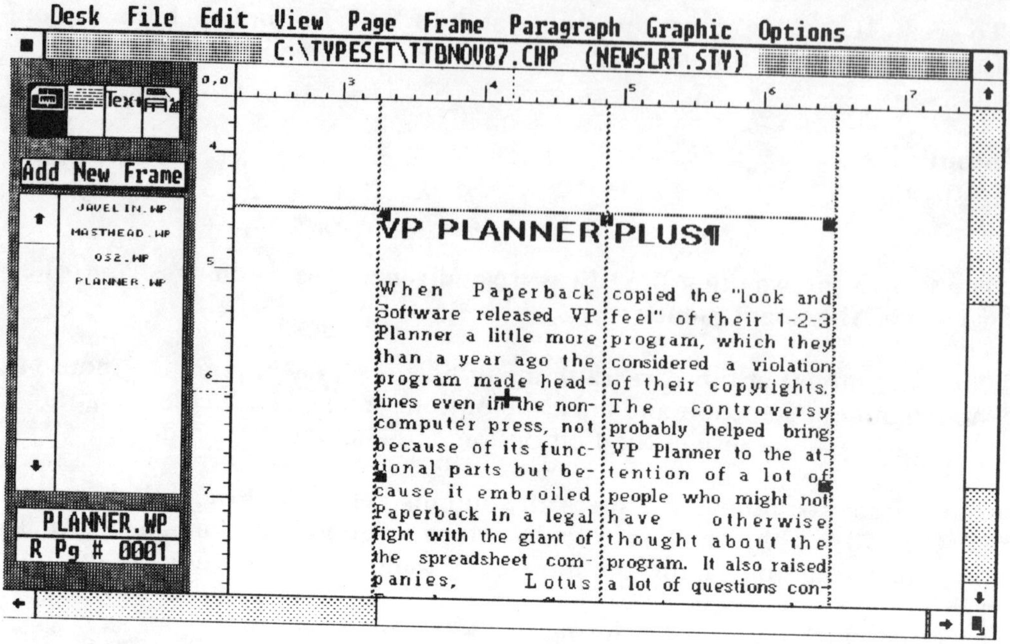

Figure 8.12

ADDING OTHER ARTICLES

Now that you have placed one article on the page, you can add the other two articles. Place Ventura into the Reduced View mode by pressing

[Ctrl/r]

Return to the Frame mode. Press

[Ctrl/u]

Select the top frame by pointing the mouse at that frame and clicking the button. Insert the text from the OS2.WP file into this frame by pointing the mouse at OS2.WP and clicking the button. The text flows into the four columns laid out for this frame.

You now want to create the headline. Change to the Paragraph mode. Press

[Ctrl/i]

Point the mouse at the first paragraph in the frame and click the button. To format this paragraph as a headline, point the mouse at the headline selection in the side bar, and click the button.

The document should resemble Figure 8.13.

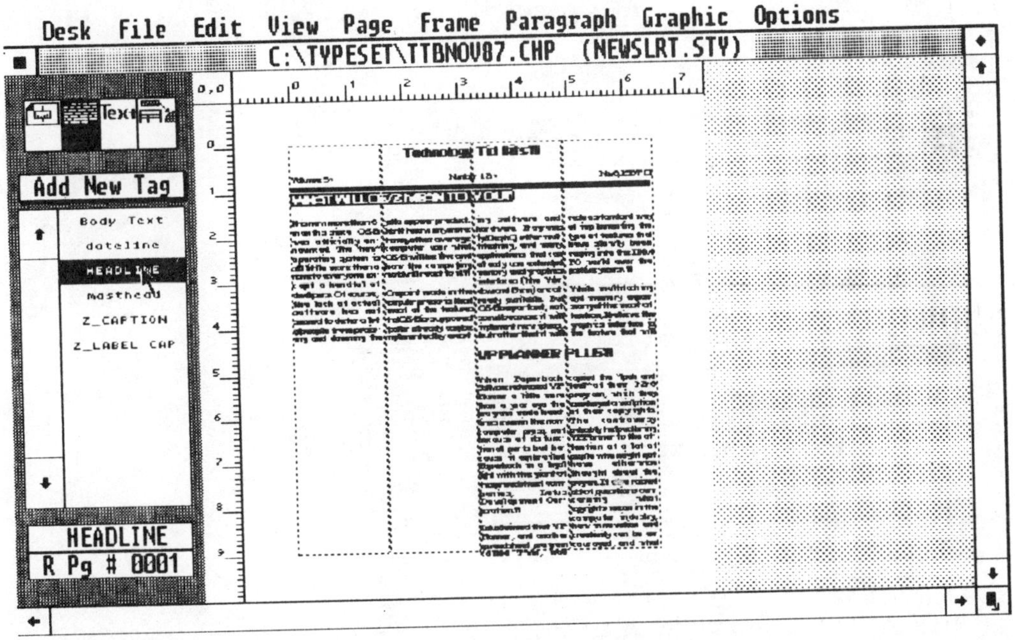

Figure 8.13

Complete the first page by repeating the process to add the last article. Enter the Frame mode by pressing

[Ctrl/u]

Select the last frame on the page by pointing the mouse anywhere in the frame and clicking the button. Then, select the text file for that frame by pointing the mouse at JAVELIN.WP and clicking the button.

The text from the Javelin article fills the final frame. To format the headline, you must change to the Paragraph mode. Press

[Ctrl/i]

Select the first paragraph in that article by pointing the mouse at it and clicking the button. Then, point the mouse at the Headline tag in the side bar and click the button. The first page of the newsletter will resemble Figure 8.14.

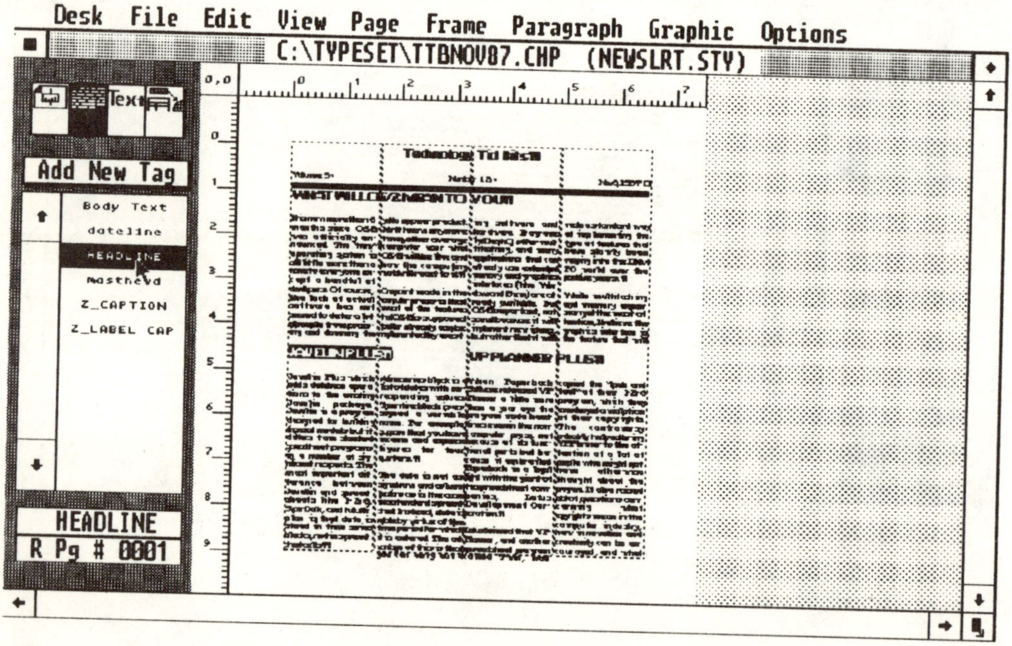

Figure 8.14

ADDING A SECOND PAGE

So far, the layout has accommodated only part of the text files loaded into the frames. Ventura placed in each frame only as much text as it could fit in the frame. To print the full text of the documents, you must add more pages to the file and include additional frames.

You may have noticed that when text is added to frames other than the master frame, Ventura does not automatically create new pages for the text. In the multiple-page document in Chapter 6, the text file was inserted into the master frame, and Ventura automatically created as many pages as were needed for the text.

In this example, each text file is assigned to its own frame. To add more pages, you must issue a special command that adds a new page. Point the mouse at the Page menu heading. At the bottom of the menu is the Insert/Remove Page option, which allows you to create the other pages onto which you will place the additional frames.

Point the mouse at the Insert/Remove Page selection and click the button. Ventura displays the INSERT/REMOVE PAGE menu.

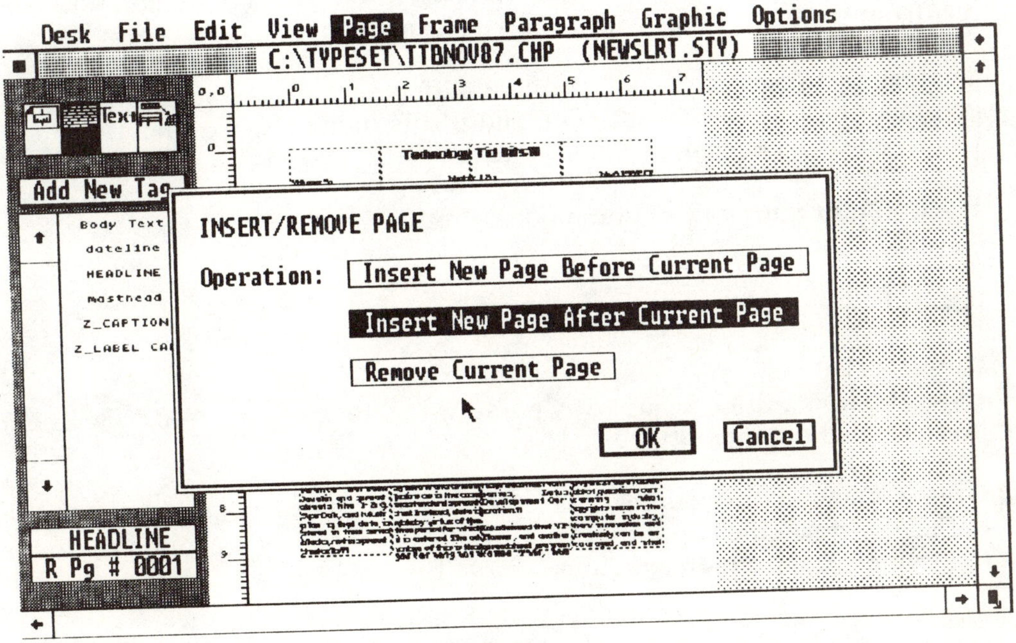

Figure 8.15

This menu allows you add a new page either before or after the current page or remove a page. Be careful when removing pages; they cannot be recalled. It is usually a good idea to save the document before you remove a page. If you make a mistake, you can abandon the change and reload the previously saved copy of the chapter.

In this case, you want to add a new page following the current page, which is the default setting and is already highlighted. Press

[return]

Ventura displays a new blank page. On this page, you will place the new frames that will contain the remainder of the text stored in the text files.

CONTINUING AN ARTICLE

Suppose you want to use the two left columns on this page to continue the OS2 article from the first page. Ventura lets you accomplish this task easily. All you need to do is create a frame. Then, select the same text file from the list that was used on the previous page. Ventura simply continues the text from the exact point where the last frame ended.

Ventura can flow text through as many different frames as you want until all text in the file is exhausted. The end-of-file marker will appear to inform you that you have displayed all the text.

Place Ventura into the Frame mode. Press

[Ctrl/u]

Enter the frame-drawing mode by pointing the mouse at the Add New Frame box and clicking the button.

Draw a frame that covers the two left columns and extends about two thirds of the way down the columns. You must leave room for a caption on top of the frame. Your screen should resemble Figure 8.16.

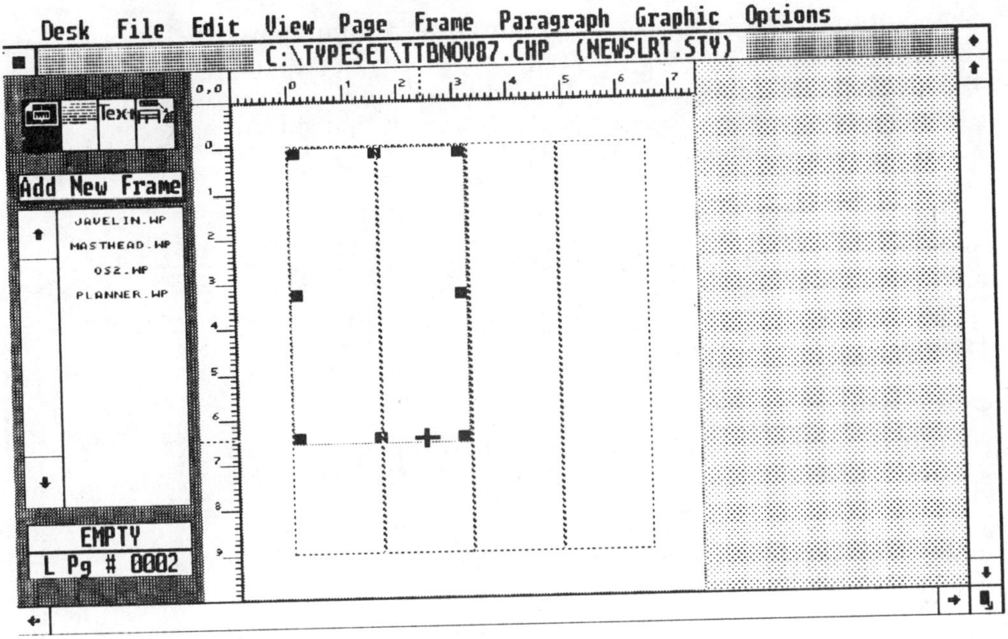

Figure 8.16

ADDING A FRAME CAPTION

The second part of the article does not begin with a headline; it simply picks up from where the last frame left off. To identify the frame as being the text from the OS2 article, you can add a caption to the top of the frame.

Point the mouse at the Frame menu heading. Then, point the mouse at the Anchors & Captions selection and click the button. For this example, insert the caption above the frame by pointing the mouse at the Above option and clicking the button.

You can now type in the caption, which will inform the reader that this text is the continuation of the OS2 story. To make the caption more interesting, use the following text attribute codes to enhance the text. The <B> stands for **bold** text, and the <I> for *italic* text. Enter

<B>OS2<I>Continued from first page
[return]

The caption frame is added to the top of the frame you have drawn. You can now finish positioning the frame. Use the frame-dragging technique to move the frame down so that the caption begins at the top of the master frame. Then, change the size of the frame so that the frame reaches down to the bottom of the master frame.

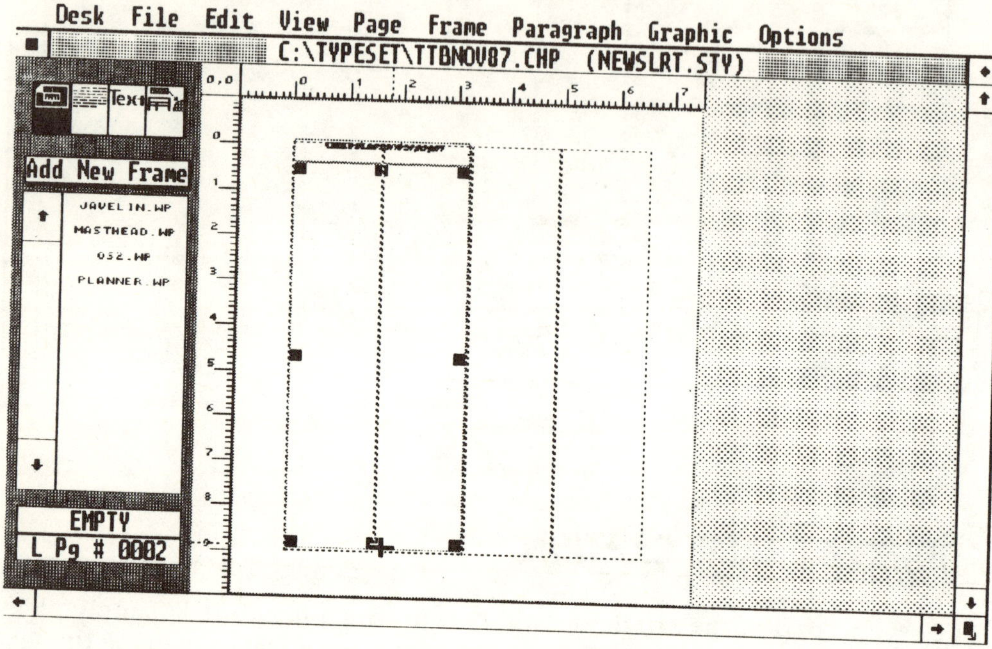

Figure 8.17

To fill the frame with text, select the text file to be used to fill the frame. Point the mouse at OS2.WP and click the button. The frame is filled with the next section of the OS2 article. Note that the frame is still formatted for a single column.

Change it to a two-column frame. Point the mouse at the Frame menu heading. Then, point the mouse at the Margins & Columns selection and click the button.

Select two columns by pointing the mouse at 2 and clicking the button. Enter the gutter width:

[down arrow] (2 times)
[Esc]
.1
[return]

The second page should resemble Figure 8.18.

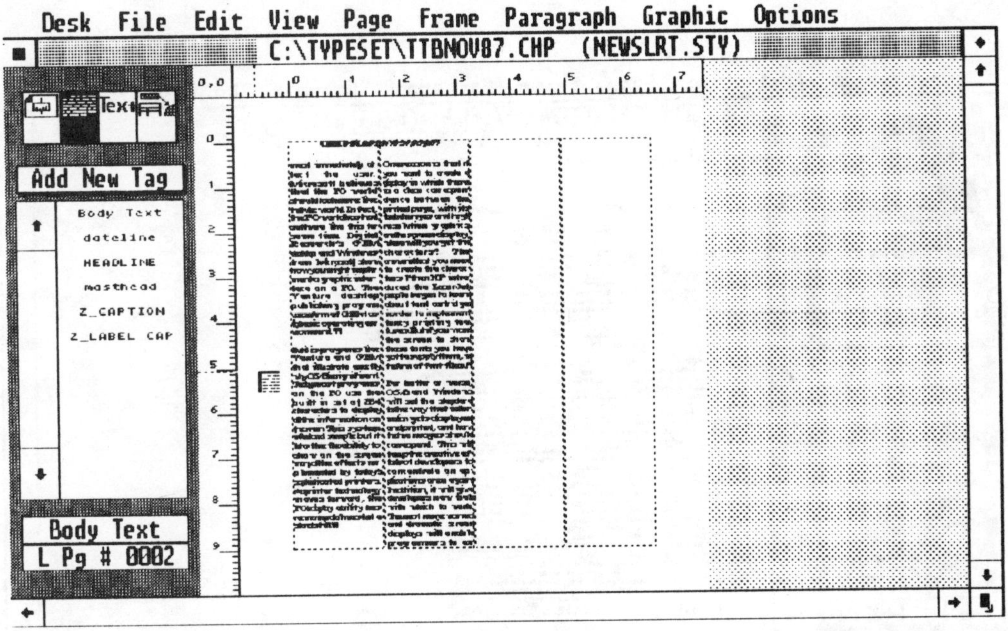

Figure 8.18

COPYING THE FRAME

Suppose you want to continue the Javelin article on the right side of this page. Since you have already laid out the left side, you can simply copy the frame to the right side of the page. Enter

[Shift/Del]
[Ins]

Use the mouse to drag the new frame to the right side of the page.

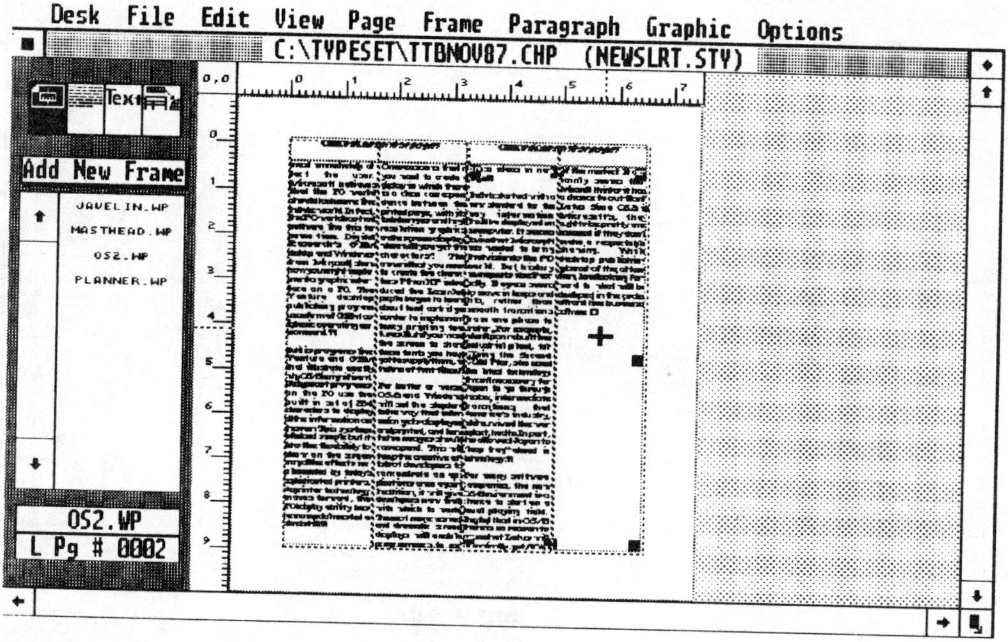

Figure 8.19

Because the copied frame was linked to the OS2 article, the last part of the article filled the frame. In this case, however, you want to make that text the next section of the Javelin article. You can make this change by selecting another text file from the list of files in the side bar.

Point the mouse at JAVELIN.WP and click the button. The text from the JAVELIN article flows into the frame. Before you continue to the next page, you will want to change the caption for the frame so that it references the JAVELIN article.

Point the mouse at the Frame menu heading. Then, point the mouse at the Anchors & Captions selection and click the button. Ventura displays the caption menu box and shows the caption copied from the other frame.

To change the caption to indicate that this frame contains the continuation of the Javelin article, you do not need to retype the entire caption. Ventura allows you to edit the caption. Press

[down arrow]

The text cursor is now located on the caption line. Use the Left Arrow key to place the cursor next to OS2. Erase the OS2, using the Backspace or Delete key, and enter JAVELIN in its place.

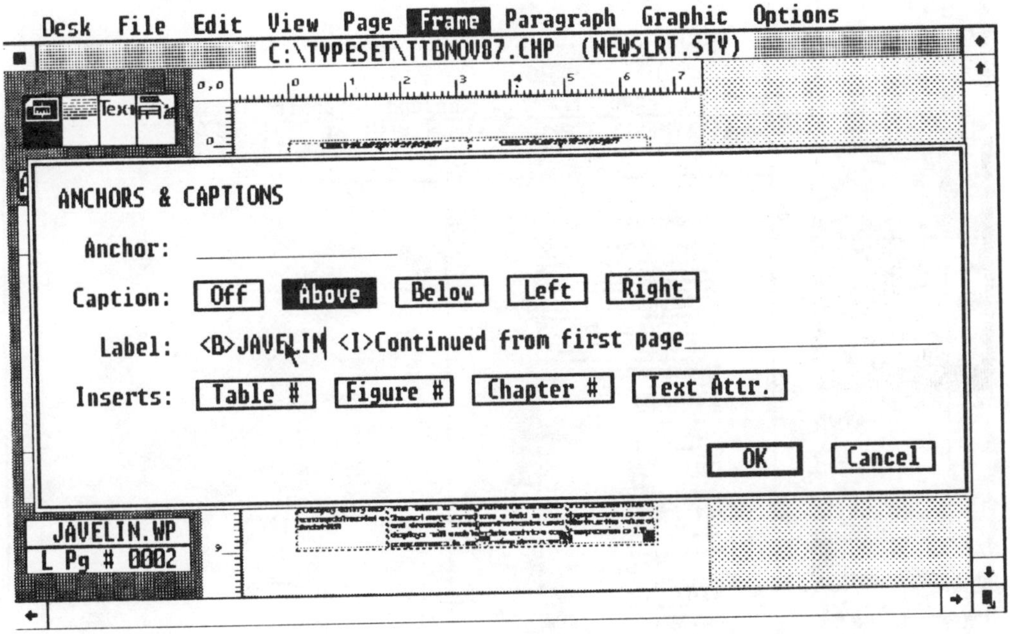

Figure 8.20

Save the new caption by pressing

[return]

You can now add a third page to the document. Point the mouse at the Page menu heading. Then, point the mouse at the Insert/Remove Page selection and click the button. Press

[return]

Because Ventura still has a copy of the dual-column frame in memory, you can begin the third page by inserting another copy of the frame. Press

[Ins]

Ventura inserts the frame and the end of the OS2 article.

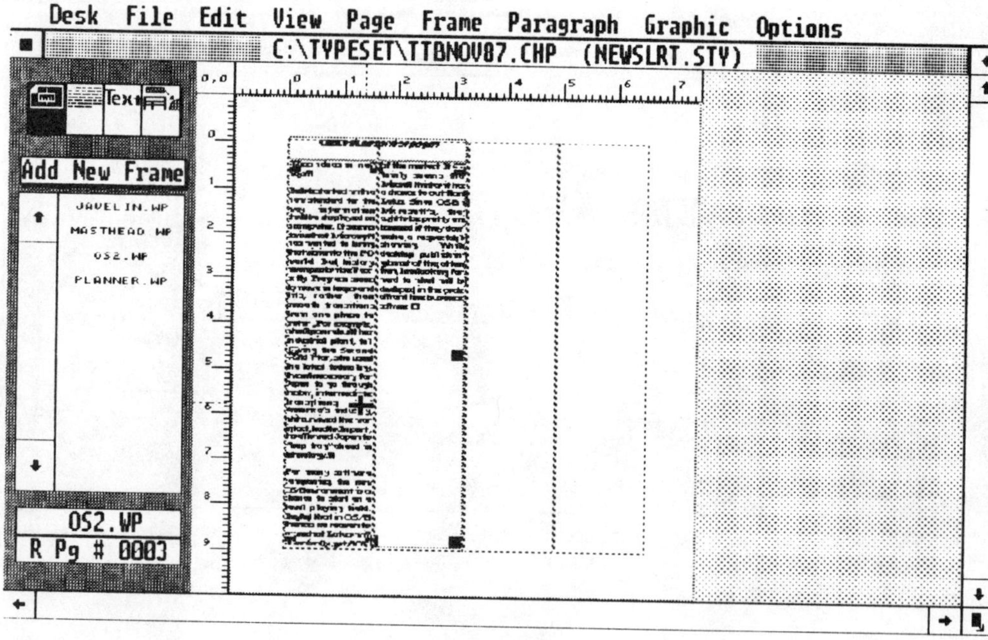

Figure 8.21

COLUMN BALANCING

The remainder of the article does not require the entire two columns. The column on the left is full, but the column on the right is less than half full (see Figure 8.21). Ventura can make the columns appear the same length if the text does not fill the entire frame. This feature is called **column balancing.**

Column balancing is helpful for two reasons. First, it improves the appearance of column text when part of a column is left blank. Second, after the columns have been balanced, you can use the text as a guide to shortening the frame to eliminate the unneeded space.

To select balanced columns, you must display the Sizing & Scaling menu by pointing the mouse at the Frame menu heading, pointing the mouse at the Sizing & Scaling selection, and clicking the button.

The displayed menu includes Column Balance as its last item. Select balanced columns by pointing the mouse at On, clicking the button, pointing the mouse at OK, and again clicking the button. The text is balanced between the two columns.

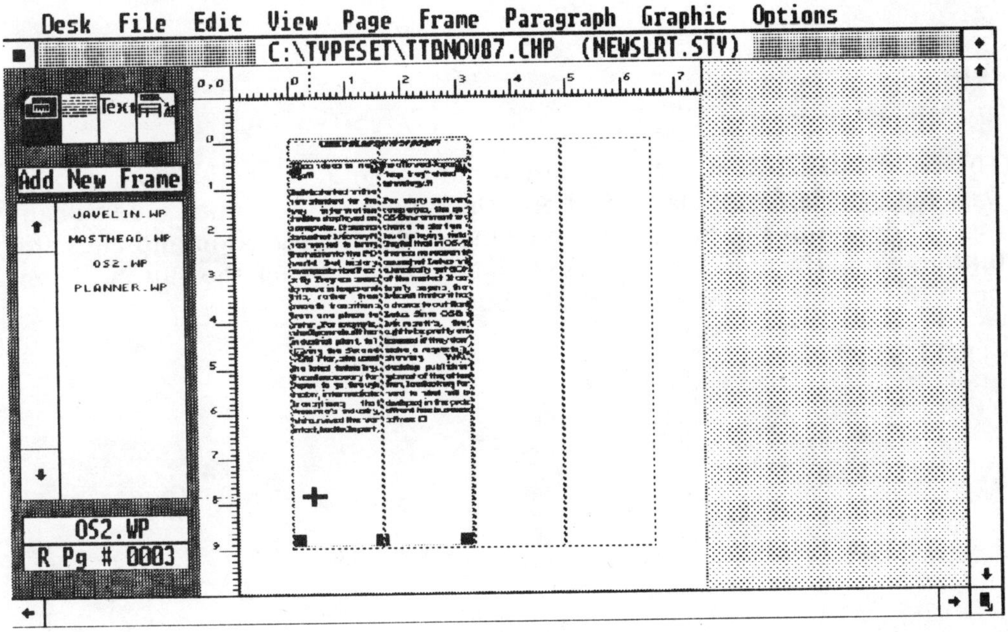

Figure 8.22

You can quickly complete the JAVELIN article by copying the frame from the right side of the previous page. To move back to the previous page, press

[Pg Up]

Select the Javelin frame by pointing the mouse at the right frame option and clicking the button. Copy the frame into memory. Press

[Shift/Del]

Move back to page 3. Press

[Pg Dn]

Insert the frame onto page 3. Press

[Ins]

The end of the Javelin article is pasted onto page 3. This frame would also look better if it were balanced. Point the mouse at the Frame menu heading. Then, point the mouse at the Sizing & Scaling selection and click the button. Point the mouse at Column Balance ON, and click the button. Then, point the mouse at OK and click the button.

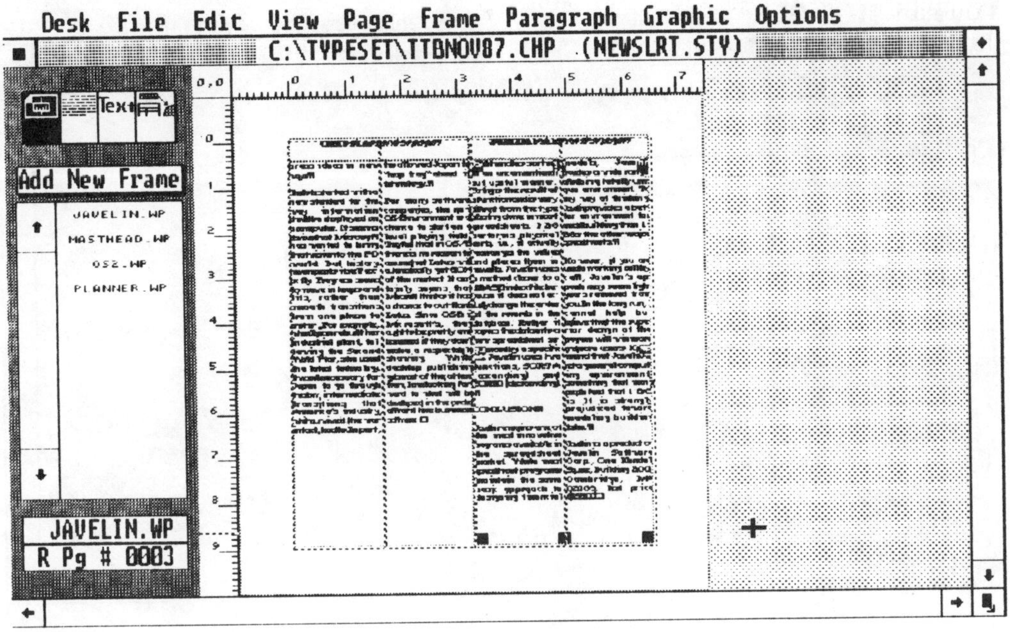

Figure 8.23

Create a fourth page by pointing the mouse at the Page menu heading. Then, point at Insert/Remove Page and click the button. Press

[return]

Insert the frame already in memory by pressing

[Ins]

Ventura inserts another copy of the Javelin frame. Because there is no more text to be displayed from that file, the frame is blank. Use the mouse to expand the frame to cover the entire page.

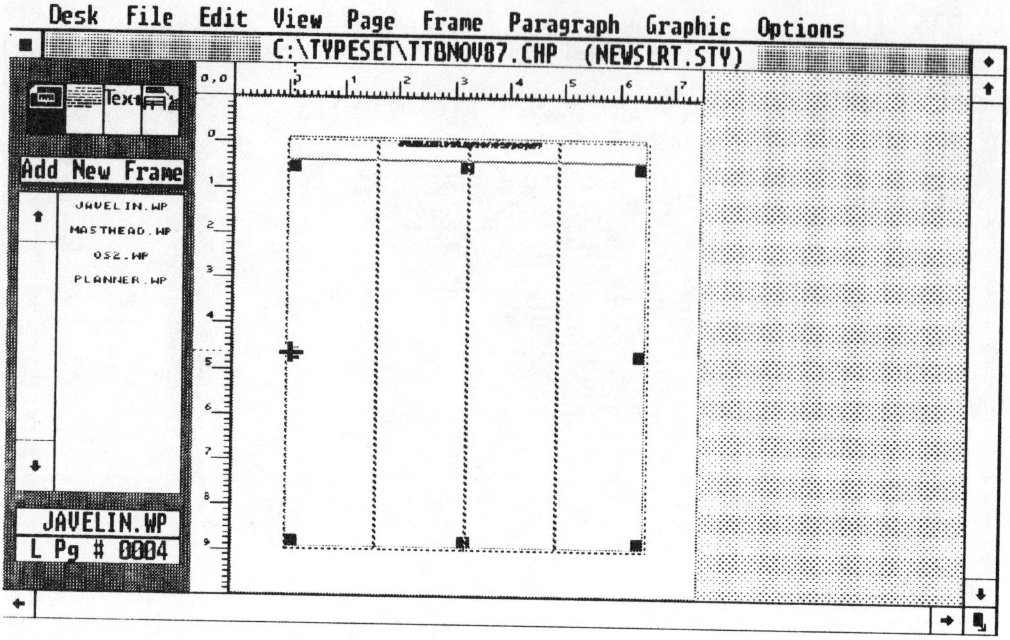

Figure 8.24

Next, fill the frame with the text from the PLANNER article by pointing the mouse at PLANNER.WP and clicking the button.

The final part of the newsletter is placed into the frame; however, the frame is only a two-column frame. Change the frame to a four-column layout.

Point the mouse at the Frame menu heading. Then, point the mouse at the Margins & Columns selection and click the button. Choose the four-column option by pointing the mouse at the number 4 and clicking the button. Then, press

[return]

The screen should resemble Figure 8.25.

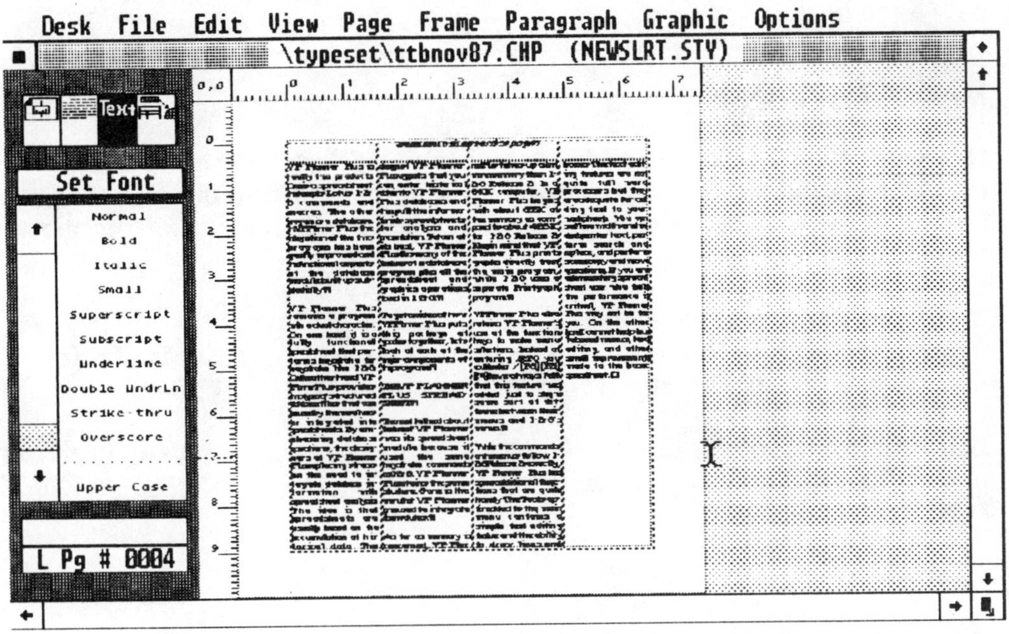

Figure 8.25

The last step is to change the caption. Point the mouse at the Frame menu heading. Then, point the mouse at the Anchors & Captions selection and click the button.

Change the caption to read VP PLANNER instead of JAVELIN. Save the revised caption by pressing

[return]

The newsletter is complete. Save the chapter by pressing

[Ctrl/s]

You can print the chapter if you want to.

SUMMARY

Newsletter Formats

Newsletters are a variation on basic multiple-page and multiple-frame documents. Newsletters do not include text placed directly into the master frame; instead, text is placed into a series of frames placed on top of the master frame.

The master frame helps with column alignment. The master frame is formatted for a column layout. The Column Snap feature ensures that frames placed on top of the master frame line up correctly.

Each frame placed on top of the master frame is used to display text from one of the articles in the newsletter.

Multiple-Frame Documents

When a text file is displayed in a frame other than the master frame, Ventura shows only as much text as will fit into the frame. You can display the rest of the text from that file at another point in the chapter by adding a frame and selecting the same text file from the file list. This process can be continued until the entire text is displayed in a series of frames.

Inserting a Page

When text is added to frames other than the master frame, Ventura does not automatically add new pages to accommodate the document. In such cases, you must manually create additional pages as required by using the Insert/Remove Page command.

Alignment Width

When frames are divided into columns, you can display a line that runs the width of the frame rather than the column by changing the overall width setting in the Alignment menu.

APPENDICES

APPENDIX A: DOS, FILES, AND WORD PROCESSORS

Unlike many programs used on microcomputers, Ventura is not intended to be used by itself. You will probably want to use a word processing program to prepare text files and graphics programs to create pictures, drawings, or other illustrations before including or formatting them in Ventura documents. In addition, you might be familiar with spreadsheet and data base programs that can be used to prepare reports, lists, and other information.

Ventura's basic premise is that it is capable of using data from all of these programs to produce typeset documents. This appendix discusses some of the basic concepts of using other applications with Ventura.

DOS Organization

The term DOS stands for Disk Operating System, which is itself a computer program. Unlike Ventura or a word processor, however, DOS is always running on your computer, even when another application such as Ventura is open. DOS performs many basic tasks required by all applications running in the computer. The most obvious job that DOS is responsible for is storing data in files on disk.

It is DOS – not your word processor, spreadsheet, or data base – that determines the syntax and structure of files and file names. To organize files on disks, DOS recognizes three basic levels of organization. The highest level of organization is called a **volume**, which refers to all data stored on a single disk – hard or floppy. DOS assigns single-letter names to all the drives on your system. The floppy disk drives are called "A" and "B"; the fixed (or hard) drives begin with the letter "C" and can go on as far as "P," but usually stop with "E," "F," or "G." As part of its basic grammar, DOS requires that all Volume names end with a colon (:) character. Thus, drives always have names like A:, B:, C:, etc.

The next level of organization is a **directory**. DOS allows you to divide a disk into several directories that act as file folders; they group related files. For example, Ventura is normally installed in a directory named VENTURA. The sample files supplied with Ventura are placed into a directory named TYPESET. It is common practice to place each program that you load onto your hard disk into its own directory: Lotus into 123, WordPerfect into WP, etc. As with volumes, DOS requires a special punctuation mark to indicate that the term refers to a directory. The character used is a backslash (\). For example, the VENTURA directory should be entered as \VENTURA. The backslash instructs DOS that you are referring to a directory named VENTURA as opposed to a file named VENTURA.

The final level of organization is the **file**—the smallest unit of organization recognized by DOS. Files names can include from one to eight characters, and DOS allows a three-character extension to be added to the name to indicate the type of information stored in the file. Ventura automatically adds extensions to indicate the purpose of files it creates. For example, chapter files have a CHP extension. Some word processing programs, such as Multimate and Word, add DOC extensions to word processing files. Others, such as WordPerfect and WordStar, do not automatically add any extension, although you are free to add them if you like.

When all the elements are combined, you create what is called a **full pathname**, which consists of the volume name, the directory name, and the file name, as in the following example:

c:\typeset\invoice.chp

This line informs DOS that on drive C in a directory called TYPESET is a file called INVOICE.CHP. DOS does not distinguish between uppercase and lowercase letters.

Wild Cards

To make operations simpler, DOS allows you to insert a wild card character to locate a group of similar files. When an asterisk (*) appears in a path name, DOS allows any characters to match the part of the file name represented by the asterisk. For example,

c:\typeset*.chp

informs DOS that you are referring to the files on drive C in the TYPESET directory that end with CHP. When used with a command, this path name instructs DOS to select all files with a CHP extension. Following is another example:

c:\wp\a*.wp

In this case, the specification informs DOS that you are looking on drive C, in the WP directory, for files that begin with the letter "A" and end with a WP extension.

Ventura allows you to use this type of DOS specification in any of its item selection menus. By understanding how to use DOS volume, directory, and file specifications, you can locate and store files in related groups, which makes Ventura operations faster and easier.

Word Processing Files

While you can directly enter information into Ventura, you are better off entering information into a word processing program.

Ventura's relationship with word processing programs is a two-way street. When Ventura loads a file prepared in a word processing program, it recognizes certain features implemented in the word processor but ignores others. In addition, when you save a Ventura chapter, text files associated with the chapter are revised by Ventura, which means that the features not recognized by Ventura are stripped out of the file.

In general, Ventura will not recognize paragraph formatting, line spacing, indents, headers, footers, footnotes, and other paragraph and page layout features. If your text file contains these features, they will be ignored and stripped out of the file when it is saved in Ventura; however, Ventura will recognize simple text attributes such as underlining, bold face, superscript, subscript, strike-through text, and hard spaces between words.

Ventura also handles spacing between paragraphs in a way not common to most word processing programs. In WordPerfect, WordStar, and Multimate, you usually insert two [return] characters to create blank lines between paragraphs. Text formatted in this manner will not appear correctly in Ventura. Remember not to add the extra [return] characters to files intended for use with Ventura. Ventura can automatically strip extra [return] characters from the document as it loads if you place a special code at the beginning of the file – **@PARAFILTER ON =** . Make sure this line is the first line of the document, or the command will not operate correctly.

You can, however, create formats in your word processing document that Ventura will recognize. This is done by entering text-based codes that Ventura can translate into formatting features.

Paragraph Tags

@Tagname

The @TAGNAME instruction is used to assign paragraphs to style sheet formats. Any paragraph that does not begin with an @ command will be formatted as body text. To begin a paragraph with an @ sign that is not meant to be a style tag name, enter @@. This situation occurs most often in writing about computer spreadsheet programs that use the @ symbol to indicate formula functions.

Note that it is not necessary for a style sheet with the tag names used in the text file to actually exist. If you load a text file with tag names not in the current style sheet, Ventura creates the tag names automatically and assigns them the same format values as the Body Text format. To indicate that these tags are not part of the original style sheet, Ventura places the tag names in uppercase letters in the style sheet side bar display.

$ Commands

Ventura does not recognize word processor formats for footnotes or index entries. To create these entries in a text file, you must use the $ commands as follows:

<$Fxxxxx>	= footnote
<$Ixxxxx>	= index entry
<$&xxxxx>	= frame anchor

where xxxxx is the text of the footnote, index entry, or anchor.

Attribute Commands

You can insert format attribute codes into your text while you are creating a document in your word processor. Ventura recognizes the following codes:

<=>	double underline
<^>	superscript
<B>	bold weight type
<D>	resume normal text
<I>	italic print
<L>	light weight type
<M>	medium weight type
<O>	overstrike
<U>	underlined text
<V>	subscript
<X>	strikeover

You can select a point size by using <P> with a number value. Entering the following text sequence changes the point size to 14 and then back to 12:

<P014>Hello<P012>

You can change the font by using <F> with a number that corresponds to the font you want to use. For information about font numbers, see Appendix B.

Spreadsheets

Ventura offers no direct way of loading information stored in spreadsheet files such as Lotus 1-2-3 WKS files or SuperCalc CAL files; however, spreadsheet programs can create text files by sending output to disk files rather than to the printer.

In Lotus 1-2-3, the /<P>rint <F>ile command will print the selected range of cells to a text file with a PRN extension. When you use the /<P>rint File command, you will be prompted to enter a file name for the output file. Remember to turn off the page breaks and margins that 1-2-3 normally inserts by using the /<P>rint <F>ile <O>ptions <O>ther <U>nformatted command to suppress page breaks, headers, footers, and margins.

In SuperCalc 4, the command for creating a text file from spreadsheet data is / Output File. To select unformatted output, use the / <O>utput <F>ile <O>ptions <R>eport <F>ormat <N>o command.

Remember, the spreadsheet program will have its own set of default drive and directory specifications, which will probably not be the same as Ventura's or your word processor's. In that case, you may want to change the defaults so you can place the PRN file in a directory that is convenient for work in Ventura. For example, if you want to place a Lotus 1-2-3 PRN text file into the Ventura TYPESET directory, you can use the /<F>ile <D>irectory command to enter C:\TYPESET as the active directory. Any / <P>rint <F>ile commands entered after this point will place the output files in the TYPESET directory.

There remains one major defect of PRN-type files. Column separation is achieved by inserting space characters between the columns. Ventura will attempt to proportionally space all characters on the line, which will disrupt the alignment. The problem can be solved in one of three ways.

The first method requires that you edit the PRN file and replace the spaces with [Tab] characters. If you are using Word, you can search for groups of spaces and replace them with tabs. For example, entering a search string of **[Space]^w** will locate all groups of space characters with two or more spaces. A replacement string of **^t** will insert tabs in their place.

The second method is to use a monospaced font, such as Courier 10-point, which assigns the same spacing to all characters. Many but not all printers support this type of font. Unless you have this type of font, you cannot solve the tab/space problem using font changes.

The third solution is to use a special utility program developed expressly to solve this problem. One such utility is called VP/TABS (available from THE LASER EDGE, 360 17th Street, Suite 203, Oakland, CA 94612).

When loading PRN files into Ventura, set the file format type to WordStar. Do not use ASCII. Ventura considers ASCII file formats as files that use two [return] characters to end each line. 1-2-3 and most other programs output text files with a single [return] character at the end of each line. If a PRN file is loaded as an ASCII format file, Ventura will ignore the [return] as a paragraph end character and create one big paragraph out of the entire text. The WordStar format will read any ASCII text file as well as actual WordStar files. Under this format, Ventura will treat a single [return] character as an end-of-paragraph code.

Text Files

A PRN file created by 1-2-3 or other spreadsheets is an example of what is called a **text file**. A text file contains standard text characters, including tabs, in which lines are terminated with one or two [return] characters. This type of file can be produced by almost any standard program. If you have access to Sidekick, you can use the Notepad command, [F4], to capture text displayed on the screen into an text file format.

Remember, text files that create columns by placing spaces between items will not line up correctly when the text is formatted in a proportionally spaced font. Spaces used in this way must be replaced with tab characters. In the ASCII coding system, the tab character is character number 9.

dBASE III PLUS

Data base information can also be copied into a text file format and loaded in Ventura. dBASE III PLUS is a very flexible program; it can create a text file of almost any format, which means that you can create text files that contain Ventura formatting codes and, most importantly, tab codes instead of spaces. This can be done quite easily in dBASE III PLUS by combining data fields with special functions.

Suppose that you have a data base containing, among other fields, three fields named CLIENT, PHONE, and CITY. You want to include a list of clients and their cities and phone numbers in a Ventura chapter. To avoid having to reenter the information, you can use dBASE to create a text file already formatted for Ventura.

The key to this process is the use of the SET ALTERNATE commands. The ALTERNATE commands allow you to select a text file as an alternate output location. In effect, when an alternate has been selected, any information that appears on the screen will also be copied into a text file. The dBASE command, LIST, will display lists of data that can be copied into the alternate file, creating the text for Ventura.

To create the list of clients mentioned as an example, you would begin by selecting an alternate file. The following command selects the file CLIENTS.WS as the alternate file. WS was selected as the extension since you will load the text as a WordStar file in Ventura. Enter

SET ALTERNATE TO C:\TYPESET\CLIENTS.WS

If you do not want the field headings to be part of the file, enter

SET HEADINGS OFF

The correct format for listing data is to replace the spaces following a data item with a tab character. The alignment in dBASE will look odd, but it will be the correct format for Ventura. Accomplish this task by using the TRIM() function to eliminate the spaces and the CHR() function to insert tabs. CHR(9) will cause a tab character to be printed. To create the necessary text file, enter

SET ALTERNATE ON
LIST TRIM(client) + CHR(9) + TRIM(phone) + CHR(9) + TRIM(city)
CLOSE ALTERNATE

You can also include a Ventura style tag code to assign a special format to the text line. For example, to add the Database style tag to a line in the file, you would enter a sequence of commands such as the following:

```
SET ALTERNATE TO C:\TYPESET\CLIENTS.WS
SET HEADINGS OFF
SET ALTERNATE ON
LIST"@DATABASE=" + TRIM(client) + CHR(9) + TRIM(phone) + CHR(9) + TRIM(city)
CLOSE ALTERNATE
```

APPENDIX B: ADDING PRINTER FONTS

One of the most fascinating features of Ventura is the ability to add fonts, which increases the variety of your formatting possibilities. Ventura supplies a basic set of fonts that can be used with your printer. The three basic font styles supplied with Ventura are as follows:

- **Dutch (Times-Roman).** The most commonly used font, Dutch letters contain lines that vary in thickness throughout different parts of the letter, and they also contain small extensions at the end of lines, called **serifs**—from the French word for foot.
- **Swiss (Helvetica).** This font is characterized by a uniform line width and a lack of serifs. The appearance of Swiss fonts is darker and cleaner than Dutch fonts. The name "Helvetica" is derived from the old Latin name for Swiss.
- **Courier.** This font is used to replicate typical typewritten text produced on a monospaced typewriter.

Adding New Fonts

One of the best ways to add fonts to your Ventura system is to use the Bitstream Fontware program and purchase Bitstream fonts for your system. Bitstream supplies fonts for the Apple LaserWriter, AST TurboLaser, Cordata LP300X, HP Laser Jet Plus and series II, and Tall Tree JLaser.

Bitstream's program allows you to create both printer and screen fonts so that your screen display will also show the new fonts you add.

One advantage of the Bitstream system is that you can create as many different point sizes as you want. A font is supplied in a single file that is then used to create fonts of various sizes. As of this writing, Bitstream offers more than 20 different fonts for Ventura. The price of each font is listed at $195.00, and a one-time purchase of an installation kit for all fonts costs an additional $95.00.

The installation kit allows you to specify the type of screen display and printer you are using, which is helpful if you have several computers that use different printers or monitor types. Suppose you have two printers – a HP Laser Jet Series II and a Cordata LP300X. The Bitstream program allows you to create fonts for both printers so that you can achieve consistent print output from both machines.

The Bitstream program begins with a list of the fonts you can create (Figure B.1).

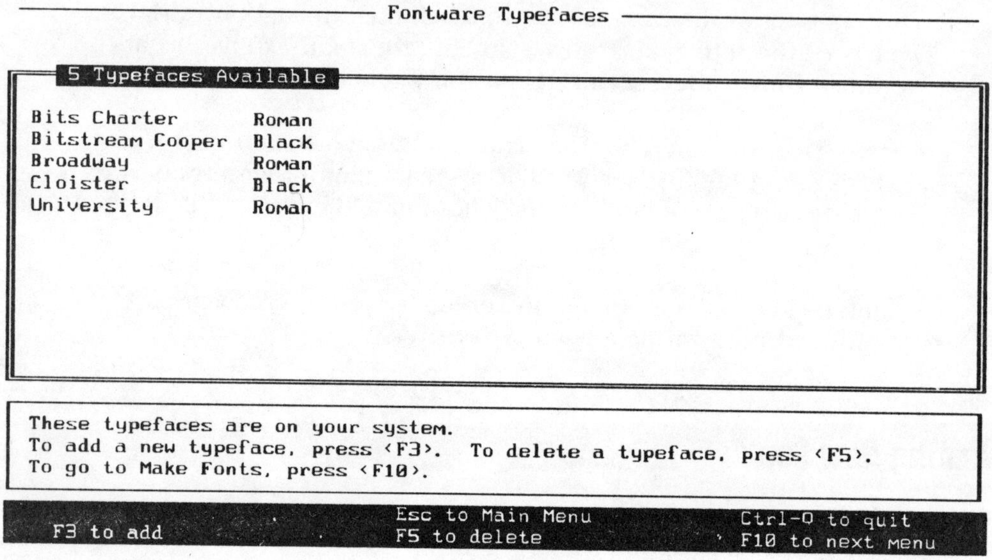

Figure B.1

You can select a series of fonts and the size that you want to use (Figure B.2).

When using a program like Bitstream, you many want to generate small sets of fonts. You can later use Ventura to merge several of these small font sets into a large font set that will serve as your default printer font setup. You also have the option of creating screen fonts that match the selected printer fonts (see Figure B.3).

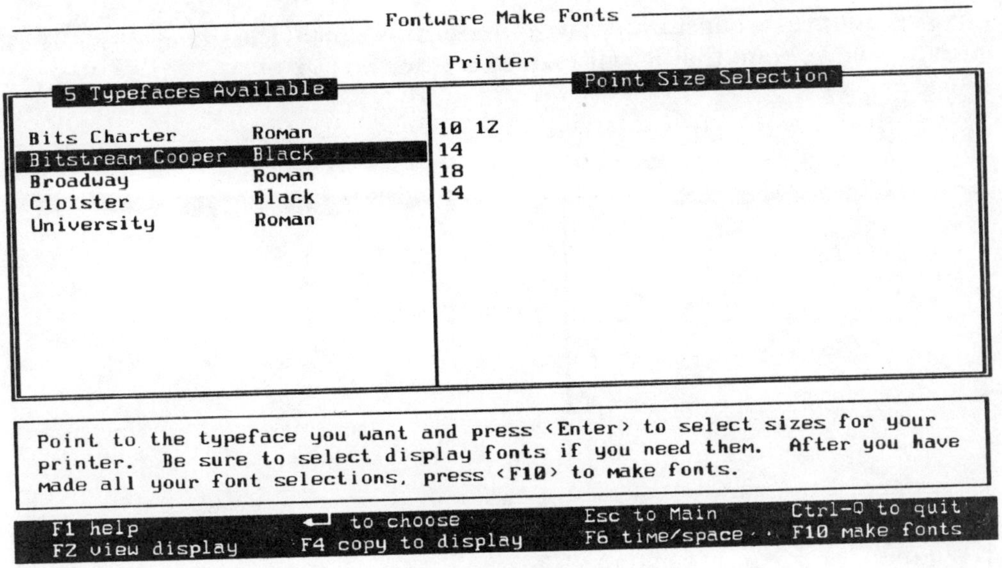

Figure B.2

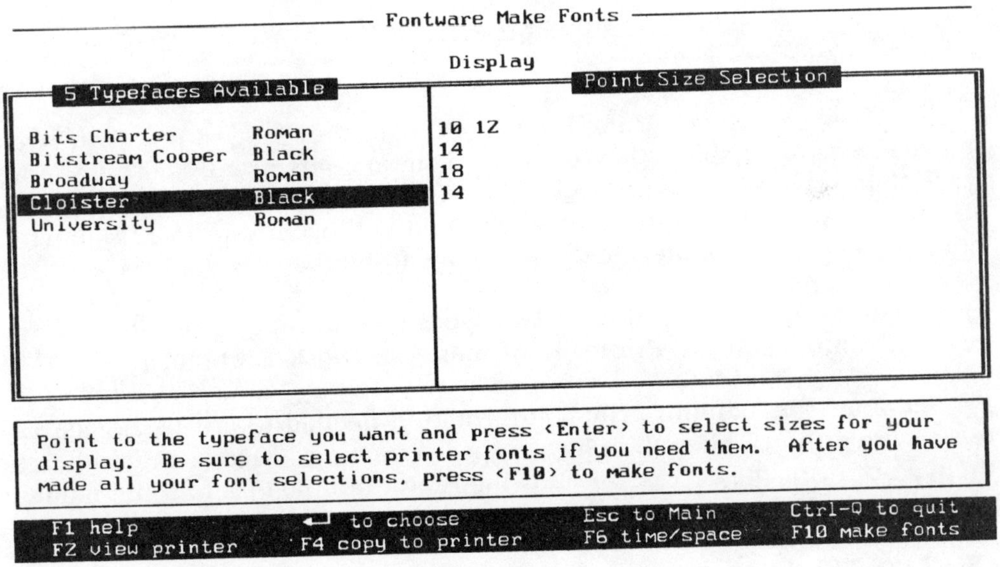

Figure B.3

Font creation can consume a large amount of time. Bitstream displays an estimate of the time that it will take to create the fonts.

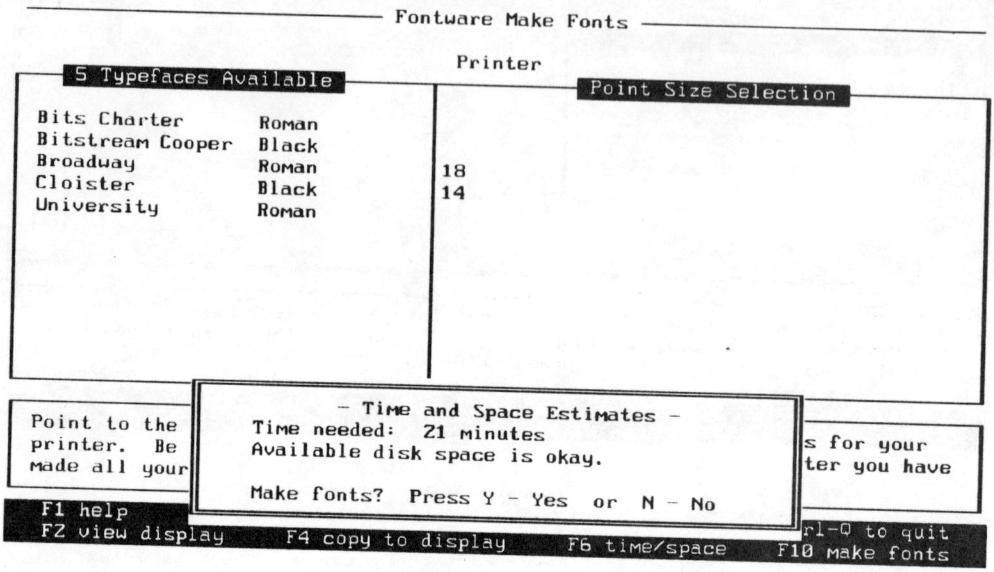

Figure B.4

Not surprisingly, the larger the fonts, the longer they take to be constructed and the more disk space they require. Printer fonts usually take up more space than screen fonts. For example, a 24-point font file may take up 120 to 180 kilobytes. The equivalent screen font will occupy 10 to 12 kilobytes. You may need several megabytes of storage to hold all the fonts you create.

The Bitstream program produces two types of files needed to integrate the new fonts into Ventura: Printer Font files and Width Table files.

Printer Font files contain printer information needed to create the characters on the printer. These files have a special naming structure that indicates the type of print they create. Following is an example of a font file name:

CENT18BP.SFP

The font is named CENT (short for Century); it is in 18-point bold type.

The other type of file is a **Width Table file**, which is the link between font files and Ventura. This file informs Ventura of important information about fonts that enables the program to display the new fonts for use with the program. Bitstream creates a width file for each group of created fonts. Following is an example of a width table file name:

HP__LJ000 WID

Bitstream simply numbers the width tables HP__LJ001.WID, HP__LJ002.WID, etc. You may want to change the names to something more descriptive; simply use the DOS RENAME command to do this. Make sure that you use the WID extension. For example,

RENAME HP__LJ000.WID HPOLDENG.WID

Once you have created the necessary width and font files, you can integrate them into Ventura.

Loading Different Width Tables

The Ventura Options menu includes two commands used for adding or changing fonts. The first is the Set Printer Info selection. The menu box for this command resembles Figure B.5.

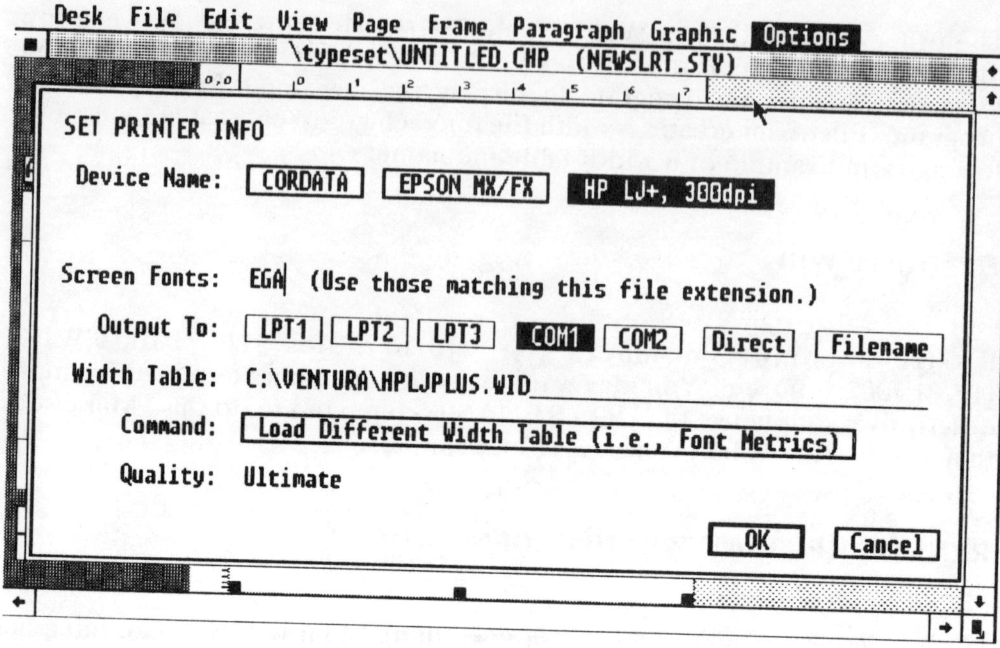

Figure B.5

The most significant entry on the screen is the name of the width table. In this example, the table is HPJPLUS.WID. This file determines the fonts available when you use the font selection menus.

To load a different font table, select Load Different Width Table, which displays a list of WID files (see Figure B.6).

The file that you select determines the available fonts. To see a list of available fonts, you can use the Add/Remove Fonts selection on the Options menu (see Figure B.7).

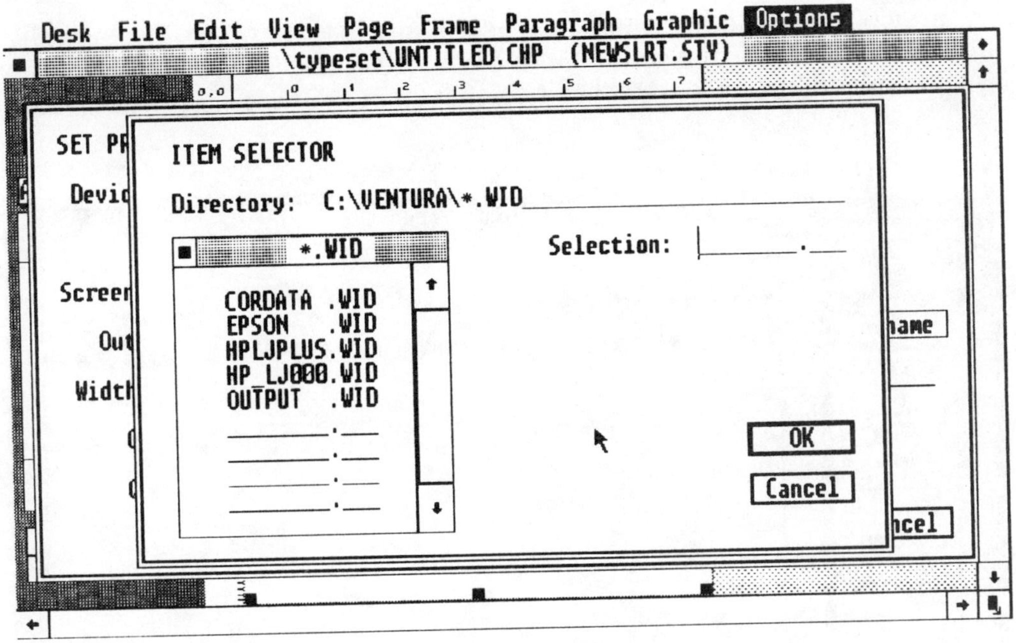

Figure B.6

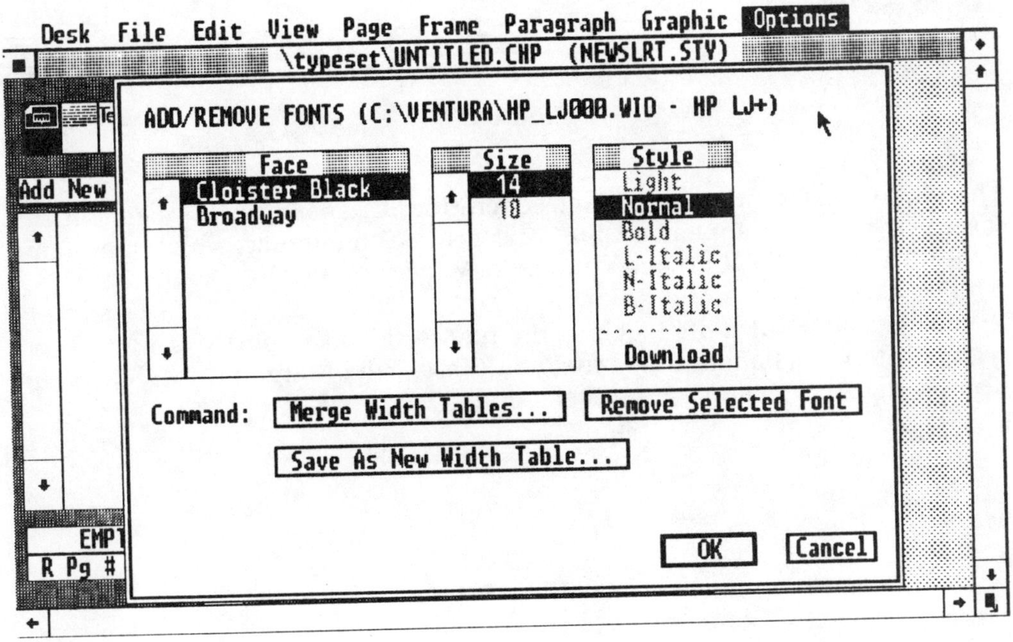

Figure B.7

The previous illustration displays two new fonts listed in the HP__LJ000.WID file. While that file is the active width file, you can select only from the fonts listed in that file. Figure B.8 shows how these fonts will appear on the screen:

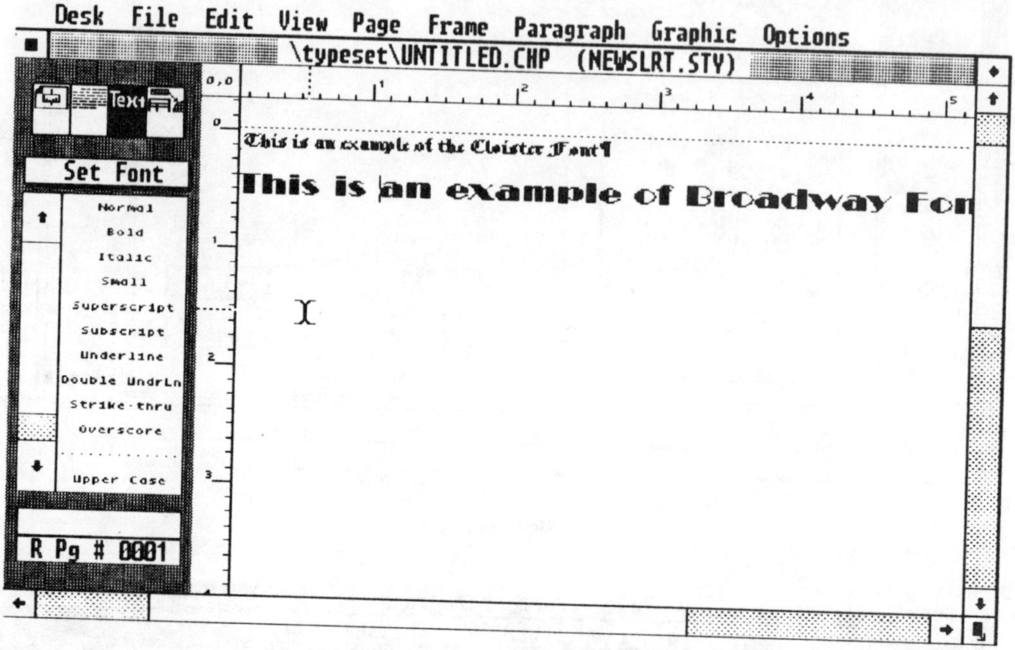

Figure B.8

Thanks to Bitstream's screen font generation, the new fonts appear on the screen as they will appear on the final printed document, which maintains Ventura's WYSIWYG (What You See Is What You Get) concept.

If you have a set of fonts (such as the one in this example) you want to integrate into your standard font file, you can use the Merge Width Tables option on the Add/Remove Fonts selection.

Suppose that the standard font width table – the one that automatically is displayed in the Set Printer Info menu – is HPLJPLUS.WID. Point the mouse at the Options menu heading. Then, point the mouse at the Add/Remove Fonts selection and click the button. Point the mouse at the Merge Width Tables option and click the button. Ventura will display the list of WID tables. Point the mouse at HPLJPLUS.WID and click the button. Ventura then adds all the fonts that would normally appear in in the HPLJPLUS.WID file to the new width table that you loaded – HP_LJ000.WID.

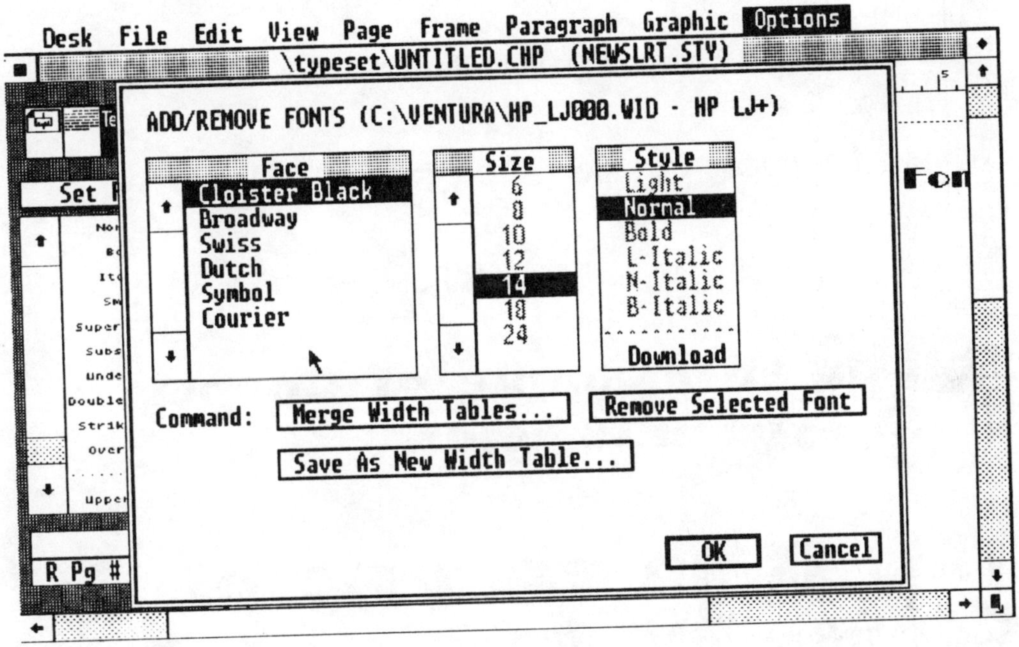

Figure B.9

If you want, you can save the new combined file under its own name using Save As New Width Table option. You can also remove unwanted individual fonts from a width table using the Remove Selected Font option.

With these commands, you can integrate and organize any new fonts you acquire.

Following are examples of Bitstream fonts.

Examples of Additional Fonts Available From BitStream

This is an example of Cloister Type in 24 Point.

This is an example of Cloister Type in 14 Point.

This is an example of University Type in 18 Point.

This is an example of UniversityType in 14 Point.

This is an example of Cooper Black Type in 18 Point.

This is an example of Cooper BlackType in 24 Point.

This is Broadway 18 Point.

This is Broadway 14 point.

This is Charter 12 point.

INDEX

A

B

C

D

E

F

G

H

I

L

M

N

O

P

R

S

T

U

V

W